Contents

Table of Contents iii
Introduction vii
Acknowledgments ix

Topics

401(k) Plans 1
900 Service 5
Accountants 9
Advertising Agencies 12
Answering Machines 15
Automatic Staplers 19
Beverage Services 22
Business Cards 25
Business Forms 29
Business Insurance 32
Calling Cards 36
Car Rental Agencies 39
CD-ROM Drives 43
Cellular Service 47
Cellular Telephones 51
Centrex Service 55
Chairs 59
Checks 63
Cleaning Services 66
Clipping Services 69
Collection Agencies 72
Color Printers 76
Commercial Printing 81
Computer Backup Systems 85

Conference Calling Services 89
Conferencing Equipment 92
Copy Paper.. 95
Cordless Telephones 99
Corporate Cards... 102
Desks.. 105
Desktop Computers.. 108
Dictation Equipment 114
Dot Matrix Printers 118
E-mail Services.. 122
Employee Drug Testing....................................... 126
Executive Recruitment Agencies 129
Fax Broadcasting Services..................................... 133
Fax Machines 136
Fax on Demand 140
Fax Servers 144
File Cabinets.. 148
Frequent Flyer Programs...................................... 151
Graphic Designers 154
Ground Shipping 157
Health Insurance 161
HMOs 165
Hotels 169
Ink-jet Printers 174
International Callback 177
International Calling 180
International Expedited Delivery............................... 184
Internet Service Providers..................................... 188
ISDN 192
Keyboards.. 196
KSU-less Phone Systems 200
Lamination Equipment 203
Laser Pointers... 206
Laser Printers 209
LCD Systems 213

BUSINESS REPLY MAIL

FIRST CLASS MAIL   PERMIT NO. 8225 WATERTOWN, MA

POSTAGE WILL BE PAID BY ADDRESSEE

Business Consumer Guide
BEACON RESEARCH GROUP INC
125 WALNUT ST STE 11
WATERTOWN, MA 02172-9931

BUSINESS REPLY MAIL

FIRST CLASS MAIL   PERMIT NO. 8225 WATERTOWN, MA

POSTAGE WILL BE PAID BY ADDRESSEE

Business Consumer Guide
BEACON RESEARCH GROUP INC
125 WALNUT ST STE 11
WATERTOWN, MA 02172-9931

Send me a FREE issue of BUSINESS CONSUMER GUIDE!

☐ Mr. ☐ Ms. _____
Name

_____
Company

_____
Address

_____
City   State   ZIP

_____
Phone number   e-mail (optional)

1. What is your primary job function/title?

2. What is your organization's primary business activity?

3. How many employees are there at your location?
   ☐ 1-10 ☐ 11-24 ☐ 25-49 ☐ 50-99 ☐ 100-249 ☐ 250+ people

4. Where do you have Internet access? (Check all that apply)
   ☐ at work ☐ at home ☐ at library ☐ no access

EBG1

Send me a FREE issue of BUSINESS CONSUMER GUIDE!

☐ Mr. ☐ Ms. _____
Name

_____
Company

_____
Address

_____
City   State   ZIP

_____
Phone number   e-mail (optional)

1. What is your primary job function/title?

2. What is your organization's primary business activity?

3. How many employees are there at your location?
   ☐ 1-10 ☐ 11-24 ☐ 25-49 ☐ 50-99 ☐ 100-249 ☐ 250+ people

4. Where do you have Internet access? (Check all that apply)
   ☐ at work ☐ at home ☐ at library ☐ no access

EBG2

Contents

Letter Folding Equipment 217
Letter Opening Equipment 220
Long Distance Service 222
LTL Shipping 226
Modems 230
Monitors 234
Multifunctional Devices 238
Music On Hold Systems 241
Notebook Computers 244
Off-site Storage 248
Office Supplies 251
Overhead Projectors 255
Overnight Delivery Services 259
Pagers 262
Paper Shredders 265
Payroll Services 268
PDAs 272
Pension Plans 276
Photocopier Controls 280
Photocopiers 284
Pointing Devices 289
Portable Printers 292
Postage Meters 296
Postal Scales 301
PPOs 304
Prepaid Phone Cards 308
Public Relations Firms 311
Recordable CD Drives 314
Recycling 319
Safes 323
Same Day Delivery Services 326
Scanners 329
Signs 333
Slide Projectors 337
Stock Photography 340

Systems Furniture 343
Telemarketing Services 347
Telephone Directory Software..................................... 351
Telephone Headsets.. 353
Telephone Systems... 356
Temporary Help Services 361
Time Clocks 364
Toll Fraud Prevention 367
Toll Free Service 371
Toner Supplies 375
Trade Show Displays... 378
Travel Agencies 382
Typewriters... 386
Uniforms.. 389
Uninterruptible Power Supplies................................... 392
Video Conferencing Services....................................... 396
Voice Mail Systems 400
Workers Compensation Insurance 404
World Wide Web Site Setup 408

TOPIC LISTING BY CATEGORY..................................... 413
INDEX 419

Introduction

About the book

If you have ever tried to buy something for the office and been stumped about whom to call or what to ask, this book is for you.

The Essential Business Buyer's Guide is designed to help buyers get a headstart on the buying process. For each topic, we review the basics to get you up to speed and then point out the key buying criteria that should influence your purchasing decision. Special buying tips, pricing information, listings of leading vendors, and definitions of technical terms help round out the advice. Altogether, this reference provides buying advice on more than 110 products and services.

Buying is all about knowing what you need and understanding what the market has to offer. Companies armed with this book will find themselves able to make better purchasing decisions more quickly.

Who we are

The Essential Business Buyer's Guide was created by the staff of the *Business Consumer Guide*, the foremost authority on business purchasing issues.

Since 1992, the *Business Consumer Guide* has helped businesses across the U.S. and Canada make better and more informed purchases of office equipment and services. Our in-depth reports offer brand-name buying recommendations, vendor profiles, purchasing worksheets, and buying tips for small and medium-sized businesses.

If you would like more information about becoming a *Business Consumer Guide* subscriber, or if you would like to order one of our detailed reports on a specific product or service please call (800) 938-0088, or write us at *Business Consumer Guide*, 125 Walnut Street, Watertown, MA 02172.

On-line buying assistance

As an additional resource for corporate buyers, we have created BuyersZone, a World Wide Web site designed to supplement the information contained in this book.

Throughout the book, you will notice a BuyersZone icon at the end of many topics. By browsing to http://www.buyerszone.com/ you will be able to find updated purchasing information, links to vendors, and user forums on these subjects.

We encourage you to use BuyersZone. The site is free, and the information is updated daily.

Contacting us

Finally, we encourage feedback. We have been helping businesses for years, but this is the first edition of *The Essential Business Buyer's Guide*. We encourage you to share your suggestions, criticisms, and comments. In particular, if there are topics you would like to see added, or areas that need some clarification, please let us know.

We also want your buying tips. If you know of ways for businesses to save money, get a better deal, or avoid problems with a purchase, share them with us. That way, we can pass along the best tips to other readers in future editions.

Via e-mail: essential@buyerszone.com

By fax: (617/924-0055)

By mail: Beacon Research Group, Inc.
125 Walnut Street
Watertown, MA 02172-4043

Acknowledgments

Over the past four years, many subscribers, colleagues, and friends have suggested that we compile our purchasing research efforts into a single book. While we have always thought this a great idea, our always-busy editorial schedule seemed to dictate that this undertaking would never see completion.

Finally, after nearly two years of starts and stops, Seth Kessler brought his motivational, managerial, and organizational skills to the task. Almost singlehandedly, Seth turned a few aging files and articles into a thriving project.

Of course, even Seth could not complete this big a task alone. Mie-Yun Lee lent her considerable skills to the work, turning our semi-coherent technobabble into something substantially more readable.

Sally Chen did a bit of everything: research, writing, and editing. Her careful explanations and diligent follow-up added a much-appreciated level of detail to our topics.

We would also like to thank all the editorial assistants who researched and drafted this volume into existence. Our dedicated colleagues include Binh Le, Dara Neumann, Meredith Scott, Marc Shedroff, and Karen Zahalka.

There are also numerous people who helped us with this book, generously sharing their insights, comments, and ideas along the way. In particular, we would like to thank: Kevin Alansky, E. B. Baatz, Michael Chasen, Andrew Douglas, Cameron Foote, Karen Kavet, Jane M. Kessler, Richard S. Kessler, Christine Litavsky, Joseph Liu, Susan Moeller, Marc T. Nobleman, Dominique Raccah, and Todd Stocke.

Finally, a big thanks to all the family members and friends who supported us through this project.

— **The Staff of the Business Consumer Guide**

401(k) Plans

A 401(k) plan is a popular type of pension fund that is funded by salary deductions. Employees choose to contribute a percentage of their pre-tax income into a fund that is invested for retirement. Employers set up and administer the 401(k), but are not responsible for setting contribution levels or investing strategies.

VENDORS

Company	Headquarters	Phone Number	Target market (# of employees)
ADP	Roseland, NJ	800/432-401K	5-1000
Alliance Capital	Secaucus, NJ	800/243-6812	25+
American Funds	Los Angeles, CA	800/421-8511	10-2,500
American United Life	Indianapolis, IN	800/528-6139	25-500
Dreyfus Retirement Life	New York, NY	800/557-401K	1-200
Federated Investors	Pittsburgh, PA	800/239-3211	25-99
Fidelity Investments	Covington, KY	800/343-9184	25-100
Gabelli Funds	Rye, NY	800/GAB-2274	25-1,000
Invesco Retirement Plan Services	Atlanta, GA	800/538-6370	25+
Lincoln National Life	Ft. Wayne, IN	800/248-0838	2-500
Nationwide Life Insurance Co.	Columbus, OH	800/367-5939	25-2,000
New England Retirement Services	Boston, MA	800/422-2808	10-2,500
Phoenix Funds	Enfield, CT	800/243-4361	25-500
The 401(K) Association	Langhorne, PA	215/579-8830	2-25
Van Kampen American Capital	Houston, TX	800/421-5666	25-1,000

Buying points

Advantages of a 401(k) plan

For a number of reasons, 401(k) plans are a very popular way for companies to provide retirement benefits to their employees. First, 401(k) plans allow individual employees, rather than the company, to determine how much money they want to invest towards retirement.

A second advantage of 401(k) plans is that the employer is not generally liable for investment results. In a traditional defined-benefit pension plan, insufficient returns on investment may require the employer to allocate additional funds to the retirement account. In contrast, 401(k) plan investments are controlled by employees, allowing each person to be as aggressive or conservative with the funds as he or she desires.

For employees, 401(k) plans also offer the advantage of transferability. Since the 401(k) is funded by employee deductions, it remains the property of the individual employee. As a result, employees can transfer the investment to a new employer if they switch jobs. Employees can also access 401(k) funds immediately in case of emergency.

Impact on employee retention

401(k) plans typically have very little effect on employee retention, since all contributions to the plan belong to employees. Individuals leaving a firm can take 401(k) funds with them to a new job.

One way to increase employee retention is to offer matching contributions to a 401(k) plan. This means the employer agrees to contribute a certain amount of money to an employee's fund for every dollar the employee contributes. These matching contributions can be vested over a period as long as seven years, to encourage employees to stay at a firm for a longer period of time.

About plan providers

There are hundreds of companies that offer 401(k) plans to businesses. Primary vendors include insurance companies, banks, third party administrators, and investment firms.

It is difficult to generalize differences across provider types. However, each provider typically has a strength in a particular aspect of 401(k) plans, whether it be administration, information or investments.

Comparing providers

Currently the 401(k) market is very competitive, with many firms actively seeking a portion of this business.

The first area to examine when comparing providers is their range of investment opportunities. Firms offering 401(k) services should not only have a good track record of investments, but should also provide a wide range of investment vehicles and options. This will allow your employees the freedom to choose different levels of risk and reward.

A second area to examine is account service. You should get a strong understanding of both setup and ongoing service fees. Find out whether these fees vary according to the amount of plan activity, and whether there are fixed minimums concerning participation levels. If fees are not all-inclusive, learn what other types of charges can be incurred, and run through a typical and worst case scenario when comparing providers. This way, you will not be surprised by the cost of maintaining a plan for your employees.

A third component to a successful 401(k) plan is properly educating employees about the risks of different investment options. To ensure that employees are happy with the plan over the long term, make sure the administrator you choose is capable of providing educational materials and answering questions from participants.

Small company plans

Until just a few years ago, 401(k) plans were usually only offered by larger firms, since the costs of designing and maintaining plans were prohibitive for smaller firms. Today, however, many mutual fund companies, banks, and insurance companies have developed 401(k) plans for firms with 25 to 200 employees.

A few plans are targeted at even smaller companies. However, firms with fewer than 25 employees will generally not find the plans to be very economical. This is because administrative expenses are primarily fixed, which means that small businesses will end up paying more on a per-person basis than larger firms. However, fees are dropping rapidly, which means smaller and smaller firms can reasonably consider signing up for a plan.

About plan limits

401(k) plans place limits on the maximum amount that can be contributed by any employee each year. Employees currently can contribute up to $9,500 (in 1996), or a maximum of 15% of salary, whichever is lower.

One drawback of 401(k) plans is that the IRS has strict rules to make sure that investment levels are relatively equal across a firm. Because lower paid employees are often less willing to invest high percentages of their salaries, firms often must set a limit on the contributions of top personnel. This can limit the attractiveness of a 401(k) plan for executives.

Pricing

Since 401(k) contributions come from salary deductions, employers need only pay administrative and start-up costs to fund the plan. While 401(k) plans can be a very inexpensive means of providing a pension, administrative costs can be significant, since participants individually direct where their funds are invested.

Generally, you can expect to pay a startup fee of approximately $10 for every plan participant. Ongoing administrative fees will vary from $30 to $70 per participant, with fees typically smaller for larger companies.

Terms

Employer matching contribution
The amount, if any, that the employer contributes to the employee's retirement. Matching contributions are usually calculated as a set percentage of an employee's contribution, up to a fixed limit.

Vesting The period of time an employee must work at a firm before gaining access to employer-contributed pension income. The employee's own salary reductions are fully vested, or non-forfeitable.

Special tips

Since 401(k) funds are targeted for retirement, the IRS has strict rules on access to these funds before age 59 $^1/_2$. In most cases, early withdrawals will incur significant penalties.

Non-profit organizations cannot implement a 401(k) plan, but can design a similar plan called a 403(b) plan.

HR Investment Consultants (800/462-0628) publishes a *401(k) Provider Directory: Small Plan Guide* that profiles 40 providers of 401(k) plans geared specifically for small businesses.

See also
Accountants, Payroll Services, Pension Plans

For more information, visit
BuyersZone
http://www.buyerszone.com/

900 Service

A 900 number is a calling service that allows companies to charge customers for information delivered over the phone. Although the concept has been somewhat battered in the past by scams and negative press, 900 numbers have quietly gained acceptance as a practical way for firms to provide technical help or post-warranty support to their customers.

VENDORS

Company	Headquarters	Phone number
Advanced Telecom Services	Wayne, PA	610/688-6000
American Telnet	Wilmington, DE	302/651-9400
AT&T	Basking Ridge, NJ	800/655-1366
BFD Productions	Las Vegas, NV	800/444-4BFD
Interactive Strategies	W. Lake Village, CA	800/870-3030
Network Telephone Services	Woodland Hills, CA	800/727-6874
Telepublishing	Boston, MA	800/874-2340
West Interactive	Omaha, NE	402/573-1000

Buying points

Rationale
900 numbers are an excellent way for companies to charge support costs to customers who need the extra service. Rather than raising prices for all customers to cover support costs, many firms have turned to 900 numbers as a simple yet effective way to directly bill users for phone assistance.

900 numbers offer the convenience of automatic billing, with charges sent to users through their regular phone bills. This can be especially helpful when services are too inexpensive to justify the costs of separate billing.

Implementing a 900 number is a delicate task, however. Firms should be careful to avoid offending their existing customers, particularly those who are accustomed to certain levels of free support. Businesses should also be aware of the reputation of 900 numbers, and be careful to explain the costs and benefits of the service to their customers before implementing a program.

How 900 service works
To use a 900 service, a caller dials a telephone number that uses 900 as the area code. Immediately upon connecting, the caller will hear a preamble explaining how the call will be billed. This is designed to allow the caller to hang up before charges begin to accrue.

After this message, callers can be handled by a dedicated 900 service center or directly routed to your company's offices.

How calls are billed
Calls made to 900 numbers can be billed in one of two basic ways. Most services charge callers according to the number of minutes spent on the phone. This fee can entail a constant per minute charge, or can vary, with the first few minutes costing a certain amount and following minutes assessed at a different rate. Calls can also be billed at a flat rate, which results in a set charge regardless of the amount of time the caller is on the phone.

Most calls are billed on the caller's local telephone bill. However, some 900 numbers allow the caller to bill the call directly to a major credit card.

About 900 service providers
Companies interested in setting up a 900 number can choose either to work directly with a carrier or to sign up with a service bureau.

Working directly with a carrier is generally an option only for larger companies that have an advanced PBX phone system. You will typically require an automated attendant system to answer incoming calls and to alert users to the charges, plus automatic number identification capabilities to identify the number that will be billed for the call. In most cases, this will require a direct T1 connection between your phone system and a long distance carrier, which will cost several thousand dollars to install and maintain on a monthly basis.

Most smaller companies will want to work with a service bureau. These companies have already made the investment in phone equipment and lines, and have 900 numbers available for almost immediate use. A 900 service bureau not only provides access to a 900 number, but can also help design a program that will comply with all regulatory requirements. Service centers can also provide office space and support for smaller companies unable to support a full calling center in their own offices.

Choosing a provider

There are several points to consider when evaluating service bureaus. These include the system capacity, service offerings, and company experience.

First, make sure that the service bureau will be able to handle the expected call volume during peak calling periods. Peak periods can arise during certain times of the day, or after a radio or television commercial. The service bureau should have enough lines and personnel to handle all the calls you expect to receive in these situations.

Another area to evaluate is the service offerings of the 900 bureau. Examine areas such as call handling capabilities, program design assistance, regulatory knowledge, and billing reports. Ideally, the service bureau should have previous experience with the type of program you would like to implement. Even better is a firm that already has similar 900 offerings currently in place.

It can also be useful to experience the service from a customer's perspective. Call other services hosted by the provider to get a sense for how well these services are implemented. Check into the collections process for delinquent customers and make sure it suits your customer base.

Finally, look into the company's background. This is particularly important since the 900 service business has seen more than its share of unscrupulous companies. Learn about the firm's clients, and how long they have been in business. It is also advised to thoroughly check references.

Legal requirements

In order to combat burgeoning problems with pay-per-call services, the Federal Trade Commission (FTC) passed the Telephone Disclosure and Dispute Resolution Act (TDDRA) in 1993. This Act sets specific requirements for advertising and operating 900 number services to prevent deceptive billing practices.

For example, all numbers that cost more than $2 per call are legally required to warn callers about these charges during the introduction, or preamble. Callers should be given the opportunity to hang up without being charged when calling these numbers.

Any service bureau you use should be able to guide your firm through the specifics of the Act to ensure that your 900 program is in compliance.

Pricing

Working with a service bureau costs between $1,000 and $2,500 in initial fees. On an ongoing basis, you will generally need to pay monthly fees and per minute charges based on the call volume received. In addition, there will usually be a carrier commission of 10% to 15% of gross revenue. The total amount paid to the carrier and service bureau usually totals close to $1 per minute.

Terms

Automatic Number Identification (ANI) A feature that identifies the phone number of the incoming caller. ANI is required with most 900 lines to identify where the call should be billed.

Dialed Number Identification Service (DNIS) A feature that identifies the 900 number that was dialed. This allows one call center to handle a variety of calls, directing calls to different support groups depending on the number that was dialed.

IP Industry term for an information provider, or the company that sets up a 900 number.

Tailored call coverage The ability to selectively block calls by state or area code.

Uncollectables A term for those callers who have not paid their 900 bill. Some bureaus can help reduce the amount of uncollectables with caller tracking equipment that denies delinquent accounts access to the service.

Special tips

Keep in mind that many companies block calls to 900 numbers on their phone systems. You may want to provide an alternative route for people at such companies to reach you, such as credit card billing via a regular or toll free line.

Avoid shared 900 numbers that require callers to dial an extension to reach your service. This can result in misdialed numbers and greater difficulties in resolving billing disputes.

Rates and terms are almost always negotiable. Talk with multiple bureaus to increase your leverage in bargaining discussions.

The publisher of *Audiotex News* (800/735-3398) also offers various titles about the 900 industry, including *The Directory of 900 Service Bureaus: How to Select One* and *Promoting Your 900 Number.* They also can refer you to service bureaus with specialties in particular areas.

See also
Fax on Demand, International Callback, Long Distance Service, Telemarketing Services, Toll Free Service

ACCOUNTANTS

Certified Public Accountants can provide businesses with a full array of financial services and advice, including audits, business financing advice, record keeping, assessments of benefit and compensation plans, and income tax preparation. In addition to providing varied financial services, an accountant can be a valuable asset in helping your business make the most of its financial opportunities.

RECORDS RETENTION

Type of records	Permanently	10 yrs.	7 yrs.	3 yrs.
Accounting records (annual financial statements, journals, tax returns and worksheets, depreciation schedules, ledgers, etc.)	●			
Accounts payable/receivable		●		
Sales records & expense records			●	
Bank statements, canceled checks & loan records			●	
Computer backup of all business records	●			
Corporate records (board minutes, incorporation documents, by-laws, licenses, contracts, leases, mortgages, trademarks, patents, etc.)	●			
Benefit, pension & profit sharing plan	●			
Payroll records & employee contracts			●	
Employment applications & resumes				●
Property records			●	

Buying points

CPA qualifications

A Certified Public Accountant (CPA) is a professional title for accountants. This title indicates that the individual has completed the necessary levels of education and licensing and has passed a national examination.

In order to retain this certification, CPAs must attend a minimum of 40 hours of tax workshops, seminars, and other forms of professional education each year to keep up-to-date on new tax regulations. This helps ensure that their work is in compliance with changing laws.

Another indication of the individual's training is membership in the American Institute of Certified Public Accountants (800/CPA-FIRM). To maintain active membership in the AICPA, members must satisfy their CPA license requirements on an annual basis. Firms are also reviewed once every three years.

Finding a CPA

Finding a CPA can be a sensitive task, since the accountant must be entrusted with the intimate financial details of your business. To find a CPA, start by speaking to a banker, colleague or lawyer that you trust. Most state societies of CPAs also offer referral services. Avoid just looking through the Yellow Pages or accepting a random solicitation.

Next, talk to the person about your industry and your firm. Make sure they have a general understanding of the type of issues that you face. Ask for references, especially of clients that are from the same industry, or are approximately the same size.

Ask references how knowledgeable the CPA is about their industry. Find out about turnaround time on requests and whether the firm is responsive to questions. Also learn if the CPA gives valuable suggestions on new approaches to financial and tax matters. Finally, find out how often the reference consults with the CPA, and how much the accountant charges for these consultations.

Pricing

Since accounting services are not a commodity, pricing depends on many variables, including the type of services rendered, the kind of tax return that needs to be filed, and the condition of your financial records.

Accounting services are generally rendered on a work performed basis. Generally, the less time the firm's staff has to spend deciphering and searching through your records, the less it will cost you in the end.

When starting a relationship, discuss the types of services you expect to have rendered. Find out exactly who will be working on your tax return, and make sure to understand the qualifications of that individual.

Special tips

Be sure all your internal records are up-to-date. Accounting firms charge extra for the time it takes to sort through and reconcile your bank statements, payables, receivables, and receipts.

There are many low-cost software options for businesses looking to automate such applications as check writing, billing/invoicing, general ledger, accounts receivable, accounts payable, payroll, bank reconciliation, inventory tracking, job-cost tracking, and financial reports. Start by asking your CPA to recommend titles that are appropriate for your business.

Be sure to ask your CPA how long different types of records should be kept, since the IRS can conduct audits of your business long after your return was filed.

See also
401(k) Plans, Corporate Cards, Payroll Services, Pension Plans

Did you know?

The first income tax form, issued in 1913, was only 4 pages in length, including instructions.

Advertising Agencies

Advertising agencies can help companies conduct ad campaigns using a wide range of media, including television, radio, billboards, Yellow Page directories, magazines, newspapers, and the Internet.

Buying points

Types of services provided
Advertising services fall into two general categories. First, agencies can help you position your product in the marketplace by producing advertisements that will generate attention.

Second, agencies can help you place these advertisements in various media, by purchasing magazine ad pages, television commercial time, or other placement opportunities.

Why work with an agency
One of the primary advantages of working with an agency is the ability to utilize an agency's creative services to create professional-looking pieces. Although a company may have talented designers in-house, they may not be fully aware of the particular requirements of a given advertising medium.

Ad agencies also make sense for companies that are developing an ad campaign for the first time or are working under strict time constraints. Media buyers can assist in identifying specific outlets in which to advertise and often have ad rates on hand for easy comparison shopping.

Over the long term, ad agencies can offer more flexibility than in-house advertising. It is much easier to replace an agency when you are not satisfied with the concepts being proposed than it is to fire an employee whose ideas are becoming stale.

Minimum advertising budgets
Companies of all sizes can use an advertising agency. However, not all agencies will be interested in handling every account. Generally, you will find that the largest agencies work with accounts that spend more than one

million dollars per year on advertising. While smaller accounts may be able to work with these organizations, they generally will not receive as much attention as they would with a smaller agency. Small regional and local firms are a better bet for companies that expect to spend less than $1 million on advertising.

Working with an ad agency makes much less sense if you have an advertising budget of less than $100,000. At such spending levels, it often makes sense to contact publications or other advertising targets directly to obtain information about their rates and audience.

Learning about agencies

There are directories that list agencies by various criteria, including advertising specialties, specific campaigns, and geographic location. Two well-known sources of information are the *Advertising Red Books*, which are published by National Register Publishing (800/521-8110), and *Adweek* Directories (800/468-2395). Local advertising clubs can also start you off with a list of agencies to contact.

The bidding process

When looking for an agency, the first step is to draw up a list of potential partners. You will want to include a mix of local and regional or national firms.

The initial conversations you hold should convey your needs to the agency and give you a sense for the agency's capabilities. Based on these conversations, you should be able to narrow your list to three or four firms.

At this point, the finalist agencies will prepare a presentation, which is known as a pitch. During the pitch they will go into greater detail about how they would handle your account.

Some bids may include a work assignment that outlines the type of work the agency expects to conduct with your account. The work assignment gives a clear sense of the media plan, the creative strategy, and production budget. In order to incorporate such information in the bidding process, the agency finalists must be given a sense for your desired media mix (i.e., what percentage will be print versus broadcast advertising) and advertising budget.

In general, the initial discussions do not incur any costs, but will require you to allocate valuable time and resources to adequately inform the agencies about your needs. For large accounts, the bidding process can easily take three months. Smaller companies should probably plan for a 6-8 week search.

Pricing

Advertising agencies historically charged a flat fee of 15% commission on all media billings. Today, the compensation varies from client to client, with most fees ranging from 8% to 12% plus some expenses.

Terms

Circulation The number of paid and unpaid copies that are distributed by a publication.

Column inch A measurement used in newspaper advertising where one unit is one column wide and one inch long.

Cost per column inch The method by which newspapers charge for advertising space. Advertisers can determine the cost of an ad by multiplying the desired ad size by this cost.

Gross Rating Points (GRP) Used to measure advertising costs for radio and television, GRP is the total number of impressions (the average number of times a target audience sees or hears an advertisement) delivered by a media schedule, expressed as a percentage (e.g., 1 GRP delivers 1% of the population).

Media kits Information packaged for advertisers that typically contains copies of the publication or information about the advertising medium, demographic information, rate sheets, and advertising restrictions and specifications.

Rate card The cost of advertising space quoted by publications. Note that this rate may be subject to negotiation for frequent advertisers.

Special tips

All published rates are negotiable to some extent. If you expect to advertise regularly in a particular publication, do not be afraid to ask for a discount based on your expected volume. Discounts are often based on ad frequency, total dollar volume, advertisements in affiliated publications, and prompt payment.

If the expense of a full-service advertising agency is more than you wish to spend, consider working with an agency on a contingency basis, or with freelancers who handle specific tasks. The best way to find freelancers is by asking for recommendations by graphic designers, public relations firms or clients with whom you currently work.

For more detailed information about the agency selection process, call the American Association of Advertising Agencies (212/682-2500). It publishes the series *A Client's Guide to...* with an issue dedicated to conducting an agency search/agency compensation.

For information on newspaper advertising, contact the Newspaper Association of America (800/651-4NAA) for a list of available resources.

Firms unfamiliar with how the industry works may want to hire a local consultant, or a service like the Advertising Agency Register (212/644-0790) to help choose an agency. By asking a lot of questions, however, you will probably be able to find out what you need to know on your own.

See also
Clipping Services, Graphic Designers, Public Relations Firms, Signs, Stock Photography, Trade Show Displays, World Wide Web Site Setup

Did you know?

Outdoor advertising grew rapidly in the 1970s because cigarettes were banned from advertising on television and radio.

Answering Machines

Almost all businesses face the problem of having to deal with phone calls that arrive after business hours. To avoid missing these calls, many small firms turn to answering machines. As technology has improved, these machines have become much more flexible at handling large volumes of messages or multiple users.

In addition, answering machines are much less expensive than voice mail systems or answering services.

PRICING

Type of answering service	Price range
Standalone cassette answering machine	$30-$120
Standalone digital answering machine	$50-$300
Voice mail service bureau (per person, per year)	$50-$90
Faxmodem with voice mailbox	$150-$400
Low-end voice mail system	$900-$2,000

VENDORS

Company	Headquarters	Phone number	Warranty
Bogen	Ramsey, NJ	201/934-8500	1 yr.
Cobra	Chicago, IL	800/262-7222	1 yr.
General Electric	Fairfield, CT	800/626-2000	1-2 yrs.
Lucent Technologies	Murray Hill, NJ	888/4-LUCENT	2 yrs.
Panasonic	Secaucus, NJ	800/545-2672	1 yr.
PhoneMate (Casio)	Torrance, CA	310/320-9810	1 yr.
Radio Shack (Tandy)	Fort Worth, TX	800/843-7422	1 yr.
Sharp	Mahwah, NJ	800/BE-SHARP	1 yr.
Sony	Park Ridge, NJ	800/222-SONY	1 yr.
Southwestern Bell (Conair)	E. Windsor, NJ	800/366-0937	1 yr.

Buying points

Types of answering machines
There are four different types of answering machines currently on the market. The least expensive models use a single tape for both incoming and outgoing messages. The problem with this approach is that callers must wait a long time before recording if the tape is filled with other messages.

More sophisticated machines use two tapes, one for incoming and one for outgoing calls. This minimizes the delay before recording, since the incoming message tape is kept wound to the appropriate place.

Newer answering machines often use digital chips to record incoming or outgoing messages. Models typically combine a digital chip for the outgoing message with tape for incoming messages.

Purely digital machines use no tape at all, recording both incoming and outgoing messages digitally.

Advantages and disadvantages of digital technology
The biggest difference between digital and tape machines concerns storage flexibility. Unlike a tape recorder, digital machines can erase one message without disturbing others on the machine. This allows important messages to be kept without cluttering the machine with less relevant messages.

A second advantage of digital machines is that sound quality can be better than with tape devices. Tape machines all suffer from some level of background hiss, particularly with the outgoing message, while digital machines typically offer a much cleaner-sounding message. However, be aware that digital technology does not automatically guarantee good sound. Some digital recorders use cheap microphones or very low sampling rates. In many cases, a cheap digital machine may sound worse than a tape machine.

A third advantage of digital units is reliability. Since these units have no moving parts, they tend to be very sturdy. In contrast, tape-based machines are relatively complex, and will tend to break down after a few years of use.

One disadvantage of digital machines concerns power failure. If the power goes out, digital machines can lose all their messages unless there is a battery backup feature.

Handling incoming calls
To keep track of when messages arrive, most firms find it very useful to have a machine that offers a time and date stamp. This records information about the time of the call before the start of each message.

Many businesses need different messages for different times of the day. Answering machines equipped with a multiple greeting feature can easily handle this requirement. In most cases, you record multiple greetings and then set specific times when each message should be played.

Some answering machines offer multiple mailboxes, allowing callers to route messages to a specific recipient. The caller simply enters a touch tone code and records the message in a specific mailbox. When people return to the office, they can play just the messages left in their mailbox.

For those who do not wish to handle individual messages, an announce-only feature allows a recorded message to be left without giving callers the option to record a response.

Key features for travelers
If you are frequently away from your office, you will want to purchase an answering machine with remote access features.

The most basic remote access feature is message retrieval. Users can pick up messages on the road by entering a touch-tone password after calling. In most cases, other touch-tone buttons allow you to skip, rewind or delete messages.

Another useful feature is remote activation. This allows you to turn on the machine via telephone in case someone in your office forgets to activate it.

One money-saving feature is toll saver, which modifies the number of times the phone will ring before the machine picks up. Typically, the machine will answer a call immediately when there are new messages. If no new messages have been recorded, the user can hang up before the machine picks up the line.

Allowable message lengths
One important specification to check with any answering machine is its recording time. Many units limit either the length of individual messages or the total amount of recording time. In either case, short recording limits can frustrate callers.

For individual messages, look for a machine that allows at least one minute per call. Even better are machines that offer 2.5 minutes per message, since this is enough for even the most detailed request.

Total recording time tends to be a bigger issue for digital machines than cassette recorders. Many digital units can only hold 4 minutes of messages, which may translate to as few as eight messages. If you suspect that this is not enough, look for a machine that offers 15 or 30 minutes of recording time.

Two-line systems
Two-line answering machines, while relatively uncommon, are available for businesses that receive calls over more than one line. However, most two-line answering machines are fairly limited in terms of capabilities. For example, many cannot pick up a call on the second line while simultaneously answering a call on the first.

Special tips

Avoid units that integrate an answering machine and a phone into a single component. If you have difficulty with one of the two, you may be unable to use the other until the problem has been resolved.

If you often find yourself trying to decipher incoming messages, purchase a machine with variable speed playback. This can reduce the bother of listening to long-winded callers and aid in deciphering messages from fast talkers.

If you are looking to replace your existing answering machine, some manufacturers offer special replacement pricing if you can show proof of ownership (either by sending the receipt or the machine to be replaced). Others offer refurbished units; be sure to check the warranty information before choosing this replacement option.

Voice mail services provided by local telephone companies may be a viable alternative to answering machines. These services provide multiple mailboxes for as little as $15 per month.

A noteworthy high-end digital answering system, the Friday by Bogen, offers voice mailboxes and other simple voice mail features at a fraction of the cost of voice mail service bureaus or low-end voice mail systems.

See also
Voice Mail Systems

Did you know?

Early answering machines used a metal arm to lift the phone receiver off the cradle and play a message into the mouthpiece. Messages were similarly recorded directly from the earpiece.

Automatic Staplers

*A*utomatic staplers can help reduce the time and effort needed to staple multiple sets of a document. They are particularly useful for businesses that do not have an office copier equipped with an automatic stapling function.

PRICING

Type of stapler	Price range
Cordless	$40-$95
Standard electric	$30-$210
Heavy-duty electric	$250-$700
Saddle stapler/long-reach electric	$430-$550

VENDORS

Company	Headquarters	Phone number	Cordless	Warranty
Boston/Eberhard Faber (Hunt Mfg.)	Statesville, NC	800/879-4868		1-2 yrs.
GBC Bates	Northbrook, IL	800/477-9900	●	1 yr.
Max USA	Garden City, NY	800/223-4293		90 days
Panasonic	Secaucus, NJ	201/348-7490	●	90 days-1 yr.
Stanley Bostitch	E. Greenwich, RI	401/884-2500		90 days-2 yrs.
The Staplex Company	Brooklyn, NY	800/221-0822	●	90 days
Swingline (Acco USA)	Wheeling, IL	800/222-6462	●	1-2 yrs.

Buying points

How they work
There are two main ways that automatic staplers can operate. Optical models have a small light beam within the model. When the light beam senses a document has been inserted, the stapler automatically binds the pages. User-activated models require the user to push a button or foot pedal to activate the machine. This allows documents to be placed more precisely, but does so at the expense of speed.

Binding capacity
Staplers can bind from 2 to 100 sheets of paper at a time, with different models offering varying capacities. A stapler's binding capacity also depends on the type of paper being stapled. Most machines can staple twenty sheets of 20 lb. (regular copy) paper without difficulty.

Stapler capacity
Some automatic staplers hold the same number of staples as a manual stapler, holding one full strip of 210 standard staples at a time. Larger models can hold 2,500, 5,000, or even 10,000 staples. However, these models require the purchase of staple cartridges rather than regular staples.

Avoiding stapler jams
Automatic staplers are not necessarily more prone to jamming than manual staplers. However, automatic staple jams do tend to be more difficult to fix, particularly in cases when a user exceeds the stapler's page capacity.

Fortunately, most manufacturers offer immediate replacement of units in need of repair, with warranty coverage renewed for each replacement unit.

To avoid jamming, users should be very careful not to remove a document until the stapler has finished its full up and down motion. Manufacturers also warn against purchasing cheap staples, which may cause jamming due to excess glue or weak metal.

Other features to consider
One of the most common automatic stapler features is cordless operation. These battery-powered units tend to be similar to their plug-in cousins, except that they usually cannot handle as many pages at once.

There are relatively few other features available with standard models, although many manufacturers can produce specialized models. Custom models can be designed to provide features such as finger activation or saddle stapling.

Noise considerations
Stapler noise levels vary from one manufacturer to the next, but usually closely correspond to the page capacity. Newer designs, particularly heavy-duty models, tend to be much quieter than older units.

Terms

Flat clinch A staple that is completely flat when closed. This allows for easier stacking of documents.

Saddle staplers Staplers that are used to fasten booklets or brochures at the centerfold.

Throat depth Indicates of how far from the edge of a sheet of paper a staple can be placed.

Special tips

Ask the dealer for a trial period to make sure the automatic stapler can handle your daily stapling needs.

Most electric staplers will need a rest period after heavy usage to prevent overheating.

Some staplers have an indicator light that glows when very few staples remain in the unit.

Be careful. Automatic staplers can puncture fingers as quickly as they do other materials.

See also
Letter Folding Equipment, Photocopiers

Beverage Services

A professional beverage service supplies bottled water, coffee, and other beverages to businesses. A beverage service representative determines what supplies are required by your office and then stocks the items in a manner that ensures the safest and most efficient utilization of space.

PRICING

Type of beverage service	One year cost
Basic coffee service	$720
Gourmet coffee service	$1,008
Bottled water service w/ cold & room temperature cooler rental	$228
Bottled water service w/ hot & cold cooler rental	$264
(Pricing estimates based on a 30-person office.)	

VENDORS

Bottled water company	Headquarters	Phone number	Areas served
Arrowhead	Monterey Park, CA	800/950-9393	California
Calistoga	Calistoga, CA	707/942-6295	California
Deer Park	Norton, MA	800/325-3337	East
Evian	Greenwich, CT	800/365-2208	U.S.
Mountain Valley	Hot Springs, AR	501/623-6671	most of U.S.
Ozarka	Dallas, TX	800/950-9397	Gulf
Poland Springs	Norton, MA	800/950-9395	Northeast
Sparkletts	Pasadena, CA	800/492-8377	West
Zephyrhills	Tampa, FL	800/950-9398	Florida

Buying points

Why use a beverage service

Most employees consume beverages, particularly coffee and water, several times a day. If employees must leave the office to get these beverages, each break can take ten minutes, resulting in a significant loss of productivity to the company.

Beverage services are designed to help a firm meet employee demands for quality beverages without leaving the office. These firms can supply bottled water, coffee, and other drinks right in your lunchroom or hallway.

Available offerings

As might be expected in the office environment, most beverage services concentrate on coffee. Bottled water is also very popular, but other beverages such as juices, soft drinks, tea, and even cappuccino are also available. Many of these services can also provide snack foods such as popcorn and chips.

For businesses that do not want to deal with cleaning cups and plates, beverage services can also supply disposable cups and other kitchen utensils. Some will even go so far as to provide refrigerators, microwaves, and storage cabinets.

Account size requirements

Beverage services can supply firms of virtually all sizes with beverages such as water and juices, since these products last a long time. In terms of coffee, most firms set a minimum consumption requirement of four pots per day before they will place and service a coffee machine in your office.

Offices with more than 100 employees may want to consider installing a vending machine to meet the range of employees' beverage and snack needs. Vending machines can greatly reduce your expenditures since employees will offset some of the costs. The vending company, which is often the same company offering the other beverage services, will help set prices for the items based on your budget.

Finding a provider

Virtually all beverage services are local providers, which can make finding a firm somewhat difficult. One option is to call the National Coffee Service Association (800/683-NCSA), which offers a referral service. The International Bottled Water Association (800/WATER-11) is also available to answer questions about bottled water service.

Pricing

Most coffee services do not charge for basic equipment. The brewing machine and water cooler are usually included as part of a service agreement with a coffee service, as long as supplies are purchased through that company. Next day delivery of supplies is also usually included as long as a minimum order size, typically about $25, is satisfied.

Cases of coffee pouches usually cost about $40 to $60 per case of 84 to 96 pouches, with each pouch producing one pot of coffee. Specialty coffees will cost more per pouch.

Bottled water services usually rent or sell coolers and require a refundable deposit for each bottle delivered. Depending on the type of cooler ordered, monthly cooler rental rates range from $10 to $15 per month. Alternatively, a cooler can be purchased outright for $200 to $300. Excluding bottle deposits, the water costs approximately $7 to $10 per 5- or 6-gallon bottle, with 3-gallon bottles costing a bit more per gallon.

Special tips

Many bottled water companies offer introductory specials like one free month of cooler rental and a couple of free bottles of water.

There is usually no delivery charge for firms that can commit to a term of at least 12 months.

If you enter into a one year service agreement, try to negotiate a guarantee that your prices will not change during the length of the term. Also find out about cancellation or delivery charges if you discontinue service before the end of the contract.

BUSINESS CARDS

*T*he typical business greeting involves a firm handshake and an exchange of business cards. After you leave, the business card is the primary symbol and reminder of who you are. It is little wonder that creating this small piece of paper can demand so much attention.

PRICING		
Paper type	Printing process	Total cost
White stock	Thermography	$15-$60
White stock	Flat print	$25-$85
White stock	Gravure	$80-$315
High-quality	Thermography	$35-$75
High-quality	Flat print	$40-$95
High-quality	Gravure	$90-$325
(Each based on a quantity of 500.)		

Buying points

Printing sources
Virtually any commercial printer can print business cards. There are differences, however, in the types of cards a printer can produce. If printers cannot handle the actual printing themselves, they will typically outsource the job to another printer.

Designing a business card
Many printers offer a range of standard business card designs. For these designs, you simply indicate the text and logo that should be printed.

For a more distinctive look, you can have business cards custom designed. Graphic designers can help not only specify the card design, but also the paper, color, and printing process.

You can also prepare a business card yourself using desktop publishing software. Consult with a printer beforehand to make sure the copy is appropriately formatted. Depending on the printer, you may need to submit camera-ready copy or a computer file.

Printing methods
There are three printing methods used to produce business cards. Although each method can be used to produce any design, there will be significant differences in the way the finished cards appear.

The least expensive process is known as thermography. The process produces raised print which is slightly shiny looking. Thermography is primarily used for business cards and invitations.

Business cards can also be flat printed. As the term suggests, flat printing simply applies ink against paper. This process is typically a bit more expensive than thermography.

Gravure printing is used for high-end designs. With this printing process, a metal plate is used to imprint the cards. The resulting card has a very clean look and is particularly well suited for displaying thin lines and crisp lettering.

Paper options
The least expensive paper used in business card printing is white card stock, which is more specifically known as white 80 pound wove cover stock. The basic price for business cards quoted by printers generally includes the cost of using this paper. Virtually all printers offer a large selection of other papers that vary in color, weight, and texture.

Choosing business card colors
Black is the least expensive and most common color used in business card printing. Some printers offer a set of "standard" colors at a nominal additional cost to the buyer, with higher charges for custom Pantone colors.

In general, printing costs will increase according to the number of colors required. This is because there are charges involved in creating the color, and in preparing and cleaning the press.

Unusual features
There are several ways to help your business card stand out.

One method is to emboss the business name or logo on the cards. Embossing raises or lowers the surface of the paper to produce an image or spell letters. This area can either be printed or left unprinted. Since embossing requires a custom die, it can add quite a bit to the total cost of the cards.

Companies can also print graphics or lettering using colored foil, which provides a very noticeable shine.

If there is not enough room to include all the information you want on one side of a card, consider printing on the back side. You may even want to consider using paper that folds into the size of a business card to double the available amount of print space.

For an unconventional look, companies can incorporate a photo in a card or produce business card magnets.

Ordering the right quantity

Seventy-five to eighty percent of the cost of printing business cards is due to pre-press work. Typesetting, preparing the inks, and setting up the press make up the bulk of the printer's expenses. In contrast, the actual printing process costs very little.

As a result, be generous when ordering cards. It is much cheaper to order more cards than you need than to reorder small sets of cards time and time again.

Most printers set a minimum order of 250 or 500 cards per name. 500 cards translates to about a five-inch stack of cards.

Printing turnaround time

The turnaround time for business cards can range from two days to two weeks. Cards using a standard template and standard colors can often be produced in a matter of days. Custom business cards generally take longer.

Business travelers who need cards printed for the next day can place a rush order with a copy shop. The shop will photocopy one business card onto card stock and then cut the printed sheets down to size. This method should only be used in emergency situations, as the print quality of the cards tends to be quite poor.

Pricing

At the low end, printing a basic set of 500 business cards costs anywhere from $30 to $65. However, better stock paper, color ink, and more expensive printing processes can dramatically drive up the cost. For example, 500 business cards sporting two colors and using high quality paper can cost more than $100.

Terms

Camera ready copy A paper printout that can be used by the printer to make plates for printing. This process typically involves taking a picture of the printout with a camera to create the plate.

Pantone color A color coding system that is widely used throughout the printing industry. This system assigns codes to a wide range of colors and specifies the mixture of basic colors required to create a particular shade.

Thermography A printing technology which sprays thermography dust on business cards to form letters and graphics. The cards are then fed through a heater which solidifies the dust to produce raised print.

Special tips

You can get more mileage out of your business cards by printing them without specific reference to the person's job title or department. These cards can still be useful even if your employees change departments or are promoted.

If your company experiences high turnover, you may want to create a business card which contains only the company or the department's general information.

If you are printing a logo that has large areas of solid color, thermography may not be the best choice. The printing process typically causes solid areas to have a pebbly look.

One easy way to create a memorable card is to design a card to read vertically instead of horizontally.

A business card with color that extends to the edge of the card costs more to print than a card that contains no print along the edges.

Some printers that specialize in business cards have pre-made dies for embossing. This can be an economical way of obtaining embossed cards without paying the high cost of custom dies.

If you do have the card embossed, ask for the die. That way, if you switch printers, the die may not have to be recast.

See also
Business Forms, Commercial Printing

BUSINESS FORMS

*E*ven in this age of computers, paper forms are widely used for invoices, purchase orders, shipping slips, and account statements.

Producing these forms requires unique equipment. Because printing, assembling, and numbering multi-part forms is a complex task, only certain printers specialize in forms manufacturing.

PRICING

Quantity and type of form	Price range
1,000 Stock impact, 3-part	$175-$201
1,000 Stock impact, 4-part	$212-$253
5,000 Stock laser, 1-part	$212-$295
5,000 Stock impact, 3-part	$395-$683
5,000 Stock impact, 4-part	$732-$935
5,000 Custom impact, 3-part	$626-$854
5,000 Custom impact, 4-part	$744-$1,012

VENDORS

Company	Headquarters	Phone number	Stock laser	Custom laser	Stock impact	Custom impact
Deluxe	St. Paul, MN	800/328-0304	•	•	•	•
John Harland	Decatur, GA	800/282-0250	•	•	•	•
McBee	Parsippany, NJ	800/526-1272	•		•	
Moore Business Forms	Vernon Hills, IL	800/323-6230	•	•	•	•
NEBS	Groton, MA	800/225-9550	•	•	•	•
Rapidforms	Thorofare, NJ	800/257-5287	•	•	•	•
Wallace	Lisle, IL	800/323-8447	•	•	•	•

Buying points

Buying business forms

Business forms are sold through three channels: direct from the manufacturer, through a distributor or indirectly through secondary channels.

In direct sales, manufacturers use catalogs and sales forces to sell their product. Because catalog ordering eliminates the middle man and because the forms produced are based on standard templates, this channel tends to have the best prices. However, you may need to call several manufacturers to find one that can print forms in the style or design you require.

Distributors work by taking orders and passing them along to the printer best suited for the job. This method saves you the effort of finding a printer that can provide the forms you need, but means that you will pay a slight markup for this convenience. Similarly, commercial printers that cannot perform the order themselves will tap outside print shops for help.

Other companies, such as software vendors, sell forms to supplement their services. They have little incentive to provide competitive pricing, so prices tend to be quite high from these vendors.

Printing company logos

Most manufacturers can easily add a company logo and name to stock forms. These forms are sold preformatted, with a small customizable area available for company information. While the cost of adding a company name is usually included in the basic price, adding a logo can cost $25 to $100 more. Orders are then grouped and printed according to the form design. As a result, stock forms tend to be inexpensive, even in small quantities.

Custom-designed forms can handle any name or logo design you require. These forms are designed to meet a company's unique needs and require a separate run each time they are ordered. Custom forms are more expensive than stock forms, and usually require a longer lead time.

Preprinted forms vs. laser printing forms

Laser printing forms is a reasonable alternative to using preprinted forms, particularly when firms often adjust their format or print few forms per day.

In large quantities, printing forms with a laser printer tends to be quite expensive. Laser printers are non-impact printers, meaning that they do not press the image into the paper's surface when printing. As a result, multi-part forms can only be made by printing each part individually and then folding them together. In high-volume situations, using preprinted forms with a dot matrix printer can be less expensive.

Electronic invoicing

Electronic invoicing is a way to automatically transfer invoicing information from one company's computer databases to those of a supplier or customer. Typically, such

Business Forms

Electronic Data Interchange (EDI) systems are established by a large company in order to manage its supplier network.

These customized systems typically require establishing an e-mail or EDI account with an e-mail/EDI provider. Increasingly, EDI options utilizing the Internet are being developed for more cost-effective delivery of this information.

An EDI system can be quite expensive and is generally only used by smaller firms when a major customer demands its implementation. However, once installed, these systems can reduce ordering time and data entry as well as reduce delivery costs.

Terms

Carbonless paper This paper is specially treated to allow information written on a form to be transferred to underlying parts without the use of carbon paper.

Crash printing This method of manufacturing forms prints an image on the first layer of a form, with the resulting pressure transferring the image to the underlying pages by carbon or carbonless paper.

Laser forms These forms are designed for printing on a laser or ink-jet printer.

Lithographic printing This printing process prints each part of a form individually.

Snap-set forms These forms are designed to be completed manually.

Stock forms These forms are pre-designed forms intended for use by multiple companies. Customization options, if any, are quite limited.

Special tips

Companies that order forms in small quantities may find it more cost-effective to search the market for a suitable match among stock designs than to order custom-designed forms.

Firms that spend more than $50,000 per year on forms should work with a direct sales agent to find ways to minimize costs. Smaller businesses will usually benefit more from the lower overhead of catalog purchases.

When designing a form, make sure it is easy to read and complete. Serif fonts are recommended for large blocks of text (like directions), while sans serif type is recommended for elements of the form that require immediate interaction with the reader (like captions or titles).

For assistance in designing forms, consider hiring a person who has been trained in their design. The Business Forms Management Association (503/227-3393) and the Document Management Industries Association (800/336-4641) offer referrals of local certified designers and tips on how to create better forms.

See also
Business Cards, Checks, Commercial Printing, Dot Matrix Printers

BUSINESS INSURANCE

*B*usiness insurance is designed to protect business against unexpected events such as robbery, fire, or accident. In some cases, business insurance may determine whether a company is able to survive such events.

Unfortunately, most businesses spend far less time investigating insurance options than they spend investigating purchases or even inexpensive office products. Some firms are left exposed to significant risks, while others simply waste money on unneeded or overlapping coverage.

INSURER RATING SERVICES

Rating service	Headquarters	Phone number	Highest ratings						Declining ratings
A. M. Best	Old Wyck, NJ	908/439-2200	A++	A+	A	A–	B++	B+	B
Duff & Phelps	New York, NY	800/395-3334	AAA	AA+	AA	AA–	A+	A	A–
Moody's	New York, NY	212/553-0377	Aaa	Aa1	Aa2	Aa3	A1	A2	A3
Standard & Poor's	New York, NY	212/208-8000	AAA	AA+	AA	AA–	A+	A	A–

Buying points

Types of coverage
The three basic types of coverage that a business requires are property, liability, and workers compensation.

Property insurance protects firms against physical damage or loss, such as fire or theft. This type of insurance will help cover the cost of repairs or replacement goods.

Liability insurance is designed to protect firms from claims brought by third parties, by providing coverage for legal defense and financial compensation.

Workers compensation is a specialized form of liability insurance that protects a firm against claims from job-related injuries or illnesses.

Many policies combine property and liability coverage into a single policy, called a business owners policy (BOP).

Choosing a policy
Before choosing a policy, firms need to consider the amount of coverage, conditions of coverage, and the method by which reimbursements are calculated.

When selecting the amount of coverage, firms must walk a fine line between too much and too little. The amount should be sufficient to cover potential losses, but not so great as to exceed the actual value of the covered property.

Conditions of coverage refer to the types of problems that are actually covered by the policy. For property insurance, some policies only cover perils listed in the specific policy. Others cover all perils that are not specifically excluded in the policy. For liability coverage, consider what types of claims are covered and how coverage is defined. Particularly important is whether a claim will be covered by a policy that was in effect at the time the incident occurred or at the time the claim was filed.

Reimbursement can be calculated on a replacement cost basis, which reimburses the policy holder for the actual cost of replacing property, or an actual cash value (ACV) basis, which starts with the replacement cost and deducts some amount for the physical depreciation of the lost or damaged property.

Selecting a broker
Finding a broker who can write business coverage is a relatively easy task. What is harder is finding a broker well suited for your company's needs. Although you may be swayed by someone offering low premiums, you are better off finding a broker whose philosophy about risk management matches your own.

It often helps to find a broker who deals with other businesses in your industry. This will help ensure that the broker understands the major property and liability issues facing your company.

Vendors
While there are many insurance companies that offer business insurance, make sure any company you

consider is financially stable and good about paying its claims.

There are several rating agencies to consult when trying to evaluate the financial strength of a given insurer, including A. M. Best Company and Standard & Poor's.

Each state has a department of insurance that handles insurance-related complaints. You can usually learn how many complaints have been lodged against an insurer; most states will also provide a summary listing the nature of each complaint.

Pricing

Premiums for property insurance depend very much on the risk of the most frequent perils. This basic rate is then further adjusted at the discretion of the insurer. Credits may be applied for good claims history or for additional loss control measures, while debits may be incurred if there are additional factors which tend to increase the firm's overall risk.

Liability insurance premiums are calculated by first placing your company into a specific business classification. This classification results in a different charge based on the type of work you perform. For example, businesses that regularly expose their employees to physical hazards, such as those common in the construction and trucking industries, have substantially higher liability premiums than businesses with many clerical workers.

A second consideration is the size of your firm, which is called your exposure base. Depending on how your business is classified, the exposure base may be measured in terms of payroll, gross sales or square footage.

The final factor is your claims history. Large firms receive an experience rating, which compares the firm's claims history against the average in the industry. Companies with a limited exposure base are subjected to the merit rating system, where the total number of claims made by similar companies is used as to adjust premiums.

Terms

Adjuster The person who is primarily responsible for determining the fate of a claim. An adjuster assesses damage and evaluates the value of a claim.

Commercial General Liability (CGL) form A basic liability policy that covers four forms of injury: bodily injury or property damage which results in actual physical damage or loss, personal injury, and advertising injury. Most companies will need to supplement their CGL with automobile insurance and workers compensation.

Deductible The amount the insured must pay towards a claim before receiving any policy benefits. Deductibles can be calculated on a per-claim or aggregate basis.

Experience rating An indication of your history of claims. Experience ratings better or worse than average will affect a firm's premiums.

Exposure base A measure of the size of a firm. The exposure base may be measured in terms of payroll, gross sales, or square footage.

Grace period The amount of time granted to a policy holder to adjust a policy to reflect the value of newly-purchased assets.

Premium The amount of money a firm must pay to obtain insurance coverage.

Umbrella insurance An excess liability policy, providing additional coverage above and beyond that offered by primary policies.

Special tips

If you are denied coverage on a claim, contact the National Consumer Helpline of the Insurance Information Institute (800/942-4242) for help.

For small to medium-sized businesses, a businessowners package (BOP) policy can be a bargain. It bundles property and liability coverage into a comprehensive package, often saving firms a substantial amount of money.

Raising the deductible is often an easy way to reduce premiums, since small claims represent a relatively large proportion of total insurance payouts. If you expect to file relatively few claims, then consider a per-claim deductible. If you expect to file many small claims, then an aggregate deductible is recommended to limit your overall costs.

Check the renewal terms of your policy so you know whether it is automatically renewed or must be renegotiated each year.

The installation of burglar alarms, fire extinguishers, smoke alarms, fire doors, and sprinkler systems are typically the most effective measures for obtaining insurance credits. Even simple changes, such as keeping duplicate records off-site, can result in reduced premiums.

If you work with independent contractors who already have sufficient levels of liability coverage, you may be able to substantially reduce your premiums by excluding them from your exposure base.

Businesses that depend greatly on top-level managers may want to consider a key person policy, which protects firms against situations such as the death or disability of an executive.

See also
Employee Drug Testing, Health Insurance, Workers Compensation Insurance

For more information, visit
BuyersZone
http://www.buyerszone.com/

CALLING CARDS

*F*or most business travelers, staying in touch means spending a lot of time on the phone. While pay phones are plentiful, high calling costs may require you to lug around several pounds of change to make your daily calls. A far better alternative is to use a calling card.

PRICING

Calls made with	Price range
Low-priced calling card	$313
High-priced calling card	$813
Cellular phone	$856
Hotel phone	$1,025
Coin phone	$1,475

(For five-hundred 2.5 minute calls between Seattle and Boston.)

VENDORS

Company	Headquarters	Phone number	Flat rates	Banded rates	Account codes
AT&T	Basking Ridge, NJ	800/882-2273		●	
Cable & Wireless	Vienna, VA	800/486-8686	●		●
Frontier	Rochester, NY	800/836-8080	●	●	●
LCI	McLean, VA	800/860-1020			
LDDS WorldCom	Jackson, MS	800/737-8423	●		●
MCI	Washington, DC	800/727-5555		●	●
Sprint	Overland Park, KS	800/877-4000	●		●

Calling Cards

Buying points

Sources for calling cards
Calling cards are offered by hundreds of companies, including most long distance and local carriers. Any card can work from any phone, and most cards can be used for both long distance and local calls.

Although some companies require that you use their long distance service in order to get their calling card, many will supply a card without concurrent long distance service.

How calling cards work
To use a card, you first must dial an access code to connect to the carrier that issued the card. An access code is usually a toll free number, but some cards (typically those issued by local carriers) allow you to connect just by dialing a zero.

Once connected to the system, you enter your account code. This tells the carrier to whom the call should be billed. After the account is verified, the final step is to dial the telephone number you want to reach. The bill is later mailed to the card owner.

Available features
Calling cards can be equipped with many features that make them easier to use.

One basic feature to look for is speed dialing. With this feature, the card user can store a set of commonly-called phone numbers for easy retrieval.

Travelers finding themselves frequently redialing a busy number will find messenger services quite helpful. These services allow a caller to record a message for delivery at a later time. Usually, the service will dial a designated phone number every 15 to 30 minutes until the call is answered and the message is relayed.

For billing purposes, account codes help allocate costs to different departments, clients or projects. Account codes can also help limit the use of corporate calling cards for personal calls.

Billing methods
Calling card bills include any of three types of charges. At minimum, each call will be billed a standard per-minute rate. Many cards also add a fixed access surcharge for each call that is placed. Finally, a monthly fee may also be charged by some services.

Your expected usage can help determine which type of billing arrangement will be best suited for you. Users who place many short calls will want to look for a card that has no access surcharge, while those who make fewer, but longer calls will want to look for low per-minute rates.

Also consider when during the day you make calls. If many calls are placed after business hours, look for a company that offers low evening rates.

Preventing calling card fraud
Calling card fraud results in millions of dollars of illegal charges each year. Although users are generally not liable for fraudulent calls, it can be very frustrating to argue about charges with the carrier.

In many cases, only the account number is stolen. Vandals "shoulder surf," memorizing the numbers they see punched in by a user. To avoid this kind of theft, try to block the phone when entering your account number.

In addition, make sure to disconnect from the carrier before leaving the phone. Otherwise, the next user can continue to charge calls to your card.

Toll restriction allows a company to block calls to certain area codes or dialing exchanges. This minimizes your exposure to theft by denying thieves the ability to reach 900 numbers or overseas locations.

Pricing

Calling cards cost more to administer than standard long distance service, and thus cost more. However, many cards are radically overpriced.

Cards with an access charge typically bill 20¢ to 35¢ per minute, plus an access surcharge of 35¢ to 65¢. Cards without an access charge typically bill 30¢ to 40¢ per minute.

Calls also vary in cost depending on the time of day and the type of call rounding used with the card. Most cards bill a minimum 30 seconds per call and round calls to the nearest full minute. Cards that round calls to the nearest six-second increment can reduce bills by 10% to 20%, on average.

Special tips

Using a calling card issued by your long distance carrier is not always the cheapest option. Even when you factor in volume discounts, cards from other carriers are often much less expensive.

Travelers who make most calls within one area code should consider a calling card offered by the local telephone company. These carriers usually provide better rates for calls placed in the local region. A secondary benefit is often shorter access codes.

Some calling cards waive the access surcharge for subsequent calls when you place multiple calls without disconnecting from the network. Inquire about the availability of this feature if you often make several calls at once.

If you issue calling cards to employees, do not share cards or a single account code. If you issue a unique account to each person, it will be much easier to activate and deactivate cards as individuals leave the firm.

See also
Cellular Service, Conference Calling Services, International Callback, International Calling, Long Distance Service, Prepaid Phone Cards, Toll Free Service

For more information, visit
BuyersZone
http://www.buyerszone.com/

Car Rental Agencies

*R*enting a car has to be one of the best bargains around. A $20,000 automobile can be less expensive to rent than a pair of in-line skates, and probably requires you to fill out fewer forms.

Although car rental is a bargain, the costs can add up. Car rental typically represents 15% of a firm's travel budget. In coming years, this percentage threatens to go significantly higher as rental rates continue to rise.

VENDORS

Company	Headquarters	Reservation number	Corporate account number	U.S. locations	% U.S. on-airport	Worldwide locations
Alamo	Ft. Lauderdale, FL	800/462-5266	800/328-8018	121	68%	193
Avis	Garden City, NY	800/331-1212	800/321-3709	1,200	NA	4,800+
Budget	Lisle, IL	800/527-0700	800/527-0700	1,050	33%	3,200
Dollar	Tulsa, OK	800/800-4000	800/800-0088	244	71%	998
Enterprise	St. Louis, MO	800/325-8007	Local offices	NA	2%	2,400+
Hertz	Oklahoma City, OK	800/654-3131	800/654-4405	1,300	100%	5,600
National	Minneapolis, MN	800/227-7368	800/227-7368	1,000	33%	5,000
Payless	St. Petersburg, FL	800/729-5377	800/729-5255	65	44%	88
Thrifty	Tulsa, OK	800/367-2277	800/331-3550	489	23%	1,141
Value	Boca Raton, FL	800/327-2501	800/327-2501	49	50%	49

Buying points

Rental options

There are seven national firms that specifically target the business rental market. Hertz and Avis are the largest, typically offering the largest numbers of cars and the most airport rental locations. Other competitors include Budget, National, Alamo, Dollar, and Thrifty.

A second option in many areas, are regional rental firms that target the leisure market. Although most leisure-oriented rental firms have fewer locations, they can often be found near airports. In addition, some offer a level of service that is comparable to the national firms. Some of the largest regional agencies are Value and Payless.

There are also a number of firms that concentrate on rentals to repair shops. Although most of these firms are located outside the airport and do not actively seek business travelers, they can be considered in a pinch. The largest firm in this market is Enterprise, which offers the largest number of rental locations of any firm nationwide.

Differences among rental car firms

The biggest difference among rental firms concerns how rapidly you can rent and return a car. In most cases, the rest of your rental will be fairly similar no matter which firm you use, since all the major rental agencies use new cars and remove them from service after about 20,000 miles.

Agencies speed the rental process in three ways. First, rental lots can be located close to airline terminals, resulting in a shorter bus ride. Major firms such as Hertz and Avis often feature on-airport lots, while other agencies such as Thrifty typically use off-airport rental centers.

Some car rental agencies also offer express pickup services to shorten rental time. This allows you to avoid the line at the rental counter, which can be very busy when many planes have recently arrived. Hertz, Avis, National, and Budget even have programs that allow customers to proceed directly to a car and drive away without waiting in any line.

A third feature that can save time is a quick return service. These allow you to return a car without waiting in line. Some firms offer automated terminals, while others staff the return lots with parking lot attendants that can record return information on a wireless computer.

Altogether, services such as these will help you save about ten minutes on each end of a trip. However, this time savings does come at a premium. Renters typically pay an additional $10 to $20 per day when choosing a firm that offers these services. As a result, you may want to limit your use of the fastest vendors to those times when you require the extra level of service.

Opening a corporate account

Corporate accounts tend to be a very good deal even for infrequent renters. There are no sign-up fees, and you can save an average of 20% on every car you rent.

In addition to lower rates, corporate accounts can provide other benefits. Many programs offer free upgrade coupons or free rental days to members. Rental firms will also guarantee cars in times of high demand for account holders, meaning a corporate renter will rarely face a situation in which no cars are available.

Rental strategies

If your firm spends more than $15,000 to $20,000 yearly on rentals, you should try to concentrate all your rentals with one firm. This will allow you to negotiate larger discounts or obtain added insurance benefits. However, if your company's usage falls below this level, it can make more sense to join the corporate programs of several agencies, so you can select the best one depending on local rates and special offers.

Rental insurance

Purchasing rental insurance from a rental agency (typically a collision damage waiver, or CDW) tends to be a relatively poor bargain. Rental firms typically will charge you several times the actual value of the insurance.

For more cost-effective coverage, you should obtain insurance through a corporate or personal credit card. Many gold cards offer auto insurance coverage to rentals made with the card. Larger firms may want to add collision and liability insurance as part of their standard insurance package, or negotiate insurance coverage as part of a rental agreement.

Pricing

Rental rates vary depending on the size of the car, availability, and the rental agency.

Most rental firms offer several sizes of automobiles, ranging from compact through intermediate and full-sized. Moving up a size is generally not very expensive, but specialty cars and vans/trucks often cost much more.

Local supply and demand also has an enormous effect on rental rates. Leisure areas such as Florida are usually very inexpensive, since the major rental agencies compete with dozens of smaller firms. Cities such as New York and Chicago tend to be very expensive, since space is limited and demand is high.

There is also tremendous variation depending on the number of reservations made for that day. Rental firms are increasingly using yield management systems to predict demand and raise prices during peak periods. This means that rates are likely to go up if there is a major convention or new tourist attraction.

Depending on the rental agency you choose, rates may be as little as one-half of the most expensive choice. For one-time rentals, Hertz and Avis are generally at the top of the price scale, with Thrifty, Dollar, and Alamo nearer to the bottom. However, corporate discounts of 20% to 25% can make even the higher-priced rental firms quite competitive.

Special tips

If you will be traveling by air to your destination, make sure to tell the rental agency. Some car rental firms charge higher rates for local renters.

If most of your firm's rentals are used in a fairly limited area, you may be able to obtain a 100 miles/day cap in exchange for lower daily rates. In this case, you can expect to save $4 to $5 per day off the standard corporate rate.

You may be able to negotiate lower corporate rates if you can guarantee reservations. Unlike hotels, most car rental agencies fail to penalize customers who fail to cancel reservations. This has resulted in an average 15% to 40% overbooking of reservations, and made fleet management quite difficult for the car rental agencies. By guaranteeing reservations, you can potentially knock off a couple of dollars per rental.

Make sure to negotiate what will happen if a retail rate is available for less than your corporate rate. Some agencies will allow you to default to the lower rate (or even less) under the corporate plan, while others will only let you switch if you agree to give up your corporate benefits.

Value is unique in offering hourly rentals in all its locations. A traveler in town for a brief business meeting can now pay as little as $1.59 per hour to rent a car, instead of having to pay a full day rate.

If you have many employees under the age of 25, negotiate ways to eliminate underage surcharges or waive an underage exclusion policy.

See also
Corporate Cards, Frequent Flyer Programs, Hotels, Travel Agencies

For more information, visit
BuyersZone
http://www.buyerszone.com/

CD-ROM Drives

CD-ROM drives are the computer version of a standard audio compact disc player. Instead of music, a CD-ROM holds computer data, ranging from information databases to business applications to computer games. A single disc can hold 650 megabytes of data—the equivalent of nearly one million printed pages or 500 floppy discs.

PRICING

Drive type	Price range
Internal 4X speed	$80-$200
Internal 8X speed	$150-$430
External 4X speed	$150-$300
External 8X speed	$300-$500

VENDORS

Company	Headquarters	Phone number	Caddy	Toll free technical support	Warranty
Apple	Cupertino, CA	800/776-2333		●	1 yr.
Chinon	Torrance, CA	800/441-0222		●	1 yr.
Hitachi	Norcross, GA	800/241-6558	●		1 yr.
Mitsumi	Santa Clara, CA	408/970-0700		●	1 yr.
NEC	Boxborough, MA	800/632-4636	●	●	2 yrs.
Panasonic	Secaucus, NJ	800/742-8086		●	2 yrs.
Plextor	Santa Clara, CA	800/475-3986	●	●	2 yrs.
Sony	San Jose, CA	800/352-7669	●	●	1 yr.
Teac	Los Angeles, CA	800/888-4923			1 yr.
Toshiba	Irvine, CA	714/457-0777			1 yr.

Buying points

Uses for CD-ROM drives
In just a few years, CD-ROM drives have grown from a niche product to a standard feature on almost all new computers. This is because CD-ROMs are useful for a number of tasks.

First, CD-ROM drives are very useful for applications that need to access large amounts of information. Products such as phone number or manufacturer directories can be placed on a CD and accessed much more quickly and cheaply than paper documents.

CD-ROMs are also a convenient way to install large programs; applications such as Microsoft Office can be delivered on one CD-ROM instead of 30 or more floppy discs. In fact, many programs now require a CD-ROM drive for installation.

The biggest downside to CD-ROM drives is that most units cannot record data. This makes CDs unable to serve as a storage medium. CD-ROM drives also run slower than a hard drive, which makes them less suitable for running applications directly from disc.

How CD-ROM drives work
CD-ROM drives all use similar technology. Essentially, a low-power laser reads information from a disc and transfers it to the computer.

The primary difference between drives concerns how fast the disc rotates. Initially, drives rotated fast enough to transfer 150 kilobytes (Kb) per second. This is now referred to as a single speed (1X) drive. Most modern drives now rotate several times as fast as the old single speed drives. Double speed (2X) drives transfer 300 Kb per second, while quadruple speed (4X) drives transfer 600 Kb per second. The fastest drives currently available are 8X and 12X models.

Rotation speed is not the only factor that affects drive performance, however. Buyers should also check a drive's data access rate, which indicates how long the drive will take to locate a specific piece of information on the disc.

Also important is the cache size, which refers to the amount of data that can be stored in a memory buffer between the CD and the computer. Because the computer can obtain data from the cache much faster than from the CD itself, a large cache can often make a drive appear to operate much faster.

Internal vs. external drives
CD-ROM drives typically are available in both internal and external configurations. Internal drives are $40 to $100 less expensive than external drives, since they do not require a case. However, you will need a vacant 5.25 inch bay in your computer to hold the internal mechanism.

External drives are often preferable if you want to share the drive between multiple computers. By simply unplugging the unit, one CD-ROM drive can be used to install programs on many computers in an office.

CD-ROM Drives

Protecting data

CD-ROM technology tends to be fairly durable. However, dust and dirt can cause permanent damage to both discs and drives.

To protect discs, many drives are designed to work with a caddy. A caddy is a special plastic case that surrounds and protects the CD. The caddy is directly inserted into the drive, so fingers never directly touch the CD.

The biggest problem with caddies is that you need an individual caddy for each CD-ROM. At about $5 apiece, this can significantly boost the cost of maintaining a large collection. However, caddies are worth the cost if many people will be handling the discs.

Terms

Access rate Measured in bytes per second (Bps), the access rate indicates how quickly the drive can find a single piece of data, such as a number from a database.

Digital video disc (DVD) A new format standard that allows for increased storage capacity on CDs, as much as 25 times that of traditional CD-ROM discs. DVD cannot be read by CD-ROM drives, but DVD drives will be able to read regular CD-ROMs. DVD is expected to launch by early 1997.

Pits and lands The series of flat and depressed areas on a CD that encode information. When a laser hits these pits and lands, it converts them into digital ones and zeros. The computer then assembles them into text, graphics, sounds, or video.

SCSI Pronounced "scuzzy." This is the interface typically used to connect a CD-ROM drive to a Mac or a PC.

Transfer rate The rate at which information is transferred from the CD to the computer, in kilobytes per second. Slower transfer rates can result in slower operation and jerky video.

Special tips

8X CD-ROM drives have quickly become the industry standard for new computers. Avoid any double and single-speed drives, since these are much slower and only a bit cheaper than quad speed alternatives.

Manufacturers may try to make a drive more appealing by claiming it has a high storage capacity. Do not let this affect your decision, because storage capacity refers only to the amount of data on the disc and has nothing to do with the drive.

Another misleading specification concerns the method of measuring the data access rate. Manufacturers that use the "full stroke" method instead of the "one-third stroke" method will wind up with higher scores. When you compare drives, make sure that both manufacturers use the same measurements.

External drives that connect to a PC through a parallel printer port will operate much more slowly than models that connect through a SCSI port.

If you find yourself using the same CDs most of the time, you may want to consider purchasing a drive that can handle multiple (4 or 5) CDs at a time. There are also CD jukeboxes for those who need simultaneous access to dozens of CDs.

See also
Computer Backup Systems, Desktop Computers, Notebook Computers, Recordable CD Drives, Stock Photography

Cellular Service

*T*o use a cellular phone, you must first sign up for cellular service. Cellular service connects your phone to a network of cellular towers, allowing you to access the public phone network from almost anywhere.

PRICING	
Type of calling	Rate per minute
High volume (>720 min./mo.)	$0.23
Medium volume (360 min./mo.)	$0.28
Low volume (120 min./mo.)	$0.45
Calls made in affiliated areas (assuming medium volume)	$0.63
Calls made while roaming (assuming medium volume)	$1.27

Buying points

The calling process

To make a cellular call, you simply dial a number on a cellular phone, and then push the "send" button. The call is transmitted via radio waves to a local tower, and then relayed to the telephone network for completion.

The term cellular refers to the fact that each tower only covers a small geographical area, or "cell." As callers move from one area to the next, calls are transferred to the adjacent tower.

Unlike regular phone service, callers incur charges for both calls they place and calls they receive. In addition, providers may charge callers for attempting a call, even if it results in a busy signal.

About the providers

The cellular market consists of two providers in every metropolitan area. Each provider is assigned a specific band of frequencies, which they use to carry their calling traffic.

In most areas, the two spectrum bands are owned by a local Bell company (such as Bell South or Southwestern Bell) and an independent provider (such as AT&T Cellular or GTE Mobilenet). In many cases, cellular service is sold under a national brand name such as Cellular One.

Finding the right plan

To find the right calling plan, you need to estimate your monthly calling volume. Think about how many calls you will make per day, including those that reach voice mail or answering machines. Also include the number of calls you expect to receive on the phone. A good estimate is to assume your calls will last about three minutes, on average. Then simply calculate your monthly minutes.

Depending on your typical calling volume, different plans will be more or less cost effective. Individuals using the phone less than 100 minutes a month (five minutes per day) are generally best off using a "security" or "basic" program. These plans charge a low monthly fee, although they generally have high calling costs—often more than 35 cents per minute.

Callers that spend more time on the phone (up to 250 minutes per month) should look for a "standard" plan. These generally offer 1-2 hours of free calling plus lower per-minute fees. The monthly charge will be somewhat higher than that of a security plan, but you should easily save more from the lower per-minute costs.

If you spend a lot of time on the phone, consider an "executive" plan. These offer several hours of free calling and quite low per-minute rates. Many executive plans also include free services such as voice mail. Monthly charges tend to be more than $150.

Comparing coverage areas

Another factor to consider when choosing a provider is the coverage area. Providers usually have similar, but not identical, service areas. If you travel to outlying areas, one provider may offer much more complete coverage than the other.

Calls made outside a provider's calling area are typically subject to roaming charges, which can be as high as $1 per minute. To make these costs more reasonable, some carriers have "affiliation" agreements that greatly reduce roaming charges in adjacent areas.

Setting up a corporate account

Businesses that intend to provide cellular phones to employees should ask about corporate plans. These plans typically require at least three, and sometimes as many as 50, phones to be activated in order to take advantage of the lower rates. In addition, charges must usually be combined for centralized billing.

National accounts are also available for companies that intend to provide cellular phones to employees across multiple states. Generally, such accounts can take advantage of substantial volume pricing discounts.

Billing statements

Cellular billing is usually handled just like a normal telephone bill, except that the cellular carrier issues the bill. Bills can be sent to each cellular user, or can be consolidated within a firm. There are even some calling plans that combine cellular service with your local or long distance telephone bills.

Most carriers bill in one-minute increments, which means you are billed for a three-minute call if your call is just two minutes and one second long. A few carriers offer 30-second calling increments, which generally translates to a 12% savings for the typical cellular user.

Types of features available

Cellular service plans are available with a wide range of features. Most require an additional fee of $2 to $10 per month, although some executive-level calling programs include features at no charge.

Cellular voice mailboxes offer callers a way to leave messages if the recipient's cellular phone is in use, turned off or out of range. They work like any answering machine, allowing phone owners to store, retrieve, and play messages.

Call forwarding allows a cellular phone user to relay calls to any designated phone number. Cellular phone users will often route calls to their office or home when they are available at these locations. This allows users to give out a single phone number.

Pricing

Cellular calls range in cost from about 20¢ per minute for high volume programs to about 75¢ per minute for infrequent users.

While per minute rates are very important, also be sure to examine the length of peak and off-peak hours. Most carriers offer lower rates for calls on nights and weekends, which may significantly reduce your bill if you make many calls after business hours.

Most carriers charge an activation fee of about $40 per phone. However, this fee can often be waived by individual account representatives.

Terms

Digital service A type of cellular service that converts voice traffic into digital codes for transmission and reception. This service vastly increases the number of phone users the carrier can support in a given area, and is often found in major metropolitan areas. To use digital service, a user must own a phone capable of both digital and analog transmissions.

Personal communications system (PCS) A fully digital wireless system that operates on a different frequency than cellular phones. While PCS provides voice transmission like cellular phones, the technology will also offer improved data transmission capabilities for equipment such as faxes, pagers, and modems. This type of service is expected to have a great impact on the cellular industry as it becomes available nationwide in the next few years.

Special tips

Since each carrier installs its cellular towers at different locations within a given region, call quality may differ from one carrier to the next. Be sure to check the call quality in areas you frequently visit before you sign up for service.

Callers who frequently travel outside their provider's area may want to look into the cost of signing up for service in other areas. In some cases, it can be cheaper to have multiple accounts than to pay roaming charges.

If your call volume substantially varies from month to month, look for a plan that increases the calling discount as your volume increases. This will ensure that you are charged a reasonable rate rate if your volume rises or drops. If no plans in your area offer this type of discounting, check if you can switch between plans if your calling patterns change. Also learn if there is a charge associated with such a switch and see what impact it has on the contract's term length.

Because of the competitive nature of the cellular industry, avoid agreements that last more than one year.

See also
Calling Cards, Cellular Telephones, Conference Calling Services, International Calling, Long Distance Service, Pagers, Prepaid Phone Cards, Toll Free Service

Cellular Telephones

*C*ellular phones offer an instant channel to communicate from virtually anywhere. Many businesses find that with cellular phones, sales reps can service accounts more easily and busy executives can make better use of downtime.

VENDORS

Company	Headquarters	Phone number	Handheld	Mobile/ Transportable
Audiovox	Hauppauge, NY	516/233-3300	●	●
Ericsson	Research Triangle Park, NC	800/227-3663	●	
Lucent Technologies	Parsippany, NJ	800/232-5179	●	
Mitsubishi	Braselton, GA	800/888-9879	●	●
Motorola	Libertyville, IL	800/331-6456	●	●
NEC	Irving, TX	800/421-2141	●	
Nokia	Tampa, FL	800/666-5553	●	
OKI Telecom	Suwanee, GA	800/554-3112	●	
Panasonic	Secaucus, NJ	201/348-7000	●	

Buying points

Types of cellular phones

There are three types of cellular phones on the market: handheld, transportable, and mobile.

Handheld phones are small units powered by internal batteries. These models weigh as little as 3 ounces and can easily fit in a pocket or purse. These factors have helped make handheld phones the most popular type of cellular phone. On the downside, handheld phones have the weakest signal strength and the shortest battery life.

Transportable phones combine a phone and a separate battery in a small bag. These models weigh two to four pounds, and offer a much stronger signal and longer battery life than handheld phones. Transportable phones are ideal for individuals who normally work out of a car, but occasionally need to take the phone with them.

Mobile phones are permanently installed in an automobile. They run off a car battery for almost unlimited talk time, and offer a strong signal for good connections in remote areas. Although mobile phones have declined in popularity, they are still installed in many corporate fleets.

Battery life considerations

Battery life for cellular phones is measured in terms of both talk time and standby time. Talk time indicates the length of time a person can speak continuously on a phone; standby time expresses how long a phone can be kept active to receive incoming calls.

Most portable phones will list at least two sets of talk and standby time. This is because most can be equipped with multiple kinds of batteries. When comparing specifications, make sure that installing a longer lasting battery will not make a phone uncomfortably bulky.

If you expect to regularly exceed the phone's battery life, look for a phone that allows batteries to be swapped mid-call. In addition, you may want to find a model that can be equipped with a car kit that allows the phone to run off a car's battery.

Assessing features

Like many other products, cellular phones suffer from "feature creep." This means that models are equipped with many more features than the average user will ever need. Rather than comparing a list of features, it can be more valuable to check how they are implemented.

Memory is one feature that deserves close scrutiny. Many phones offer the convenience of alphanumeric memory, which identifies phone numbers with accompanying name tags. Check how many letters can be saved per name tag (we recommend a minimum of eight) and whether numbers can be retrieved by a name search or by scrolling.

Another feature to consider is the ringer control. There is nothing more annoying than receiving an incoming call during an important meeting.

Cellular Telephones

While most phones come equipped with ringers that can be turned off, more advanced models offer silent flashing lights or vibrating alerts to signal calls. For those who might forget to turn a ringer back on, a phone with an escalating ringer can be a quite useful feature.

Design considerations

Cellular telephone manufacturers face the distinct challenge of intelligently cramming many features into a compact design. When comparing models, buyers should focus on two aspects of a phone's design.

The first is the keypad. Above all, a keypad should be easy to use, with keys well spaced and easy to push. Features such as a backlit keyboard, differently-shaped keys, and a raised bump on the 5 key can be helpful for dialing numbers. It should also be easy to toggle between alpha and numeric entry, with automatic muting of tones when entering information. A lock can help prevent inadvertent use.

Also pay attention to the display. Check how many digits can be displayed at a time—ideally you will be able to view a full phone number, including the area code, without scrolling. You should also check the glare on the display and keypad under bright outdoor lighting conditions; higher end models are often equipped with an adjustable contrast for easier viewing.

Pricing

In the cellular industry, phones are used as bait to entice people to sign up for service. As a result, few buyers have to pay full price for a phone. Dealers often get large commissions from cellular carriers for signing up new customers and activating service. These commissions allow dealers to dramatically mark down the prices of cellular phones—often to virtually nothing. (Note: Phone buyers in California will not find "free" phone offers, as laws there prohibit this kind of bundling.)

Keep in mind, however, that free phones tend to be low-end models with only the most basic features. For the newest models, price tags can be as high as a few hundred dollars.

Terms

Numeric assignment module (NAM) An encrypted phone number that is assigned to each phone by a cellular service provider. Some phones can be programmed with two (dual-NAM) or more (multi-NAM) phone numbers. This allows a user to sign up for service in different calling areas and avoid roaming charges when visiting those areas.

Personal communications system (PCS) A fully digital wireless system that operates on a different frequency than cellular phones. While PCS provides voice transmission like cellular phones, the technology will also offer improved data transmission capabilities for equipment such as faxes, pagers, and modems. This type of service is expected to have a great impact on the cellular industry as it becomes available nationwide.

Special tips

The practice of bundling cellular equipment and services can make the purchasing process quite confusing. Make sure that the service package is right for your calling patterns before buying a phone. Over time, you will spend far more on service than the amount you save because of a discounted phone.

If you spend a lot of time talking on a handheld while in the car, make sure that you can get a car adapter to power the unit from the car battery.

Digital phones may allow you to obtain better rates in areas that offer digital cellular service. However, check with your local provider first; most areas have not yet installed digital networks.

Shop around when choosing a dealer. Some dealers will offer services such as free loaners for broken phones and free pickup and delivery of phones. Some dealers are also willing to take in used phones and credit their value toward the purchase of a new phone.

Companies interested in providing cellular telephones for users located throughout the country may want to turn to a cellular carrier for the purchase. Working with a single carrier allows firms to strike a better deal for both equipment and service than by working with multiple dealers and carriers.

When transporting your cellular phone, make sure there is some sort of mechanism on the phone that will prevent accidental battery drain from keys that are inadvertently pressed for a long time.

See also
Cellular Service, Cordless Telephones, Pagers, Telephone Systems

Centrex Service

*C*entrex is a phone company service that provides phone system features to businesses that do not want to purchase their own phone system. Centrex service uses a portion of the phone company's central office equipment to direct calls for an office.

CENTREX EQUIPMENT VENDORS

Company	Headquarters	Phone number
Comdial	Charlottesville, VA	800/347-1432
Cortelco	Corinth, MS	800/288-3132
DBA	Vancouver, British Columbia	800/473-2800
Deka	Santa Clara, CA	408/567-1900
Newtronix	Brooklyn, NY	718/331-2600
Vodavi	Scottsdale, AZ	800/843-4863

Buying points

How Centrex works

In a regular PBX phone system, calls travel from each extension through a central "switch." The switch determines whether calls go to an outside phone number, an inside extension or even an accessory such as a voice mail system. The switch also controls the use of features, such as putting a call on hold.

Centrex works very similarly to a business PBX, except that the switch is located at the phone company's local office instead of in your building. Calls travel from your extension and go outside the building until they reach the local telephone company office. At this point, the switch directs a call to an outside line, back to the office to another extension, or to accessory systems such as voice mail.

Advantages of Centrex

The main advantage of Centrex is that it converts phone system costs from a large capital investment to a monthly charge. This is advantageous for businesses that are short on cash, or for firms that expect to move or need a much larger system in the near future.

A second advantage of Centrex is that your firm is not responsible for maintaining or servicing the equipment. This means that costs are very predictable, allowing firms to accurately budget phone system costs far into the future. In addition, there is less chance for catastrophic failure, since the phone company maintains the switch around the clock for hundreds, even thousands, of customers.

Centrex also makes sense for businesses that are spread over a large geographic area. Centrex allows you to use the current phone company infrastructure to connect different buildings, rather than having to construct your own network of wires. This often makes Centrex appealing for colleges and government organizations that are spread over multiple buildings.

Centrex disadvantages

The greatest disadvantage of Centrex is that it is almost always more expensive over time than owning a phone system. No matter what type of deal you arrange, buying a phone system will almost always cost less in the long run.

A second issue with Centrex is that you need to deal with the phone company's bureaucracy each time you need to add extensions or change features. If you have ever had difficulty getting a phone line installed, you know that the local phone company is not always the most responsive firm for urgent requests.

Centrex also tends to be more difficult to use than a good PBX system. Modern PBXs are equipped with proprietary phones to access features and direct calls. These phones are designed specifically to work with the features available on the system. In contrast, Centrex can work with either regular telephones or specially designed Centrex-compatible phones. Accessing Centrex features with a regular phone can be a fairly cumbersome process. While Centrex phones are much better, they can still fall short when compared to the best PBX phones.

Other claims
While Centrex certainly has some advantages, many of the claims of its proponents are less than convincing.

One common Centrex claim is that the system can handle any level of growth, since the phone company switch is much larger than any individual business. While Centrex does tend to be very expandable, switches do run out of room. Fast growing areas may grow to capacity, requiring major upgrades to the system before further expansion is possible. In addition, modern PBXs are very expandable, making this claim less relevant for businesses that are considering a new phone system.

A second Centrex claim is that your phone system never becomes obsolete, since the phone company continually upgrades the system. Unfortunately, phone companies are not always very consistent about upgrading all their equipment. Some switches get frequent upgrades, while others wait a long time for capabilities such as ISDN or even caller ID. Depending on the priorities of the local phone company, your firm could wait a long time to get a specific Centrex feature or capability.

Buying service
When buying Centrex, there are three areas to examine. The first is which features or feature packages you will use. Since the phone company charges for every feature, it makes sense to give some thought to this, since you do not want to order features that will remain unused.

A second area to consider is what equipment you will use to access the Centrex service. Although Centrex works with ordinary phones, it requires complex codes to access each feature. For example, you may need to push *72 to forward a call to another extension.

As you might imagine, remembering all these codes is not an easy task. As a result, most firms buy special Centrex phones that allow the user to push a "forward" button rather than *72.

Centrex phones are available from many phone system manufacturers. It is also possible to buy Centrex-compatible equipment such as voice mail systems, paging systems, and call accounting systems for situations where the Centrex service option does not offer the functionality you require.

The term of agreement is a third area for consideration. Both the phone company and its Centrex agents will do their best to sign your firm up for terms as long as 7 to 10 years. While the first year costs may appear quite enticing, you would do well to take the big picture into account before making a decision. Make sure to learn what penalties will be incurred if you want to end a term agreement early; these fines can often be quite hefty.

Pricing

Centrex pricing varies from state to state and is, in many cases, determined by a state regulatory board.

Pricing should range from $17 to $20 per line on a monthly basis. While many options come standard, advanced options such as voice mail may cost an extra $5 to $20 for each person per month. Finally, expect installation charges to be about $50 per line, with lower prices in highly competitive areas.

Phones made to take advantage of various Centrex features usually cost between $175 and $400 each.

Terms

Customer premise equipment (CPE) Telephone equipment that is kept at the business location, rather than at the local phone company. PBX systems are a type of CPE.

Direct inward dialing (DID) A Centrex feature that allows customers to directly dial an employee's extension without calling the main company number. DID is a very useful feature for reducing the workload on attendants, but is also commonly available for use with PBX systems.

Extension A telephone on a phone system or Centrex system. Many calls in a business are made between extensions. These calls are normally free, since they do not use the public phone network.

Private branch exchange (PBX) A telephone switch that directs calls for a company. PBX systems are the primary alternative to Centrex service.

Switch Equipment that routes calls according to what number is dialed on a phone. Switches are used by the phone company to route call traffic, as well as by businesses to route calls within a firm. Centrex uses a portion of a central office switch to provide businesses with features that are similar to a PBX.

Special tips

Centrex providers often use a very low first-year price to persuade budget-conscious businesses to sign up for the service. Rates are often raised dramatically in subsequent years. Make sure to ask how rates will change over time.

When signing up for Centrex service, try to negotiate some sort of package deal to include all the services you want for a single price.

See also
KSU-less Phone Systems, Telephone Systems, Voice Mail Systems

CHAIRS

*A*nyone who has sat in an uncomfortable chair can attest to the aches and pains that can develop from prolonged sitting. While having an uncomfortable chair may be bearable in a reception area, it is unacceptable for the work environment.

Many workers spend up to seven hours a day seated in a chair. With this kind of continuous use, having the right chair is critical to productivity. The wrong chair can distract people from the job at hand and worse, potentially result in long-term physical harm.

				VENDORS

Company	Headquarters	Phone number	Budget	Mid-range	High-end
Bodybilt	Navasota, TX	409/693-7000			●
Creative Office Seating	Philadelphia, PA	215/684-1770	●	●	
Eck Adams	St. Louis, MO	800/333-7328	●	●	●
Girsberger	Smithfield, NC	800/849-0545		●	●
Global	Marlton, NJ	800/220-1900	●	●	●
Grahl	Coldwater, MI	517/279-8011		●	●
HAG	Greenboro, NC	800/334-4839		●	●
Haworth	Holland, MI	800/344-2600		●	●
Herman Miller	Zeeland, MI	616/654-8600		●	●
Steelcase	Grand Rapids, MI	800/333-9939		●	●

Buying points

Finding the right chair
The best way to find a good chair is to have it tested by the person who will be using the chair.

To check for a proper fit, start by ensuring that the person's feet can rest firmly against the ground while the thighs remain level on the seat cushion. The chair should be rounded in front to avoid reducing circulation below the knee. The seat cushion, or seat pan, should feel comfortable, and the person's weight should feel evenly distributed throughout the seat. In addition, the back rest should feel comfortable; a contoured backrest will often provide greater lumbar support.

Also, check that a number of different seated positions can be accommodated comfortably. If the user often leans back, make sure that doing so does not result in any neck tension. To promote good posture when leaning forward, it can be helpful to have a chair that has a forward tilt, which will place the hips a few degrees higher than the knees. Finally, arm rests, if available, should be designed in a manner so the chair can be pulled up close to a computer keyboard or desk surface.

You should also consider the work environment in which the chair will be placed. There are different types of chair casters depending on the floor surface. While hard wheel casters are appropriate for a carpeted office, soft wheel casters are preferable for other floor materials to avoid damage.

Purchasing multiple chairs
If you are outfitting the entire company, it is not practical to provide each person with a custom-fitted chair. Instead, you will want to find a chair that is adjustable enough to fit most people in the firm. This means that the chair is capable of supporting different positions, tasks, and body shapes.

Adjustability can be accomplished in two primary ways. An active chair allows the user to fix the chair in various positions, while a passive chair adjusts to fit the body's actions. The superiority of each type has been a source of ongoing debate; you will need to decide which you prefer.

At minimum, the chair should be equipped with a lift that can raise and lower the seat height, and an adjustable backrest. Some models also include separate parts for the lower and upper back. Armrests can be made to move back and forth, as well as up and down. There are even chairs whose seat backs can be adjusted in and out to accommodate different length legs.

When to use a furniture dealer
Most companies purchasing mid- to high-end furniture will go through a dealer to furnish their office. Dealers typically sell products from one of the three largest furniture vendors, and then complement this line with a select number of smaller vendor lines.

Advantages of working with dealers include their ability to obtain a wide variety of designs and offer samples for prospective buyers to examine. Companies planning to place a large order will even be able to bring a few models into the office for evaluation by the staff.

Buying from a catalog
Buying furniture from a catalog is an option for companies interested in purchasing budget to mid-market furniture. Leading catalog marketers include National Business Furniture, Quill, Reliable, and Viking.

Because catalog vendors do not have the high overhead of a dealer showroom, seating is typically priced 20%-40% lower than the manufacturer's suggested retail price. Pricing becomes even better when you purchase multiple units.

However, buying via catalog does mean that you will be unable to try out the furniture before you make your purchase. At best, distributors will send fabric swatches and wood chips to help with product selection. If you are planning on purchasing seating through a catalog, make sure to try at least one chair before buying multiple units. Keep in mind that if you later decide that you want to return your purchase, you are likely to be responsible for return shipping. In addition, you may be subject to a restocking fee of as much as 15 percent.

Buying from a superstore
Superstores offer many advantages for businesses buying low-end seating. These stores buy products in bulk, allowing them to sell at very low prices. In addition, models are available right on the floor, allowing you to try them out before you buy. Finally, superstores often provide immediate and free delivery.

Despite these advantages, many superstores can be a poor choice for many firms. The furniture on display is generally designed for use in a home office, and does not offer the comfort or durability of better designs. In addition, selection tends to be fairly limited.

Pricing
Most offices should expect to pay $250 to $350 for a good office chair. While top-of-the-line chairs can cost as much as a few thousand dollars, they generally will not be substantially more comfortable than a $300 chair.

For the budget-conscious, less expensive chairs are available for around $100 per model. Leaders in the low-end market include Global and Wallace. Budget seating is primarily sold through catalogs and superstores.

Special tips
Make sure to ask whether parts can be replaced in your office when repairs are required. If shipping is necessary, ask who will be responsible for freight charges, as they can be quite substantial.

Dealers selling large numbers of products in a given line often get better prices from the manufacturer, which should give you more room to negotiate.

Aggressive discounting is rampant in the dealer channel. Even if you are buying only one piece of furniture, you can still expect to receive about a 30% discount off the suggested retail price. As the volume of your purchase increases, the discount should continue to increase to nearly half the original list price.

If you will be buying many chairs at a time, it is fair to ask for a few samples to be brought to the office for in-house trial. Employees can then vote for the chair they prefer.

While a standard chair will be adequate for most people, it may be necessary to buy special chairs or chair accessories to support the needs of very small or very tall workers, as well as particularly heavy employees.

If you happen to like a particular line of furniture but are not thrilled with the dealer, call the vendor directly to learn of other dealer locations. With most larger manufacturers, you will have several dealers to choose from in a metropolitan area.

A chair that meets or exceeds BIFMA/ANSI standards is one that has been subjected to a series of tests for durability. This can be a good indicator of overall construction quality.

Most mid-market and high-end chairs are designed to last about 10 years, and are constructed to allow for the replacement of parts such as headrests or armrests.

See also
Desks, File Cabinets, Systems Furniture

For more information, visit
BuyersZone
http://www.buyerszone.com/

Did you know?

Many office workers spend as much time in their chair as they do in bed.

CHECKS

When businesses run low on checks, most turn to their bank for a refill. The assumption seems to be that since the banks are holding the money, they are also the ones to issue the checks.

However, there is no real reason to purchase checks from your bank. Independent check printers firms can print checks that are just as valid and accepted as the ones you obtain from your bank.

VENDORS

Company	Headquarters	Phone number	Stock laser	Stock impact	Traditional 3 per page	Traditional one-write
The Check Store	Lakewood, CO	800/424-3257	●	●	●	
Checks in the Mail	New Braunfels, TX	800/733-4443	●	●	●	●
Current	Colorado Springs, CO	800/204-2244	●	●	●	
Custom Direct	Cincinnati, OH	800/272-5432			●	
Deluxe	St. Paul, MN	800/328-0304	●	●	●	●
Image Checks	Little Rock, AR	800/562-8768	●	●	●	
John Harland	Decatur, GA	800/282-0250	●	●	●	●
McBee	Parsippany, NJ	800/526-1272	●	●		●
Moore	Vernon Hills, IL	800/323-6230	●	●		
NEBS	Groton, MA	800/225-9550	●	●	●	●
Rapidforms	Thorofare, NJ	800/257-8354	●	●	●	●
Wallace	Lisle, IL	800/323-8447	●	●		

Buying points

Check printers
Check printing is not a particularly difficult process. Any company can print checks as long as they have magnetic ink for check processing, and the ability to number checks consecutively for accounting purposes.

Although many firms get their checks from the bank, there are almost no banks that print these checks themselves. Instead, banks turn to companies that specialize in check printing. In addition to serving banks, these check printers also sell directly to check users.

Different types of checks
Companies generally have the choice of buying either traditional or computer-generated checks.

Traditional checks are designed to be completed by hand or with a typewriter. They are typically arranged three on a page, with a stub for reference. An alternate design, called one-write checks, adds a carbon strip on the back of each check to record relevant information on a ledger. With one-write checks, users can issue checks without having to write the recipient and the amount elsewhere.

Computer-generated checks are designed to be used with a computer-based accounting program and a printer. Single sheet designs are intended for laser printers, while dot matrix printers generally use continuous form designs. For businesses that need multiple receipts, dot matrix printers can also print onto carbonless multi-part checks.

Preventing check fraud
The easiest way to prevent fraud is to include color copy protection on the checks. This process incorporates additional lines into the check's background image in what is called a pantograph. When a check is copied, the resulting image will produce a "void" mark.

Where to purchase checks
Checks are available from three primary sources: direct sales catalogs, local forms distributors, and banking or accounting service providers.

Direct check vendors primarily sell through catalogs. By eliminating the middle man, these vendors tend to provide the best value for companies buying only a few thousand checks at a time. Direct vendors can handle simple customization such as logos, but usually do not offer custom designs.

Local distributors are typically used for higher volume purchases, or situations where a special design is required. Distributors do not print the checks themselves, but will work with one or more printers to complete the job. This method saves you the time of having to find a suitable printer, but usually results in somewhat higher prices than a direct vendor.

Banks and software vendors only sell checks to supplement their other services. They have very little incentive to provide competitive pricing, since checks are not their main line of business. As a result, prices from these vendors tend to be quite high.

Pricing

Businesses can expect to save anywhere from 20% to 70% off bank prices when buying checks from catalogs or local distributors. You can expect to pay $70 to $100 for 1,000 checks. Companies buying 5,000 checks at a time will pay about $250 for impact checks, and $300 for laser checks.

Terms

Impact checks Checks that are designed to work with daisywheel and dot matrix printers. Each check usually consists of multiple parts and comes attached to the next for continuous printing.

Laser checks Checks designed for use with a laser printer. They are typically arranged with one or three checks per sheet. The three on a page design costs less per check, but can be difficult to use if you usually print just a few checks at a time.

Traditional three per page checks These checks come ready for use in a seven ring check binder, and can be completed by hand or with a tabletop check machine.

Special tips

Most firms should plan on buying enough checks for nine months to one year. Small firms may want to order a slightly larger supply, since prices are significantly higher for quantities of less than 1,000 checks.

If you require checks in quantities of more than 10,000, or if you need custom designs, you may want to consider working with larger forms printers. Direct sales vendors include Data Documents (800/228-9277), Duplex (815/895-2101), Standard Register (800/232-0981), and UARCO (800/877-5939). Manufacturers who sell through distributors include Ennis Forms (800/972-1069) and General Business Forms (847/677-1700).

When buying computer checks, make sure they are compatible with the software you use. You can usually specify what program you use, or send a voided check to the firm to find a close match.

See also
Business Forms, Commercial Printing, Laser Printers, Payroll Services

Cleaning Services

Cleaning services are contracted to periodically clean office space, usually after business hours. Since the firm may be responsible for closing your office at night, choosing a cleaning service requires some care.

VENDORS

Company	Headquarters	Phone number	States served	Number of offices
CleanNet USA	Columbia, MD	800/735-8838	10 states	13
Coverall	San Diego, CA	800/799-1911	25 states	49
JaniKing	Dallas, TX	800/552-5264	34 states	70
Maid Brigade	Atlanta, GA	800/722-MAID	30 states	245
Maid to Perfection	Baltimore, MD	800/648-6243	12 states	76
OPEN Cleaning Systems	Phoenix, AZ	800/777-6736	AZ, CA, WA	3
ServiceMaster	Memphis, TN	800/255-9687	50 states	3,600
Tower Cleaning Systems	Valley Forge, PA	800/355-4000	36 states	30

Buying points

Finding a service

Although looking for a cleaning service can be as easy as turning to the phone book, you should first consider services that nearby firms use. Since transportation costs are often a large factor in determining fees, you may be able to save money by using a firm that already works at a nearby building or office.

When speaking with a service, learn about the types of firms the service works with before describing your cleaning requirements. Ideally, the firm should service accounts that have office space similar to yours.

Firms that pass this initial screen should then be walked through your office and provided with a detailed list of the cleaning tasks and information on how often they must be completed. The cleaning service can then estimate how much time the job will take and how much should be done on a daily or weekly basis.

To ensure that bids are comparable, create a standard bid format. The request should ask for a breakdown of supply costs and the time needed to complete each task.

Also make sure to notify the services that they will be involved in a competitive bidding situation. This can help you receive a more competitive price quote.

Assuring peace of mind

It is critical to check references and a company's history since cleaning services will generally work in an unattended environment. Start by learning how long the company has been around. Consult references, and ask how employees are hired.

Also check that the service is adequately insured and bonded. This will reduce your liability in the event of an accident or damage to property. Bonding allows you to recover damages from the cleaning company for theft if you can prove that the company is responsible for any loss.

Providing supplies

One of the issues you will need to address is who will provide the cleaning and maintenance supplies. Supplies such as bathroom tissue, paper towels, wastebasket liners, and liquid soap can either be purchased from local janitorial supply and office supply dealers, or provided by the cleaning service.

Small firms often do not buy enough supplies to qualify for free delivery from janitorial supply vendors. In these cases, you will probably be better off obtaining supplies from the cleaning service, unless a distributor is located close to your firm.

Signing a contract

You should have a written agreement when you hire a service to clean your office. This agreement should include detailed descriptions of the cleaning specifications and work standards you have agreed upon. Cleaning specifications include descriptions of the cleaning area, frequency, and supplies. Work standards refer to the level of security and supervision provided. Also include information on insurance requirements, rate change information, and payment schedules.

Pricing

A single worker can clean approximately 1,800 square feet per hour, which translates into yearly rates of between $0.60 and $1.80 per square foot, according to a study conducted by the Building Owners and Managers Association (BOMA) International. Bids should usually vary no more than 6¢ to 15¢ per square foot, since costs are generally the same for competing cleaning services.

These prices will vary depending on local conditions, as well as the type of cleaning to be done. Companies utilizing union labor will generally charge 35% to 40% more than non-union firms.

It is not advisable to hire a company whose prices are much lower than average. Since about 80% of a cleaning service's costs cover labor, a low bid typically means that either the bidder has not accurately assessed the workload or plans to cut corners.

Special tips

For greater leverage in bidding, you may want to band several offices together to obtain a group quote.

It is usually a good policy to avoid asking a cleaning service to tidy work areas. Organizing what may look like unorganized clumps of paper strewn across a desk can create chaos in the office.

If employees tend to pile work on the floor, have the cleaning service only dispose of items found in the wastebasket. Other items destined for disposal should clearly be marked as trash.

Cleaning is a very local business, with few national brands. Even well-known firms such as ServiceMaster and JaniKing can provide inconsistent levels of service since they are franchise operations.

Dissatisfaction with a cleaning service usually arises more from miscommunication than from poor service. You should make sure that you and the vendor have a common set of expectations.

Prices on maintenance supplies vary 30% across different grades. Ask for free samples before purchasing supplies.

BOMA (800/426-6292) published a cleaning study in 1990, with useful tips and pricing. A new study is expected by the end of 1996.

See also
Office Supplies, Recycling

Clipping Services

*W*hether you are interested in monitoring the press coverage your company receives, or whether you are just interested in keeping abreast of developments in your industry, a clipping service can be a valuable service. By clipping articles for many clients at the same time, clipping services can offer extensive search capabilities for relatively little money.

VENDORS

Company	Headquarters	Phone number	Coverage
Allen's Press Clipping Bureau	San Francisco, CA	415/392-2353	National
Bacon's Clipping Bureau	Chicago, IL	800/621-0561	National
Burrelle's Press Clipping Service	Livingston, NJ	800/631-1160	National
Carolina Clipping Service	Raleigh, NC	919/833-2079	Regional
Clipping Bureau of Florida	Clearwater, FL	813/442-0332	State
Colorado Press Clipping Service	Denver, CO	303/571-5117	Regional
Garden State Press Clipping Bureau	Red Bank, NJ	908/842-1616	Regional
Luce's Press Clipping	Mesa, AZ	800/528-8226	National
Mutual Press Clipping Service	Harrisburg, PA	717/671-3870	State
New England Newsclip Agency	Framingham, MA	508/879-4460	National
Texas Press Clipping Bureau	Dallas, TX	214/969-5570	National

Buying points

How clipping services work
A clipping service essentially acts as your company's eyes and ears in the press. Based on your search instructions, human readers scan printed materials for matching references. Clips are then collected and sent to you with information about the publication in which they appeared.

Uses for a clipping service
Public relations firms have traditionally used clipping bureaus as a way to monitor client coverage, but companies also use these services for marketing and competitive analysis.

Types of media coverage
Clipping services track coverage in many different types of media including daily and non-daily newspapers; trade, consumer, and professional magazines; newsletters; and newswire services. Some services also scan television and radio broadcasts.

While most services focus on covering domestic media, some services monitor foreign media.

Clipping services vs. online searches
Clipping services offer three primary advantages over online searches. First, they offer greater coverage. Clipping services are often the only source for coverage of limited-interest publications such as local or town newspapers. Moreover, clipping services will search for references in the published piece rather than in the abstracts some publications use online. Clipping services can also monitor advertising.

A second advantage is timeliness. Through your fax machine, you can receive clips from major metropolitan papers on the same day they are published. Online services sometimes take several weeks to get articles on their service.

Finally, clipping services can provide the actual clip for your review. This means that you can see how much space was given to the text of the article or to any accompanying graphics or photos.

Online searches can be a more effective resource if your company does not need the most recent information, or does not require comprehensive monitoring. In addition, online services offer firms a great deal of flexibility in their searching and cost much less. They are also the only source for historical searches.

Choosing the right clipping service
There are approximately 45 national, regional, and state clipping services in the market. The three largest clipping services are Bacon's, Burrelle's, and Luce's.

Differences between companies relate primarily to their coverage and their fees. National providers cover many more sources than regional or state bureaus; however, the smaller bureaus will usually offer more comprehensive coverage of local press. In addition, regional providers typically charge less than national companies and offer faster delivery of clips to your desk.

Other services

Some services analyze clips for information such as editorial slant, circulation, and effectiveness. This can be done for your company on a stand-alone basis, or on a comparative basis against your competitors.

Pricing

Clipping services charge a monthly service fee plus the cost of each clipping. The monthly fee varies depending on the number of publications monitored. You can expect to pay $100 to $240 each month, plus $0.70 to $1.30 for each individual clipping.

Additional charges may be incurred if the clipping runs over multiple pages of a publication, or if you require coverage of foreign publications.

Special tips

Make sure to ask if there is a minimum term before signing up with a service. Some of the national providers require a 3-month minimum commitment.

Check if there are additional charges for monitoring more than a certain number of search topics.

To learn of clipping services in your area, consult a local public relations association.

See also
Advertising Agencies, Public Relations Firms

Collection Agencies

Collection agencies specialize in collecting payment from overdue accounts. Businesses can hire collection agencies to help reduce their bad debt, improve their cash flow, and lessen the workload for billing departments.

VENDORS		
Company	Headquarters	Phone number
Accent	Omaha, NE	402/391-5285
CCS	Newton, MA	800/CASH-FLOW
Checkrite	Midvale, UT	800/234-7800
CRW	King of Prussia, PA	800/581-5947
Dun & Bradstreet	Wilton, CT	800/234-3867
Frost-Arnett	Nashville, TN	615/256-7156
GC	Houston, TX	713/777-4441
Nationwide	Atlanta, GA	602/379-2222
Payco	Brookfield, WI	414/784-9035

Buying points

How collection agencies work

At a certain point, bad debt becomes a drain on a firm's finances. Most firms bring in collection agencies to collect on debts that that are more than eight months old, although a few bring in agencies after only three months.

Collection agencies can collect debts in one of two ways. For larger debts, they will typically send letters and make phone calls to the delinquent account. Smaller debts may not justify the cost of phone calls, and a collection agency will be limited to simply sending threatening letters.

Choosing a service

Choosing a collection service can be a difficult task, since it is often hard to predict how successful a firm will be with delinquent accounts.

The first area to investigate is how the agency expects to collect debt. You should examine the letters that will be used and judge whether they will be effective with your customer base. Also ask about the training that telephone collectors receive to ensure they understand requirements imposed by the Fair Debt Collection Practices Act.

Next, investigate how your company will interact with the service. Find out how information about delinquent accounts will be transferred to the agency. Learn when collected funds will be forwarded, and what information will be available detailing the collection progress and success rates. Finally, find out how you can stop collections if you receive payment or credit an account.

A third area to investigate, particularly when collecting from individuals, is skiptracing. This refers to a method a collection firm uses to find debtors who have moved or can no longer be reached at their billing phone numbers or addresses. Agencies should have access to online search capabilities and telephone databases to help locate these debtors.

A final area to investigate is the firm's reputation. You should check references, particularly from clients that are in a business similar to yours. Also investigate whether the firm complies with state licensing or bonding laws.

Before hiring an agency

Before hiring a collection agency, there are several steps you can take to reduce the amount owed to your firm.

First, be careful when offering credit. Carefully check credit references of each new account and make sure you do not extend more credit than the firm can handle.

When extending credit, clearly explain the terms of the transaction. Make sure that customers know when you expect payment, and clearly detail any credits or penalties for early or late payment.

Also make sure to follow up with all overdue accounts. Do not expect customers to police themselves; instead, make sure to promptly send statements and reminders of payment due dates.

As accounts become late in paying, institute a series of overdue notices. You should schedule regular written and oral reminders before even considering a collection agency. This will not only help save money, but will also avoid the ill will that can be generated when using a third party to collect the funds.

As a final step, set an absolute due date before the account is turned over to a collection agency. Do not extend this date, but do give the debtor warning of this final payment date.

Pricing

Debt collection is usually done on a contingency basis. This means that the agency keeps a percentage of money that is collected from a debtor. Commissions usually range from 10% to 30% of the recovered amount. Other agencies require an upfront fee and then take a lower percentage of the recovered amount.

The advantage of contingency billing is that you do not pay for uncollected debts. However, some agencies will not offer contingency services for small debts. In these cases, you will typically pay a fixed fee for a series of letters or calls.

Terms

Dunning Letters that are sent from the collection agency on behalf of the creditor. The attorney dunning process refers to the last letter that is sent from a lawyer outlining upcoming legal action.

Forwarding The process of transferring a debtor's account from one collection agency to another agency in a different part of the country. Forwarding occurs when an agency is not licensed to do business in the state where a debtor is located.

Write-off rate The accepted amount of bad, uncollectable debt firms should expect as a simple risk of issuing credit. With low profit transactions, firms should aim for rates of less than one percent. With high profit transactions, firms should aim for rates of less than five percent. Also called charge-off rate.

Special tips

When assigning a third-party firm to collect an overdue account, provide the company with all the information you have about the debtor, including an itemized breakdown of all contacts between your organization and the debtor's business or home.

Some states require collection agencies to be licensed in their state before they can pursue debtors. Contact the American Collectors Association (612/926-6547) or a particular state's collection agency administrator for specific details on state requirements.

The Fair Debt Collection Practices Act (FDCPA) is designed to protect consumers from undue harassment from collectors. Any third-party

Collection Agencies

agency, individual, or attorney should understand the requirements imposed by the FDCPA rules. This act does not yet pertain to "in-house" collectors or employees of creditors, but that may soon change.

To increase the agency's chances of tracking down an individual or business, always ask for the customer's physical address (even if you are sending the materials to a Post Office box), phone number, and social security number. It can also help to work with a credit reporting agency. All of this information will be helpful in tracking down individuals even in the event of nonpayment, even if they have closed their P.O. box or changed their address and phone number.

See also
Accountants

Color Printers

*C*olor printers allow you to produce color documents from any computer. Color can highlight areas of text or graphs, or can be used to create photo-realistic images on a page.

PRICING

Color printer type	Price range
Dye sublimation	$5,000-$20,000
Ink-jet	$200-$10,000
Laser	$5,000-$15,000
Solid ink	$4,500-$10,000
Thermal wax	$850-$15,000

VENDORS

Company	Headquarters	Phone number	Dye sublimation	Ink-jet	Laser	Solid ink	Thermal wax
3M	St. Paul, MN	800/844-8816	•				
Apple	Cupertino, CA	800/538-9697		•	•		
Canon	Costa Mesa, CA	800/848-4123		•			
Digital	Maynard, MA	800/777-4343					•
Epson	Torrance, CA	800/289-3776		•			
Fargo	Eden Prairie, MN	800/327-4622	•				•
Hewlett-Packard	Palo Alto, CA	800/752-0900		•	•		
IBM	Southbury, CT	800/426-2468			•		
Kodak	Rochester, NY	800/235-6525	•				
LaserMaster	Eden Prairie, MN	800/805-7549		•			
Lexmark	Lexington, KY	800/358-5835		•	•		
Mitsubishi	Cypress, CA	714/220-2500					•
Okidata	Mt. Laurel, NJ	800/654-6651		•			
QMS	Mobile, AL	800/523-2696			•		
Seiko	San Jose, CA	800/888-0817	•				
Tektronix	Wilsonville, OR	800/835-6100	•	•	•	•	•
Xerox	Rochester, NY	800/349-3769			•		

Buying points

Uses of color
Color printers can be used for a variety of tasks in the office. A traditional use is to proof color documents before they are sent to a commercial printer. This can help businesses avoid costly mistakes or poor color choices.

However, color printers are increasingly being used for projects beyond just proofing. Businesses can produce an impressive range of customized marketing materials on color printers, including color transparencies, color report covers, and color graphs.

Types of color printers
There are five different types of color printers on the market: ink-jet, laser, solid ink, thermal wax, and dye sublimation.

Ink-jet models are the least expensive type of color printer. These models spray tiny drops of ink onto a page to create an image. Output can be quite good on very smooth paper, but deteriorates on rougher stock. Colors also tend to be vulnerable to smudging and running, particularly immediately after printing. For busy offices, ink-jets are typically not fast enough, printing only 1 to 2 pages per minute.

Color laser printers use the same toner-based printing process as black and white laser printers, except that they require toner in four different colors. These models produce very crisp documents, with none of the smudging or wetness of a dense ink-jet page. Color laser printers can also be used as a regular black and white laser printer. On the downside, color lasers are very expensive, with models typically starting at $5,000.

Solid ink printers melt solid blocks of ink, which is then sprayed onto a page. This printing process results in very bright colors, but fine lines and text tend to be a bit imprecise.

Thermal wax printers work by melting wax from ribbons and applying the wax to a page. Thermal wax printers work very well with transparencies, and are often used by businesses to create vibrant color presentations. On the downside, printing tends to be very slow, with long waits to warm up the printer and fill in a page. Thermal wax technology is also not very well suited for printing on paper, with most models requiring extra-smooth paper to obtain a high-quality image.

Dye sublimation is a high-end color printing technology that produces near-photograph quality output. These printers use heat to directly transfer dye from a ribbon. The technology is often used to create proofs before printing, or by image-reliant businesses (e.g., advertising, graphic design) to create final client presentations. However, dye sublimation printers are quite expensive, with most machines costing $5,000 or more.

About printer languages
Color printers are generally used to produce fairly complex output. As a result, color printers need to be

equipped with fairly high-end printer languages.

The most common language used by color printers is PostScript. PostScript is a printer language that describes images the same way no matter what type of printer is receiving the instructions. As a result, a PostScript document will look the same whether printed on a cheap laser printer or a professional quality imagesetter.

Some printer manufacturers choose not to pay PostScript's high licensing fees, and instead use a clone interpreter to convert the PostScript language into printer commands. Clone versions of PostScript tend to work fine most of the time, but may run into difficulty with some complex images.

The major alternative to PostScript is Hewlett-Packard's PCL language. PCL cannot be used with Macintosh computers, and is not as popular as PostScript among high-end printers. It is, however, the most common language used in color ink-jet models.

Printing resolution

Resolution refers to the number of dots that can be placed in an inch. However, dots per inch is not always such a straightforward guide to quality among color printers. Depending on the process used to create different colors, a printer's resolution should be interpreted differently.

All color printers create different colors by mixing cyan, magenta, and yellow in various combinations. One way to mix colors is called dithering. In this process, dots of cyan, magenta, and yellow are placed close together to create the effect of a given color. Because the eye does not see each individual dot, it is fooled into seeing the desired color.

In contrast, continuous tone printing combines cyan, magenta, and yellow in varying amounts on top of one another to form a dot of the appropriate color. Since continuous tone printing does not require multiple dots to give the visual impression of a single color, it can create very good looking output at much lower resolutions. In fact, most continuous tone printers print at just 300 dpi.

Dithered images need much smaller individual dots to create the same quality image. To compete with continuous tone printers, dithering printers typically offer resolutions of 600 dpi or even 1200 by 600 dpi.

Printing speed

Color printers are not known for their speed. Color images require three or four times as much processing and printing time as black and white images. In addition, color documents are usually much more complex than the typical one-color page.

Color lasers are typically the fastest type of color printer. Most have a rated speed of 3 to 4 pages per minute (ppm), although most documents will take substantially longer to output.

Thermal wax and dye sublimation printers tend to be much slower.

These machines must heat and apply the colors to a page, which increases both warm-up times and printing times. Only a few thermal wax machines offer a rated speed of 2 ppm, and most actually operate at well under 1 ppm. Dye sublimation printers are even slower, with output speeds generally measured in minutes per page.

Ink-jet and solid ink models typically print at about one page per minute, although there are versions available that can work at higher speeds.

Paper sizes

Virtually all color printers can handle 8.5 x 11 inch sheets. However, not all can create a letter-sized document with edge-to-edge printing, which is known as a full bleed. To obtain a full bleed on an 8.5 x 11 inch sheet, you must typically print on a larger-sized sheet and then trim it to size. Laser printers generally cannot handle the larger "Super A" pages to produce a full bleed, although most thermal wax and dye sublimation models offer this feature.

Far fewer printers are capable of printing on 11 x 17 inch, ledger-sized sheets. To obtain a full bleed on ledger paper, you will need a printer capable of printing on the slightly larger "Super B" sheets.

A few models are equipped to handle rolls of glossy paper or transparency film. These are most often found with dye sublimation and thermal wax printers.

Pricing

Color ink-jets are the least expensive type of color printer. Low-end models start at under $300, and even expensive versions rarely exceed $1,000.

Color lasers and solid ink models start at about $4,500. High speed models and large format (ledger) models range as high as $20,000.

Thermal wax printers are much more variable in price, ranging anywhere from $875 to $4,000 in cost.

Dye sublimation printers are generally the most expensive type of color printer, starting at about $7,000 and rising to well over $10,000. However, there are a few low-end models available for as little as $1,500.

Terms

Consumables Toner, cartridge, developer or any other parts of the printer that must be periodically replaced.

Continuous tone A printing technology that combines inks to form a dot of the appropriate color on the page. Continuous tone printing is primarily used with dye sublimation printers, but some other designs also utilize this technology.

Resolution The number of dots appearing on a printed page. Dots are measured in dots per inch, or dpi. An example of this is 600 by 600 dpi output, which indicates 600 dots per inch in both horizontal and vertical directions. This can also be written as simply 600 dpi.

Special tips

If you frequently print documents that combine text and color on a page, stay away from low-end ink-jets that are equipped with three-color cartridges. These models mix cyan, magenta, and yellow to produce black ink. The results are generally a deep, greenish-blue hue rather than black. A better choice is to pay an additional $200 to $300 for a four color ink-jet that includes cyan, magenta, yellow, and black in a single cartridge.

When calculating the cost of a color printer, make sure to factor-in the ongoing costs of operation. On a per page basis, laser printers and solid ink printers tend to be the least expensive to operate. Most cost anywhere from 25¢ to 60¢ per page with 50% sheet coverage. Thermal wax printers tend to be substantially more expensive to operate. Printing costs range from $0.50 to $1.25 per page. Dye sublimation printers are the most expensive of all. All models cost at least $2 per page, and large format printers can be as much as $8 per page.

See also
Desktop Computers, Dot Matrix Printers, Ink-jet Printers, Laser Printers, Stock Photography

For more information, visit
BuyersZone
http://www.buyerszone.com/

COMMERCIAL PRINTING

*A*lmost every firm requires the use of a commercial printer for creating brochures, manuals, catalogs, or stationery. Whether producing full-color graphics or black and white flyers, commercial printers can fulfill your printing needs.

VENDORS

Quick printer	Headquarters	Phone number	Number of locations
AlphaGraphics	Tucson, AZ	520/293-9200	304
American Speedy	Troy, MI	810/614-3700	467
Kinko's	Ventura, CA	800/2-KINKOS	850+
Kwik Kopy	Cypress, TX	713/373-3535	870
Minuteman	Farmingdale, NY	516/249-5618	850
Nightrider	Houston, TX	713/440-6464	NA
PIP Printing	Agoura Hills, CA	818/880-3800	621
Quick Print	Wichita, KS	316/636-5666	214
Sir Speedy	Mission Viejo, CA	714/348-5000	880

Buying points

How the printing process works

Printing begins with the submission of materials to the printer. Computer files or high-quality printouts are generally acceptable formats. These will be converted to printing plates that are used in the actual printing.

The second step of the printing process is production, where the printer runs the project on a printing press using printing plates, paper and ink.

During postpress, printed pages are collated, folded, trimmed, and bound to create the finished product.

Types of printers

Commercial printers fall into one of three broad groups, based on the type of printing equipment they operate. Large commercial printers generally handle high-volume, four-color print jobs. Although they can take orders of all sizes, they are typically best suited to running jobs that produce a minimum of 50,000 impressions, or sheets.

Small commercial printers are equipped to print materials of limited complexity in lower quantities. These printers deal in quantities up to tens of thousands of pages, and primarily produce materials needing one or two colors.

Quick printers form a subgroup of the small commercial printer category, catering to clients who need fast turnaround times. This is an area where franchising has become popular, with companies such as Kwik Copy, PIP Printing, and AlphaGraphics being some of the most popular.

Printers also specialize in many other niches. For example, business form printers specialize in printing continuous-form materials such as invoices, shipping statements, and purchase orders. Other printers specialize in printing materials such as books, newspaper inserts, or glossy post cards.

Looking for a printer

When choosing a printer, you should try to find a printer that can easily handle the volume and number of colors in the job. Depending on the size and type of the press they run, printing costs for the same job can vary dramatically across printers.

For low volume black and white projects, it is often best to use a printer that offers electrostatic printing. This essentially involves a high-end copier, which stores the images to be printed as digital files. Electrostatic printing is good for quantities up to 5,000 impressions.

For higher volumes, you will generally want to use a printer that has an offset sheet press. These come in a wide range of sizes, starting at 8.5 x 11 inch and rising to 17 x 22 inch and beyond. The best press for a given job depends on the size of the piece, but you will want to choose a size that wastes a minimum amount of paper. For two-sided printing, perfecting presses are often very efficient, since they can print both sides of a sheet in a single pass.

Web presses are designed for the largest jobs. These machines use a continuous roll of paper. They tend to be difficult and expensive to set up for a job, but are very fast once they are running. Web presses are typically a good choice for runs of 200,000 impressions or more.

Beyond the presses, also investigate the scheduling process at the printer. Some printers do not rigidly schedule each press, allowing you to jump in with a small job and get it done very quickly. Other printers schedule very carefully, requiring long lead times before a job can be finished.

A final area to investigate is service. There are many areas where a printing job can go wrong. An effective liaison will help manage the process smoothly, provide information as needed, and troubleshoot when necessary. It can be worthwhile to check references and learn about the weaknesses of each rep or printing firm before assigning critical print jobs.

Pricing

For a printer, determining the cost of a given print job is not terribly difficult. An economic value can quickly be obtained by taking into account the press used, the plates made, the ink used, the paper, and the quantities run. Determining the market value of a print job, on the other hand, is a very inexact science. How much of a markup the printer assesses depends on the firm's current capacity and desire for business. A busy printer may offer a quite ordinary price, while a printer with an idle press may price below cost to maintain cash flow.

For businesses that spend a minimum of $50,000 per year on printing, it is possible to negotiate guaranteed rates for a fixed length of time.

Terms.

Electrostatic printing A printing process similar to that used by everyday photocopiers. It has recently become a major competitor to offset lithography for very short printing runs.

Flexographic press A process used to print on materials such as plastic bags. These presses use rubber plates with printed areas raised in relief.

Ganging Term used when a printer runs a variety of different jobs together for more efficient production.

Gravure printing A high-quality printing technique that uses direct contact between an etched copper plate and the paper. This technique is rather expensive because the plate has a relatively high cost. However, it is the best way to print high-quality materials such as brochures and annual reports.

Impression A term used to describe a sheet produced by a printing press.

Offset lithography A popular printing method that can print materials with a variety of textures. This process is also economical in its use of ink and the time required to set up a press.

Perfect binding A binding process which uses glue to hold the pages in place. During this process, the left edge of each sheet is roughened, and then glue is applied. A cover is then placed over the pages, keeping everything in place. It is most often used to create paperback books.

Screen printing A printing method often used for non-flat goods. This method is best equipped to print on items such as mugs and clothing.

Signature A group of images that appear on a printing plate. The signature is arranged in such a way that the pages will appear in the right order after they are folded and trimmed.

Special tips

Since printers use different types of equipment, they are not well suited to handle every print job. Take the time to understand a printer's limitations before assigning a project.

Make sure to ask if the printer will run a given job in-house. It will be more cost effective to find the appropriate printer for a job than to have a printer serve as a middleman and send the job to another company.

When designing marketing materials, it is often very productive to consult a printer about the size of a brochure or document. In many cases, a printer can suggest slight alterations in size that will dramatically cut the cost of printing by using a press more efficiently.

Glossy paper is particularly good in reproducing photographs, since the ink sits on the surface of the paper, rather than spreading into the paper fibers.

See also
Business Cards, Business Forms, Checks, Lamination Equipment

Computer Backup Systems

*E*very year thousands of businesses lose computer data because of fires, floods, or burglaries. Many more experience smaller losses from system crashes, accidental erasures, or computer viruses. Computer backup systems help businesses avoid these catastrophes by providing a safe way to maintain important files.

PRICING		
Type of computer backup	Equipment cost	Cost of storage
Removable cartridge drive	$200-$500	$0.08-$0.13/MB
3.5" MO drive	$375-$700	$0.02-$0.10/MB
Travan QIC tape drive	< $500	$0.02/MB
CD-R drive	< $1,000	$0.03/MB
DAT tape drive	$1,000-$1,400	< $0.01/MB
5.25" MO drive	$1,200-$2,400	$0.03-$0.09/MB
8 mm tape drive	$1,600-$2,000	< $0.01/MB
DLT tape drive	$3,500-$7,000	< $0.01/MB

VENDORS						
Company	Headquarters	Phone number	Types of tape drive	3.5" MO drive	5.25" MO drive	Removable cartridge drive
Exabyte	Boulder, CO	800/442-4392	QIC, 8 mm			
Fujitsu	San Jose, CA	800/626-4686		•		
Hewlett-Packard	Palo Alto, CA	800/752-0900	QIC, DAT		•	
Iomega	Roy, UT	800/697-8833	QIC			•
Micro Design Int'l. (MDI)	Winter Park, FL	800/228-0891		•	•	
Olympus	Melville, NY	800/347-4027		•	•	
Pinnacle Micro	Irvine, CA	800/553-7070		•	•	•
Quantum	Milpitas, CA	408/894-4000	DLT			
Seagate Technology	Scotts Valley, CA	408/438-6550	QIC, DAT			
SyQuest	Fremont, CA	800/245-2278				•

Buying points

The need

In many businesses, the information stored on computers is irreplaceable. Customer databases, tax records, marketing materials, and intellectual property may all be stored on computers throughout the office.

Unfortunately, files stored on a computer are always at risk. Hard drives crash, systems get infected with viruses, and files are accidentally erased. If none of these events have occurred at your firm, you should consider yourself very lucky.

Even worse catastrophes can wipe out the information on several computers. Burglaries, fire or natural disasters can cause your business to lose the computers and all the files they contain.

Backup systems are designed to protect against both system failures and business catastrophes. By storing copies of data outside the office, you can keep your files safe at all times.

Types of backup

There are two basic ways to back up computer data. The most common is to record a copy of your data onto some type of removable storage. This can vary from a simple floppy disk to removable cartridges and tapes. These should be taken off-site each day, to maintain a safe copy in the event of disaster.

A second type of backup uses network connections to back up business data. In this case, a firm sends a copy of files to a remote system via a phone line or Internet connection. The information is thus guaranteed to be stored off-site.

Removable storage options

The least expensive type of removable storage is a floppy disk, since all computers are equipped with a disk drive. Unfortunately, floppy disks do not hold enough information to easily back up most modern computers.

A second type of storage is a removable cartridge drive, such as a SyQuest drive, or an Iomega Zip or Jaz drive. Cartridge drives hold anywhere from 88 megabytes (MB) to 1.2 gigabytes (GB) of data, making them quite adequate for backing up most individual computers. They also can access data very quickly, making it easy to retrieve individual files that may have been erased or lost. On the downside, cartridges tend to be fairly expensive, making the drives impractical for backing up many computers.

For computer networks and large hard drives, tape storage is often the most practical backup option. Tape formats can handle up to 40 GB of data on a single reel, and tape drives can write data at very high speeds. Tape is also fairly economical, costing less than a cent per MB of storage. The biggest drawback with tape is that the data is not easily accessible. While you will find tape to be a lifesaver if your hard drive is wiped out, it is often very time consuming trying to locate one lost file.

A fourth type of removable storage is an optical or magneto-optical (MO) drive. These drives record on removable disks that hold anywhere from 650 MB to several GB of data. The fastest growing type of optical storage is the recordable CD drive, or CD-R, which allows you to record data onto a disc that can be played in any CD-ROM player. Unfortunately, current CD-R technology does not allow you to erase old data, which makes the system better suited for permanent archiving of records rather than daily or weekly system backups.

Tape drives

For most firms, tape drives are the best choice for completely backing up a computer system. Because of their low cost and high storage capacities, most firms use tape for at least a portion of their backup strategy.

Quarter inch cartridges (QIC) are one of the oldest tape drive standards in the industry. While older QIC formats hold only a few hundred MB of data, the newer Travan QIC format can hold up to 2 GB of uncompressed data. The biggest drawback is that QIC tape drives can be very noisy, which can make running the backup very unpopular in the office.

Digital audio tape (DAT) drives are designed for companies with somewhat larger backup needs. Using a 4 mm tape originally designed for digital audio players, DAT drives can handle 1 to 4 GB per cartridge. These drives are especially well suited for businesses that need to back up numerous small files. There are also drives built around 8 mm videotapes, which hold a bit more than DAT drives but otherwise have quite similar performance characteristics.

The newest tape drives for the PC market are called digital linear tape (DLT) drives. These emerged from mainframe storage systems, and are typically used in very large backup systems. DLT drives tend to start at about $2,000, but can store 20 GB or more. They are especially well suited for backing up large files such as databases, but are not as fast when storing many small files.

Software

Most tape drives come equipped with software that allows unattended backups of a single computer or a small network. For larger networks, you generally have to buy third party software that works with the backup drive and the network operating system.

Software must be able to handle problems during backup and recovery. It should allow recoveries to be made from any individual tape or disk, and should be tolerant of user mistakes, such as files that are left open, by alerting the user rather than crashing or aborting the backup.

Terms

Data compression A technique that allows more data to be stored on a given tape. Most manufacturers assume a 2 to 1 data compression rate can be achieved (i.e., 2 MB of data on 1 MB of tape), but actual results may vary.

Gigabyte (GB) A measure of data storage equivalent to 1,000 megabytes

(MB) or approximately 1 billion bytes of data.

Helical recording A way to write information to a tape that involves spinning the writing head in the reverse direction to the tape movement. Helical scan drives can hold more information on a given tape length than a standard recording head. VCRs are a common example of helical recording.

Incremental backup A backup method which only records the files on a system that have changed since the last backup. Incremental backups require much less storage space, but take longer to restore after a crash or disaster. Many businesses conduct full backups each week, while conducting the quicker incremental backups each day.

Jukebox Large networks often need more storage capacity than is available in a single tape. A jukebox automatically loads and unloads tapes from the player during a backup.

Native capacity The storage capacity of a drive when no compression techniques are used. Comparing drives based on their native capacity eliminates differences in manufacturer assumptions concerning file compression.

Special tips

Make sure to test the recovery process soon after your purchase.

Some businesses have backups seem to go as planned for months, only to find that no data was recorded when an emergency arises.

Avoid systems that connect to the computer through the parallel printer port. These transfer data much more slowly than devices using a SCSI or IDE connection.

Tape drives require frequent cleaning to remain in working condition. Buy a tape head cleaner to prolong the life of the head, and set a schedule for cleaning the drive.

Tapes that are frequently used should be retired after about one year.

Businesses should use a backup routine that keeps at least one complete set of data off-site at all times. In many cases, the best approach is a grandfather-father-son approach, which records three complete versions of all data. If a backup does not go as planned, this means there are still two recent copies of the data available.

See also
CD-ROM Drives, Desktop Computers, Notebook Computers, Recordable CD Drives

Conference Calling Services

*M*ost phone systems are not much use when more than two or three people need to participate in the same conversation. Conference calling services allow you to join many people from multiple offices into a single conversation, creating virtual meetings even when participants are thousands of miles apart.

Company	Headquarters	Phone number	Document conferencing
A Better Conference	Palm Springs, CA	800/569-0788	●
ACT	Golden, CO	800/228-3719	●
AT&T	New York, NY	800/232-1234	
ATS	Overland Park, KS	800/234-4546	
The Conference Center	Cambridge, MA	800/825-2578	
Conference Pros	Houston, TX	800/522-3377	
Confertech	Westminster, CO	800/525-8244	●
Connex International	Danbury, CT	800/426-6639	●
MCI	Cedar Rapids, IA	800/475-0600	●
Sprint	Westwood, KS	800/366-2663	

Buying points

Types of conference calls

There are three main ways a conference call can be arranged. The primary difference among them relate to how participants are initially connected.

In an operator-assisted conference, an operator calls and connects each individual participant to the conversation. Participants must be at a designated phone number at a certain time.

A second option is a toll free meet-me conference. Each participant dials a specific toll free number established for the conference. This gives participants greater flexibility in terms of their location, but requires advance planning to acquire a number and notify people of the number to dial.

A third type of conference service is a toll meet-me conference. This works essentially the same as a toll free meet-me conference, but the participants dial a regular number instead of a toll free number. With this arrangement, each participant pays for the cost of making the phone call.

Conferencing features

There are a number of features provided by conferencing services that can help you more effectively manage a teleconference. For example, the service can conduct a roll call to ensure all participants are onboard, monitor phone calls to provide assistance as needed, or broadcast fax agendas or documents prior to a meeting. Some services even offer subconferencing, where a few participants can leave the main discussion for a private conversation.

For groups working on a common project, document conferencing can be a useful tool. This feature allows participants to view the same document on a computer screen. It can be helpful if you need to edit a presentation or agree upon specific wording.

For international conferences, companies may find translation services to be useful. Many of the largest long distance carriers offer interpreters for dozens of languages to help facilitate communication.

Conferences can also be recorded on tape for later review. Some service bureaus can even keep a recording of the conference available for playback to later callers.

Large conferences

A conference that will have more than one hundred participants has unique demands, which not all service bureaus will be able to meet.

Firms should look for two basic features when planning such a conference. First, a service bureau should be able to restrict talking capabilities to a few key people. This will help keep the conversation coherent.

However, the service should also give listeners an opportunity to voice their opinions. This can be done either by offering a voting mechanism which immediately tallies responses to questions, or by allowing individuals to signal to the operator when they have a comment. Participants can then be queued to pose questions at the appropriate time.

Pricing

Pricing for conference calls depends on the call type, conference length, and number of participants. Rates may also vary according to the time of day the conference call is conducted. A basic conference involving 8 people lasting 50 minutes will generally cost between $100 and $200.

Special tips

The best way to save money on conferencing is finding a carrier that offers volume discounts to monthly callers and lower off-peak rates. Large discounts typically require a substantial monthly minimum commitment.

If you frequently make conference calls, you may want to consider purchasing a conferencing bridge. These systems combine multiple lines into a single call without a significant loss in sound quality. Although conferencing bridges are not cheap, they make sense for firms that spend $2,000 per month or more on conferencing services.

See also

Calling Cards, Cellular Service, Conferencing Equipment, International Calling, Long Distance Service, Prepaid Phone Cards, Telephone Systems, Toll Free Service, Video Conferencing Services

Conferencing Equipment

Conferencing equipment allows multiple people gathered in one room to participate in the same telephone call. This equipment is often used to conduct a group meeting with people outside the office.

			Type of unit	
Company	Headquarters	Phone number	Portable	Installed
AT Products	Harvard, IL	800/848-2205	●	●
Coherent	Leesburg, VA	800/443-0726	●	●
Gentner	Salt Lake City, UT	800/945-7730	●	●
NEC	Irving, TX	800/TEAM-NEC	●	
Polycom	San Jose, CA	800/765-9266	●	
Shure	Evanston, IL	800/447-4873	●	●
Sound Control	Norwalk, CT	203/854-5701		●
U.S. Robotics	Skokie, IL	847/676-7010	●	

Buying points

How they work

Conferencing units consist of microphones and speakers that broadcast and pick up voices much like a fancy speakerphone. These units are designed so that multiple people in one room can easily hear and speak to callers without having to huddle around a telephone handset.

The equipment usually consists of an all-in-one portable unit that is placed at the center of a table and is connected to a regular phone cord. Some models also have additional microphones to better capture all the voices in the room.

For permanent installation of conferencing equipment in a room, some vendors sell installed conferencing units. This type of equipment requires custom installation, with speakers and microphones strategically wired throughout a room.

Sound quality

Most regular speakerphones operate in "half-duplex" mode, which mutes the speaker whenever the microphone is activated. This is designed to prevent feedback from overwhelming a call.

The problem with half-duplex is that it severely disrupts the natural flow of conversations, since only one person can speak at a time. If anyone in the group makes a sound, the phone cuts off the voice of the remote participant. This can result in choppy sounding conversations, with words frequently cut off when people speak simultaneously.

In contrast, most conference equipment operates in full-duplex mode, allowing both parties to speak at once. To do this, the equipment uses a digital signal processor, or echo canceller, which digitally prevents feedback by eliminating the caller's voice from the microphone pickup. Essentially, the echo canceller "hears" the caller's voice and removes this sound from the microphone input signal. With this type of conferencing equipment, both parties can talk and listen without experiencing the awkward breaks of a speakerphone conversation.

Purchasing choices

The biggest factor when choosing conferencing equipment is to make sure that the unit operates in full duplex mode. Although most units now offer this capability, there are a few models on the market that are nothing more than expensive speakerphones.

Next, look for a system that is designed for the appropriate room size you will be using. If the system will be used with large and small groups, look for expansion modules that can accommodate larger numbers of participants. Wireless microphone systems are also an option for conference participants who will be walking while speaking.

It is best to test the equipment in the environment where it will be used to make sure the sound level is acceptable and that the microphones can reach all participants. You should also check that the conferencing equipment is compatible with your current phone system. If you cannot get the equipment on a trial basis, you may want to consider renting the equipment at first.

Pricing

If you are looking to buy a conferencing system, expect to pay a minimum of $400 to $1,000 for a portable unit. For custom installations, prices can range from $1,500 to tens of thousands of dollars.

Special tips

Some phone systems are capable of connecting three or more parties together into a single conversation. Instead of buying conferencing equipment, it may be practical to connect two (or more) internal extensions with an outside caller for small conferences.

When multiple people are participating on one end of a conversation, it can be helpful to have each person identify themselves when making a comment. Voices are often hard to distinguish over the phone.

See also
Conference Calling Services, ISDN, Telephone Systems, Video Conferencing Services

COPY PAPER

Copy paper is a basic business staple guzzled like water by busy offices. Although one white sheet may appear to look much like another, there is more variation in paper than the untrained eye might expect.

VENDORS			
Company	Headquarters	Phone number	Minimum order
Nationwide Papers	Stamford, CT	203/358-6600	$300
The Paper Mart	East Hanover, NJ	201/884-2505	none
ResourceNet Int'l.	Covington, KY	606/655-2000	$250
RIS Paper	Long Island City, NY	718/392-8100	varies
UniSource	Valley Forge, PA	610/296-8000	$300
WWF Paper	Bala Cynwyd, PA	800/345-1305	$75
Zellerbach	Miamisburg, OH	800/509-5603	$300

Buying points

Variations in copy paper

There are four specifications primarily used to describe paper. The weight is often the simplest to find. This figure, typically 20, 24, or 28 pounds (#), indicates the approximate thickness of the paper.

Opacity indicates how much light will shine through the paper. This typically ranges from 80 to 92 percent, with greater numbers indicating greater opacity.

A third specification is brightness, which indicates the paper's ability to reflect light. Like opacity, brightness ranges from about 80 to 92 percent. To the eye, brighter sheets will appear more white.

The fourth point of comparison is smoothness. Smooth paper can make print look cleaner, and gives documents a finished look. Smoothness can be represented with a number, but is usually indicated with a descriptive word, such as "vellum" or "smooth" finish.

Branded papers

Paper mills manufacture and market different types of paper under various brands. Each branded paper typically meets a different combination of the above-mentioned specifications. In addition, branded paper is usually backed by some kind of guarantee about its ability to work in office equipment.

Differences between two brands of paper with the same specifications are minimal. Due to improved manufacturing processes and tighter specifications in mills, paper is now a true commodity.

As a result, if you buy branded paper, consider switching brands to take advantage of price fluctuations. By finding similar papers from other manufacturers, you will be able to take advantage of lower prices when you encounter them. Buying brands that have similar paper characteristics can save you up to 10% in paper costs.

Generic paper

Generic paper is paper that falls below specifications set by paper manufacturers. The problem is usually due to slight variations in paper color or thickness. This paper is then sold to a "seconds" house that packages the sheets for sale.

Generic paper can be typically identified by the plain carton in which it is packaged. Identifying labels, if any, usually indicate that the product is xerographic or multipurpose copier paper, without mention of a specific paper mill.

Generic paper is absolutely fine for most types of office equipment. The exception is high speed copiers, or any equipment handling more than 40 sheets per minute. The reason for this is that high-speed machines have very narrow tolerances for paper thickness. Because generic paper is often paper that specifically fails thickness specifications, it will be more likely to cause paper jams.

For slower machines, however, generic paper offers substantial savings.

You should be able to save 35% in paper costs by buying generic rather than name brand paper for fax machines, laser printers, and slower photocopiers.

Purchasing paper

Currently, most companies purchase paper from contract stationers and office supply stores. These sources generally offer paper at quite competitive prices, although you should shop around to make sure you are getting a good deal.

Companies that go through more than 100-150 cartons of paper yearly have a bit more flexibility when shopping for paper. For these companies, paper merchants that specialize in buying and selling paper can be an attractive source.

Pricing

Superstores often sell copy paper at a very thin profit margin to attract customers, with the expectation that other, more profitable goods will be purchased. As a result, superstores can be tough to beat for companies that purchase less than 10 cases of paper at a time.

Prices from paper merchants can vary considerably. Quotes for branded paper can range from $37 to $52 per carton for ten cases of 20 lb. paper. For 40 cases (or one skid) of paper, prices are slightly better, with quotes ranging from $36 to $40 per carton.

Terms

Acid-free sheets Paper that is produced without using acid in the manufacturing process. These sheets are more suitable for long-term storage since they are less likely to yellow and decay over time.

Basis weight The weight of a ream of paper in its standard size.

Bond paper Paper sold in weights of 20 to 34 pounds.

Caliper Measurement of how many thousandths of an inch, or points, thick a certain number of sheets is. This figure is utilized most often in reference to file folders.

Grain The direction in which the paper fibers are directed, which can be determined by seeing which direction the paper tears most easily. Virtually all copy paper is grain long.

Ream A standard amount of copy paper equivalent to 500 sheets.

Smoothness Measured on a numeric Sheffield scale, this figure indicates the texture of the paper.

Special tips

While laser printing tends to look the same on almost any kind of paper, ink-jets are very sensitive to the type of paper that is used. Ink-jet printers using smooth paper will produce noticeably better output, particularly with complex graphics, as the ink is less likely to "feather" or be absorbed by the paper.

Paper needs to be stored appropriately to maintain its quality. Overly humid or dry conditions can affect the paper's ability to run cleanly through machines.

Specialty paper vendors distribute papers that are preprinted with fancy borders, backgrounds or trim. Some of the major national vendors include On Paper (800/820-2299), Paper Direct (800/272-7377), and Paper Showcase (800/843-0414).

> **Did you know?**
>
> Paper is made from the papyrus plant by taking thin slices of the plant, laying them side by side, and then soaking, pressing, and drying the resulting sheet.

See also
Color Printers, Ink-jet Printers, Laser Printers, Paper Shredders, Photocopiers, Recycling

Cordless Telephones

A cordless telephone is a phone that uses radio waves to transmit conversations from the handset to a base unit plugged into a phone line. Cordless phones give individuals the flexibility to move around in an office while staying on a call.

PRICING

Type of cordless telephone	Price range
2-channel	$52-$90
10-channel 46-49 MHz	$40-$240
10-channel 900 MHz	$180-$310
25-channel 46-49 MHz	$60-$400
25-channel 900 MHz	$150-$500
Wireless phone system (per user)	$800-$2,500

VENDORS

Company	Headquarters	Phone number	25+ channels	900 MHz	Wireless systems
Cobra	Chicago, IL	312/889-3087	●	●	
GE	Indianapolis, IN	800/626-2000	●	●	
Lucent Technologies	Basking Ridge, NJ	800/451-2100	●	●	
Nortel	Raleigh, NC	800/4-NORTEL			●
Panasonic	Secaucus, NJ	800/545-2672	●	●	
Phonemate (Casio)	Torrance, CA	310/320-9810	●		
Radio Shack (Tandy)	Fort Worth, TX	800/843-7422		●	
Sharp	Mahwah, NJ	800/BE-SHARP	●		
Sony	Park Ridge, NJ	800/222-SONY	●	●	
Southwestern Bell (Conair)	E. Windsor, NJ	800/366-0937	●	●	
SpectraLink	Boulder, CO	303/440-5330			●
Uniden	Fort Worth, TX	817/858-3596		●	

Buying points

Types of cordless phones
For small offices and home users, there are two types of cordless technology. Most older and less expensive phones transmit in the range of 46 to 49 megahertz (MHz). These phones offer ranges of 500 to 600 feet.

Newer cordless models use the 900 MHz frequency, which reduces line static and allows for longer calling ranges. 900 MHz phones offer ranges of 1,500 to 1,600 feet.

There are also cordless phones designed for use with corporate PBX phone systems. These units typically use the PCS frequencies that have been set aside for new mobile communication systems, allowing them to handle extremely wide calling ranges and many simultaneous users.

Avoiding call interference
To avoid call interference, look for a cordless phone that can transmit on multiple channels. This refers to the number of different frequencies the phone can use to handle conversations.

Until recently, 10 channels were considered the norm for cordless phones. However, the FCC recently increased the number of channels available for cordless phones. Most units now offer at least 25 channels, while a few offer as many as 60 channels.

With any multichannel phone, look for an autoscan feature. This automatically scans all the available channels at the beginning of a call, selecting the channel with the clearest reception. Some phones offer a channel memory feature, which remembers which channel works best in a given environment for faster call placement.

Preventing eavesdropping
Most cordless phones now incorporate digital technology to prevent calls from being picked up deliberately or by mistake. This technology spreads a single conversation over multiple frequencies.

A few models now also offer voice scrambling, which prevents even a determined snoop from picking up your conversations.

Battery life
Generally, you can expect a phone to last four to eight hours on a single charge. More sophisticated phones generally require more power to operate and, therefore, have a shorter battery life.

If you expect to use a cordless phone for long periods of time, look for a model that uses a dual battery system. This will allow you to swap in a new battery rather than interrupt a conversation for recharging.

Also be sure that any phone you choose has some sort of low battery indicator to avoid losing an important call.

Cordless phones for PBX systems
Regular cordless telephones can be plugged into most PBX phone systems. However, they often do not have enough range or enough channels to be used throughout a large office.

A new technology called unlicensed personal communications services (UPCS) can create wireless phone systems within an office. These wireless systems can cover anywhere from 500,000 to 4 million square feet.

If you are looking for a wireless system, the best place to start is with your current phone system vendor. Integrating a wireless phone system from another manufacturer can be difficult, and often limits the number of features you can obtain.

The wireless phone market is currently dominated by Lucent Technologies (formerly AT&T), Nortel, and SpectraLink. As the technology becomes more popular, expect other major phone system manufacturers to enter this market.

Pricing
Cordless phones range in price from $40 to $500. The variation in price will depend primarily on the number of channels, the transmission frequency, security features and other calling features. At the low end of this range are 10-channel models that operate at 46-49 MHz. At the high end are 900 MHz models that operate on 25 or more channels and offer a full spectrum of features.

Pricing for wireless phone systems varies considerably depending on the type of system being considered. They range in price from $800 to $1,500 per user.

Terms

Automatic access protection code A digital security code that helps prevent unauthorized access by other cordless phone users in your area.

Multichannel operation A feature that automatically seeks the clearest channel to minimize interference and maximize the phone's performance.

Special tips

Many cordless phones will not work during a power outage, since the base unit requires power to transmit signals. As a result, you should always keep some standard phones available in case of a blackout.

Two-channel cordless phones are very inexpensive, but offer very poor sound quality. Almost any business will be disappointed by the sound quality of these phones.

Some phones have LCD displays that can display the phone number being dialed or the length of the call. Some can even work with Caller ID to indicate the phone number of incoming calls.

See also
Cellular Telephones, KSU-less Phone Systems, Telephone Systems

Corporate Cards

*I*f your company has employees who travel regularly, you need some way to efficiently handle T&E (travel and entertainment) expenses. No approach seems perfect. Cash advances do not encourage frugality, yet reimbursing personal credit card charges can lead to administrative headaches.

Designed specifically for business travelers, corporate cards offer one of the easiest ways to address this situation. Corporate cards ease cash flow concerns and offer itemized bills for greater accountability and better purchasing oversight.

VENDORS

Company	Phone number	Charge Card	Credit Card	Number of ATMs Worldwide	Centralized billing	Distributed billing
Air Travel Card	800/222-4688	●		0	●	
American Express	800/528-2122	●		100,000	●	●
Diners Club	800/999-9093	●		190,000	●	●
First Bank VISA Business Card	800/344-5696		●	250,000	●	
First Bank VISA Corporate Card	800/344-5696	●		250,000	●	●
GE Capital Corporate Card	800/338-7587		●	220,000	●	●
MasterCard Business Card	800/727-8825		●	405,000	●	●
MasterCard Purchasing Card	800/727-8825		●	405,000	●	●

Buying points

How they work

Corporate cards are essentially company-sponsored credit or charge cards. The primary difference between corporate and personal cards is that corporate cards offer a great deal more flexibility in terms of charges, billing, and payment. Moreover, because corporate cards are used companywide, they offer summaries of information that could otherwise take hours to compile from numerous personal charge slips.

Liability for purchases

Probably the greatest concern facing a company considering corporate cards is the issue of liability. Although most firms will attest to the steadfastness, honesty, and loyalty of their employees, fewer companies would be willing to be held absolutely accountable for all charges made on a corporate card.

Recognizing this, corporate card vendors offer varying levels of liability. This can range from a policy where the company assumes primary responsibility for all charges, to one where the issuing vendor assumes ultimate responsibility for all unpaid charges. Like an insurance policy, the per year costs of maintaining a corporate account will vary according to the amount of liability the corporate card vendor assumes.

Corporate card acceptance

Most cards can be used for a wide variety of travel expenses, including hotel stays, meals, and retail purchases. Virtually all corporate cards can also be used to obtain cash advances from an extensive network of automated teller machines. The exception to this rule is the Air Travel Card, which can only be used with airlines.

For domestic travel, there is little difference in acceptance among cards. However, for international travelers, the acceptance rate tends to vary greatly. VISA and MasterCard are the most universal, with about 12 million vendors accepting these cards globally. If less developed areas of the world are frequented by your firm's employees, you should make sure the card you choose is widely accepted in these locations.

Billing options

Card issuers generally offer a great deal of flexibility when it comes to billing. When comparing billing options, there are two primary considerations to keep in mind.

The first is the type of balance that will be maintained. There are two types of cards available: charge cards and credit cards. Charge cards often have no spending restrictions, but come with the expectation that bills will be paid in full every month. In contrast, credit cards allow firms to roll over their expenses, but at hefty interest rates—ranging as high as 20 percent. If your firm expects to carry balances regularly, you are probably better off using personal credit cards, which typically charge lower interest rates.

Another consideration is who will be paying the bills. Payment can either be centralized or distributed. With centralized payment, all employee charges are consolidated for payment by the company. To ensure that only the appropriate charges are paid, individual statements can be issued to employees for review. Many vendors also offer the option of making individual cardholders responsible for payment, with consolidated expense reports forwarded to the company.

Reporting features

One of the major benefits of a corporate card comes in the form of tailored expense reports and analyses. These reports can offer some much-needed relief to overworked accounting departments by replacing the need to individually record each expense.

The type and frequency of reports vary greatly. Data can be reported according to variables such as vendor, city, cardholder or expense type. Reports are typically issued monthly, with some cards offering quarterly and year-end recaps.

In addition to the paper reports, corporate card vendors have recently begun offering expense data on diskette for additional in-house analysis.

Special tips

Keep in mind that most aspects of a corporate card are negotiable. This includes the per card fees, the type of liability maintained, the late payment fee, the interest rates, and the cash advance fee. By shopping around, you will be able to find significant savings.

Companies interested in keeping a tight rein on how a card is used can restrict various aspects of the card. For example, you can choose to limit the maximum amount of cash that can be withdrawn from an ATM. Some cards will also allow firms to limit purchases to certain categories of goods such as airline tickets. For purchases where the card is not authorized for use, charges will be rejected.

One popular benefit of corporate cards is automatic insurance protection. From the vendors' perspective, insurance is a good benefit to offer because it is not often used (which means it is not very expensive to maintain), but is valued fairly highly by customers. As a result, most vendors offer travel accident, lost baggage, and buyer's protection insurance.

The most desirable type of insurance is coverage for rental car collision damage. Most corporate cards provide primary coverage, as opposed to the secondary coverage offered by most personal credit cards. This means the corporate card covers all damage, instead of just the damage not covered by the driver's personal auto insurance policy.

See also
Accountants, Car Rental Agencies

Did you know?

In 1958, the original cardboard American Express card was referred to as the "Purple Card."

DESKS

*B*uying a desk often seems like merely a matter of choosing style and size. If you know the look you want, the purchase should be simple.

Unfortunately, buying a desk involves more than just a good eye. Variations in quality can mean the difference between a desk that lasts for decades and one that winds up in the trash the following year.

VENDORS

Company	Headquarters	Phone number	Price range - Budget	Price range - High-end	Materials - Laminate	Materials - Veneer	Materials - Metal
Allsteel	Aurora, IL	800/764-2535	●	●	●	●	●
Bevis (Hunt Mfg.)	Philadelphia, PA	800/477-4446	●		●		
The Bukstaff Co.	Oshkosh, WI	800/755-5890	●	●	●	●	
GF Office	Canfield, OH	216/533-7799	●	●	●	●	●
Haworth	Holland, MI	800/334-2600		●	●	●	
Herman Miller	Zeeland, MI	616/654-8600	●	●	●	●	●
HON	Muscatine, IA	800/833-3964	●	●	●	●	●
Invincible	Manitowoc, WI	800/558-4417		●	●		●
Krueger Int'l.	Green Bay, WI	414/468-8100	●	●	●	●	●
La-Z-Boy	Monroe, MI	313/241-4700	●	●		●	
Miller Desk	High Point, NC	800/438-4324	●		●	●	
Vogel Peterson	Garden Grove, CA	800/942-4332	●	●	●		

Buying points

Types of desks
The primary difference among desks is the material used in their construction. Desks are typically made from wood, laminate or metal.

While wood is considered to be the best looking-material, it tends to scar and must be treated to maintain its appearance. As a result, most desks are made of laminate, which is a plastic finish applied to a wood core. Laminate comes in a wide array of patterns, from wood grain to color finishes, and is available in the budget and mid-market segments. For even greater durability, some businesses prefer metal desks.

Key parts of a desk to examine
A good way to check the quality of any desk is to examine the construction of the drawers. Higher quality drawers will have a sturdy suspension, using metal rollers and guides. Make sure that the drawers open and close smoothly when bearing weight. Also check to see if the drawers slide out to their full length, allowing the user to fully utilize the space.

With wood desks, continue to examine the drawers to assess the quality of construction. Higher-end desks will have drawers that are assembled using an interlocking dovetail construction rather than staples or glue. In addition, the bottom of the drawers will use a wood veneer or heavy plywood sheet rather than a plastic melamine sheet.

When considering laminate desks, examine the type of laminate used. A thick, high pressure laminate withstands stains, scratches, watermarks, and other day-to-day office abuse much better than a thinner laminate. In addition, more expensive desks typically have rounded corners rather than regular squared-off corners.

The primary indicator of quality for metal desks is the gauge of steel used in their manufacture. This can be assessed by simply feeling how solid the construction is and checking a desk's overall weight. One area to examine in particular is how the drawers look when they are closed. If the desk is not set right, you will see a gap where the drawer meets the desk.

Working with a computer
The most important factor when buying a desk that will be used with a computer is to make sure that the keyboard can be placed at a comfortable height. A normal desk height of 29 to 30 inches can result in great discomfort when working at a computer for long periods of time. To address this issue, the desk should be equipped with either a keyboard platform (preferably adjustable), or legs that can be adjusted.

Also consider how computer wiring is managed. Some desks are equipped with wiring holes. These allow wires to be dropped through the worksurface so they do not hang over the edge of the desk. Other desk manufacturers address this issue by adding channels along the edge of the desk to funnel the wires. Some manufacturers have even developed a storage area for a surge suppressor so it can be kept safely out of the way of errant feet.

Desk longevity
The warranty can give a good sense for the life expectancy of a desk. Mid-market desks typically come with warranties of 5 to 15 years, while high-end desks are designed to last several decades.

The edges of a desk typically show the most wear, especially at the corners and at the center near the chair. You may want to check the edge surface to test its resistance to chipping.

Pricing
Desks range in price from $80 to $10,000 depending upon the material used, the quality of construction, design features, and the amount of storage space. Average prices are between $300 and $1,500.

Special tips
If the desk will be used for conferences or group work, look for a model with a deep overhang to provide more leg space for coworkers.

You can get considerable discounts if you buy more than one desk at a time.

One attractive option for low cost, but high-end desks is to buy remanufactured furniture. Vendors replace worn parts and refinish surfaces to remove damage. Limited availability generally makes this a better solution for smaller companies.

Sales are generally slowest during the summer, making it the best time to negotiate a deal on furniture.

See also
File Cabinets, Chairs, Systems Furniture

For more information, visit
BuyersZone
http://www.buyerszone.com/

Desktop Computers

*B*uying a computer can be an overwhelming process. There are so many components to consider that it can be difficult to know what to get, let alone how much you should pay. Even if you have bought a computer fairly recently, the rapid pace of change in this industry means that older guidelines may not hold much weight anymore.

VENDORS

Company	Headquarters	Sales number	Technical support number
Acer	San Jose, CA	800/239-2237	800/445-6495
Apple	Cupertino, CA	800/538-9696	800/SOS-APPL
AST	Irvine, CA	800/876-4278	800/727-1278
Austin (IPC)	Austin, TX	800/752-4171	800/752-4171
Compaq	Houston, TX	800/888-5858	800/652-6672
Dell	Austin, TX	800/727-3355	800/727-3355
Digital (DEC)	Maynard, MA	800/344-4825	800/344-4825
Gateway 2000	N. Sioux City, SD	800/846-2042	800/846-2000
Hewlett-Packard	Palo Alto, CA	800/752-0900	970/635-1000
IBM	Somers, NY	800/426-2968	800/772-2227
Micron	Nampa, ID	800/347-3490	800/438-3343
MidWest Micro	Fletcher, OH	800/572-8844	800/572-8844
Packard Bell	Chatsworth, CA	800/733-5858	800/733-4411
Quantex	Somerset, NJ	800/652-0566	800/864-8650

Buying points

PC vs. Mac

The first decision when choosing a computer is whether to purchase an IBM-compatible PC or a Macintosh system.

PCs currently dominate the business computer market, particularly in large firms and financially-oriented departments. PCs tend to be inexpensive, and can run the widest range of software. In addition, newer operating systems such as Windows 95 have helped make PCs easier to use and set up.

Macintosh models have less than 10% of the overall market, but are very strong in the educational, graphics, and multimedia industries. Macs are very easy to use and require less technical knowledge for tasks such as networking or connecting peripherals. However, some software is not available for Macs, and system prices tend to be higher than similarly-equipped PCs.

Overall, the best choice for you depends on the work you will be doing. If businesses that are similar to yours use Macs or PCs, you are probably best off making the same choice.

Choosing a computer

Once you make the Mac versus PC decision, the next task is finding the right brand and model.

Currently there are many brands of PCs on the market, ranging from well known companies like Compaq and IBM to no-name brands assembled in spare rooms. The Mac market is not nearly as diverse, but there are a few firms that compete with Apple in the segment.

When deciding among brands, it is important to understand that computers are simply a combination of very standard parts. By mixing together processors, disk drives, and other hardware in various combinations, manufacturers can create a system to meet almost any need. No company really makes faster or better computers; the primary difference is in the components that are used.

As a result, it is critical when choosing a computer to understand what type of components you require. By getting the processor, memory, hard drive, and video support you need, you can be sure that the computer will be up to the task.

Type of processor

A computer's processor is the "brain" of the machine, controlling what the computer thinks and does. In many ways, your choice of processor will affect the performance and capabilities of the computer more than any other component.

The most popular processor currently on the market for the PC is the Intel Pentium chip. Pentiums are available in a number of different clock speeds, ranging from 75 MHz to as high as 200 MHz.

For higher performance, Intel also makes a faster and more expensive chip called the Pentium Pro. The

Pentium Pro is specifically designed for systems that use the Windows NT operating system. It tends not to be a good choice for computers that want to run the older DOS or Windows 3.1 operating systems.

Besides Intel processors, businesses have very few choices for PC processors. The Cyrix's 6x86 is one of the more notable competitors, offering performance about equal to a Pentium at a lower price. However, systems using the Cyrix chip tend to be very difficult to find. Another alternative is the AMD 5k86, which so far has not shown any appreciable advantage over the Pentium.

Buyers interested in a Mac will be choosing among Motorola/IBM's various PowerPC chips. The fastest PowerPC chip is the 604e, while the 603e and 601 offer less performance at lower prices. These chips offer clock speeds ranging from 60 MHz to more than 240 MHz.

Memory

Memory, also called RAM, is the workspace for the processor. A computer with lots of memory has plenty of room to run multiple applications. In contrast, a system equipped with less memory requires the processor to waste time shuffling data to make room for the next set of data. If memory space is very limited, the processor may even need to temporarily store data on the hard drive, a process that significantly slows the entire system.

As a result, the amount of memory in the computer can have a dramatic effect on how fast the processor operates. Most new computers are equipped with at least 8 megabytes (MB) of memory. This is enough to load most operating systems and run most programs, albeit slowly. However, most users will want more memory. We strongly recommend at least 16 MB as a working minimum. Users who keep more than one program open at once should consider equipping a computer with 24 to 32 MB of memory.

Adding memory to a computer costs only about $10 per MB, and memory can easily be bought and installed after the purchase.

Storage space needs

Most computers come equipped with a hard drive to store applications and documents. Hard drives have dramatically dropped in price over the last few years, to the point where few systems are even offered with anything less than an 800 MB drive. High-end systems commonly offer storage capacities as large as 2 gigabytes (GB).

If this sounds like a lot of storage, consider that applications now routinely take as much as 10 to 25 MB apiece. An operating system such as Windows 95 will occupy as much as 50 MB. Complex files, such as sound, graphics or video, can occupy as much as 100 MB.

With hard drive space available for less than 30¢ per megabyte, it does not make sense to skimp on a hard drive. We recommend buying at least a 1 GB hard drive for new business computers.

Desktop Computers

Video needs

On Windows-based PCs, video performance plays a critical role in how fast the computer appears to operate. Even with a Pentium-class processor, you may find yourself twiddling your thumbs if the system takes a long time to redraw images on the screen.

The key to video performance is the video card. The card determines the number of colors the monitor will display, as well as the resolution and the speed at which the images appear.

Most systems today come with cards that can handle eight-bit color, which means the monitor can display 256 colors simultaneously on a screen. For users requiring more realistic images, many systems can be equipped with video cards offering 16-bit or 24-bit color. These can display 65,000 or 16.7 million colors, respectively.

To handle the enormous amount of data that comes with displaying so many colors, good video cards include specially-designed processors and memory (video RAM). Cards typically come equipped with one MB of video RAM. However, if you expect to use a large monitor or need to display many colors, look for a card with 2 or 4 MB of video RAM.

Where to buy a computer

Computers are sold through a variety of channels, including retail stores, direct vendors, mail order firms, computer stores, and value added resellers (VARs).

Retail stores tend to have fairly attractive pricing, but offer a limited choice of models and almost no advice. They are usually a good choice only if they stock exactly what you need.

Direct sales vendors such as Dell and Gateway 2000 are significant players in the computer market. These firms sell direct from the factory, and tend to combine good prices and attractive service policies.

Mail order stores are most suitable for very knowledgeable consumers. Buying via mail order can result in the best bargains, but also presents the greatest risk of receiving a sub-par system. As a result, businesses buying through mail order should be careful to investigate both the firm and the model before making a purchase.

Computer stores are often a good source for advice and technical help. Most computer dealers stock a wide number of models, plus most important peripherals. However, dealers tend to be more expensive than other sources.

VARs generally have the highest level of knowledge about systems, particularly in setting up computer networks. While you can expect to pay a 10% premium for the service and advice of a VAR, you will receive on-site assistance to help set up the system and fix any problems that may arise.

Pricing

The processor is the single most expensive component in a computer.

As a result, the age and the market supply of a processor have a major effect on pricing. In the first few months after a new processor is introduced, production lines are usually not fully up and running at top speed. This is a bad time to buy, since prices are very high and there may be unresolved compatibility problems with some systems.

Once a processor is superseded by a faster chip, its price tends to drop dramatically. This is usually the best time to buy. Although further price cuts are inevitable, waiting any longer risks shortening the useful life of the computer. Purchasing just after the introduction of a new chip gives you the best combination of price and leading-edge technology.

No matter where you buy, keep in mind that this is an extremely competitive industry. Any vendor will be willing to negotiate with you, especially if you can be flexible in terms of configurations or accessories, or if you are buying multiple units.

Terms

Clock speed The number of instructions a processor can execute per second. Clock speed is measured in millions of instructions per second (megahertz, or MHz). It is a good indicator of performance only when comparing the same type of chip.

Gigabyte (GB) One thousand megabytes of data. A gigabyte is equivalent to approximately one billion words.

Operating system A basic program controlling how you can use and operate the computer. All Macs use the MacOS. PCs can work with a much greater range of operating systems. Older operating systems include DOS and Windows, while newer ones include Windows 95, Windows NT, and OS/2. There are also a number of less popular operating systems for technical users.

Resolution The number of dots of light that appear on a monitor. A higher resolution means that more dots appear on the screen, allowing a larger image to be displayed on a given monitor.

Special tips

Computer systems follow a very predictable pattern of price reductions. In many cases, waiting just a few months can bring significant savings. Intel, which makes the majority of processors, typically announces price reductions during the second month of every quarter. Computer buyers generally reap the benefits of these announcements within six weeks.

Because computer technology changes so fast, it is usually not worth upgrading a computer. Although you can often inexpensively upgrade one component, other components will be inferior to those found in newer models.

Computer manufacturers often charge much higher amounts for computers that are very expandable. If you do not expect to add accessories to a computer, you can often save money by purchasing a less-expandable slimline model.

Desktop Computers

See also
CD-ROM Drives, Color Printers, Computer Backup Systems, Dot Matrix Printers, Fax Servers, Ink-jet Printers, Keyboards, Laser Printers, Modems, Monitors, Notebook Computers, Pointing Devices, Recordable CD Drives, Scanners, Uninterruptible Power Supplies

For more information, visit
BuyersZone
http://www.buyerszone.com/

Did you know?

Today's desktop PC, which costs about $2,000, has the same processing power as a 1970s Cray 1 supercomputer, which sported a million dollar price tag.

Dictation Equipment

*D*ictation equipment serves as a way to capture ideas by recording a voice instead of writing or typing. The equipment is often used in businesses that bill on an hourly basis, since it can minimize the time spent by high-paid employees on any project. Dictation is also commonly used in businesses where writing is impractical, such as medical services and emergency response units.

VENDORS				
Company	Headquarters	Phone number	Analog	Digital
Dictaphone	Stratford, CT	800/447-7749	●	●
Lanier	Atlanta, GA	800/708-7088	●	●
Olympus	Melville, NY	800/221-3000	●	
Panasonic	Secaucus, NJ	201/348-7000	●	
Philips/Norelco	New York, NY	516/921-9310	●	●
Sanyo	Chatsworth, CA	800/421-5013	●	
Sony	Montvale, NJ	800/686-7669	●	●
VDI	Hampton, NH	603/926-3100		●

Dictation Equipment

Buying points

Uses of dictation

Dictation is primarily useful in two situations. The first situation is when taking notes is difficult or too time consuming. In these cases, a recorder is often the easiest way to capture all the information that is needed. For example, dictation is often used while traveling, when other forms of note-taking would be impractical.

A second use of dictation is to shift the time burdens of typing. Dictation minimizes the time needed to take down information at the expense of increasing the total work required to get everything on paper. It is most valuable, therefore, when low-salaried employees are available to transcribe the work of higher-paid executives. In companies where such a transcribing arrangement is not available, dictation is typically much less efficient than writing or using a computer.

Available technologies

There are two types of dictation equipment. Analog equipment is a variation of a basic tape recorder, using magnetic impulses to store sounds on audio tape. With the emergence of small tapes and miniaturized electronics, recorders have shrunk to the point where they are smaller than a wallet and can weigh as little as five ounces.

Digital dictation equipment stores sounds on computer hard drives. Although digital equipment is generally not portable, it allows for much more flexibility in retrieving, prioritizing, and managing files. Recordings can be accessed out of order, and portions can be erased without disturbing other parts of the recording. Digital dictation can also be accessed via phone for travelers out of the office.

Buying an analog system

Purchasing an analog system tends to be a fairly simple task. For recording, users have a choice between pocket recorders or desk units. Pocket recorders typically have a built-in microphone, while desk units also can accept an external microphone.

Most equipment is standardized on microcassettes, which are among the smallest type of recording tape available. However, there are other tape designs on the market, which means that you will need to check that all the equipment you buy can use the same tapes.

One of the most important features to look for is indexing. This allows the person doing the recording to add a tone to the tape at the beginning or end of each dictated message. These tones allow the transcriber to easily find the beginning of each document, or even queue documents in a particular order.

A second feature to consider is voice activation. This feature automatically starts the recording process when the user begins to speak. Voice activation saves tape as long pauses are no longer recorded. However, the first few syllables of each recorded segment are often distorted.

Determining digital system requirements

Digital dictation systems are quite complex, with many different capabilities available depending on your firm's needs. To get an accurate estimate for your system requirements, you will need to collect information such as the number of phone lines that will connect to the system, the peak dictation demands on the system, the typical turn-around time for dictation, and the average length of each dictation. These figures will help determine the amount of storage space required as well as the usage demands on the system.

Transcription equipment

Transcription equipment is used to help typists convert dictated messages into written text. Buyers should look for equipment that allows the transcriber to easily modify the speed and volume at which the dictated information is conveyed. In addition, the model should be able to utilize indexing tones on the recording. Finally, these models should have foot controls so the transcriber's hands do not have to move from the keyboard to control playback.

Purchasing channels

The majority of low-end dictation units are sold through office equipment dealers and retail outlets.

Larger, centralized systems typically require much more service and support. While dictation equipment dealers do exist, most of these systems are sold by direct sales forces. This allows the company to tailor a centralized system for your office structure. If you are buying large numbers of recorders and transcribers, you should make sure to deal with a large dealer or the manufacturer.

Pricing

Analog dictation systems range in price from about $79 for a standard portable microcassette recorder to $3,000 for an advanced transcriber.

Digital dictation equipment costs considerably more than its analog counterparts, running anywhere from $1,000 to $60,000. In fact, systems can exceed $100,000 depending on the number of ports, lines, and trailers required.

Terms

Conference recording A feature that allows the user to adjust the microphone sensitivity to record a conference. The dictation setting minimizes background noises, while a conference setting allows the microphone to pick up all voices in the room.

End-of-tape alert A feature of many analog systems that signals when the tape needs to be flipped to the other side.

Ports The connections between a centralized dictation system and a phone system. The number of ports indicates the maximum number of people that can access the system via phone at any one time.

Trailers The prompts and questions a digital dictation system will ask when users access the system by phone.

Special tips

Pay attention to the design of recording units. Some units have record buttons that could be accidentally activated when you attempt to play back a document. This could cause unintended erasure of important notes.

People just beginning to dictate notes or letters will initially find it quite awkward. Rather than giving up, users should continue to practice; it becomes much easier to do over time.

Voice recognition systems are available for converting voices to computer text. Standalone models cost $400 to $6,000, while PC-based systems are $4,000 to $8,000. These systems are offered by companies including Dictaphone, Dragon Systems (617/965-5200), Norcom (800/225-0866), and Philips.

See also
Desktop Computers, Telephone Headsets

> **Did you know?**
>
> Studies indicate that, on average, people can speak their thoughts at approximately six times the speed of writing.

Dot Matrix Printers

*D*ot matrix printers use a set of closely spaced pins and a ribbon to print letters or other characters on a page. Unlike laser printers or ink-jet printers, dot matrix printers actually impact the page to print a character, much like a typewriter. This allows them to print through multi-part forms, rather than just printing on the top sheet.

VENDORS

Company	Headquarters	Phone number
AMT	Camarillo, CA	805/388-5799
Apple	Cupertino, CA	800/776-2333
Brother	Somerset, NJ	800/276-7746
C. Itoh	Tustin, CA	800/877-1421
Dataproducts	Simi Valley, CA	800/980-0374
Digital	Maynard, MA	800/777-4343
Epson	Torrance, CA	800/BUY-EPSON
Genicom	Chantilly, VA	800/436-4266
Lexmark	Lexington, KY	800/891-0395
Mannesmann Tally	Kent, WA	800/843-1347
Okidata	Mt. Laurel, NJ	800/654-3282
Output Technology	Spokane, WA	509/536-0468
Printer Systems Int'l.	Newton, MA	617/928-3580
Star Micronics	Piscataway, NJ	800/506-7827
Texas Instruments	Dallas, TX	800/TI-TEXAS

Buying points

Common applications for dot matrix printers

While laser printers have become the office standard for letters and proposals, dot matrix printers remain an important part of back-office operations in many firms. Dot matrix printers are commonly used for printing invoices, purchase orders, shipping forms, labels, and other multi-part forms. Dot matrix printers can print through multi-part forms in a single pass, allowing them to quickly produce more pages than even high-speed laser printers.

Choosing a printer

The first consideration when choosing a printer is the number of pages you expect to run through the machine. Low-volume dot matrix printers sell for only a few hundred dollars; however, these machines are not designed for high-volume printing. If the printer will be used to print more than 50 pages per day, make sure to get a machine designed for high-volume usage.

A second consideration is the number of parts in the forms to be printed. A good rule of thumb is to look for a printer that can just handle the number of parts you need to print. This will ensure that the printer does not work harder than it must to print through the parts, thereby increasing the life of its printhead.

9-pin vs. 24-pin printers

The first generation of dot matrix printers used a grid of nine pins to create each character. The print quality from these models is acceptable, but certainly not impressive.

As dot matrix printers began to compete with daisy wheel printers and the first laser printers, firms introduced 24-pin models. By more than doubling the number of pins, printed documents approach typewriter quality.

Today, however, the tide has shifted back to 9-pin designs. Although 24-pin models offer high-quality images, they tend to be slower and more expensive than 9-pin models. In most cases, documents printed on dot matrix printers do not need to look perfect, so 9-pin models do just fine.

There is very little quality difference between 9-pin and 24-pin models if the documents will be printed in draft mode.

Printing papers

Most dot matrix printers are designed for use with tractor feed paper. This continuous paper is bordered on the right and left sides by paper strips with a series of holes. These holes are used to guide the paper through the printer by aligning pages with two tractor feed belts found in the unit.

Since dot matrix printers are often used with several different forms, many can be equipped to hold two tractor feeds at a time. Forms can then be easily switched in and out of the printer without needing to reload sheets.

Many dot matrix printers can also handle single cut sheets, including bond paper, letterhead, and envelopes. If you expect to print these materials, make sure the model is equipped with a friction-feed mechanism in addition to the normal tractor feed. Friction feed works like a typewriter, holding sheets tightly against a roller.

Pricing

Most dot matrix printers are priced between $500 and $1,000, with light-duty or older models that cost less, and heavy workhorses that are far more expensive.

Replacement ribbons will be your only consumable cost with a dot matrix printer. Ribbons are not very expensive per page if you do the majority of your printing in draft mode. If you expect to print in very high volumes, compare the cost of replacing printer ribbons over the life of the unit.

Terms

Characters per inch (cpi) A measurement that indicates the width of printed characters. The usual pitch is 10 to 12 cpi.

Characters per second (cps) The number of characters a printer can print per second. Low-cost models operate at 200 to 300 cps, while faster models operate at more than 1,000 cps.

Continuous paper Paper that comes in a folded stack of pages with tractor-feed holes on each side. In most cases, the tractor feed strips are perforated for easy removal. Also known as fanfold paper or computer printout (CPO).

Cut-sheet feeders A printer accessory that automatically feeds regular sheets of paper into a machine. Machines without a cut-sheet feeder can usually accept plain paper, but require that sheets be fed one page at a time.

Draft mode A printing feature that allows for faster printing by using fewer pins to create each character on a page.

Lines per minute (lpm) A measurement of the speed, or throughput, of a dot matrix printer.

Tractor feed A guide used to draw paper through the printer mechanism by matching holes in the paper with spokes on the feeder.

Unidirectional printing A type of printing in which every line is printed from left to right. This means that no printing occurs as the printhead returns from right to left. Bi-directional printers print in both directions, which results in faster printing but sometimes lower quality output.

Special tips

When printing on thick forms or sheets, look for a printer with a very straight paper path to avoid jamming. In most cases, this translates to a printer that feeds from the bottom and outputs finished documents from the top of the machine.

Dot matrix printers can be quite noisy, so you may want to consider purchasing an optional stand or acoustical cover to reduce the noise.

Wide-format printers are available for offices that print onto 14 x11 inch computer paper.

While color ribbons are available for many dot matrix printers, check the output quality before buying in bulk. The print quality is generally not that good.

See also
Business Forms, Color Printers, Desktop Computers, Ink-jet Printers, Laser Printers, Typewriters

E-Mail Services

*E*lectronic mail is rapidly becoming one of the most important methods of business communication. By using e-mail, businesses can quickly send messages to the millions of firms already on-line across the globe, often for less than the price of a letter, phone call, or fax message.

VENDORS		
Commercial online service	Headquarters	Phone number
America Online (AOL)	Vienna, VA	800/827-6364
CompuServe	Columbus, OH	800/848-8990
Microsoft Network (MSN)	Redmond, WA	800/386-5550
Prodigy	White Plains, NY	800/776-3449
Dedicated e-mail service	Headquarters	Phone number
AT&T	Bridgewater, NJ	800/242-6005
MCI	Washington, DC	800/872-7654
Sprint	Overland Park, KS	800/736-1130
Internet service provider	Headquarters	Phone number
AT&T WorldNet	Bridgewater, NJ	800/967-5363
PSINet	Herndon, VA	800/827-7482
UUNet	Fairfax, VA	800/488-6384

E-mail Services

Buying points

Where to obtain e-mail service

Currently, there are three types of services offering e-mail: commercial online services, Internet service providers (ISPs), and dedicated e-mail services.

Commercial online services are private online networks offering e-mail and other services. Members typically pay a monthly fee and are given a certain number of free hours to spend on-line. Besides e-mail, these services provide news, chat rooms, and software libraries. The biggest services include America Online (AOL), CompuServe, Prodigy, and Microsoft Network (MSN).

Internet service providers are firms that provide a connection to the Internet. By dialing into an ISP's computer, businesses can browse the World Wide Web, set up a home page or send e-mail. Most ISPs are small outfits, serving a local or regional area. However, there are a few major national players, including AT&T WorldNet and UUNet.

Dedicated e-mail services are online services set up by the major long distance carriers: AT&T, MCI, and Sprint. Dedicated services concentrate only on communication needs, providing e-mail, fax, and telex capabilities.

Choosing an e-mail provider

There are three main considerations when choosing an e-mail service provider: ease of use, features, and reliability.

One major consideration is how easy the service is to set up. Setup can range from a simple installation procedure to a very involved undertaking. Commercial online services are generally fairly easy to set up. On the other hand, businesses using an ISP may need to have some degree of computer knowledge to get started.

A second area to examine is the features that are available with the service. For example, some services allow you to send e-mail over the service using the same computer program you use for internal e-mail messages. Others require you to use a proprietary e-mail application, which can make it more difficult to forward messages or send copies to coworkers. Other popular features allow you to compose messages off-line, or to send computer files attached to your messages.

A third area to consider is message reliability. With commercial on-line services and dedicated e-mail services, you can be fairly certain that your message will be delivered in a timely manner if the message is sent to another account on the same service. However, messages traveling on the Internet may be delayed by traffic or routing problems. As a result, businesses may want to use the same service as the intended recipient if they often need to send very urgent messages.

Sending computer files via e-mail

Most e-mail programs have an option called file attachment. File attachment allows you to send virtually any type of computer file along with your e-mail message.

When sending, you must consider how the file is sent. All computer files must be encoded before they can be sent as an e-mail attachment. In turn, these files must be decoded at the receiving end. Unfortunately, different programs use different encoding formats. The sender and recipient must be able to utilize the same format for a transfer to be successful.

Accessing e-mail from the road
As individuals become addicted to e-mail, it can be very difficult to give up the ability to send or receive messages while on the road. If employees need to access e-mail on the road, look for an e-mail provider that offers multiple points of presence (POPs) across the country. This will allow a traveler to dial a local number to access his or her e-mail account from many locations.

An alternate solution is to look for a provider that offers a toll free access number. This will allow you to dial into the network without paying a toll charge. However, be aware that costs for the toll free call will eventually be passed along to you through the service charge. Accordingly, such numbers should be used for only short periods of time.

Pricing
E-mail service can be quite inexpensive, particularly for businesses that are careful to minimize the number of hours they spend on-line. Commercial service providers generally charge a monthly fee of $10 for five free hours on-line, and $2 to $3 for each additional hour. You can expect to send or receive about 300 messages in the five hour window if you are careful about composing messages off-line.

Internet service providers tend to be slightly more expensive. The monthly fee is generally about $20. However, many services offer unlimited usage, which can result in lower overall charges for frequent e-mail users.

Dedicated e-mail services usually charge a fee for each message, based on a flat rate or a per character charge. The average rate is about 50¢ per message.

Terms

Domain name The address used to route e-mail on the Internet. Commercial online services and dedicated e-mail services require you to use their domain name (such as aol.com), while most Internet service providers give you the option to establish your own domain name.

Off-line composing Writing e-mail messages without actually being connected to the service. These messages can then be queued to be sent as soon as you log onto the system. Off-line composing helps minimize the amount of time you spend on-line.

Point of presence (POP) A physical location that offers local dial-in service to the network. A service with many POPs allows travelers to access the service without incurring expensive toll charges.

E-mail Services

Special tips

Free e-mail service is available from two e-mail service providers: Juno (800/799-JUNO) and FreeMark (617/492-6600). Both services require users to complete a profile before receiving the service. This profile is then used to send advertisements that appear when you access your account. Advertisements typically occupy only a portion of the screen and change about every 30 seconds.

See also
Internet Service Providers, Modems, World Wide Web Site Setup

Did you know?

Thirty-six percent of Fortune 500 company executives surveyed say they look at employee e-mail messages, according to the Society for Human Resources Management.

Employee Drug Testing

Most employers are acutely aware of the negative impact drug use can have in the workplace. To combat substance abuse, drug prevention programs are increasingly prevalent. Moreover, in industries where safety issues are of prime concern, there are now federal mandates for drug testing programs. However, drug testing remains a highly sensitive topic that raises numerous legal issues.

Buying points

Constraints of drug testing programs

Drug testing programs are mandatory for companies that are regulated by the U.S. Department of Transportation (DOT), including those in the aviation, mass transit, railroad, and motor carrier industries. However, there is very little federal regulation of companies in other industries.

Employers will need to refer to state statutes for specific testing guidelines. In some states, there are few regulations concerning the types of testing allowed and the conditions under which an employee can be tested. A number of other states only recognize results from federally certified laboratories and have strict guidelines to protect the privacy of employees.

Substances detectable by drug tests

The DOT requires routine testing for five substances: marijuana, cocaine, PCP, amphetamines, and opiates.

In most industries, the largest drug problem is alcohol. However, alcohol testing, which often requires blood, breath or saliva analysis, is not mandatory under current federal guidelines.

Common drug tests

The most common drug test is urinalysis. The test is quite cost-effective and can accurately detect the presence of the five substances listed by the DOT. However, while urine tests can detect drug use, they cannot determine the amount of the drug used, when the drug was taken, or the drug's effect on that particular employee.

Less common drug tests are blood and hair sample tests. These are generally more expensive and more complicated to administer.

When drug tests are usually performed

Depending on the company's needs, testing is usually done under one or more of the following conditions: 1) before employment or during a probation period; 2) when there is reasonable suspicion of drug or alcohol abuse; 3) as part of a routine physical, often required by federal regulations; 4) during random testing; and 5) while monitoring employees during drug rehabilitation or counseling.

Providers of drug testing

There are currently 75 urine drug testing laboratories certified by the U.S. Department of Health and Human Services (HHS). While not every state has its own certified laboratory, most laboratories have 20 to 30 collection sites across the country. The Center for Substance Abuse Prevention (800/WORK-PLACE) can provide a listing of the federal certified drug testing laboratories.

Occupational health clinics within hospitals or occupational health consultants can also provide consulting and testing services. However, many of these agents charge fees that are substantially higher than drug testing laboratories.

Choosing a urinalysis lab

There are quite a few factors to consider when choosing a lab. First, find out if the laboratory has been certified by any federal or state agencies. In general, you can be certain that the 75 HHS-certified laboratories meet the minimum standard of quality. Additionally, there may be a number of local laboratories certified for state programs.

The next step is to see how the laboratory operates. Observe how specimens are handled and learn about the standard processing procedure. In general, laboratories should have quality assurance and quality control programs that monitor and ensure the accuracy of performance in specimen processing and analysis.

Make sure to check the staff's credentials. While state requirements vary, there are nonetheless a number of minimum standards that should be met. The director should have an advanced degree in chemistry or toxicology and the technical staff should have formal training as laboratory technicians or comparable on-the-job training and experience.

Finally, the laboratory should be able to offer technical assistance and sound advice about drug testing. In the event of a legal dispute over test results, the laboratory should be able to defend its testing method, operational procedure, and the validity of test results.

Time needed to complete a drug test

Results are usually provided within 2 to 3 days after the specimen is picked up. Companies should avoid having results reported by telephone since this method may not be completely secure. Instead, companies should ask for results to be reported via mail parcels marked "Confidential."

Laboratories can also provide electronic reporting if results are needed immediately.

What to do if an employee tests positive

Companies subject to federal drug-testing regulations are required to immediately remove an employee who tests positive for substance abuse from safety-sensitive functions such as driving a commercial vehicle. The employer is also required to provide a list of counseling and rehabilitation services to the employee. Additionally, the employee must be evaluated by a licensed substance abuse professional and pass a return-to-duty test before returning to work. Finally, the employee must undergo a series of follow-up exams for a period of up to five years.

In some states, it may be a violation of state statute if an employer fires a worker after the first positive result without offering a second chance to the employee.

Pricing

Depending on the number and type of tests administered, drug testing costs can range from as little as $20 to a few hundred dollars per specimen. The good news is that the market for drug testing is fairly competitive and companies can expect similar rates from all laboratories. Volume discounting is also available to large clients.

Special tips

Questions concerning DOT regulations can be obtained via its helpline (202/366-3784) or via fax at (800/225-3784).

The Institute for a Drug-free Workplace (202/842-7400) offers two publications: *Guide to State Drug Testing Law* and *Avoiding Legal Liability: The 25 Most Common Employer Mistakes in Addressing Drug Abuse.*

To reduce the cost of testing, you may want to form an alliance with other companies in your region that are interested in establishing drug testing programs.

See also
Business Insurance, Health Insurance, Workers Compensation Insurance

Did you know?

From 1991 to 1993, the highest rates of illicit drug use were reported for construction workers, food preparation workers, and waiters and waitresses.

Executive Recruitment Agencies

*E*xecutive recruiting firms, or executive search consultants, help businesses find the right executive for a specific job. These firms have extensive contacts throughout an industry, and are able to find individuals suitable for a position and willing to move to a new firm. As professional networkers, executive recruiters can increase your "connections" when looking for the right hire.

VENDORS

Company	Headquarters	Phone number
Allerton Heneghan & O'Neill	Chicago, IL	312/263-1075
Bishop Partners	New York, NY	212/986-3419
Cejka & Company	St. Louis, MO	314/726-1603
Coleman Lew & Associates	Charlotte, NC	704/377-0362
Diversified Search	Philadelphia, PA	215/732-6666
Hayden Group	Boston, MA	617/482-2445
Hockett Associates	Los Altos, CA	415/941-8815
Pendleton James & Associates	New York, NY	212/557-1599
Preng & Associates	Houston, TX	713/266-2600
Norman Roberts & Associates	Los Angeles, CA	310/552-1112
Ward Howell International	New York, NY	212/697-3730

Source: *Executive Recruiter News*, Kennedy Publications

Buying points

When to consider executive recruitment

Executive recruitment firms are best used for positions that are unusual or highly sensitive. Recruiters can find candidates that will fit a position without calling attention to your company or requiring candidates to circulate a resume.

Types of firms

To hire executive level candidates (salaries of $100,000 or more), most businesses will use a retainer firm. These firms are given the exclusive right to fill a job opportunity. They provide a thorough recruiting and interviewing process in a highly confidential setting for both the candidate and prospective employer.

For mid-level positions (salaries of $30,000 to $70,000), companies will often turn to contingency firms. Contingency firms do not have exclusive arrangements with a particular client, receiving payment only if someone is hired from their listing. As a result, contingency firms tend to circulate a candidate's resume quite a bit more widely. In order to prevent candidates from going directly to the employer, the contingency firm will not give exact details about an opening to the candidate. As a result, well-suited candidates presented to your firm may not have any interest in the job.

Length of the process

A recruiting assignment usually takes three or four months, although it can vary tremendously based on the number of candidates and the difficulty of finding a match. However, keep in mind that candidates may not be able to begin a job as quickly as traditional hires, due to current job obligations.

Locating an executive recruitment agency

There are several sources available to help locate executive recruitment agencies.

First, there are directories of executive recruiters. Kennedy Publications (800/531-0007) offers *The Directory of Executive Recruiters*, which is cross-indexed by management function, industry and geography. Similarly, the National Association of Personnel Services (703/684-0180) offers the *Directory of Personnel Consultants by Specialization*.

Associations of executive recruiters can also be a good source for referrals. The Association of Executive Search Consultants (212/398-9556) and International Association of Corporate and Professional Recruiters (502/228-4500) offer referral and complaint services about member firms.

Of course, the best route is to get recommendations from peers in the same industry who have used a particular agency before.

Questions to ask

Before choosing an executive recruitment firm, you should ask a series of questions to learn whether a given firm fits your needs.

Start off by getting a sense for how well the firm understands your industry. Ask about what types of contacts they have and their past successes with the type of position you are trying to fill. Also make sure to find out if there are firms that will be off-limits in the search.

Next, ask about the structure of the arrangement, including whether the firm will require an exclusive listing, and whether the screening process will include interviews. It also helps to learn about the exact nature of the work they will do to fill the position.

Finally, get a clear understanding of the cost and obligations of the executive recruiting firm. Ask how much you will need to pay up front, and what guarantees the firm will make about new hires. Also find out how much it will cost to hire more than one candidate identified during the search process.

Pricing

Executive recruiters usually charge a fixed fee to conduct a search. This fee is usually set at 25% to 35% of the recruit's first-year salary.

When working on a retainer, these firms are generally paid one-third of their fee when the search is initiated. The remaining two-thirds is paid over the course of the assignment regardless of whether the position is filled.

Contingency firms typically use the same rates, although no fee is paid unless the candidate is actually hired.

Some executive recruiting firms perform their services for a flat fee or for actual time spent up to a certain maximum. Firms also tack on out-of-pocket expenses for travel and communication, which can amount to as much as 10% to 15% of salary.

Terms

Boutique firms Firms that specialize in placing candidates for a particular industry or job specialty. This is in contrast to generalist firms that will seek to meet any hiring need that arises.

Completion rate The percentage of searches conducted by a retainer firm resulting in a hire. Recruiters typically claim success rates that range from 60% to 100%.

Fallout A situation when an agency-provided candidate is hired for a position that was not part of the original search request. Payment for such a hire varies from one recruiter to the next, and should be negotiated in advance.

Guarantee A promise made by a search firm to replace a failed candidate within a certain period of time if the reason for leaving is due to an error on the recruiter's part.

Off-limits policy A policy that prevents a recruiter from approaching executives in a particular firm to fill a position. As a courtesy, recruiters will often agree not to recruit executives from a client firm for a period of one to two years. Also known as blockage.

Retainer An account that a client establishes to cover recruiter fees and expenses. This retainer is typically paid in monthly, quarterly or yearly installments.

Special tips

Since recruiters are not licensed, make sure to check references before signing any contract.

Working with a boutique firm can often lead to better quality hires, since the firm will have a better sense of trends and job movement within the industry.

To avoid being hit with unexpected charges, learn exactly what expenses will be billed before agreeing to use a firm.

Learn about any guarantees a firm will offer if the hired candidate leaves the firm in less than one or two years.

It can take a lot of time to get recruiters up to speed on your firm's culture and particular job requirements. As a result, take the time to screen recruiters carefully, with the expectation of a long-term relationship.

To protect your firm from having employees wooed away, you may want to establish an off-limits policy with any recruiting firm that you hire.

Although most recruitment fees are based on compensation, you may want to consider paying a flat rate to avoid potential conflicts of interest.

See also
Temporary Help Services

Did you know?

Executive search firms were formed after World War II when an expanding economy caused a shortage of skilled labor.

Fax Broadcasting Services

*F*ax broadcasting services can help minimize the effort needed to fax a document to many recipients. Rather than tying up your fax machine for hours, you can simply send a single copy of the document to the fax broadcasting service, and the service will send the fax to a list of designated recipients.

VENDORS		
Company	Headquarters	Phone number
Ansaphone	Boston, MA	800/782-7587
AT&T	Parsippany, NJ	800/242-6005
Cable & Wireless	Vienna, VA	800/486-8686
ITC	Denver, CO	800/685-1995
LDDS WorldCom	Jackson, MS	800/737-8423
MCI	Piscataway, NJ	800/999-2096
Mediatel	San Francisco, CA	415/882-4300
Sprint	Kansas City, KS	800/366-3297
TSI	Atlanta, GA	800/329-9898
Xpedite Systems	Eatontown, NJ	800/966-3297

Buying points

How fax broadcasting works
To use a fax broadcasting service, you first provide the service with a list or lists of fax recipients. When you want to broadcast a fax, you simply fax or modem the document to the service and specify which list should receive the fax. The service then sends the fax to the recipients on that list at the designated time.

Most services will send a confirmation report once a broadcast is concluded. This report will usually include the time of transmittal for each fax and a status report for each recipient.

Updating the broadcast list
All services allow you to update broadcast lists, but have different methods of doing so. Some companies offer software that allows users to update a list directly by dialing up the service via modem. In other cases, the user can fax or send modifications to the service and the firm will input the changes. Most companies charge a fee of 25¢ to 35¢ per addition if updates require labor on their part.

Fax broadcasting service providers
Most long distance carriers provide fax broadcasting. Fax broadcasting is sometimes offered as a loss leader, with the companies hoping to make up the difference by interesting customers in other, more expensive services.

There are also companies dedicated to providing advanced fax services. These bureaus typically offer a wide variety of faxing capabilities. Pricing can also be quite competitive from these providers.

Choosing a provider
Because most services offer the same features and customer support, differences in rates are the main criteria for choosing a vendor. Rates are typically charged per minute of faxing time.

To identify the best vendor for your needs, you should first calculate your expected usage. Estimate how often you will use the service, the average length of a fax, the number of recipients, and the frequency with which the recipient list will be updated. Then use these numbers to compare different services.

Once you have an idea which two or three services offer the most competitive base rates, examine monthly charges or minimums, the cost of special features, and any discounts. Firms expecting to use the service fairly extensively should be able to negotiate better rates.

Pricing
Services structure their rates in a variety of ways. In addition to a monthly fee, most services charge based on the number of pages sent, the number of characters sent, or the total transmission time. A typical page of text contains about 2,500 characters and takes about 45 seconds to send. Additional pages require about 30 seconds apiece to send. Pages that include graphics slow transmission speeds considerably.

Fax Broadcasting Services | 135

If most of your faxes can be sent during non-business hours, you should consider a service that offers lower rates for evening faxes. The most economical services offer rates as low as 25¢ per minute during peak hours and 19¢ per minute during off-peak hours.

Special tips

Make sure to inquire about any monthly minimum requirements. It can be quite costly to use a service with a monthly minimum if your expected usage is light or sporadic.

Look for the smallest billing increment when comparing services. Some services offer rounding to the nearest second or six seconds. Smaller billing increments can reduce the total cost of calls as much as 20 percent.

Companies that intend to send many international faxes should closely examine the discount structure. Often, discounts only include domestic faxes.

Giving your faxes a non-urgent status can save money. These faxes are sent during lulls in the day and are billed at lower rates.

Check the company's policy for incomplete transmissions. Generally, you should not be charged for faxes that do not go through completely.

See also
Fax Machines, Fax Servers, Fax on Demand, International Calling, Long Distance Service

Fax Machines

*F*ax machines enable companies to send documents almost simultaneously across town, across the country, or halfway around the world. In most cases, faxes are a cost-effective alternative to overnight delivery, and much faster option than regular mail.

VENDORS

Company	Headquarters	Phone number	Ink-jet	Laser	Thermal	Thermal transfer
Brother	Somerset, NY	800/284-4357		•	•	•
Canon	Lake Success, NY	800/OK-CANON	•	•		
Hewlett-Packard	Palo Alto, CA	800/HP-HOME-8	•			
Muratec	Plano, TX	214/403-3300		•	•	•
Okidata	Mount Laurel, NJ	800/OKIDATA		•		
Panasonic	Secaucus, NJ	800/843-0080	•	•	•	
Pitney Bowes	Stamford, CT	203/381-7000	•	•	•	
Ricoh	West Caldwell, NJ	800/63-RICOH	•	•	•	
Sharp	Mahwah, NJ	800/BE-SHARP		•	•	•
Toshiba	Irvine, CA	800/GO-TOSHIBA		•	•	
Xerox	Rochester, NY	800/275-9376	•	•		

OPERATIONAL COSTS

Pages received per day	Ink-jet fax	Laser/LED fax	Thermal fax	Thermal fax with 50% of pages photocopied
20	$1,200	$1,000	$900	$1,700
50	$2,900	$2,600	$2,300	$4,200
100	$5,900	$5,200	$4,600	$8,500

(Five-year operating costs.)

Buying points

How fax technology works
A fax machine works by scanning each outgoing page and converting the image into a series of light and dark dots. This pattern is then translated into audio tones and sent over regular phone lines. The receiving fax "hears" the tones, pieces the grid together, and prints the total compilation of dots. The resulting document is a black and white likeness of the original page.

The costs of sending
One of the hidden costs of a fax machine is phone time. Fax machines that have higher sending speeds, though typically more expensive, will often pay for themselves in reduced phone charges.

The majority of installed fax machines transmit at a speed of 9,600 bits per second (bps). This results in sending times of 15 to 60 seconds per page.

A newer transmission standard, called V.17, allows faxes to be sent at 14,400 bps to similarly equipped machines. Although V.17 tends to add a few hundred dollars to a machine's cost, this feature will pay for itself if your company faxes more than 30 pages a day. To ensure compatibility with older machines, V.17 machines are equipped with a fallback mechanism that allows them to send and receive at the regular 9,600 bps speed.

Another way to reduce transmission costs is to purchase a machine that incorporates advanced data compression protocols. Compression protocols reduce sending times by minimizing the amount of data needed to describe the page being sent. Virtually all fax machines are equipped with a basic compression protocol called Modified Huffman, or MH. However, machines equipped with the more advanced Modified Read (MR) or Modified Modified Read (MMR) protocols can send documents as much as 25 percent faster.

Some machines use proprietary sending or compression protocols to speed transmissions. However, be aware that these protocols will only work when sending to or from same brand models. Unless you fax between two offices equipped with the same model, proprietary protocols will not noticeably reduce your overall sending costs.

Printing options
Probably the biggest difference between fax machines is the method used to print incoming faxes. Most older and cheaper fax machines use thermal printing. This means that a small heating element within the machine is used to mark heat-sensitive paper. The process is very simple and reliable, with almost no moving parts to break or wear out.

Unfortunately, most people find thermal paper very unpleasant to use. The paper is stored on rolls, which results in curled pages after printing. In addition, the paper's waxy coating is difficult to write on, and the thermal image tends to fade over time.

As an alternative to thermal paper, most manufacturers now offer fax machines that can print on plain paper.

The least expensive types of plain paper fax machines print using ink-jets. These machines produce acceptable text, but tend to be very slow. As a result, ink-jets are usually not a good choice if you receive many faxes each day.

A more expensive type of plain paper fax uses a laser or LED printing engine to produce images. These faxes incorporate the same basic technology as a laser printer, using toner to produce a high-quality image on plain paper. In addition, laser/LED printing is quite reliable, with few service needs beyond toner and paper. On the downside, laser faxes tend to be much more expensive than thermal or ink-jet machines.

There are also a few machines on the market that use thermal transfer technology to print on plain paper. Thermal transfer machines use heat to transfer ink from a ribbon or sheet to the page. While these models do offer reasonable output, drawbacks include noisy operation and mediocre print quality.

Memory features
Another aspect of the machine to consider is its available memory. Memory allows a fax machine to store incoming or outgoing pages, enhancing the utility of the unit.

One of the most useful memory features is out-of-paper reception. This saves incoming faxes in memory if the machine runs out of paper.

Quick scan allows you to scan a document into memory before beginning a transmission. Since this feature uses the stored image when sending, you no longer have to wait for the fax to go through the machine before you can retrieve the original.

Dual scan uses memory to allow sending and receiving features to operate at the same time. For example, a user can scan an outgoing fax into memory while a fax is being received. The scanned fax is then sent directly from memory when the phone line becomes free.

The amount of memory required to hold a page depends on the density of the image. In general, however, you can expect 512 kilobytes to hold about 20 to 25 pages. If you find that the memory is not enough, most models accept additional memory cards.

Service needs
Fax machines, especially thermal models, tend to be very reliable. With breakdowns uncommon during the five-year lifetime of a machine, many businesses are better off not signing up for service and applying the savings to repairs in case a problem does arise.

Fax machines do need to be periodically cleaned. This consists of cleaning the scanning window and any dust filters.

Pricing
Fax machine prices vary depending on the printing process used. Thermal faxes are the cheapest, starting at $150.

For plain paper faxing, ink-jet models are available for about $300, with basic laser models available for about $600. For about $1,600 you can get a laser model with the 14,400 bps transmission speeds and the MMR sending protocol.

Like most office machines, faxes are often purchased with service contracts to provide protection against the cost of repairs or replacement. Fax service contracts cost about $100 per year for plain paper models.

Terms

Group 3 The international standard for fax machine compatibility. Virtually all regular fax machines are Group 3 machines. There is also a Group 4 designation for fax machines that can operate over digital lines. These are very uncommon, but can dramatically reduce sending costs between two offices that both use digital lines and faxes.

Special tips

If you expect to receive more than 50 faxed pages per day, a service contract may make sense. Make sure you can get a backup machine in case of breakdown.

Firms that receive faxes on legal-sized paper should look for a machine with two paper drawers. This will allow legal- and letter-sized faxes to be printed on the appropriately-sized pages without having to switch paper trays.

Many fax machines can be connected to a computer to serve as a printer, faxmodem or computer scanner. However, make sure that the fax machine can perform all of the printing and scanning functions you require before buying it for these functions. For example, if you are looking for a combination printer and fax, check if you can print onto envelopes or labels.

When comparing fax machines, ignore the page transmission times listed in the specification sheets. Manufacturers do not use the same pages for benchmarking transmissions, which makes the numbers virtually impossible to compare.

See also
Fax Broadcasting Services, Fax Servers, Fax on Demand, Ink-jet Printers, Laser Printers, Modems, Multifunctional Devices

For more information, visit
BuyersZone
http://www.buyerszone.com/

Did you know?

The first fax machine was patented by Scottish inventor Alexander Bain in 1843. It worked over a telegraph line, using electromechanical pendulums at each end to transmit an image.

Fax on Demand

*F*ax on demand technology enables companies to respond to requests for information 24 hours a day, even when there is no one at the office. These systems automatically fax frequently requested information to customers or prospects at their request, freeing employees to conduct more important tasks.

VENDORS

Company	Headquarters	Phone number
Active Voice	Seattle, WA	206/441-4700
Bogen	Ramsey, NJ	201/934-8500
Brooktrout Technology	Needham, MA	800/333-5274
Carmel Connection	Fremont, CA	510/656-0222
Copia International	Wheaton, IL	800/689-8898
Expert Systems	Atlanta, GA	770/642-7575
Ibex Technologies	El Dorado Hills, CA	916/939-8888
Info Systems	Downview, Ontario	416/665-7638
Malibu	Malibu, CA	310/456-8940
Telekol	Waltham, MA	800/797-0123

SERVICE BUREAUS

Company	Headquarters	Phone number
!nfaxamation	Denver, CO	303/820-3677
Accu-Weather	State College, PA	814/237-0309
Intelemedia	Richardson, TX	214/994-0700
MacroVoice	Boca Raton, FL	407/994-9781
Prairie Systems	Omaha, NE	800/888-3151
SpectraFax	Naples, FL	813/643-5060

Buying points

Basics
Fax on demand systems use an automated voice system to allow callers to identify which documents they would like faxed to them. Using a telephone keypad, the caller indicates the documents of interest. In many cases, the caller then punches in the fax number to which the documents should be sent. The fax on demand system then faxes the documents to the specified number.

Types of systems
These days, most fax on demand systems are PC-based, operating on a Windows or Macintosh computer with a fax board. However, stand-alone systems are still available, and are often favored by those who do not relish the idea of making sure all the components work together.

There are also fax on demand systems that work in conjunction with existing voice mail systems. These use the installed voice mail equipment to store documents and answer calls.

Faxing methods
There are two fax on demand calling modes: direct and indirect. Most systems are capable of handling both modes.

With direct calling, a caller must access the system by using a telephone that is attached to a fax machine. After the documents are selected, the caller presses the "start" button on the fax machine to begin retrieval. Both the document selection process and the fax transmission process occur during a single call.

In the indirect calling mode, the caller telephones from any phone, enters the document number, inputs a fax number, and then hangs up. The system then faxes the requested documents to the specified fax number.

Most businesses now prefer the indirect calling method, since it does not require users to dial from their fax machine. However, the indirect calling method does mean that your firm must pay for the faxing charges.

Choosing a system
Finding the best system for your needs requires an understanding of your expected usage, both in terms of the number of documents you intend to store and the number of callers you expect to use the system at one time. Defining these parameters can help you identify the size hard drive and the number of telephone lines you will need.

To help gauge use on an ongoing basis, the system should generate reports that can indicate the most popular documents being ordered, peak hours of usage, and caller profiles. Such reports should not only be useful for tracking usage, but also be helpful for understanding which documents callers most often choose.

Another item to consider is the backup features of the system. In the event of power failure or other break down, you will want a system that will not require reprogramming. It should also be easy to back up the system to avoid losing documents.

Also check how easy it is to expand the system. Look into the cost of increasing the number of documents stored on the system and the cost of adding phone lines. Although a greatly expandable system may cost a few hundred dollars more, it can be well worth the initial investment.

Transmission standards
Fax on demand systems should be equipped with the latest faxing technologies to ensure the fastest transmission times. This means that faxes should utilize 14,400 bit per second transmission speeds and advanced faxing protocols such as MMR and ECM. While it can be useful to find a system that offers fine resolution transmissions for clearer looking faxes, keep in mind this will result in longer faxing times and higher calling costs.

Creating a fax catalog
Almost any computer document can be sent by a fax on demand system. However, it must first be converted into a format suitable for faxing. Often, this is as easy as "printing" a document into the fax on demand system. Instead of creating a paper reproduction, the fax on demand system will store the document as a fax-compatible file.

Each converted document then must be tagged with a unique identifying document number that callers can use to access the file. A "catalog" describing each document and listing its access number can then be constructed to inform callers about what is available on the system.

Service bureaus
Companies that do not want to purchase a system can turn to a fax on demand service bureau. These service bureaus have all the equipment necessary to manage a fax on demand system for your company and can guide you through the process of setting up a system. On an ongoing basis, however, these services can be a costly way of providing fax on demand.

Pricing
A standard fax on demand system costs between $1,000 and $2,500. Higher-end systems, equipped with more lines and greater storage options, can cost $5,000 and more.

Charges for a fax on demand service bureau typically consist of start-up and ongoing monthly charges. Start-up fees vary according to the system requirements and can vary from less than $50 to more than $500. Ongoing monthly fees range from $35 to $150, with additional charges of $0.10 to $1 per minute for direct faxing. There are also rate discounts and credits for high-volume usage.

Special tips

If possible, try to implement a system that does not require a caller to first order a catalog before ordering documents. Such systems require two calls to access information, and tend to discourage customers from using the system.

Check what you are faxing. What may look terrific as a four-color brochure may be unreadable when sent via fax.

A useful benchmark for estimating your needs is to assume that a one-page document will require 40 to 60 kilobytes (KB) of storage. An accompanying verbal description will take 20 to 40 kilobytes.

Gray pages take longer to transmit than black or white pages. As a result, try to avoid shading when designing a fax page if transmission times are a concern.

Firms can limit overuse of a system by limiting the maximum number of documents that can be faxed at one time, restricting faxes to certain area codes, or capping the total number of documents that can be sent by the system.

Some systems are capable of guiding callers in multiple languages. This can be a useful option for companies with a diverse or international client base.

Companies interested in using fax on demand as a lead generation tool may want to sign up for Caller ID or have callers dial a toll free number. That way, the caller's telephone number will be recorded, allowing for follow up by phone.

See also
Fax Broadcasting Services, Fax Machines, Fax Servers, Long Distance Service, Toll Free Service

Fax Servers

*C*ompanies that often fax computer-generated documents may want to consider purchasing a fax server. Fax servers allow multiple users to fax documents directly from their computers, thus eliminating the need to print out the document and physically run it through a fax machine.

VENDORS

Company	Headquarters	Phone number	Hardware	Software	Both
Alcom	Mountain View, CA	800/801-8000		●	
Biscom	Chelmsford, MA	800/477-2472		●	
Brooktrout	Needham, MA	617/449-4100	●		
Castelle	Santa Clara, CA	800/289-7555			●
Cheyenne	Roslyn Heights, NY	800/243-9462		●	
GammaLink (Dialogic)	Sunnyvale, CA	800/755-4444	●		
Global Village	Sunnyvale, CA	800/736-4821			●
Intel	Santa Clara, CA	800/538-3373		●	
OAZ	Fremont, CA	800/638-3293			●
Optus	Somerset, NJ	908/271-9568		●	
RightFAX	Tucson, AZ	602/327-1357		●	
Traffic USA	Boca Raton, FL	800/840-0708		●	
Trio	Raleigh, NC	800/880-4400		●	
U.S. Robotics	Skokie, IL	800/USR-CORP	●		
Wildcard Technologies	Richmond Hill, Ontario	800/661-8210			●

Buying points

When to buy a fax server
Fax servers can help minimize the effort needed to send faxes. If your firm mostly faxes computer-generated documents, a fax server can eliminate the time needed to print the fax, walk to the printer, and then walk to the fax machine. A networked fax server is also more efficient than giving a faxmodem to each employee, since it allows many people to share a common set of phone lines and fax equipment.

Fax servers are less useful to firms that send many handwritten faxes or that do not have a computer network. In these cases, the smaller time savings derived from using a fax server is often not enough to offset the total expense of the system.

How a fax server works
A fax server consists of three components: fax hardware, which sends and receives fax signals over a phone line; server software, which manages the hardware and keeps tabs on incoming and outgoing faxes; and client software, which allows users to send faxes from any networked PC.

Most systems are installed on a server on a computer network. The hardware and server software can either be installed on a server that is already used for other tasks, or on a dedicated fax server.

A few all-in-one systems do not need to be installed on a network server. Instead, these systems come in their own box, and link directly to your network. All-in-one systems are generally more expensive than server-based systems, but are simpler to install.

Network compatibility
The first consideration when choosing a fax server is to make sure that it can work with the different parts of your existing computer network.

Start by examining the server software. Many fax servers are designed to run on high-powered server operating systems such as Novell NetWare, Microsoft Windows NT Advanced Server, or IBM OS/2 Warp Server. You will need to match the server operating system you use with the type of fax server you purchase.

Once you match server operating systems, the next step is to make sure that the client interface can be installed on all the computers in your network. Most fax software will run on DOS or Windows computers; you may have more trouble if some computers on the network run Macintosh or UNIX operating systems.

A final compatibility consideration concerns the network protocols. Some fax servers are only compatible with major network systems from firms like Novell, IBM, and Microsoft. You may have more difficulty finding a compatible fax server if you run Banyan Vines, Artisoft LANtastic, or other less popular network systems.

Hardware considerations
One of the most important hardware considerations is the number of

phone lines the system can handle. Most systems start by offering one, two or four fax lines per fax board. One line is fine for small networks (2 to 20 people) with light faxing needs, while two lines will usually accommodate at least 40 people. After that, you can expect to add one fax line for every 50 people using the system. Keep in mind that while most systems offer a great deal of flexibility when adding lines, expansion can be much more costly than purchasing the appropriately-sized system upfront.

A second hardware feature to think about is speed. Most systems can transmit and receive at 9,600 bits per second (bps). However, systems that offer 14,400 bps transmission can save money by reducing phone charges, particularly if you send more than 100 fax pages per day. A few systems operate at only 4,800 bps, and should be avoided.

Compression is a final consideration when evaluating hardware. This indicates how efficiently the fax board can compress the amount of information that must be sent with each fax. The best compression protocol is called MMR, which can reduce sending times up to 15% when sending to similarly-equipped machines.

Software features

Beyond the hardware, you should also look at fax server software.

The most important feature concerns how easy it is to send a fax from the desktop. The best systems incorporate sending functionality into any application. In most cases, sending a fax should be as simple as choosing "print" from the application menu. Less effective are standalone applications that require you to open a special utility each time you want to send a fax.

Also examine how well the software manages faxes. Examine whether the program provides phone books for storing frequently-dialed fax numbers, and whether faxes can be queued to send later in the day. Also check how the system alerts users of fax problems, such as a busy number, that may prevent a fax from being transmitted.

Handling incoming faxes

Although fax servers are very good at sending faxes from many computers, they tend not to be as good for routing incoming faxes. Many firms just print incoming faxes, and then manually deliver them to the right person. While this is a foolproof system, it does not exactly live up to the efficiency promises of fax server systems.

One effective routing technique is to purchase direct inward dialing (DID) fax lines for each person. These lines assign unique fax numbers to each person, even though all incoming faxes are still sent to one fax server. Most fax servers can read the DID number from incoming calls and route the fax to the appropriate person. Unfortunately, monthly fees for each DID line can make this routing method prohibitively expensive.

Another approach is to add routing codes to the fax number for each person. This requires the sender of a fax to dial a routing code after the fax machine connects to the fax server. Since most senders will not wait around to enter a routing code, this technique is likely to work for only a small minority of incoming faxes.

A third technique is to run incoming faxes through optical character recognition (OCR) program. The OCR program "reads" the fax cover page, and sends the fax to the appropriate mailbox. As you might expect, difficult-to-read handwriting makes this system less effective than one might hope.

Pricing

Fax servers generally cost $900 per phone line, including hardware and software. All in one systems tend to be a bit more expensive, costing about $2,500 for the first phone line and $500 for each additional line.

Terms

Class 1 and Class 2.0 These two standards are used by fax software to control fax hardware. Class 2.0 is generally considered a bit more effective, but it is best to buy hardware that works with both standards.

Fax board A peripheral card containing the phone line connection and hardware that enables the server to send and receive faxes.

Faxmodems Modems that include fax sending and receiving capabilities. Many faxmodems have trouble connecting with standalone fax machines. Dedicated fax boards, which are designed specifically for faxing, tend to be much better.

MMR (Modified Modified Read) This compression protocol allows faxes to be sent in less time. MMR is considered better than MR (Modified Read) and MH (Modified Huffman).

T.30 This is a relatively new addressing protocol for routing incoming faxes to the appropriate recipient. T.30 is now available with some fax machines, but remains too rare to be useful as a general routing tool.

V.17 This is the technical term for 14,400 bps fax transmissions. A V.17 compliant fax server can help save money on long distance charges for outgoing faxes.

See also
Desktop Computers, Fax Broadcasting Services, Fax Machines, Fax on Demand

FILE CABINETS

*I*f it were not for file cabinets, there would be mounds of paper stacked on desks, tables, and floors in offices everywhere (or at least more mounds than there are now). File cabinets help keep documents, correspondence, and reports organized and protected.

PRICING

Type of file cabinet	Price range
2-drawer vertical file	$20-$400
2-drawer lateral file	$300-$650
5-drawer vertical file	$500-$700
5-drawer lateral file	$800-$1,300
Fireproof vertical file	$800-$1,700
Fireproof lateral file	$1,000-$3,000

VENDORS

Company	Headquarters	Phone number	Lateral	Vertical	Fire-resistant	5-drawer
Fireking	New Albany, IN	800/457-2424	•	•	•	
HON	Muscatine, IA	800/833-3964	•	•	•	•
Leader/General Metalcraft	Dover, DE	302/678-3454		•		
Martin	Florence, AL	205/767-0330	•	•		•
Meilink	New Albany, IN	800/MEILINK	•	•	•	
O'Sullivan	Lamar, MO	800/327-9782	•	•		
Sauder	Archbold, OH	800/537-8560	•	•		
Sentry	Rochester, NY	800/828-1438		•	•	
Steelworks	Des Moines, IA	800/383-7414	•	•		

Buying points

Types of file cabinets
There are two main types of file cabinets on the market. The traditional file cabinet is called a vertical file cabinet. These have anywhere from two to five drawers per cabinet. Letter- or legal-sized files are stored facing the front of the drawers.

An alternate design is a lateral filing cabinet. These cabinets are much wider than standard designs, allowing files to be stored front to back or side to side in the drawers. They are also not as deep as vertical cabinets, allowing them to serve as wall partitions or credenzas.

Vertical file cabinets are often preferred in offices where wall space is a premium. Although vertical files do not hold as much as a lateral file, they take up much less wall space and feature drawer depths ranging from 15 to 28 inches.

Lateral files are more flexible in terms of filing. They can usually hold legal and letter-sized files in the same drawer, while vertical designs must choose one or the other. Lateral drawers are also bigger, holding about one-third more files than a standard vertical unit, with cabinets available in widths from 36 to 42 inches.

Checking for quality
When examining a cabinet, the first area to check is the suspension system that holds the drawers. Even when filled with weighty files, well-built cabinet drawers should open and close smoothly.

As a safety feature, it can be useful to look for some mechanism to keep the file cabinet from tipping over when multiple drawers are pulled out. The best units use counterweighted drawers and internal locking devices that allow only one drawer to open at a time.

The more use a file cabinet receives, the more likely it is to be damaged. A higher, thicker, more durable grade of steel will protect internal and external components of your file cabinet from damage.

Warranty
Most companies offer a 3- to 15-year replacement warranty for any damage caused by equipment defects. Some units now have lifetime warranties, with the manufacturer agreeing to replace any part broken during normal use. In general, the length of the warranty is a good indication of the file cabinet's durability and life expectancy.

Other filing options
If your storage needs exceed your available filing space, you may want to consider a mechanical filing system. These consist of rolling cabinets that can store many more files in a set amount of floor space. To access the files, you simply roll or move the cabinets apart to create an aisle.

For businesses working on a tight budget, open shelving is another option. Open shelving consists of sets of shelves placed side-by-side and on top of one another. With open fronts, all files are easily accessible, and it is inexpensive to add shelves as your business expands.

Fire and impact resistance

There are specially tested file cabinets that have been found to be fire and/or impact resistant by Underwriters Laboratory. This means that the cabinets can maintain an interior temperature of less than 350°F for one hour even in a 1700°F fire. Some cabinets can even protect computer disks and media tapes, which must be kept below 125°F to avoid damage. Such cabinets, however, are generally quite expensive.

In many cases, a safe can be a less expensive alternative for safely storing particularly important files.

Pricing

The cost of a file cabinet depends on the materials used, the number of drawers, the dimensions, and the lock. A two-drawer file cabinet ranges in price from $20 to $600, with a lateral file costing almost $200 more than the least expensive vertical file. A five-drawer cabinet will cost $500 to $1,300. Fire and impact resistance can add $400 to $500 more to the cabinet price.

Special tips

File cabinets can be purchased as part of systems furniture. Most manufacturers offer cabinets in different colors, designs, and materials to fit in with the rest of the system design.

Check the internal width of drawers before buying. Some cabinets are slightly wider, which is more forgiving for users who tend to overstuff file folders.

Consider buying used file cabinets from dealers or auctions for extra savings. Since older units are typically made with high-quality materials, they can be a good bargain. Be careful to check for dings and dents, however.

While an office superstore can be an easy source for buying file cabinets, furniture dealers often exhibit a wider range of options.

See also
Chairs, Desks, Systems Furniture

Frequent Flyer Programs

*A*irline frequent flyer programs reward frequent travelers with free travel. Although a somewhat ridiculous incentive, these programs have revolutionized customer loyalty programs. In fact, they have been so successful that they have saddled airlines with the enormous task of managing millions of customer accounts and trillions of accrued miles. While it is a simple matter to sign up for programs and receive credit for flights, finding the best program to use can take a bit more work.

VENDORS

Frequent flyer program	Phone number	Mileage minimum per flight	Minimum flight award level	Amex	Diners Club	MC/ Visa
Alaska Mileage Plan	800/654-5669	500	20,000			●
America West FlightFund	800/247-5691	750	20,000			●
American AAdvantage	800/882-8880	500	25,000			●
Continental OnePass	713/952-1630	500	25,000	●	●	●
Delta SkyMiles	800/323-2323	500	25,000	●		
Midwest Express Frequent Flyer	800/452-2022	500	20,000			●
Northwest WorldPerks	800/44-PERKS	500	20,000		●	●
Southwest Rapid Rewards	800/445-5764	1 credit	8 round trips/yr.	●	●	
TWA Frequent Flyer Bonus	800/325-4815	750	20,000			●
United Mileage Plus	605/399-2400	500	25,000		●	●
USAir Frequent Traveler	800/872-4738	500	25,000	●	●	●

Buying points

Earning miles
Frequent flyer programs work by having members accrue miles. Members can then "cash in" these miles for travel once they meet a desired award level.

There are two primary ways to earn miles. The first is to travel. Most airlines give out miles based on the length of the trip. This means that frequent flyer points are granted in rough proportion to how far you travel. There are a few airlines, notably Southwest, that base awards on the number of segments flown.

Many programs allow members to supplement these totals with miles earned through affiliate programs. Many travel-oriented businesses, including hotels, car rental firms, credit card companies, long distance services, and even other airlines, will award miles to a given program based on total spending amounts.

Getting a ticket
While almost all airlines base awards on mileage, one frequent flyer mile does not bear equal weight across all programs.

A domestic round-trip ticket is the standard of comparison for award plans. Most airlines currently set a 25,000 mile requirement for a ticket, although a few, including America West, Northwest, and TWA, offer some tickets at just 20,000 miles.

There is much greater variation in awards for international travel. Award requirements range from 35,000 to over 75,000 miles depending on the airline and the destination.

About prestige programs
Prestige programs are designed to keep frequent travelers flying with one airline. They provide very substantial benefits to travelers flying at least 25,000 miles a year with one airline. Such benefits include bonus miles, free upgrades, and waiving of travel restrictions.

The biggest perk for prestige programs is free cabin class upgrades. Upgrades allow frequent travelers to pay for a coach ticket while actually traveling in business or first class, if seats are available. As travelers achieve higher prestige levels, they typically receive more opportunities to upgrade, and have a better chance of getting into the roomier seats.

Travelers who fly more than 100,000 miles per year should try to join a program that has a super-prestige level, requiring very high mileage levels to qualify. This is because you stand to gain more if there are fewer members in a program vying for the same benefits. Exclusive programs such as Delta's Platinum Medallion and United's 1K flyer offer perks such as multiple upgrades and priority standby only to members that qualify for these super-prestige levels.

Reading the fine print
The airlines have increasingly been adding restrictions to their frequent flyer programs. The most common restriction has been the addition of

expiration dates for miles. Most programs now issue miles that expire three years after acquisition. However, there are a few airlines, including TWA and USAir, that issue miles that do not expire at all. This can be especially important for travelers who do not fly very often.

Blackout dates and limited seating capacity are two other common restrictions that can affect use of a program. In some cases, travelers may finally accrue enough miles for their dream vacation, only to find there are no seats available. To avoid this problem, check the fine print in the program booklet to learn about hidden restrictions.

Debating mileage ownership
More than 90% of all companies allow employees to keep miles earned while on business trips. Because frequent travel makes heavy demands on personal life, miles are seen as an easy way to increase employee morale and mitigate the negative effects of travel. While company ownership of frequent flyer miles can be asserted, the ill will likely to be generated and high administrative costs make it a fairly unpopular course of action.

Pricing
Membership in a frequent flyer program is absolutely free regardless of your level of participation. Some airlines do require a minimum level of usage in order to keep an account active.

Special tips

Travelers who frequently take short trips should check the minimum mileage awarded by each program. While most airlines credit a minimum 500 miles per trip or segment, TWA and America West offer 750-mile minimums.

Charge cards such as American Express let you accrue miles for every dollar charged, then award them to the frequent flyer program of your choice.

To stay abreast of the frequently changing frequent flyer industry, consider subscribing to *InsideFlyer* (800/209-2870) or *Frequent Flyer* (800/DIAL-OAG).

Always keep ticket stubs until a flight has been recorded on your account. This makes it easier to obtain credit in the event of a mix-up.

See also
Car Rental Agencies, Hotels, Travel Agencies

Graphic Designers

Graphic designers can help convey a message not only through text but also through the use of color, illustration, and photos. Successful designs can conjure up an impression about a company or product even before a single word is read.

Buying points

Hiring a graphic designer

Graphic designers can help companies create any type of visual materials including corporate logos, brochures, descriptive literature, and packaging graphics.

Traditionally, graphic designers worked with printed materials. However, many have now expanded their work to include video, computer graphics, and other emerging media.

Choosing a graphic designer

Probably the most important factor in choosing a graphic designer is finding someone with whom you can communicate easily. Since creating any design will require extensive brainstorming and considerable feedback, it is critical that the designer be able to understand your priorities and concerns.

It is also important that the designer's style is to your liking. While some designers are very good at creating eye-jarring effects, others prefer more understated looks. Although a designer may be able to create a range of works, there is usually a certain style the designer prefers. Understanding this preference can help in the selection process.

Finally, the designer should have experience in the particular medium that will be used. Although a designer may be very talented in creating brochures, this person may not be equally adept at designing a World Wide Web site or an advertisement. This is because each medium has a unique set of design requirements that can take some time to master.

Conducting the selection process

Begin by developing a list of designers to contact. Collect names from colleagues, commercial printers, even other graphic designers.

You will then need to contact each designer and describe the project that needs to be completed. A phone interview is usually sufficient for determining if the designer's experience, availability, and interest are enough to warrant a more in-depth discussion.

During the next round of interviews, designers should bring samples of their work. Limit yourself to about five interviews, allotting about 30 to 60 minutes per interview. You want to get a feel for the designer's style, creativity and ability to offer solutions to specific problems.

Before finalizing your selection, make sure to contact references to get a sense for the quality of the work, the designer's overall process, and pricing.

Understanding your needs

It is critical that a designer have a solid understanding of your firm, its target audience, and its position in the marketplace. Many designers use a questionnaire to get answers to key questions about a new client.

You may also want to collect information yourself to help answer these questions. Memos, press releases, and existing marketing materials can inform designers about your company. In addition, you can collect ads and materials from your competitors to provide an industry perspective and ensure that your company is uniquely positioned.

Providing concepts

A designer will generally sketch out one to three concepts for a given project. Based on client feedback, the designer will then further develop a given concept in greater detail.

It is possible for a designer to provide more concepts or to fully develop more ideas, but doing so will incur more expenses.

Writing copy

When designing work that incorporates a lot of text, graphic designers will often work in tandem with a copy writer. The writer drafts the accompanying text while the designer focuses on the look of the piece.

Rather than hiring a writer, some firms simply choose to write the text in-house. This is often done as a budget-saving move. However, companies should be certain of their writing capabilities before embarking on this path.

Copyright ownership

The issue of copyright ownership opens a Pandora's box in the area of design. In most cases, a designer will do a project on a "work for hire" basis where the results become the property of the client. However, ownership is not always that simple.

For example, preexisting photos and illustrations used in a design are usually licensed by the client, which leaves ownership in the hands of the original author. This effectively means the client is renting the creative work. If the designer is commissioned to do a project specifically for a client, then the client will usually retain unlimited reproduction rights of the work.

Since there are so many hazy areas with regard to copyright ownership, and since this can affect pricing, it is worthwhile to discuss and decide upon ownership of the copyright early in the process.

Pricing

A designer typically submits an estimate based on initial discussions with a potential client. While this may only be an estimate, make sure to review the budget to avoid any unexpected costs down the road. Also ask whether outside vendors are part of the budget, and discuss the impact of substantial changes on the project's cost.

Billing for most projects is done on an hourly basis. Rates range from $50 to $75 per hour for new designers, $75 to $100 per hour for mid-level designers, and $100 to $150 per hour for high-level designers. Be wary of designers billing less than these amounts: they are unlikely to be able to support themselves in the business over the long term.

Special tips

Carefully examine a designer's portfolio to see how various design problems were addressed. A good designer should be able to show a range of designs that do not have a cookie-cutter feel.

It can sometimes be helpful to collect other designs that you like, to give the designer a sense for the look you desire.

The hourly rate for a well-established graphic designer will be considerably greater than that for a designer from a smaller shop. However, that does not necessarily mean that the more expensive graphic designer is more talented. Do not let hourly rates convince you of a person's skill level; instead check portfolios and references carefully.

Get it in writing. Issues of payment schedules, ownership, and project timelines should be put in writing to avoid potential headaches.

It is important to get company consensus on a design concept early in the process. Do not wait until the project is near completion to solicit important opinions, since this often results in changes that add considerably to the bill.

See also
Advertising Agencies, Public Relations Firms, Stock Photography, Trade Show Displays, World Wide Web Site Setup

Ground Shipping

*W*hen packages do not need to get there overnight, businesses often turn to ground shippers. Ground shippers handle the same types of packages as overnight delivery services without the high price tag. Most ground shipments weigh less than 150 pounds and are delivered within two to six days.

VENDORS

Company	Headquarters	Phone number	Pickup charges	Delivers to Post Office boxes	Package tracking	Proof of delivery by fax
RPS	Pittsburgh, PA	800/ROADPAK	$6/week	Redirects	●	●
UPS	Atlanta, GA	800/PICK-UPS	$6-$8/week	Redirects	●	$1
U.S. Postal Service	Washington, DC	800/222-1811	$4.95/pickup	●		

Buying points

Varying delivery range
Three carriers currently offer nationwide ground shipping: Roadway Package Service (RPS), United Parcel Service (UPS), and the United States Postal Service.

differences among these services are quite minimal. All three shippers can deliver packages to every business and residential address in the U.S. However, the Postal Service is the only firm that can ship to Post Office (P.O.) boxes or military addresses. UPS and RPS must arrange a different drop-off point for these packages, a service which requires an additional fee and can delay delivery times.

Pricing differences
All three carriers use a similar rate structure, with differing rates according to the shipping distance and package weight. Although the rates are generally quite similar, there are some pricing variations worth considering.

For packages that will be delivered within 250 miles, the Postal Service is usually the least expensive option. Similarly, RPS and UPS are typically better options for greater distances, except for packages that weigh less than three lbs. These can be sent via the Postal Service's Priority Mail service for a flat rate of three dollars.

For businesses spending $500 to $1,000 a week, the best rates can be obtained by negotiating a contract with RPS or UPS. The Postal Service cannot offer negotiated rates, which makes it less suitable for larger shippers.

Low-volume users can generally save money by splitting shipping among the three carriers, using weight and the package's destination to determine the least expensive option for a given package.

Differences in delivery time
RPS and UPS deliver virtually all packages within six days. Transit times depend on distance, with local packages requiring one day, and cross-country deliveries requiring the full six-day period. A zone map for your local area will indicate the shipping time required for all areas of the U.S.

The Postal Service offers two delivery schedules for packages. Priority Mail packages are delivered in one to three days anywhere in the continental U.S. Packages sent via the standard delivery schedule (formerly Parcel Post, now part of the Standard mail classification) will arrive at their destination in 6 to 14 days.

What can and cannot be delivered
You can send virtually any item via ground shipping as long as it is packaged properly and falls within weight and size restrictions. UPS and RPS accept packages that weigh less than 150 lbs., with a combined maximum length, width, and girth of 130 inches. The Postal Service has a 70 lb. weight limit and a 108 inch maximum length, width and girth for packages.

In terms of preparation, the Postal Service requires shippers to affix postage, which means packages must be weighed and shipping fees calculated before the package is picked up. UPS will bill your company, meaning that you only need the weight and the type of service indicated on the package. RPS has the easiest shipping preparation requirements. They simply require you to affix an RPS label to the outside of the package.

Comparing tracking features
Tracking helps businesses locate the delivery status of packages. The Postal Service does not track packages and can only verify delivery by sending confirmation through the mail. RPS and UPS affix bar codes to packages so they can be easily tracked with a phone call. Fax confirmation of delivery is also possible. UPS responds the day after delivery, whereas RPS faxes confirmation after the shipping forms are returned to its headquarters.

Negotiating discounts
UPS and RPS discounts are based on weekly shipping volume, average number of zones traveled, percentage of commercial versus residential deliveries, and the average weight of the package. You should be optimistic about your expected shipping volume during negotiations, because this will be the primary factor determining the amount of your discount. If you do not meet your estimates, the carrier will subsequently readjust your rates. You can expect 3% to 6% discounts for volumes up to $1,000 per week, and 10% discounts for larger accounts.

The Postal Service only offers discounts on bulk shipments of identical mailings. Discounts for Standard deliveries can reach up to 25% for mailings of 300 pieces or 2,000 lbs. within a specific region. Priority Mail discounts are only 5% for mailings of 500 pieces or more.

Pricing
All ground shippers charge rates that vary according to the distance a package travels. The country is divided into zones and shipping charges are determined by the number of zones crossed. Prices range from $2.50 for a one-pound package to $50 for 100-pound shipments.

Each carrier also assesses charges for picking up packages. Infrequent shippers may prefer the Postal Service's $4.95 charge per pickup. RPS charges $6 for each week that a pickup occurs, while UPS assesses a weekly $6 to $8 fee for maintaining an account. To avoid pickup charges, it is also possible to drop off packages at your local RPS, UPS, or Postal Service office.

Special tips

The Postal Service generally charges more than RPS and UPS for services such as extra insurance or call-tag service.

It makes sense to negotiate discount rates before you establish an account. The carrier might offer larger discounts to win your business.

The Postal Service offers reduced shipping rates for libraries, schools, and non-profit organizations. You will need to show proof of exemption from federal taxes to your local post office to receive these rates. Also, directories and bound materials weighing one to ten ponds can be mailed at discounted rates.

The Postal Service can make pick-ups on the same day they are arranged, whereas RPS and UPS need one day's notice to schedule a pick-up.

Packages to Alaska and Hawaii are charged air rates by UPS and RPS, and ground rates by the Postal Service.

See also
International Expedited Delivery, LTL Shipping, Overnight Delivery Services, Postage Meters, Postal Scales, Same Day Delivery Services

For more information, visit
BuyersZone
http://www.buyerszone.com/

Health Insurance

*E*mployees usually rank health care coverage as the most important of all employee benefits. Yet it is also an attractive benefit for many employers. By pooling risk, businesses can purchase health coverage at a much lower cost than individuals. In addition, tax benefits make health care a very cost-effective way to compensate employees.

In spite of the growth of managed care options such as HMOs and PPOs, traditional health insurance remains a popular method of providing health care coverage.

Buying points

Pros and cons of traditional health insurance

The biggest advantage of traditional health insurance is the flexibility it provides employees. Individuals can visit any doctor or hospital they want, and receive coverage for any treatment covered under the policy.

The major drawback to traditional insurance is its cost. Because there are few oversight or cost-saving measures, premiums for traditional insurance tend to be higher than for other plans. Traditional insurance is also expensive for employees, since most plans require patients to pay costly deductibles and co-insurance with each visit.

Finding the right plan

The first step in choosing health insurance is to find a good broker. The majority of group health insurance is "written," or sold, by brokers who are self-employed or work for an independent agency. These independent brokers typically offer products from 5 to 15 insurers. While many people can recommend a broker, the broker you choose should be very experienced in dealing with firms of similar size and in the same industry.

Although most brokers try to find the best deals for their clients, a few are not so ethical. Some brokers may try tactics such as "papering the market" to lock up your business. In this situation, a broker asks for bids from nearly every insurance provider. Since insurers will only issue one quote to a business seeking coverage, this effectively prevents your firm from getting coverage from another broker.

Other brokers may not present policies fairly. Brokers may offer a computerized search that purports to compare "all" policies on the market. However, these computer searches can be rigged to recommend only the policies that the broker primarily sells.

Evaluating policies

Since there are many ways a policy can be written, it is important to carefully examine the fine print before signing any agreement.

To start, make sure that deductibles and co-insurance do not drastically exceed what employees can pay. Be wary of policies that require co-insurance of more than 25% of the cost of treatment, or those that continue to charge co-insurance for charges in excess of $10,000.

Next, check what types of conditions are covered. Some policies limit coverage to specific conditions or set artificially low limits on the maximum payment. Check provisions for long-term illnesses, as well as restrictions for pre-existing conditions. Also make sure that the policy offers at least $1 million of coverage, since the costs of treating catastrophic illnesses can easily reach these astronomical amounts.

Also watch out for low reimbursement levels. Some policies pay a set maximum per procedure, which may be far less than what a physician or doctor actually charges. If the claim payment falls short of the bill, the patient can be left paying the difference. To avoid this, you may want to check with a physician to see if reimbursement levels from the insurer you are considering are within the normal billing range.

Checking financial stability

When choosing a policy, it is very important to make sure the insurance firm backing the policy is financially secure. Hundreds of insurance firms have gone out of business in the last five years, leaving many companies with unpaid medical bills.

There are five rating agencies that evaluate the financial stability of insurance companies: A.M. Best, Duff & Phelps, Moody's, Standard & Poor's, and Weiss Research. All publish rating books, which can be examined at many libraries. Ideally, you should examine an insurer's rating both over time and across services.

Be wary of insurers that simply tout one good rating as evidence of their stability, since the other rating services may find areas of concern.

Also keep in mind that ratings can be a bit misleading. The rating services have created many different levels of "A", allowing even fairly weak insurers to claim the cherished "A" rating. As a result, make sure to find out what grade (AAA, A++, etc.) really indicates a top ranking.

Claims paying ability

An equally important area to investigate is the insurer's willingness to pay claims. Some insurers tend to be late or negligent with claims payments. Others are responsive to small claims, but tend to drag their feet when it comes to major settlement. In either case, firms will want to avoid insurers that may leave them holding the bill.

Unfortunately, this is much more difficult to determine than financial health, since there are no ratings available. Brokers will often have the best knowledge about the claims history of an insurer. In addition, each state has a department of insurance which may provide information on the number of complaints lodged against a particular insurer.

Pricing

Traditional health insurance costs an average of $3,850 per employee per year, according to the Foster Higgins 1994 National Survey of Employer-Sponsored Health Plans.

In terms of out-of-pocket costs, health insurance can vary depending on how you choose to structure the policy. Deductibles typically range from $250 to $1,000, with co-insurance ranging from 20% to 50% for the first $2,000 to $10,000.

Terms

Blue Cross/Blue Shield A loosely affiliated group of health insurance providers. Blue Cross/Blue Shield plans were initially non-profit organizations, but today, many are not very different from regular insurance companies.

Co-insurance The part of a health care bill that is shared between the insurer and the patient. For example, co-insurance often requires the patient to pay 20% of the first $5,000 of health care costs for the year. This means that a patient may owe as much as $1,000 towards the cost of treatment. Most policies use co-insurance to reduce the insurer's share of smaller claims.

Deductible The initial fee that a patient pays for health care before insurance coverage begins. Deductibles can be fixed on a per treatment, individual or family basis.

Managed care A term used to describe all programs that try to control health costs by limiting unnecessary treatment. HMOs, PPOs, point of service plans, and utilization review are all forms of managed care.

Utilization review A cost management technique that normally requires the patient or doctor to first contact a reviewer at the insurance company to get expensive procedures approved. In many cases, the reviewer may require a second opinion before proceeding. In some situations, a reviewer may ask for a change in the physician's treatment plan before authorizing coverage.

Special tips

Small businesses that have difficulty finding coverage directly from insurers may want to contact their state department of insurance to learn about small business group health providers in their area.

As an alternative, small businesses can join an association that offers group benefits for their members. Companies should be careful to scrutinize the operations of such organizations to ensure that all funds are handled appropriately.

Brokers designated as Registered Health Underwriters (RHU) have completed relevant coursework and passed a series of exams concerning the health insurance industry. You can get a list of RHU brokers in your area by calling the National Association of Health Underwriters (202/223-5533).

Watch out for hospital indemnity policies and dread disease policies. Hospital indemnity policies pay for each day you are in the hospital. Unfortunately, most do not provide enough coverage to even pay the typical daily cost of a hospital stay. Dread disease policies cover particular illnesses, but tend to be far more expensive than the likelihood of contracting one of these diseases would suggest.

Sometimes it is difficult to determine which insurance company actually underwrites a policy. Some policies are administered by a large insurer, but are financially backed by a smaller and less stable firm. National Underwriter publishes *Who Writes What*, a listing of the financial backer of every insurance policy.

See also
Business Insurance, Employee Drug Testing, HMOs, PPOs, Workers Compensation Insurance

For more information, visit
BuyersZone
http://www.buyerszone.com/

Did you know?

Health insurance first became popular in World War II as an effective way to attract scarce workers without violating the wartime freeze on salaries.

HMOs

*R*ising health care costs have forced many businesses to reevaluate their choice of employee health coverage. Instead of relying on traditional fee-for-service medicine, an increasing number of firms have switched to managed care networks as a way to reduce costs. The most popular of these is the health maintenance organization, or HMO.

PRICING

State	Avg. family premium per month	State	Avg. family premium per month
Alabama	$365.57	Montana	NA
Alaska	NA	Nebraska	$382.26
Arizona	$394.11	Nevada	$435.27
Arkansas	$326.82	New Hampshire	$435.87
California	$377.87	New Jersey	$463.73
Colorado	$384.49	New Mexico	$337.72
Connecticut	$506.62	New York	$403.12
Delaware	$546.68	North Carolina	$429.53
Florida	$318.77	North Dakota	$369.30
Georgia	$394.34	Ohio	$350.93
Hawaii	$378.17	Oklahoma	$389.41
Idaho	$357.39	Oregon	$349.95
Illinois	$392.56	Pennsylvania	$389.58
Indiana	$370.96	Rhode Island	$366.49
Iowa	$409.10	South Carolina	$414.49
Kansas	$411.49	South Dakota	$350.00
Kentucky	$392.72	Tennessee	$349.26
Louisiana	$395.37	Texas	$415.46
Maine	$473.32	Utah	$375.70
Maryland	$393.24	Vermont	NA
Massachusetts	$468.89	Virginia	$390.92
Michigan	$386.91	Washington	$396.31
Minnesota	$402.66	West Virginia	NA
Mississippi	NA	Wisconsin	$396.52
Missouri	$384.88	Wyoming	NA

Source: SMG Marketing Group, 1994

Buying points

Description

An HMO is a health care organization that signs up doctors and hospitals into a network. Members pay a set per-person fee which gives them access to the HMO's services.

There are two basic features of an HMO. First, HMOs require members to choose a primary care physician who performs basic health check-ups and approves visits to other physicians.

This gatekeeper system represents both the best and the worst of HMOs. While this structure helps minimize costs, it can be unpopular with some patients. This is particularly true of people who currently use doctors outside the HMO network, since they must switch physicians to receive coverage.

Second, HMOs will generally only cover the expense of visits to doctors and hospitals that are part of the network. Visits to non-participating doctors must often be paid by the member.

Recently, some HMOs have developed a more flexible type of coverage. A point of service plan allows members to visit non-network physicians. While visits outside the network are more expensive, the HMO does provide some level of coverage.

Type of coverage

Virtually all HMOs cover hospital care and emergency care. Most also cover outpatient care, which includes routine exams, lab work, and office visits.

However, other areas of an HMO plan can differ significantly. Treatments such as prenatal and postpartum maternity care, prescription drugs, and ambulance service may or may not be included in the plan. Pay particular attention to the provisions concerning long-term treatments such as mental health or substance abuse; some HMOs offer insufficient coverage in these areas.

Programs also vary widely in defining what constitutes an emergency, from strictly life threatening conditions to any sort of health concern. HMOs are often reluctant to cite specific guidelines in this area, but you may want to ask about specific examples. Would a child's high fever qualify? A perceived heart attack? An allergic reaction?

Assessing physician quality

The quality of physicians participating in the network can be the most difficult aspect of an HMO to assess, although it is arguably the most important.

First, inquire about the screening process that is used to sign up physicians. A screening process should ideally include checks of the doctor's background, including analysis of any previous malpractice issues.

Also ask how many physicians have been certified by the American Board of Medical Specialties. In order to be certified, a physician must demonstrate competency in a specialty by passing tests or meeting training requirements. Ideally, 85% or more of the physicians should be board-certified.

A final statistic to evaluate is the physician turnover rate. This can give you a good indication of the likelihood that you will be forced to switch doctors. The turnover rate can also indicate how satisfied physicians are with the rules for treatment and reimbursement within the network. Better programs usually have a turnover rate of less than three to five percent.

Pricing

HMOs cost an average of $3,485 per employee per year, according to the 1994 National Survey of Employee-Sponsored Health Plans by Foster Higgins. HMOs are less expensive, on average, than traditional fee-for-service health insurance plans, but more expensive than preferred provider organizations.

Terms

Capitation The annual per-person HMO membership fee. Most HMOs set at least two capitation figures, one for individuals and one for families.

Deductible The amount the employee must pay for each HMO visit. HMOs typically set deductibles of $50 or less.

Exclusive provider organizations (EPO) Similar to an HMO, an EPO is a managed health care program that requires members to use doctors within the network. However, EPOs are not governed by most state and federal HMO regulations. As a result, certain medical conditions may not be covered by an EPO.

Point of service plans HMO plans that allow members to obtain coverage for care outside the network. Point of service plans encourage members to use doctors within the HMO network by paying a greater percentage of the cost of treatment. Also known as open-ended HMOs.

Primary care provider The doctor who is responsible for determining the care an HMO member receives. HMO patients must consult their primary care providers before seeing any other doctor or receiving any treatment. This policy limits the use of expensive specialists and is thought to help control health care costs.

Staff model A type of HMO that operates its own health clinics and hires its own doctors. This model has become less common over time, as more HMOs contract services from independent physician practices.

Special tips

Examine how second opinions are handled and how disputes in treatment are settled. Quality HMOs should have a set procedure in place for airing disagreements before a grievance board.

Some plans sign up doctors simply to boost their numbers. To get a better sense of the availability of doctors in the network, ask what percentage of the doctors are actually accepting new patients.

If the HMO is owned by a commercial insurance firm, you can examine the fiscal ratings of the company through reporting agencies such as A.M. Best or Standard & Poor's.

The National Committee on Quality Assurance (202/955-3500) issues report cards on HMOs.

Businesses have created purchasing coalitions to share information about the quality of care offered by local health care providers. To locate one in your area, contact The National Business Coalition on Health (202/775-9300).

See also
Business Insurance, Employee Drug Testing, Health Insurance, PPOs, Workers Compensation Insurance

For more information, visit
BuyersZone
http://www.buyerszone.com/

Did you know?
As late as 1972, HMOs were still illegal in 38 states.

HOTELS

*I*t can be difficult for business travelers to minimize hotel costs. Unlike vacationers, business travelers usually cannot schedule trips for off-peak periods or hotel specials. They also tend to require a high level of service and amenities during their stay.

Despite these restrictions, there are many options business travelers can pursue to limit costs without compromising their stay.

PRICING	
Type of accommodation	Typical rate per night
Business hotels	$52-$480
Limited-service hotels	$47-$135
Suite hotels	$140-$219
Extended-stay housing	$20-$90

U.S. CITIES WITH THE MOST HOTEL ROOMS		
City	Number of hotels	Number of rooms
Las Vegas	225	87,267
Orlando	311	85,924
Los Angeles	627	78,984
Chicago	377	68,365
Washington, DC	352	66,356
New York City	230	61,823
Atlanta	374	58,737
San Diego	385	46,453
Anaheim	352	44,320
San Francisco	301	42,700
Source: Smith Travel Research, 1995		

VENDORS

Hotel	Reservation number	Limited service hotels	Business hotels	Number of locations
Best Western	800/528-1234	•	•	3,462
Budgetel	800/428-3438	•		120
Clarion/Quality	800/221-2222		•	158
Courtyard	800/321-2211		•	256
Days Inn	800/325-2525	•	•	1,694
Doubletree	800/222-8733		•	116
Fairfield	800/228-2800	•		239
Hampton	800/426-7866	•		564
Hilton	800/445-8667		•	349
Holiday Inn	800/465-4329		•	2,096
Howard Johnson	800/654-2000		•	550
Hyatt	800/228-9000		•	172
Marriott	800/228-9290		•	948
Radisson	800/333-3333		•	328
Ramada	800/272-6232	•	•	114
Residence	800/331-3131	•		198
Sheraton	800/325-3535		•	386
Travelodge	800/225-3050	•	•	367
Westin	800/228-3000		•	66
Wyndham	800/822-4200		•	65

Buying points

Matching hotel to need

Hotels have traditionally differentiated themselves in terms of price, allowing travelers to choose among budget, midrange, upscale, or luxury lodgings. However, when choosing a hotel, it can be helpful to look beyond price and consider hotels according to the level of service they provide.

The majority of hotels follow the traditional, full-service model. These hotels feature full-sized lobbies, hotel restaurants, and meeting rooms. They are useful for business travelers who expect to meet with clients in the hotel.

However, many business travelers simply need a place to spend the night. Limited service hotels offer a less expensive option for individuals who do not expect to be at the hotel past breakfast. These hotels offer attractive, full-sized rooms, but do not include on-premise restaurants or meeting rooms.

Other travelers spend a lot of time working or meeting customers in their rooms. In these cases, it often makes sense to stay in a suite that has separate sleep and work areas. Suite hotels typically offer suites for about the same price as a traditional hotel room, allowing businesses to conduct in-room meetings or interviews in a professional environment.

Extended-stay hotels offer an economical alternative for business travelers who find themselves in one location for several days. Extended-stay units are equipped much like small apartments, offering small kitchenettes and additional living space for travelers.

Availability of office equipment

As more business travelers try to get serious work done on the road, a hotel's selection of business amenities has become increasingly important.

One very common amenity is the use of a fax machine and photocopier. While most hotels make these machines available via the front desk, some now provide this equipment in the room, or on specially designated floors. In addition, as hotels upgrade their phone systems, they are increasingly making voice mail boxes available to guests.

For more significant business needs, hotels often rent equipment such as overhead projectors or computer equipment. However, keep in mind that although hotels can secure equipment and services for you, they tend to charge a bit extra for the convenience.

Assessing individual hotels

Mobil and the American Automobile Association (AAA) publish two of the most popular hotel rating guides, although both cater to leisure travelers rather than businesses. Zagat's also offers a guide to major hotel chains.

You may also want to consult the directories offered by hotel chains. These typically detail the type of amenities offered by individual locations, with details on meeting rooms, restaurants, and the type of business amenities that can be found in each location.

Chains vs. independents

Hotel chains offer several advantages over individually-owned hotels. The primary advantage of chains is that firms can negotiate discounts based on the total volume of business they conduct with a hotel chain. Travelers may stay only a few nights in any single property, yet still be considered a valued account. Even if specially negotiated discounts are unavailable, chains often offer upgrades or special perks to frequent visitors through affinity programs.

Another advantage of chains is that they offer a similar level of service throughout their properties. Travelers can be assured of a certain level of quality without specific knowledge of a particular property.

Independent hotels are best suited for companies that frequently travel to one city and can take the time to find appropriate lodgings. Firms will generally find that independent hotels are much more willing to negotiate discounts. In addition, there are loose co-marketing agreements between independent hotels that can act much like affinity programs from a large chain.

Easy ways to obtain better rates

There are many ways to get reduced lodging rates when traveling for business. The first way is to request a corporate rate. Many hotels have reduced rates for business travelers, but only offer the rate if you ask. Travelers may also be able to receive special discounts as a member of various organizations or as a trade show or conference attendee. It also makes sense to ask about any ongoing special programs, since these may provide rooms for less than the quoted rates.

Travel agencies can also be a good source for hotel discounts. Agencies can often obtain more competitive rates for their clients because they book rooms in bulk. As a result, smaller firms that do not conduct much travel can avail themselves of lower "preferred" rates they might not be able to obtain otherwise.

Negotiating special rates

Firms that conduct a fair amount of travel may want to consider negotiating specific discounts. Hotels begin offering discounts at about 50 person-nights per year, with sizable discounts for firms that stay 200 person-nights or more per year.

Travel agents will typically conduct these negotiations on a company's behalf. However, companies can also approach hotels directly.

Pricing

Room cost varies depending on hotel and region. Business travelers can get rates as low as $20 per night for extended-stay housing to rates as high as $300 to $400 per night for luxury business hotels.

Travelers should expect to pay about $15 to $20 more for a room equipped with business amenities.

Terms

Corporate rate   The room rate given to business travelers, which is generally 15% to 20% lower than published rates. Corporate rates are given rather freely to most corporate customers.

Preferred rate   A rate that is individually negotiated by a travel agency based on the total agency bookings with the hotel. Preferred rates can be up to 40% off the published rates.

Rack rate   This rate is the standard, published rate for each room.

Special tips

Lower rates are sometimes available by reserving directly with a hotel rather than by going through the reservation line. Also, travelers have a greater advantage asking for discounts when reserving a room over the phone than when inquiring about room availability in person.

Make sure to sign up for any frequent stay programs. You may even be able to obtain airline frequent flyer miles with your stay.

In situations where you will be holding a small meeting, a suite hotel can be a less expensive alternative to renting a full meeting room at the hotel.

If you are looking for extended-stay housing in a particular area, contact local convention and visitor bureaus (CVBs), area Chambers of Commerce, and tourism offices.

Make sure to inquire about the availability of a regular phone jack if you plan to use a modem during your stay. Many hotels have phone systems that do not use the modular jacks required by peripherals such as modems or fax machines.

Find out about phone charges before using the phone. Hotels have historically charged outrageous rates for phone calls. Even if you use a calling card, learn if there are any added hotel surcharges before using the card.

See also
Beverage Services, Car Rental Agencies, Corporate Cards, Frequent Flyer Programs, Travel Agencies

Did you know?

Eighty-three percent of travelers say they work harder than their bosses on business trips; almost the same percentage of bosses (85%) say they work harder than their staff, according to a telephone survey of 500 Hyatt business traveler customers.

Ink-jet Printers

*I*nk-jet printers spray small droplets of ink onto a page to create a printed image. They are among the least expensive printers currently on the market, yet are capable of producing high-quality images, even in color. For this reason, ink-jets have become a popular option for homes and businesses with relatively low-volume printing needs.

VENDORS

Company	Headquarters	Phone number	Color models 4-color	3-color
Apple	Cupertino, CA	800/776-2333	●	●
Canon	Costa Mesa, CA	800/848-4123	●	●
Epson	Torrance, CA	800/947-8247	●	●
Hewlett-Packard	Palo Alto, CA	800/752-0900	●	●
Lexmark	Lexington, KY	800/358-5835	●	●
Mannesmann Tally	Kent, WA	800/843-1347	●	
Okidata	Mt. Laurel, NJ	800/OKIDATA	●	
Olivetti	Bridgewater, NJ	908/526-8200		●

Buying points

About the technology
There are two ink-jet technologies currently on the market. Most ink-jets work via hydraulic pressure, spraying tiny droplets of ink onto a piece of paper. The ink cartridge and printhead move horizontally across the page, filling in images as a sheet of paper is drawn through the machine.

Canon's patented Bubblejet printers use a slightly different printing technology. In a Bubblejet, the ink is heated to a very high temperature, creating bubbles of ink. Once the bubble reaches a certain size, the ink is forced through a nozzle onto the page.

Assessing print quality
Ink-jet printers typically print at 300 or 360 dots per inch. This resolution is roughly the same as that of a low-end laser printer, creating good text and decent graphics. Some models offer even higher resolutions, making twice as many passes across the page to produce 600 x 300 or 720 x 360 dpi output.

One problem with ink-jet printing is that the liquid ink is easily absorbed by paper fibers. This "wicking" can blur the final image, making ink-jet documents appear less crisp than laser printed versions.

To produce crisp-looking output, ink-jet printers require very smooth paper. This can be purchased from the manufacturer, or from third-party paper suppliers. However, smooth stock is more expensive than regular white paper.

A second problem is that ink-jet pages are susceptible to smudging. Users must be careful handling pages just out of the printer, and should make sure that pages do not get wet.

Printing in color
Although color printing is still uncommon in most printer segments, it has been embraced by the ink-jet crowd. Most ink-jet printers now offer color capabilities, simply requiring the user to swap a color cartridge for the regular black cartridge.

Color ink-jets come in two varieties. Low-end designs use a three-color cartridge. These combine cyan, magenta, and yellow inks to produce any color in the spectrum.

The problem with three-color models is that the black areas of an image do not come out very black. The three colors combine to form a greenish-brown tinge, rather than a true black. This is especially noticeable on documents that include black text.

Four-color models get around this problem by adding black to the color cartridge. Most businesses will find this upgrade worth the extra cost. Four-color models are about $200 to $300 more than three-color models, but produce much better looking documents if you combine color and text.

Handling multiple users
Although ink-jets are inexpensive and colorful, they are not always suitable for use by many people in the office.

One of the main drawbacks to using an ink-jet model in the office is speed. Because the ink must be sprayed onto each line of a document, few ink-jet models can print more than two pages per minute. This pace is reasonable for one or two users, but is quite slow if several people want to use the printer at once.

A second problem with ink-jet printers is network compatibility. Most ink-jet models do not come equipped with any way to connect to a computer network. Models are equipped with a parallel port and a serial port, which allow them to connect to two computers at once. However, to support print jobs from multiple people, you will have to designate one computer as a print server.

The few ink-jets that can be connected to a computer network tend to be much more expensive. You can expect to pay an additional $300 to $500 for an ethernet or token ring interface.

Pricing

Low-end monochrome ink-jets typically cost $200 to $300. The addition of color can add a few hundred dollars to that cost. Depending on your needs, a color ink-jet can cost anywhere from $400 to $2,500. Features such as additional paper trays, network interface or additional memory can substantially increase the total cost of a printer.

Terms

Bubblejet printing A patented form of ink-jet printing developed by Canon. The print quality of modern ink-jets and Bubblejets is quite similar.

Printer Control Language (PCL) The language used to communicate instructions between the computer and the printer. Most ink-jet printers use a version of Hewlett-Packard's PCL printer language.

Resolution The level of detail that can be printed by a printer, measured in dots per inch (dpi). Most businesses use a 300 or 600 dpi printer.

Special tips

Do not turn off an ink-jet printer by unplugging it. The printhead is programmed to park and cap properly before the machine is shut off. If you unplug the printer, the printhead can be damaged.

Look into recycled cartridges as a less expensive alternative to buying new cartridges. Quality among third-party vendors can vary, however, so make sure any purchase is accompanied by a guarantee.

Color cartridges are significantly more costly than black-only units. Make sure to use the black-only cartridge when printing text.

See also
Color Printers, Copy Paper, Desktop Computers, Fax Machines, Multifunctional Devices, Notebook Computers, Portable Printers, Toner Supplies

International Callback

Because of various regulations and billing practices, it is generally more expensive to make calls to the U.S. from a foreign country than to make calls from the U.S. to that same country. International callback services take advantage of this discrepancy by allowing overseas travelers to make calls from foreign countries while paying U.S. rates. They use special software to establish a U.S. dialing presence for the traveler, who can then make calls for much lower rates.

VENDORS		
Company	Headquarters	Phone number
America Telefone	New York, NY	800/321-5817
Globaltel	Norcross, GA	770/449-1295
ITC	Meriden, CT	800/638-5558
Kallback	Seattle, WA	800/959-KALL
PrimeCall	Seattle, WA	800/698-1232
Telegroup	Fairfield, IA	800/338-0225
USA Global Link	Fairfield, IA	515/472-1550

Buying points

The international callback process

To use international callback services, you will need to first sign up with a U.S.-based callback service. You then provide an itinerary of phone numbers where you can be reached during an upcoming trip.

When you need to make a call during the trip, you dial a special pre-assigned number in the U.S. and hang up after the phone starts ringing. You are not usually charged for this call, because it never actually connects. However, the ringing signals the service to call you back at the number specified on your itinerary.

When the callback comes through, the call is patched to a second open line. With this open line, you can dial any domestic or international phone number as if you were in the U.S.

Calling economics

Although international callback requires you to use two lines at once (one to the callback service, and one for the outgoing call), the economics of international calling means that this is often cheaper than the direct-dialing alternative.

International callback tends to be less of a bargain if you can obtain discount services within a foreign country. For example, offices located overseas can often obtain volume calling rates that are less than those of a callback service. International callback is also not always less expensive in countries with very competitive telecom services. For example, international callback can be a poor choice when calling from Britain, while it often results in huge savings when calling from South American locations.

Providers

The international callback market is fairly recent in origin. Although there are some big players, they tend not to be firms that you have encountered in other telecommunication fields. In most cases, major carriers are unwilling to jeopardize their relationships with international partners for the smaller callback market.

Some of the bigger companies in this industry include Kallback, Telegroup, and USA Global Link.

Is callback service legal?

Although it is being contested in various courts, callback service remains legal as of the date of this publication. Some countries do occasionally block calls to callback services, but the services have become quite adept at countering this tactic.

Pricing

Callback services charge rates that range from 25¢ to $2.00 for each line in the connection. As a result, you will pay anywhere from about 50¢ to several dollars per minute depending where you are and where the call is going. Calls to the U.S. tend to be a bit less expensive, with rates as low as 35¢ per minute from some countries.

When comparing prices across callback services, make sure to identify any hidden charges. Since this industry is so unregulated, billing practices can vary tremendously from one company to another. Some callback companies charge only for completed calls, others charge for every call (even when you reach a busy signal), and others begin billing you from the moment you pick up the callback. Many firms also require a minimum monthly commitment, which may make the service impractical for infrequent travelers.

Special tips

Ask about customer service hours for the callback service. Make sure these hours include the times when travelers will be calling from overseas locations.

Although many firms require upfront subscription charges, they are often quick to waive this fee.

Obtain a sample billing statement to ensure that the report contains information you need to allocate business costs.

Check the minimum call length and billing increment for calls. Assuming the same rates, smaller increments mean greater savings. You can expect to save approximately 10% by using a service that bills in 30-second increments instead of one-minute increments, and 20% with a service that uses six-second increments.

Inquire about the credit policy for poor-quality connections.

See also

Calling Cards, International Calling, Long Distance Service, Prepaid Phone Cards, Toll Free Service

INTERNATIONAL CALLING

*I*nternational calling programs offer discounted rates for firms calling or faxing businesses in other countries. These programs are often bundled with domestic long distance programs, but can also be purchased separately to better fit particular calling patterns.

PRICING

Calls from the U.S. to:	Typical per-minute rates
Brazil	$0.76-$1.41
China	$1.05-$2.19
England	$0.40-$0.70
France	$0.40-$0.86
Germany	$0.40-$0.84
Japan	$0.40-$0.96
Mexico	$0.68-$1.39

VENDORS

Company	Headquarters	Phone number
AT&T	Basking Ridge, NJ	800/222-0400
Cable & Wireless	Vienna, VA	800/486-8686
Frontier	Rochester, NY	800/836-8080
LCI	McLean, VA	800/860-1020
LDDS WorldCom	Jackson, MS	800/539-2000
MCI	Washington, DC	800/950-5555
Sprint	Overland Park, KS	800/877-7253

Buying points

The calling process
International calls generally work much like regular long distance calls. Instead of an area code, callers dial an international access code and country code (and city code where needed) to direct their call. A few countries (primarily very small, undeveloped nations) cannot be dialed directly, and require an operator's assistance to place a call.

As the international call is placed, it can be relayed in one of two ways. Most calls are relayed along wire or fiber optic cables submerged under the ocean. Others are conveyed by satellites to the desired country. Once the call has reached the foreign country, it is relayed over the local network to its final destination.

About the market
The largest players in the international calling market are the same firms that dominate the domestic long distance market. AT&T has long been a leader in international calling, with other major international carriers including Cable and Wireless, Frontier, LCI, LDDS WorldCom, MCI, and Sprint.

In addition to these major carriers, there are numerous resellers and aggregators who also offer international calling services. These providers typically lease excess international capacity from one or more of the larger carriers and resell it to businesses.

Accessing countries
Access refers to the number of countries a caller can reach using a particular carrier. Although virtually all carriers can connect you to major industrialized countries, there are differences if you call very small countries, particularly less developed regions of Africa, central Asia, and countries of the former Soviet Union. Carriers will generally provide a list of the countries they serve, allowing you to identify whether the firm can meet all your needs.

Sound quality
Quality problems can be a major issue during international calls, with calls frequently suffering from crackles, hissing, echoes, and other symptoms of line degradation. This can be especially problematic with fax calls, since excessive noise can result in an overly long or dropped connection.

Although there are differences in the types of lines used, call quality is generally most dependent on the compression techniques used by the carrier. Many inexpensive carriers heavily compress calls to fit more traffic on a single line. Although this lowers the cost of the service, it can dramatically reduce the quality of calls.

Unfortunately, it can be very difficult to predict the amount of compression used on any given line. For voice calls, you can simply decide whether the quality is acceptable. For fax calls, you may want to examine transmission times to make sure that international faxes do not take much longer to send than domestic faxes.

Program features

As with domestic calling programs, international calling programs frequently offer features such as call accounting and detailed billing reports.

Call accounting requires callers to enter a code to complete each call. This code allows firms to allocate costs to different individuals, departments, or clients.

Detailed billing reports break out the details of international calling for analysis. You will be able to see the length and cost of each call, and will be able to compare the cost across countries or from individual offices.

Where to obtain service

Most firms obtain international service from the same carrier that handles their domestic long distance service. However, given the significant differences among providers, this may not always be the best choice. By dedicating lines to international calls or by programming your phone system to route international calls over another carrier, you may be able to save money, improve call quality, or both.

If your company regularly spends $750 or more per month on international calls, it makes sense to consider all the available international calling programs, regardless of your current carrier. If your firm spends less than that per month, you will probably want to restrict your search to the programs offered by the carrier you currently use for long distance service. Make sure that you do sign up for a program, however. Other-wise, you may find your company paying extremely high international rates simply because you do not belong to a specific international calling program.

Signing up

Before joining any program, make sure that you understand the terms and restrictions of the agreement.

First and foremost, find out if you will need to sign up with the same carrier for both domestic and international calling. Find out about any fees (installation or monthly) associated with the program, the minimum term length you must commit to, and any penalties for breaking the contract. Ask about any current promotions or volume discounts that can help lower your bill. Finally, determine what types of billing formats are available, and whether operators (customer and technical service) are available 24 hours a day.

Pricing

Pricing for international calling tends to vary much more than for domestic calling. Within a program, rates usually differ by country, with different prices for peak and off-peak calling.

Prices range from 15¢ per minute to $4.66 per minute depending on the country called and the carrier used. In many cases, changing programs can result in savings of 50% or more.

As with long distance calls, international rates are negotiable. Volume discounts are the most common area of negotiation. In general, it is more difficult to obtain concessions on specific international rates.

Terms

International access code A code used to indicate that a phone call will go outside the U.S., Canada, and the Caribbean. In the U.S., the international access code is 011. This code can also be used by many phone systems to route international calls to the appropriate international carrier.

Peak rates The rates charged for calls made during the hours of greatest demand. Because of differences in time zones, countries often have very different hours during when peak rates are charged.

Switches A telephone switch directs traffic in the telephone network, ensuring that a call reaches its intended destination. However, calls that must be routed through many switches can become degraded, resulting in lower sound quality. Most domestic calls require one or two switches to reach their destination. International calls typically go through three to four switches.

Special tips

One of the more interesting features offered by carriers is interpreters. These interpreters conference in on an international phone call to assist in translation. Costs range from $4 to $7 per minute, including the cost of the call. AT&T is particularly strong in these services, offering interpreters at a moment's notice for most major languages.

Most calling programs charge a minimum of 30 seconds per call, with six second rounding thereafter. Programs that round calls to the next full minute will be 20% more expensive, on average.

While term agreements are very common in this market, we recommend that you avoid any contract requiring more than a one-year agreement.

See also
Calling Cards, International Callback, Long Distance Service, Toll Free Service

INTERNATIONAL EXPEDITED DELIVERY

*U*nlike domestic overnight delivery, international expedited shipping is far from a commodity business. Shipping products to a foreign country requires dealing with issues such as foreign regulations, multiple time zones, and, in some cases, foreign couriers. In spite of these hurdles, carriers manage to deliver packages in remarkably little time, even overnight to many locations.

PRICING

U.S. to:	Letter-sized	5 lbs.	25 lbs.
Asia	$20-$71	$33-$89	$98-$366
Europe	$20-$36	$31-$89	$86-$180
S. America	$20-$41	$33-$111	$98-$281
Mexico	$22-$50	$45-$60	$50-$134
Canada	$7-$53	$9-$60	$19-$123

VENDORS

International program	Phone number	Money-back delivery guarantee	Weight limit
Airborne International Express	800/ABX-INTL	●	70 lbs.
Burlington International Express	800/CALL-BAX		none
Burlington Time Definite Premier	800/CALL-BAX		none
DHL Worldwide Priority Express	800/CALL-DHL	●	none
Emery Time Definite Express	800/323-4685	varies	none
FedEx International Priority	800/247-4747	●	varies
RPS RPSAir	800/ROAD-PAK	●	150 lbs.
TNT Express	800/558-5555		none
UPS Worldwide Expedited	800/782-7892	varies	varies
UPS Worldwide Express	800/782-7892	varies	varies
U.S. Postal Service Global Priority Mail	800/222-1811		4 lbs.
U.S. Postal Service International Express Mail	800/222-1811		varies

International Expedited Delivery

Buying points

Differences across carriers

One of the key differences among carriers concerns how shipments are handled. Not all international shipments are handled throughout the delivery by the same carrier that picked up the shipment. Subcontractors are often employed by carriers to deliver to areas not covered by their regular service network. This can mean that packages will take longer to be delivered, since they must wait to be handed off to another firm. Depending on the location, this might mean that a subcontracted package is not delivered until the following day.

DHL, Federal Express, TNT, and UPS have delivery networks in most major industrial countries. As a result, these carriers directly handle a large number of international packages. Firms such as Airborne, Burlington and Emery subcontract a much higher proportion of packages. While these firms deliver their own shipments in a few countries, you can expect that most overseas packages will be delivered by another firm.

Variations in transit times

Because of the vast distances involved, overnight delivery remains the exception rather than the rule for international deliveries.

Most carriers provide overnight service only from the U.S. cities that serve as the carrier's international hub. These usually include New York for Europe, Miami for South America, and Los Angeles or San Francisco for Asia. Some carriers also have limited overnight service (selected European or Asian cities only) from secondary hubs such as Atlanta, Boston, or Philadelphia. In some cases there may be a dramatic difference in delivery times between carriers if one company flies directly from your city while another does not.

Deliveries from other cities normally require at least two days. Most carriers can reach major Asian, European and South American metropolitan areas in two business days, with delivery to the rest of western Europe and east Asia available in three days.

Shipments to smaller countries, including those in Africa, Central Asia, and Eastern Europe, take significantly longer. Most carriers only serve major cities, and often use the country's postal system to reach remote locations.

Customs

Documents of no monetary value are not subject to customs approval. This means that customs will not unduly delay delivery of reports, presentations or other similar documents.

However, the customs approval process usually does affect the shipment of equipment and supplies, whether they are for internal use or resale. These dutiable goods potentially spend more time waiting to pass through customs than in the air. As a result, the ability of a carrier to quickly move shipments through customs is a critical consideration. Unfortunately, it is difficult to identify which carrier has the best customs technique since the process differs depending on the country, the frequency of shipments, and even the type of goods being sent.

To ensure faster customs review, you should, at minimum, look for a carrier that directly employs customs brokers in the countries where you will be shipping.

Tracking packages

If the carrier that picks up the package delivers it to its destination, it is usually quite simple to determine the location of the package in transit. Tracking tends to be somewhat spottier with subcontracted shipments. Most tracking systems are not well integrated across carriers, meaning that en-route tracking will usually not be available in these situations.

Volume discounting

Delivery rates are almost always negotiable, with the expected shipping volume having the biggest effect on the size of available discounts. For moderate volume shippers, 15% to 20% discounts are typical.

A simple way to increase your volume is to consolidate your shipping with one carrier. However, make sure the carrier you choose can meet all of your domestic and international shipping needs.

For low volume shippers, discounted rates may be unavailable. In these cases, it is advisable to split traffic among various carriers depending on the shipping cost and times for the particular item being sent.

Pricing

Sending packages overseas is not cheap. Expect to pay about $30 for a letter-sized document, $80 for a 5-lb. package, and $200 for a 25-lb. shipment. Prices vary considerably according to the destination country and carrier.

Terms

Customs brokers Agents who work with government shipping officials on behalf of specific carriers to expedite shipments through customs.

Dutiable shipments International shipments that are subject to taxes when entering the destination country. These packages must be sent through customs, which can result in a considerable delay in delivery.

Special tips

Air freight forwarders can be a cost-effective alternative for infrequent international shippers. These firms secure space for shipments using commercial airlines and overnight carriers. As volume shippers, freight forwarders often offer better pricing than companies can obtain on their own.

If international shipping makes up a large portion of your shipping bill, consider consolidating all traffic with DHL. While it tends to be expensive for domestic shipments, DHL offers substantial (20%+) discounts on domestic rates for companies using their international programs.

If you are located in or around a carrier's gateway city, you may be able to ship non-dutiable documents overnight or at special discounted rates. DHL (Chicago, Los Angeles, Miami, New York), Federal Express (New York, Washington, DC), TNT (Chicago, Los Angeles, Miami, New York, San Francisco), and UPS (Chicago, Los Angeles, Miami, New York, San Francisco) offer overnight delivery special programs for packages being sent from the indicated cities.

See also

Ground Shipping, LTL Shipping, Overnight Delivery Services, Postage Meters, Postal Scales, Same Day Delivery Services

Internet Service Providers

*I*nternet service providers (ISPs) provide users access to the Internet for sending e-mail, browsing the World Wide Web, and downloading software. Unlike commercial online services, who have substantial amounts of proprietary content for users to browse, ISPs primarily function as a conduit to the Internet.

VENDORS

Company	Headquarters	Phone number	24 hour live technical support	POPs
ANS	Elmsford, NY	800/456-8267	•	38
AT&T	Bridgewater, NJ	800/967-5363	•	200+
BBN Planet	Cambridge, MA	800/472-4565	•	311
GNN	Vienna, VA	800/819-6112		650
IDT	Hackensack, NJ	201/928-1000	•	< 500
MCI	Washington, DC	800/955-6505	•	300
Netcom	San Jose, CA	800/501-8649		230+
PSINet	Herndon, VA	800/827-7482	•	300
UUNet	Fairfax, VA	800/488-6383	•	300

Buying points

ISP options

It is estimated that there are more than 2,000 Internet service providers scattered around the country. These range from two-person shoestring operations to national companies with thousands of employees and billions of dollars of network infrastructure.

Connecting to the ISP

Depending on your expected usage, you can connect to the Internet via a dial-up line or via a dedicated data line.

If only one person will typically browse the Internet at a time, you should be fine with dial-up service. This means that you use a modem and a regular phone line to connect to the provider. A regular 28,800 bits per second (bps) modem is acceptable for most browsing; however, users who regularly visit graphic-intensive sites may want to consider using an ISDN connection to the ISP. ISDN offers connection speeds up to 128,000 bps, but requires an ISDN "modem" and ISDN service from your local telephone company.

When examining ISPs, make sure they offer a dial-up number in your local calling area. This will reduce phone charges for the connection. You should also inquire about the number of modems the ISP has to handle incoming calls. A good rule of thumb is that there should be one modem for every ten customers.

Businesses that will have several people simultaneously using the Internet will want to consider a dedicated line. Dedicated lines directly connect your office to the Internet service provider. You pay a relatively high monthly charge, but do not pay for each minute of connection time.

The smallest dedicated lines are 56K lines, which can handle 2 or 3 simultaneous users. However, most users will want to purchase a fractional T1 line, which can be increased to handle higher loads in 64,000 bps increments. A full T1 can handle dozens of simultaneous users, and even larger T3 connections are available for the largest firms.

Differences between ISP networks

Most Internet traffic is carried on large national networks that cross the country. Individual ISPs connect to this backbone via data pipes of varying sizes. If the provider uses too small a pipe, you may face long waiting periods when accessing other parts of the Internet.

To avoid this problem, check the size of the data pipes used by the ISP. Many smaller services use a single T1 line, a data line capable of handling up to 1,544,000 bits of information per second. While this may sound like a lot, several dozen simultaneous users can easily overwhelm this link. Most business sites will be better off looking for a provider that uses multiple T1 lines, or even larger T3 lines.

Firms should also look into the provider's network redundancy. Ideally, a provider will have more than one connection to the Internet backbone, so you can send and receive e-mail and browse outside sites even if one link is down.

Finally, check the number of connections, or "hops," between your provider and the Internet backbone. Many providers connect to the backbone through another provider. Using an Internet provider that is more than two steps removed from the Internet can slow the speed at which you can access other sites.

Customer service concerns

Finding an ISP that offers strong customer service tends to be a real challenge. Many providers fail to live up to their service promises, with users often encountering long waits for help.

If you are just obtaining dial-up service, your risk is fairly limited. If you are not satisfied with your ISP, you can usually just sign up with another service. The only real difficulty is notifying people of your new e-mail address.

If you are installing a dedicated line, you are making a much longer-term commitment. Make sure to check references to gauge how much support you can really expect to receive from the provider.

Pricing

Internet service providers tend to offer Web and e-mail access at quite low rates. The cheapest service is a basic shell account, which typically offers unlimited browsing for about $10 or $15 per month. The problem with shell accounts is that you cannot use graphical browsers, which means you cannot take advantage of most of the attractions of the Web.

For full graphical access, you need to obtain a SLIP or PPP account. These allow you to use popular browsers such as Netscape Navigator or Microsoft Internet Explorer while connected to the ISP. SLIP/PPP accounts costs $20 to $40 per month. Not all offer unlimited access, but most set fairly high usage limits per month.

Terms

Point of presence (POP) Pronounced "pop." A physical location maintained by an ISP that provides a local connection to the Internet. You should make sure the ISP has a POP in your local calling area to avoid costly phone charges.

T1 line A dedicated phone line that carries 1.544 million bits of information per second. A T1 line can be used to connect a user to an ISP, or to connect an ISP to other locations on the Internet. T1 lines can be shared among multiple users; this is called fractional T1 service.

T3 line A very large dedicated line that carries 45 million bits of information per second. T3 lines are most often used by ISPs to connect to the Internet backbone.

Upstream provider The national network the ISP uses to connect to sites around the country. In some cases, an upstream provider may actually be another Internet provider that, in turn, maintains a connection to one of the national networks.

Special tips

If you will want to access e-mail while traveling, look for a provider that offers a national network of POPs. This will allow business travelers to access e-mail or Web sites from many locations.

Most ISPs can help you establish your own domain name (e.g., www.buyerszone.com) as an e-mail account or Web site. However, make sure not to pay too much for this service. The Internet registry charges $100; you should not pay much more than a $20 surcharge to an ISP for help with registration.

See also
E-mail Services, ISDN, Modems, World Wide Web Site Setup

Did you know?

The reason why the Internet has no "center" is that it was originally set up by the Department of Defense as a decentralized network so it could survive a nuclear war.

ISDN

*I*SDN is a digital telephone service that provides high-speed voice and data transmission to any other ISDN user. This service has recently gained in popularity, particularly for those telecommuting or accessing the Internet.

SERVICE VENDORS

Company	Phone number
Ameritech	800/832-6328
Bell Atlantic	800/570-ISDN
Bell South	800/858-9413
Cincinnati Bell	513/566-DATA
GTE	800/4-GTE-SWS
Nevada Bell	702/688-7280
Nynex	800/GET-ISDN
Pacific Bell	800/4-PB-ISDN
Rochester Telephone	716/777-1234
SNET	203/771-5111
U.S. West	303/896-8370

EQUIPMENT VENDORS

Company	Headquarters	Phone number	Mac	PC
3Com	Santa Clara, CA	800/NET-3COM	•	•
Ascend	Alameda, CA	800/922-0119	•	•
Boca Research	Boca Raton, FL	407/997-6227		•
Gandalf	Cherry Hill, NJ	609/461-8100	•	•
IBM	Armonk, NY	800/772-2227		•
Motorola	Huntsville, AL	205/430-8000	•	•
U.S. Robotics	Skokie, IL	800/550-7800	•	•

ISDN

Buying points

Defining ISDN
ISDN stands for Integrated Services Digital Network. Unlike most digital lines that directly connect two locations, ISDN is a switched service that allows you to dial any other subscriber on the ISDN network.

In its basic configuration, ISDN provides two high-speed channels. This allows users to exchange data and hold a voice conversation simultaneously, using the same connection. Alternately, the two channels may be combined to double the data capacity.

Speed
ISDN connections allow for much faster data transfers than ordinary analog lines. An ISDN BRI line consists of two bearer channels and one data channel. Each bearer channel can carry 56,000 or 64,000 bits per second (bps), depending on the local provider. This is in marked contrast to the fastest analog modems which operate at top speeds of only 28,800 to 33,600 bps.

In practice, ISDN's advantage over analog lines is even more pronounced. ISDN lines dial and connect extremely fast, often in less than a second. Once connected, the line is perfectly clear, which means that transmission occurs at the full transmission rate of 56,000/64,000 bps. In contrast, analog modems are often forced to step down to 20,000 bps or slower transmission rates to accommodate lower quality phone lines.

In some areas, ISDN channels can be combined, or "bonded," to create a single 128,000 bps connection. This offers connections that are nearly five times as fast as a typical 28,800 bps analog modem.

Practical applications
ISDN applications are growing as the service becomes more popular and accessible.

One popular use is connecting to online services or the Internet. ISDN allows for much faster downloading of graphics, audio, and video, which can minimize wait times. Although ISDN connections are not available from all online providers, an increasing number now offer them.

ISDN is also becoming popular for telecommuting. An ISDN line in the home can be used to connect to a corporate network for much less money than a dedicated line. Yet ISDN is much faster than a regular modem, allowing home-workers to access databases or other large applications from corporate servers without encountering painfully slow response times.

A third use of ISDN is for video conferencing. Regular telephone lines are too slow for most current video conferencing applications. However, one or more ISDN connections is often enough for desktop video conferencing. Software on the market is increasingly targeted for ISDN service, with a new ISDN-based standard emerging to permit different video conferencing systems to communicate with each other.

A final use of ISDN is as a backup for a dedicated data connection. Because

ISDN terminals can dial and connect so quickly, critical data connections can be shifted to an ISDN backup if a main line goes down. Since ISDN is a dial-up service, businesses will pay much less keeping an ISDN line available for backup than paying for a second dedicated line.

Necessary equipment

Using ISDN requires an ISDN terminal adapter, or "modem," at both ends of the connection. This device translates computer data into the appropriate signals for ISDN. Although not technically modems, these units are manufactured by modem companies and are packaged to look like standard analog modems.

Getting service

ISDN service is purchased from your local telephone service provider. It is not available in all areas, so you should call the telephone company before purchasing any equipment.

Setting up an ISDN line tends to be very complicated. There are dozens of ways to implement ISDN, depending on what equipment is installed at the local telephone company exchange. Most local telephone services have special help lines for businesses purchasing ISDN service.

Alternatives to ISDN

Although ISDN is much faster than an analog modem, it is not the only high-speed connection option on the market.

One emerging alternative is the cable modem. These modems work on the coaxial lines installed by cable companies. Cable modems promise speeds five to ten times as fast as ISDN, although they are still in the testing phase.

Another promising technology is ADSL, or Asymmetric Digital Subscriber Line. ADSL is a new way of using standard telephone lines for high-speed transmissions. ADSL will allow speeds of up to 6.1 million bits per second downstream (to the user) and 640,000 bps upstream. ADSL should become available in some areas in 1997.

Pricing

ISDN installation fees vary depending how far you are from a local telephone company office. You can expect to pay anywhere from $40 to $400 for installation.

Once installed, you must pay a monthly ISDN fee, which can range from as little as $15 to more than $100 per month.

Currently, most ISDN plans do not charge per minute for local calls. However, some telephone companies are now switching to per minute or per hour charges for ISDN calls due to heavy usage.

ISDN terminal adapters start at approximately $300 for the most basic units. Units designed for networks or multi-line routing can easily rise above $2,000.

Terms

Basic rate interface (BRI) The standard ISDN interface offered by the local telephone company. It includes two B channels (56/64 kbps each) and a data channel (16 kbps) for directing the call.

Bearer (or B) channel A line that carries data or voice. Bearer channels carry 56 or 64 thousand bits per second, depending on the local configuration.

Bonding A process that allows two bearer channels to be joined together to transmit a single 128 kbps data stream.

Data (or D) channels A line used to carry signal information about incoming and outgoing calls.

Kilobits per second (Kbps) A measurement for the speed at which data can be transferred, in thousands of bits per second.

Special tips

Intel offers a national availability hotline (800/538-3373x208) to help you find out whether ISDN service is available in your area.

Keep in mind that a bonded connection often results in two simultaneous long distance charges, thus increasing your phone bill.

Do not replace all of your conventional phone lines with ISDN lines. ISDN terminals need an external source of power, which means that you will be unable to use the phone if the electricity goes out.

See also
Conference Calling Services, Conferencing Equipment, Desktop Computers, Internet Service Providers, Long Distance Service, Modems, Telephone Systems, Video Conferencing Services, World Wide Web Site Setup

KEYBOARDS

*I*f you have ever used a computer for any length of time, you are probably quite familiar with the importance of a good keyboard. Long stretches of typing can cause wrist pain or muscle strain for almost any user. In most cases, users should be able to find a keyboard that allows for greater efficiency or less muscle strain at a very modest price.

VENDORS

Company	Headquarters	Phone number	PC	Mac	Dvorak	Chording	Custom designs
Adesso	Los Angeles, CA	213/294-4300	●	●			
Apple	Cupertino, CA	800/776-2333		●			
Datadesk	Bainbridge Island, WA	800/755-7185		●			●
Ergonomixx	Kensington, MD	800/784-1047	●	●			
Genovation	Irvine, CA	714/833-3355	●				●
Health Care Keyboard	Milwaukee, WI	414/536-2160	●	●	●		
Infogrip	Ventura, CA	800/397-0921	●	●		●	
Key Tronic	Spokane, WA	800/262-6006	●	●			
Microsoft	Redmond, WA	800/426-9400	●				
MicroSpeed	Fremont, CA	510/490-1403	●	●			
SIIG	Fremont, CA	510/657-8688	●	●			●

Buying points

Types of keyboards
Traditional keyboards share the same basic design: flat rows of keys plus a row of function keys. For added functionality, some models have a few special keys or include an integrated numeric keypad.

New keyboards are designed to minimize injuries and to provide a more efficient work environment. Some offer split or tilted designs, while others include independently contoured keys, integrated palm supports, or built-in pointing devices.

Features
If you currently use an older keyboard, it is often well worth the cost to get a larger model with more keys. Full-sized keyboards typically include 15 function keys, a full numeric keypad, as well as arrow keys that move the cursor.

If your desk does not have room for a mouse, you may be interested in finding a keyboard that includes a built-in pointing device. Many models incorporate trackballs, touchpads, or mini-joysticks into the keyboard, to allow users to direct a cursor without taking their hands off the keyboard.

Also useful are extra keys that can be programmed with short-cuts, or macros. These allow you to perform common tasks without using a mouse or a combination of several keys. Among the most common extra keys found is a Windows 95 key, which opens the operating system's Start menu.

A fourth feature is an adjustable keyboard. Many newer models can be split down the middle or tilted to accommodate different hand positions. Few people agree on the ideal setup, but these adjustable models offer users a great deal more flexibility.

Compatibility
Virtually any computer can accept a third-party keyboard. However, not all keyboards can be used with all computers.

To ensure compatibility, you simply need to make sure that the new keyboard uses the same plug as the old model. IBM-compatible PCs can work with a keyboard that uses a PS/2 or serial port; Macintosh-compatible keyboards need an ADB connector.

Preventing repetitive stress injuries
Computer users who sit at a keyboard for hours at a time or type in an improper position can wind up with repetitive stress injuries (RSIs).

Although their usefulness has been debated, a few keyboard designs may help users avoid such injuries. Generally, these keyboards are designed to help keep the user's wrists parallel to the desktop. Designs include keyboards that split between the two hands, and keyboards that tilt away from the body.

There are also a number of ergonomic devices that can help combat repetitive stress injuries, including therapeutic support gloves, arm support guides, reverse slant wrist guides, and adjustable keyboard drawers. These items can generally be found in computer and office supply stores.

Users should also sit properly and employ good work habits to avoid injury. Furniture should always be adjusted so the keyboard sits at or below elbow level. If a desk is too high, consider a keyboard tray. Furthermore, users should often take breaks from typing. Experts recommend that users who type extensively should, at minimum, take a five-minute break from typing every 30 minutes.

Alternatives to the standard QWERTY keyboard layout
Almost all keyboards use the same layout, placing the QWERTY keys in the upper left-hand side of the keyboard. Unfortunately, this turn-of-the-century design may not be the most efficient for a modern PC.

The most widely accepted alternate keyboard layout is the Dvorak layout. This design places the most commonly used letters in the home row, which reduces the distance your fingers must travel and supposedly increases overall typing speed.

Most operating systems can implement a Dvorak layout via software. To see which letters are found on which keys, you will need to buy stickers, switch keys or purchase a new Dvorak keyboard.

More radical designs do away with the whole concept of hitting one key to get a letter. Chording keyboards usually include 5 to 7 keys on a single layout, allowing you to generate any character with one hand by pushing combinations of keys. Of course, chording layouts require quite some time to get used to, and cannot be used with standard keyboard designs.

Pricing
Keyboards cost anywhere from $75 to $200 depending on what features are included. Specialty keyboards that adjust or tilt can add hundreds of dollars to the price.

Terms
Carpal tunnel syndrome (CTS) One of the most common repetitive stress injuries. It occurs when nerves passing through the wrist are restricted due to an unnatural typing position.

Home row Where your fingers are supposed to rest when typing. It is the middle row on most keyboards.

QWERTY A term used to indicate a standard keyboard layout. Also known as classic or typewriter layout.

Repetitive stress injury (RSI) An injury that arises from repeated movements that place unusual stress on a body part. While carpal tunnel syndrome is the most highly publicized ailment, bursitis, tendinitis, and tenosynovitis are also quite common.

Special tips
Notebook computer users who regularly work in one location should

definitely consider a full-sized keyboard for greater productivity and increased typing comfort.

If one computer is shared among several people, it can be difficult to properly adjust an ergonomic keyboard's position. In these cases, it may be worthwhile to purchase a keyboard for each user.

Keyboards used in dirty areas can be protected by inexpensive plastic covers. These allow you to type without removing the cover.

You can clean a keyboard by shaking it upside down. You will be surprised by the amount of debris that is collected.

See also
Desktop Computers, Notebook Computers, Pointing Devices

Did you know?

The QWERTY arrangement used in most keyboards was originally designed to avoid jamming typewriters by separating the most commonly struck key pairs.

KSU-less Phone Systems

Small businesses that need more than one or two phone lines may want to consider a KSU-less phone system. These phone systems bridge the gap between basic telephones and full-fledged phone systems.

VENDORS		
Company	Headquarters	Phone number
ATC	Charlottesville, VA	800/347-1432
DBA Telecom	Bellevue, WA	800/473-2800
MacroTel	Boca Raton, FL	407/997-5500
Panasonic	Secaucus, NJ	201/392-4222
SBC	St. Louis, MO	800/255-8480
Telematrix	Tamarack, FL	800/462-9446
TT Systems	Yonkers, NY	914/968-2100

KSU-less Phone Systems

Buying points

Understanding the technology

Most small phone systems use a central control unit, called the key system unit (KSU), to provide features that are not available with ordinary phones. For example, a central unit typically allows users to make calls to another in-office extension, and prevents other users from accidentally picking up a line that is being used.

These key systems require professional installation and maintenance. All outside telephone lines must connect to the KSU, as well as all inside extensions. Configuring and wiring these phone systems can be nearly as costly as the phones themselves.

KSU-less phone systems are designed to provide the features of a small phone system in a decentralized manner. These phones contain proprietary circuitry that allow them to communicate to one another without requiring a central cabinet.

Installation and expansion issues

The greatest advantage of a KSU-less system is that installation is very simple. Most KSU-less systems plug directly into regular phone jacks, without any need for separate wiring. However, KSU-less phones do require an external power source.

In terms of growth, KSU-less systems tend to be quite limited. Most systems can be expanded to 3 lines and 8 extensions, although some models can handle as many as four lines and 16 extensions.

If you expect to expand beyond these limits, KSU-less systems are usually not a good choice. Most small key systems can be upgraded to a larger key system cabinet, which allows you to save your investment in phones and circuit cards. In contrast, KSU-less phones cannot be upgraded for use with a larger system.

Calling features

KSU-less systems typically offer the features you would expect on a low-end phone system. All models offer basic phone system features such as hold and speed dialing. In addition, most KSU-less systems offer advanced features such as paging, conference calling, and call privacy. Many phones can even be equipped with music on hold systems.

KSU-less systems usually are not able to work with accessories such as voice mail or automated attendant. However, these features are generally also not available on inexpensive key systems.

Pricing

KSU-less systems generally cost between $130 to $225 per phone. Comparable key systems generally start at $250 per phone including installation. The savings from buying KSU-less phones can quickly exceed $1,000 on a typical eight-phone system.

Terms.

Extension Each telephone in a phone system.

Key system A type of phone system for small offices. Key systems use buttons, or keys, to access different outside lines.

Lines Connections to the outside phone network. The number of lines determines the number of incoming and outgoing calls that can simultaneously occur.

Special tips

KSU-less systems require a separate power supply, meaning that when the power goes out, so does the telephone system. To remedy this, look for a system with centralized power or a rechargeable battery option, which not only provides back-up power in cases of emergency, but also recharges itself when the power comes back on.

Make sure any KSU-less system you are considering is compatible with the type of telephone wiring used in your office. The system should also be able to work with telephone accessories such as answering machines and modems.

KSU-less systems are not permanently wired into your office. These phones can easily be unplugged and moved to a new location, or sold. This flexibility allows you to treat a KSU-less system much like any other business machine, rather than as a permanent investment in your premises.

See also
Cellular Telephones, Cordless Telephones, Telephone Systems

For more information, visit
BuyersZone
http://www.buyerszone.com/

Lamination Equipment

*L*amination equipment applies a protective plastic coating to paper documents or other easily-damaged materials. A laminating machine has many uses in the office, from extending the life of much-handled papers to producing durable name tags and business cards.

Company	Headquarters	Phone number
Apollo	Ronkonkoma, NY	800/777-3750
Boston (Hunt Mfg.)	Philadelphia, PA	800/283-1707
GBC	Northbrook, IL	800/477-9900
Global Equipment	Port Washington, NY	800/645-1232
IBICO Binding	Elk Grove, IL	800/323-5373
Royal/Olivetti	Bridgewater, NJ	908/526-8200
Seal Products	Philadelphia, PA	800/257-7325
Smith Corona	New Canaan, CT	800/448-1018
USI	Branford, CT	800/243-4565

Buying points

Types of laminators
There are three major categories of laminators.

Personal models are designed for infrequent, small laminating jobs such as business cards, name tags, and small note cards. These are often sold to homes or individual users.

General office models are larger units intended for documents such as charts, menus or legal transcripts. They are more expensive, and can often handle bulkier or wider materials.

High-end industrial lamination equipment is designed to operate at high speeds for long periods of time. These models are often used in businesses that must produce large quantities of laminated cards or documents.

Choosing a laminator
Laminators utilize a fairly simple technology with few differences among units. As a result, buying is usually a straightforward press.

The first consideration is the size of the documents you will need to laminate. Smaller units are often less expensive, but may be unable to handle full-sized sheets or oversized documents.

A second consideration is adjustability. If you expect to laminate materials of different thicknesses and sizes, you need a machine with adjustable temperature controls and motor speeds to properly seal any object. Simpler machines lack these controls, and may only be suitable for a specific material size or thickness.

A final consideration is how the machine will be used. If you expect to laminate many items at once, you can choose a model that combines heating and motor controls in a single on-off button. The downside of these models is that there is often a long warm-up time after the machine is shut off. For intermittent use throughout a day, it often makes sense to buy a unit that has a separate motor switch, allowing you to maintain the heating surface at the correct temperature when you are not laminating.

Speed
Laminating machines come in a range of speeds. Low-end models can take as long as 30 seconds to process a letter-sized document, while high-end models can take less than 10 seconds to process the same job.

Where to purchase a laminating machine
Basic laminating machines are available at office supply stores. For industrial machines, you will usually need to contact the manufacturer to find a local distributor.

Supplies
In most cases, the only accessory you will need is a protective shield of plastic that encloses the document to be laminated. Plastic is available in both pouches and rolls.

Most personal and office models use file-jacket-like pouches, which means that each document must be individually inserted into the plastic. Since pouches are made to house a given document size perfectly, specific pouches need to be purchased for different-sized lamination jobs.

Industrial machines generally use rolls, which significantly cut down on the time needed to prepare a document for laminating.

Pricing

The lamination equipment market is fiercely competitive. As a result, similar models from different manufactures generally cost about the same.

Depending on the features of the laminator and the documents to be laminated, the cost of the equipment can range from as little as $70 for a personal model to as much as $300 for a general office model. The industrial models, generally used in a production setting, cost well over $1,000.

Laminating accessories such as pouches or rolls can significantly drive up the cost of operating a laminator. Depending on the size of the pouches, the accessory cost can range from less than $20 for a box of 100 credit card size pouches to nearly $150 for two large rolls.

Terms

Carrier This is a piece of folded white cardboard with a non-stick coating on the inside used to transport a pouch through the laminator.

Co-polymer film A lamination film consisting of different adhesive resins. It is formulated to adhere to various types of materials including paper, plastic, and metal.

Encapsulation The process by which an item is heat sealed within layers of plastic film, thus protecting it from dirt and changes in climate.

Pouch Two sheets of pre-cut, pre-sized plastic sealed together on the top edge and open on three sides.

UV (ultraviolet) film A lamination film that has an ultraviolet block mixed into the co-polymer adhesive to protect documents from damaging rays.

Special tips

A less expensive alternative for infrequent lamination needs is to use self-adhesive pouches and sheets. These are available in a variety of sizes. Pouches cost approximately 25¢ for each 4 x 5 inch sheet, with a letter-sized pouch costing approximately $1.50. Alternatively, quick copy centers often offer lamination services.

Not all photographs can be laminated in any machine. Low-quality photographic paper can melt when put through a laminator, smearing the photo beyond recognition.

See also
Business Cards, Business Forms, Commercial Printing

Laser Pointers

*L*aser pointers shine a pinpoint beam of light across a large room. They are designed to provide presenters a simple and elegant way of pointing out details on a screen while giving them the freedom to roam across a room.

PRICING

Pointer type	Price range
Pen-style	$39-$229
Commercial size	$198-$399

VENDORS

Company	Headquarters	Phone number	Warranty
Apollo	Ronkonkoma, NY	800/777-3750	1 yr.
Beta Electronics	Columbus, OH	614/792-1181	1 yr.
Emerging Technology	Little Rock, AR	501/375-2227	2 yrs.
Laserex	Scottsdale, AZ	602/951-6969	1 yr.
Lyte Optronics	Santa Monica, CA	800/255-9133	2 yrs.

Buying points

Uses for a laser pointer
Laser pointers can be used for emphasis when presenting slides, maps, video, charts or other projected images. They provide a clear way to point out details on an image without standing right at the projector or blocking the screen. Laser pointers are particularly useful for detailed photos or maps, where the audience may not immediately notice important details.

How a laser pointer works
A laser pointer projects a red or orange dot on the screen. The size of the dot varies, but most are no more than a few inches in diameter. Some models offer a larger dot size for very large presentations.

Except in a very smoky or dusty room, the beam is not visible to the audience.

Types of laser pointers
Laser pointers come in two sizes. The smaller units are about the size and weight of a pen, while the larger "commercial" versions are about the size of a flashlight.

Choosing a laser pointer
The three main considerations when purchasing a laser pointer are the power output, the wavelength, and the battery life.

Power output indicates the brightness of the laser pointer. Measured in milliwatts (mW), power output varies from 3 mW to 5 mW, the highest allowable power limit for a laser pointer.

The advantage of higher power beams is that the dot will be visible even on very bright projected images. The 5 mW models are designed for use with bright LCD projectors and overhead projectors.

Another purchasing factor is the wavelength of light used by the laser pointer. Low-end beams often use a 680 nanometer (nm) wavelength, which is effective to about 150 feet. Laser pointers with lower wavelengths, such as 630 nm, offer brighter images and an effective range of up to 250 feet.

Battery life for laser pointers typically ranges from three to five hours. However, commercial models are designed to last anywhere from 15 to 30 hours.

Batteries
Most pocket-sized laser pointers take standard AAA batteries, while commercial lasers use standard 9-Volt or D batteries. Some models offer an indicator that warns you about low battery level before the beam shuts off.

Pricing
When laser pointers were first introduced in 1991, the average retail price was near $300. Now, the average price is under $100.

Special tips

A pulsating beam feature is available with some laser pointers to add emphasis to a presentation. It can also be useful to conceal a shaky hand. However, this effect decreases battery life.

A few laser pointers can be equipped for infrared transmission. By connecting an infrared receiver to a computer, a PC-based presentation can be controlled with the pointer.

Make sure not to directly point a laser beam at someone's eyes. Although beams tend to be fairly safe, they can damage the retina in some instances.

See also
LCD Systems, Overhead Projectors, Slide Projectors

Laser Printers

*D*espite promises of a paperless office, almost every document that is created on a computer is eventually printed. As a result, the printer remains a critical component of any computer system. Among the different types of printers, laser printers provide the fastest, most efficient way to reproduce text and images, offering high resolution and quick speeds at a relatively low cost.

PRICING

Printer type	Typical price range
Personal laser printers	$370-$1,100
Network laser printers	$1,500-$5,000

VENDORS

Company	Headquarters	Phone number	Fax back number
Apple	Cupertino, CA	800/776-2333	800/462-4396
Brother	Irvine, CA	800/276-7746	800/276-7746
Canon	Costa Mesa, CA	800/848-4123	800/526-4345
Digital (DEC)	Maynard, MA	800/777-4343	800/777-4343
Epson	Torrance, CA	800/289-3776	800/922-8911
Genicom	Chantilly, VA	800/436-4266	NA
Hewlett-Packard	Palo Alto, CA	800/752-0900	800/231-9300
Kyocera	Somerset, NJ	800/232-6797	800/459-6329
LaserMaster	Eden Prairie, MN	800/688-8342	NA
Lexmark	Lexington, KY	800/891-0331	606/232-2380
NEC	Boxborough, MA	800/388-8888	800/366-0476
Okidata	Mount Laurel, NJ	800/654-3282	800/654-6651
Panasonic	Secaucus, NJ	800/854-4536	800/222-0584
QMS	Mobile, AL	800/523-2696	800/633-7213
Texas Instruments	Dallas, TX	800/336-5236	800/848-3927

Buying points

How they work
A laser printer uses an electrostatic process similar to a photocopier. The laser charges areas of a photosensitive image drum. Toner particles are then attracted to these areas of the drum. By rolling this drum against a piece of paper, the printer creates an image on a page. In the final stage, heat is used to fuse the toner to the paper.

Types of laser printers
Laser printers run the spectrum from small, personal laser printers to giant network models. Personal laser printers are designed to be used by a single person or a few people in an office. They are small, relatively slow, and can handle only a few types of paper.

Network laser printers are designed to be used by many people across a firm. These printers are generally equipped with an interface that allows them to directly connect to a local area network. Network printers generally operate at speeds of 15 to 30 pages per minute, and can handle a variety of paper sizes and types.

Checking compatibility
Most offices with IBM-compatible PCs will want to look for a printer that uses PCL5. This language, originally developed for Hewlett-Packard printers, is the de facto standard in the industry. Watch out for low-cost printers using older PCL versions such as PCL4; these printers are fine for basic text, but will not handle some complex images.

The most popular alternative to PCL is called PostScript. This is a very powerful language that will produce the same image regardless of the equipment it utilizes. However, printers equipped to handle PostScript are usually quite a bit more expensive than PCL printers. Look for a PostScript-compatible printer if your office regularly sends work to service bureaus for outputting, or if your network includes any Macintosh computers.

About printing speed
Manufacturer reports of printer speeds are often somewhat misleading. Most advertisements tout the printer's engine speed, which is given in terms of pages per minute. Unfortunately, this speed simply refers to the maximum number of sheets the printer can physically churn out per minute, not the typical speed of the printer in use.

For files that use many fonts or incorporate complex graphics, the speed of the printer's processor tends to be much more significant than the engine speed. When printing graphics, a large portion of print time is spent waiting for the processor to calculate where to place each dot on the page to create the desired image.

Because processor speed is not easily measured and is rarely advertised, you need to look at the type of processor to get a sense for the overall speed of the machine. In general, processors using RISC technology are the fastest available. Inexpensive machines often use 80186, 68000, or 68020 chips, all of which are relatively slow.

Acceptable printer resolutions

Resolution for laser printers is measured in dots per inch, or dpi. This refers to the number of dots, both vertically and horizontally, that are printed per inch of paper.

For many years, 300 dpi printing was considered the standard for office documents. However, many printers now offer 600 dpi resolution, which translates to a four-fold increase in print quality. Fine lines and dark curves look better at 600 dpi, but text will look very similar at either resolution. Buyers looking at PCL printers will need to purchase a model equipped with an extended version of PCL5, called PCL5e, for 600 dpi capability.

Printers that boast printing resolutions greater than 600 dpi are nice to have, but are not necessary for most offices.

Paper tray basics

When purchasing a laser printer, do not overlook basics such as paper feeding. Most users will find paper trays that hold fewer than 250 sheets to be too small for the office environment. Better are printers with two paper trays, since one tray can be filled with letterhead, legal-sized or scrap paper. Such features will allow you to leave the printer unattended for longer periods of time.

A manual feed tray is also very helpful for printing envelopes, labels or card stock. If you will be frequently printing envelopes, a dedicated envelope feeder can be a reasonable option.

Pricing

The cost of a laser printer will vary depending on whether you purchase a personal or network laser printer. Personal laser printers start around $400 and can go above $1,000. Network laser printers usually fall into the $1,500 to $4,000 range.

The cost of consumables for a laser printer, over the printer's life, will often far exceed the printer's initial purchase price. The cost for consumables, including toner, drums, developer, ozone filters, and corona wires, can range from $700 to $3,500 per 100,000 pages. As a result, it makes sense to calculate the price of these consumables, especially toner cartridges, before making a purchase.

On the other hand, service and repair costs tend to be minimal for laser printers. If you can keep the model clean, you are unlikely to face any serious breakdowns.

Terms

LED A printing technology that utilizes a light beam instead of a laser. LED and laser technologies work in the same way and produce very similar quality output.

Pages per minute (ppm) A measurement that refers to the printer's engine speed.

Resolution The level of detail that can be printed by a printer, indicated in dots per inch (dpi). Most businesses use a 300 or 600 dpi printer. 1,200 dpi models are available for those needing professional-quality output.

RISC (Reduced Instruction Set Computing) A type of processor that uses fewer instructions to complete the printing process. RISC processors can be much faster than ordinary processors.

Smoothing An image enhancement feature. With smoothing, the printer fills in the jagged edges of an image with small dots to create a smoother looking line.

Special tips

Printers vary greatly in their ability to handle heavy paper. While a printer may be equipped with a manual paper tray for such jobs, it is wise to check its capabilities before you buy.

Checking processor speed is especially important when considering a PostScript printer, since this complex language requires tremendous processing power for fast outputting.

An additional factor that contributes to printing speed is the printer's memory, or RAM. Particularly when printing complex graphics, equipping a printer with additional RAM can speed the printing process significantly.

Keep in mind that your warranty remains in effect even if you do not purchase consumables (toner, etc.) produced by the original manufacturer. This is required by law.

Hewlett-Packard has recently introduced a new printer language, called PCL6. More printers should be equipped with this language in the coming months.

Look for a printer that is Energy Star compliant. These printers should save you a modest amount in electricity bills each year and are likely to last longer, since lower energy usage translates to lower demands on the cooling system.

See also
Color Printers, Desktop Computers, Dot Matrix Printers, Ink-jet Printers, Multifunctional Devices, Notebook Computers, Portable Printers, Toner Supplies, Typewriters

For more information, visit
BuyersZone
http://www.buyerszone.com/

LCD Systems

*F*or many businesspeople, there is nothing more frightening than the prospect of a bad presentation. We fear boring our audience, losing our notes, and finding mistakes in the materials at the last minute.

In this war for attention, LCD (liquid crystal display) presentation systems have emerged as the newest high-caliber weapon. These systems project a computer screen's image onto a wall. With an LCD system, you can easily bring the power of a multimedia presentation to groups of any size.

Company	Headquarters	Phone number
ASK	Lyndhurst, NJ	800/ASK-LCD1
Buhl	Fairlawn, NJ	201/423-2800
Dukane	St. Charles, IL	800/676-2485
Eiki	Lake Forest, CA	800/242-3454
Epson	Torrance, CA	800/289-3776
In Focus	Wilsonville, OR	800/294-6400
NEC	Boxborough, MA	800/NEC-INFO
nView	Newport News, VA	800/775-7575
Proxima	San Diego, CA	800/447-7692
Sharp	Mahwah, NJ	800/237-4277

Buying points

Differences between panels and projectors

An LCD panel is a translucent screen surrounded by a plastic frame. The entire device is about the size of a hard-cover book and looks much like an Etch-A-Sketch. To use it, you simply place the LCD panel on an overhead projector and connect it to a computer. Light shines through the panel, projecting an image of the computer screen onto a wall or a screen.

LCD projectors are a more recent innovation, with the first models introduced just a few years ago. Essentially, these devices combine the functions of an LCD panel and an overhead projector into a single unit. The LCD projector sits on a table and projects a computer screen image for group viewing. The projector market has grown even faster than the panel market, with projectors making up 65% of the combined panel and projector market in 1995.

The main benefits of choosing a panel over a projector have always been greater portability and lower prices. Despite the maturing of projector technology, panels still weigh less, are smaller, and cost less than projectors.

As a result, panels are a good investment if you know that a quality overhead projector will always be available at your destination. However, many overhead projectors are not bright enough to work with an LCD panel.

For most other situations, projectors make more sense. Projectors are much less bulky than carrying both a panel and an overhead projector, and allow you to travel without worrying about what equipment is available at your destination.

What can be connected

LCD systems are primarily designed to work with a computer. They allow you to project presentations directly from a PC, using programs such as Microsoft PowerPoint. They can also be used to show anything that appears on a computer screen, serving as a group tutorial on how to use a specific program.

Many LCD systems can also accept video from a laser disc player, camcorder or VCR. If the system can be connected to both sources at once, you can easily alternate between video and computer images. This can create a very impressive show.

Brightness considerations

The brightness of a projection unit affects how easily images can be seen. Brightness is measured in terms of ANSI lumens, which range from about 100 on a dim model to over 400 for the brightest color models. If you need to project images in a well-lit room, look for projectors providing at least 300 ANSI lumens. Models rated at about 200 ANSI lumens are acceptable for presentation in a relatively dark room.

Similarly, the brightness of the overhead projector determines the appearance of images from an LCD panel. Overhead projectors should project a minimum of 4,000 lumens when used with an LCD panel.

Types of light sources

LCD projectors use a lamp to project a viewed image. There are currently two different types of lamps available: halogen lamps and metal halide lamps.

Halogen lamps are much less expensive than metal halide lamps, costing about $30 versus $400 for a metal halide model. However, halogen lamps tend to project a somewhat yellow-tinged light, which may be noticeable with images where color accuracy is very important. Metal halide lamps project a more blue-white light and last about 15 times as long as halogen lamps, making their high unit price more reasonable.

Showing color presentations

Many LCD systems are able to display one to two million colors at a time. This is fine for color bar charts or graphs, as well as short video clips. However, users concerned with projecting true-to-life video or still photos will want a system that offers a full palette of 16.7 million colors. Keep in mind, however, that many notebook computers cannot handle 16.7 million colors at once, so check the computer's output capabilities before buying.

Features to look for

One popular feature is a remote control. This allows the presenter to roam about the room while controlling what appears on the screen.

Many LCD panels and projectors can be equipped with speakers or audio outputs to complement a presentation. While internal speakers are louder and better sounding than notebook computer speakers, do not expect concert-quality sound. For higher-quality audio, most models can be connected to external speakers.

Finally, some models offer a zoom feature that enlarges a portion of the screen for detailed viewing.

Pricing

LCD systems range in price from under $1,000 to over $10,000. Low-end units typically do not offer audio or video capabilities, while high-end models offer bright images and can accept signals from a range of video and audio sources.

You can anticipate paying near list price for new models. Once a model has been on the market for a while, you can expect to get 10% to 15% off the list price if you are purchasing one unit, and as much as 20% off if you are buying in bulk (three or more machines). Prices vary among dealers so it usually pays to shop around.

Renting units costs $250 to $400 per day.

Terms

ANSI lumens An industry standard measurement of a LCD projector's brightness. Some companies still advertise non-ANSI lumens, but this term is relatively meaningless since reported measurements are not always comparable.

Image size The maximum size of a projected image. Most projectors are designed to display an 8-foot diagonal image, while some machines can project up to a 33-foot diagonal image.

Resolution The number of screen pixels that can be displayed by the LCD system. Most units have a resolution of 640 by 480 pixels, which projects a standard VGA computer screen. Higher-resolution models are useful if you need to project more of a screen, such as a full layout of a drawing or document.

Screen markup A feature that allows users to digitally draw on a screen to highlight areas of interest, much like an overhead marker.

Special tips

To eliminate the need to haul around a notebook computer, a few models offer memory presentation. This allows presentations to be stored within the unit and played without a computer. The presenter either inserts a disk into the machine or a PC card into a PCMCIA slot.

Make sure you thoroughly test an LCD system before you buy it. Rather than having a dealer set up the unit for you and show you how it works, do it yourself from beginning to end with the equipment you plan to use.

Project an image you are very familiar with, such as your company logo, so you can compare the image quality of different models. You should also try out each piece of equipment at several distances from the screen.

Look for a machine that is equipped with a separate remote; models that use a detachable control panel for their remote control put you at risk of disabling the whole machine if the remote is lost.

See also
Laser Pointers, Notebook Computers, Overhead Projectors, Slide Projectors

Letter Folding Equipment

Anyone who has manually folded invoices or brochures knows the prodigious amounts of time such tasks require. Letter folding equipment can help automate a very time-consuming part of the process, by providing a quick way to prepare materials for envelope stuffing.

PRICING

Type of letter folder	Price range
Personal folder	$200-$300
less than 20,000 sheets per hour	$600-$2,900
more than 20,000 sheets per hour	$1,000-$6,000

VENDORS

Company	Headquarters	Phone number
Ascom Hasler	Shelton, CT	800/243-6275
Duplo	Santa Ana, CA	800/255-1933
Francotyp-Postalia	Lisle, IL	800/341-6052
Martin Yale	Wabash, IN	219/563-0641
MBM	N. Charleston, SC	800/223-2508
Neopost	Hayward, CA	800/624-7892
P.F.E., Int'l.	Kennesaw, GA	800/949-7334
Pitney Bowes	Stamford, CT	800/672-6937
Profold	Sebastian, FL	800/770-3653

Buying points

Uses
Letter folding equipment helps minimize the amount of time spent by mailing departments or small businesses when preparing large volumes of outgoing mail. Letter folders are also useful for folding brochures or other materials.

Types of feeders
Low-end letter folding equipment is fed manually. With this equipment, a user can typically keep pace with a person stuffing envelopes. This can translate to a speed as fast as a couple hundred pieces per hour.

For larger volumes of mail, automated letter folders operate at speeds varying from 1,500 to more than 4,000 sheets per hour. These models typically incorporate an automatic paper feeder for faster operation.

Friction feeders move paper by using rubber wheels. This technology is relatively inexpensive, but can result in smudging when used with freshly printed sheets. Friction feeders also wear out with use, making them less practical for use in a high-volume production setting.

Vacuum, or air suction, feeders use air to pull paper into the folder. These feeders are much more effective in handling coated, glossy papers, and can be used quite effectively with newly printed papers. However, vacuum feeders tend to be quite expensive, and are generally only available on high-volume machines.

Paper handling
Letter folding machines can make numerous kinds of folds, including standard business letter folds (called a c-fold), accordion folds (a z-fold), double folds, single folds, right angle folds, and brochure folds.

Most machines can fold several sheets of paper together at one time. However, feeders usually have trouble handling stapled sheets. This means that you may need to feed stapled sheets through the folders by hand.

Features
Letter folders are fairly straightforward pieces of equipment. However, there are some features to look for that can help process mailings even more effectively.

A batch counter prevents the machine from folding more sheets than desired. Some models will automatically stop folding once a certain number of sheets have been run. There are also total counters available that can indicate how many sheets have already been folded, with stackers available to neatly hold the folded documents.

Inserters can help further automate the mailing process by inserting documents into envelopes. To ensure the appropriate forms are inserted in the right envelope, some folder/inserter models utilize optical mark recognition (OMR) technology. OMR-equipped models are particularly useful when sending invoices or statements of different page lengths to clients.

Companies that find they often need

to fold certain documents will find memory settings useful. These settings allow the user to record as many as fifteen custom folding jobs into memory to facilitate the processing of a recurring project. For example, this feature can be used to set paper guides when folding odd-sized jobs, which can be more practical than having to adjust the paper guides each time.

Pricing

Folders start at approximately $200 for a personal desktop model and are readily found in office superstores or mail order catalogs. Commercial folders are much more expensive, starting in the thousands of dollars, and are sold by mailing equipment vendors. As with other expensive pieces of mailroom equipment, high-end letter folders can also be leased from the manufacturer.

Terms

Accordion fold A fold that folds a page into thirds in the shape of a Z. Also known as a Z-fold.

Brochure fold A type of fold that reduces the paper to half its original size with two one-quarter folds on either side.

Double or double parallel fold A type of fold that denotes the sheet is folded back onto itself twice.

French fold A type of fold that indicates one vertical and then one horizontal fold. This usually requires two passes through a folding machine.

Letter fold Also known as a standard or c-fold, this folds a sheet into thirds, with the two end segments folded on top of one another.

Paper guides This feature aligns odd-sized paper stock for folding.

Special tips

Make sure to test equipment with the type of paper that will be folded. Models are not all equally adept at handling thin, glossy or carbonless paper.

Check how paper jams are handled. Better-designed machines can release rollers for easier access to the problematic sheet.

Friction paper feeders need regular maintenance for optimal performance. One key maintenance step is eliminating static which can cause sheets to stick together or wrap around the rollers. In addition, cleaning the rubber rollers will prevent them from cracking, and will remove ink and talc buildup that can cause feeding and folding problems.

A jogger helps align stacks of paper for folding and is recommended for dissipating static electricity.

If you will be renting or leasing folding equipment, find a dealer that offers a range of low- to high-end models. This will make it easier to obtain upgrades mid-way through your contract.

See also
Automatic Staplers, Letter Opening Equipment, Photocopiers

Letter Opening Equipment

While firms often spend thousands of dollars to automate their outgoing mailing operations, few companies put much thought into improving incoming mail operations. Yet dealing with incoming mail is often a very time-consuming process.

Automatic mail openers are designed to reduce the time spent opening incoming mail. They vary from handheld, battery-operated models to heavy duty desk models that can handle 600 envelopes per minute.

PRICING

Type of letter opener	Price range
Battery operated	$6-$20
Less than 300 envelopes per minute	$60-$1,700
More than 300 envelopes per minute	$700-$5,000

VENDORS

Company	Headquarters	Phone number	Chad	Slit
Ascom Hasler	Shelton, CT	800/243-6275	●	●
Boston (Hunt Mfg.)	Philadelphia, PA	800/283-1707	●	
Francotyp-Postalia	Lisle, IL	800/341-6052	●	
Martin Yale	Wabash, IN	219/563-0621		●
Neopost	Hayward, CA	510/489-6800		●
Omation	Mountain View, CA	415/966-1396	●	
Panasonic	Secaucus, NJ	201/348-7490	●	
Pitney Bowes	Stamford, CT	800/672-6937	●	

Letter Opening Equipment

Buying points

Types of letter openers
There are two types of letter openers: chadders and slitters.

Chadders use cutting wheels to slice off $1/8$ inch from the top of an envelope. These models tend to be fairly inexpensive, but run the risk of damaging the contents of an envelope.

Slitters work by cutting through the top seam of the envelope. Because this process is more complex than that used by chadders, slitters tend to be more expensive. Slitters typically command a $1,000 to $2,000 premium over equivalent chadder designs.

Durability
Automated mail openers are considered to be quite durable, and should not require a service contract. Service, when required, usually just involves fixing a jammed machine. To avoid service calls, you simply need to empty the unit's catch tray daily so the holding capacity is not exceeded. If your firm expects to process more than 2,000 pieces a day, make sure steps are in place to ensure that the tray is emptied at regular intervals during the day.

Larger mailing items
Most models are equipped to handle up to 6 x 10 inch (#10) envelopes. Higher end models can handle envelopes up to 9 x 12 inch in size and up to $3/8$ inch thick.

Features
Probably the most useful feature a company can look for is an automated feeder to convey pieces through the machine. Joggers can also be useful to settle the contents, minimizing the chance of having the tops of checks or other important materials sliced off.

For monitoring purposes, there are also counters available to count the number of pieces being processed each day. Firms may also like the ability to stamp incoming mail with the time or date to keep track of when mail has arrived.

Special tips

One way to reduce the cost of purchasing a letter opener is to find used or refurbished machinery. Pitney Bowes models tend to be the easiest to find in the used market, with reliable units available for as little as $800. Slitting machines tend to be much more difficult to find on the used market, since the technology is still relatively new.

Many models offer "feathering" cuts that reduce the likelihood of receiving painful paper cuts when emptying envelopes.

In addition to testing units with mixed size mail, try using openers with different materials ranging from regular paper to kraft to Tyvek envelopes.

See also
Postage Meters, Postal Scales

Did you know?

The average person will take nearly 15 minutes to open 100 letters by hand.

LONG DISTANCE SERVICE

U.S. businesses currently spend more than $70 billion per year for calling privileges, with the bulk of this amount going to long distance carriers. Finding a carrier and a program well-suited to your company's calling pattern can help save your company hundreds of dollars each year in long distance fees.

PRICING	
Number of minutes	Average cost per minute with a national carrier
250	15.0¢-24.6¢
500	15.0¢-24.6¢
1,000	15.0¢-24.6¢
2,500	14.6¢-24.3¢
5,000	14.6¢-22.3¢
10,000	14.0¢-22.0¢
25,000	13.0¢-21.0¢
50,000	12.8¢-21.1¢

VENDORS			
Company	Headquarters	Phone number	Market share (1995)
AT&T	Basking Ridge, NJ	800/222-0400	53%
Cable & Wireless	Sterling, VA	800/486-8686	1%
Frontier	Rochester, NY	800/836-8080	1%
LCI	McLean, VA	800/860-1020	1%
LDDS WorldCom	Jackson, MS	800/539-2000	5%
MCI	Washington, DC	800/950-5555	18%
Sprint	Overland Park, KS	800/877-4646	10%
Source: Federal Communications Commission			

Buying points

Choosing a carrier
There are literally hundreds of long distance carriers on the market, ranging from giants like AT&T to small, virtually unknown resellers.

For most smaller firms, the differences across carriers are fairly minor. You will generally get the same sound quality, service arrangements, and overseas access no matter what firm you choose. The biggest difference is for larger firms, since larger carriers are often better able to handle complex data communication requirements.

Price should be a primary consideration for companies looking for basic phone service. Rates vary depending on when you call, where you call, and how many calls you make. By looking for a program that is designed for your calling patterns, you can often save a substantial amount on charges.

To get a sense for rates, examine a recent phone bill. You will be able to get a sense for your overall calling pattern, as well as the average cost per minute. Then learn about programs from other carriers to see how your rates might improve.

Service considerations
While price is important, you must also make sure that a long distance provider offers the service you need.

The first thing to check is the hours of technical and operator support. Some firms only offer support during business hours, which can create problems if your firm often works evenings or nights. If you use services such as collect calling or operator-assisted international dialing, make sure that operators are available when you need them.

It is generally very difficult to assess the likelihood of a major network failure. If you are very concerned about the prospect of calling problems, you may want to split your traffic across two different carriers. An alternate solution is to keep access codes for different carriers to use in emergency situations.

Switching carriers
Once you decide which program you want to join, you simply need to contact the long distance provider. The carrier will handle the process of notifying the local provider about switching lines. It should take about a week to become established with a new carrier. This switch should not be noticeable by anyone except your accounting department.

If you ask, your new carrier will often cover the cost to switch, which is typically $5 per line. In addition, carriers often provide a 30 or 60 day satisfaction guarantee, which includes a free switch back to the original carrier if you are dissatisfied with the new service.

Comparing programs
To compare calling plans with different rate structures, you will need to calculate your effective cost per minute. Examine a recent telephone

bill and add the total number of minutes spent on direct-dialed interstate long distance calls. Then, calculate your total interstate and monthly charges, making sure to exclude any taxes and international, intrastate, and calling card calls. Divide the cost into your total number of calling minutes to determine your effective cost per minute. This figure can then be used in comparisons with other programs.

Negotiating better rates

Getting a better deal for your company simply requires asking for additional discounts. Depending on the size of your account, you will have varying success in negotiating lower rates or waived fees. If you run into resistance, you may be able to negotiate by guaranteeing a minimum monthly call volume or agreeing to use the carrier for a set number of years. However, such commitments on your part should be entered into judiciously.

You may have more luck if you work with one sales rep assigned to your account rather than a customer service representative; often, sales reps have more authority to approve special discounts.

Pricing

Your usage and per minute rates most directly affect the charges you will pay. Long distance carriers offer their best customers a rate of about 10¢ per minute; you should keep this in mind while researching different programs.

There may also be monthly charges that can range from $5 to $25 per month. Often, these charges are waived if a minimum billing level is attained.

Terms

Access codes A five digit code that can be dialed to access a specific carrier's network for outgoing calls. Also known as a 10XXX code.

Banded rate program A calling program that bills varying per-minute rates according to the distance a call travels. As a result, a business will pay less for a call to a neighboring state than one going to a distant state. Banded plans can be efficient for businesses that make most of their calls within the local region.

Dedicated service A type of long distance service offered to high-volume customers that requires installing a dedicated telephone line to the long distance provider's network. Dedicated service costs less per minute than regular switched service, but commands high installation fees.

Flat rate program A calling program that bills the same per-minute rate for all domestic calls. This type of plan can be particularly cost-effective for businesses that place calls to destinations all across the country.

Off-peak rate The rate charged during non-business hours. Some companies have multiple off-peak rates, with different prices for evening and night-time/weekend calls.

Long Distance Service

Peak rate The rate charged during regular business hours. These are typically the highest rates for a given program. Peak hours are not defined consistently across carriers; companies should check how they are defined before signing up with a carrier.

Switched service A long distance plan that uses regular phone lines for placing calls. Outbound calls must be "switched" by your local provider to access the long distance carrier of your choice.

Special tips

Never agree to sign up for a plan without getting written information about the program. It can be quite difficult to get full disclosure about rates, discounts, and monthly charges over the phone.

If you negotiate any special discounts or waivers for your account, make sure to get them in writing. You can turn to this document in the event that they are not honored.

If you rarely make operator-assisted calls, you can save money by subscribing to a carrier that does not offer this service.

Access codes allow you to make phone calls using another carrier's network if your long distance lines go down. Simply dial the access code for a carrier like AT&T (10288), MCI (10222), or Sprint (10333) and then dial the number directly. You will be billed for these calls by your local telephone carrier. However, do not use these lines regularly, as the rates are quite high.

Reevaluate your service every 12 months; programs change rapidly, and a great deal last year may no longer be such a good buy.

Larger firms can cut their long distance calling costs by installing a T1 line, or dedicated line, which provides twenty-four direct connections to your long distance carrier. Dedicated service rates are 3¢ to 4¢ lower per minute than regular switched service, but upfront installation charges can be quite costly. Dedicated lines are generally recommended for companies spending $5,000 or more a month on long distance calling.

Think your lines were "slammed," or switched to another carrier without your authorization? You can dial 700/555-4141 to learn which long distance carrier is serving your phone lines.

See also
900 Service, Calling Cards, Cellular Service, Conference Calling Services, International Callback, International Calling, Prepaid Phone Cards, Toll Free Service

For more information, visit
BuyersZone
http://www.buyerszone.com/

LTL Shipping

*S*mall package delivery services such as UPS are not equipped to handle especially heavy or bulky deliveries. For these items, businesses usually turn to less than truckload (LTL) carriers. These companies commonly ship items weighing 600 to 1,000 pounds, and can be relied on for delivering packages up to 10,000 pounds.

VENDORS

Company	Headquarters	Phone number	Automated rate information
ABF	Fort Smith, AR	800/346-3617	800/367-2237
Consolidated Freightways	Menlo Park, CA	415/326-1700	NA
Conway Transportation Systems	Menlo Park, CA	415/854-7500	NA
Freightways	Rosemont, IL	800/USE-TNT-0	NA
Nationsway	Denver, CO	800/822-NWTP	800/822-NWTP
Overnite	Richmond, VA	804/231-8000	800/368-5035
Roadway Express	Akron, OH	800/ROADWAY	800/ROADWAY
Yellow Freight	Overland Park, KS	800/610-6500	800/610-6500

Buying points

How the market works
The LTL market is very fragmented and competitive, with profitability very dependent on delivery efficiency. As a result, LTL carriers typically operate through a hub system. An LTL carrier picks up packages from multiple customers, transports these items to a local terminal, and then consolidates goods traveling the same route.

Many LTL carriers only serve specific geographic regions, which increases the chance of conveying full loads. If a shipment is sent to a location outside a carrier's normal service area, the trucking company will arrange to transfer the shipment from the edge of its service area to another LTL for final delivery. This practice is called interlining.

Finding a reliable carrier
With so many different LTL carriers on the market, it can be difficult to know which one to choose. However, there are several industry measurements that you can use as a proxy for reliability.

The first consideration, particularly for longer distance shipments, is the delivery schedule and the number of times the package will be interlined. Longer shipping times and more interlining often suggest that a shipper cannot efficiently deliver your shipment. This may result in higher costs, and creates more opportunities for something to go wrong during interline transfers.

A second statistic to consider is on-time delivery. This indicates how often a firm meets its declared delivery schedule. A good firm will typically quote on-time delivery rates in the mid to high nineties.

A final area to examine is the claims/damage ratio. This ratio measures the percentage of revenue paid out in claims for problems caused by loss, damage or theft. The industry average is 1.25% to 1.4%. You should use a company with a similar or lower ratio.

Available features
One of the most popular features offered by LTL carriers is expedited delivery, the shipping industry's equivalent of a rush job. To deliver packages faster, carriers bypass their hubs, which decreases shipping time but adds substantially to the overall cost.

Another popular feature is shipment tracking. Shippers that offer tracking services have radio networks that keep all trucks in constant communication with headquarters. This allows the carrier to locate your shipment at any time.

Saving money on LTL shipping
When using an LTL shipper, always ask for a discount. Simply asking can save you up to 15%, even on single shipments. For firms that ship large amounts, discounts of 35% to 60% are not uncommon.

Companies that do not frequently use LTL carriers can access higher levels of savings by combining their shipping volume with other companies, either by joining a shippers association, such as Merchant Shippers Cooperative Association (603/226-0144) or NASSTRAC (202/393-5505).

Another option is to use a logistics management company. These companies place shipments and negotiate discounts based on the total shipping volume of their client base.

Pricing

Determining delivery charges for LTL shipments is much more complex than for small packages. In addition to the weight of the shipment and the distance it must travel, you must also specify a shipping classification. Shipments are classified on a scale from 50 to 500, according to a package's density, value, fragility, and storage requirements, with higher numerical ratings indicating higher per pound transportation costs. To learn the class of your shipment, you can consult an LTL carrier or you can purchase the *National Motor Freight Classification* listing through the American Trucking Association (703/838-1700).

The final cost will include accessorial charges. These are extra charges for services such as storage, contacting the recipient, or delivery to companies without loading docks.

Terms

Consignee The intended recipient of the package.

Truckload carriers These carriers focus on shipments that fill an entire truck or specially-designed trailer.

Special Tips

Cost-effective alternatives to LTL shipping are the Multiweight and Hundredweight programs offered by RPS and UPS. These programs offer a discount for multiple packages totaling 200 pounds or more that are all going to the same address. As long as each package meets individual UPS/RPS size requirements, you will get 10% to 20% off the regular UPS/RPS rates. This is often cheaper than sending a full pallet via an LTL carrier, although you will need to individually label and pack each box.

If packages need to arrive at their destination in a hurry, consider using an air freight forwarder. These services specialize in the immediate delivery of heavyweight goods via air. Companies are often able to secure a much better rate for delivery than if they were to work through a branded national overnight delivery service.

Routing guides can help you identify which carriers serve a particular area. *The American Motor Carrier Directory* (800/547-8753) and the *National Highway Carriers Directory* (847/634-0606) offer guides that cover the nation. If you only need information on one city, consult the *Official Motor Freight Guide* (800/621-4650).

Establishing an account can reduce costs. Not only will you get discounts, but you are also billed later instead of having to pay in advance. This can be helpful if a problem arises with your shipment.

If you have to ship goods more than 1,000 miles, you may want to consider a national LTL carrier over a regional carrier. These firms offer the advantage of not having to interline packages traveling long distances.

See also
Ground Shipping, Overnight Delivery Services, Postal Scales, Same Day Delivery Services

For more information, visit
BuyersZone
http://www.buyerszone.com/

MODEMS

A modem is a device that allows computers to communicate over ordinary phone lines. Modems convert the digital signals of a computer into audio tones, giving you the ability to transfer data and access online information.

VENDORS

Company	Headquarters	Phone number	Faxback number	Warranty	Toll free technical support
AT&T	Largo, FL	800/482-3333	800/870-2221	2 yr.	●
Boca Research	Boca Raton, FL	407/997-6227	407/995-9456	5 yr.	
Global Village	Sunnyvale, CA	800/736-4821	800/890-4562	5 yr.	
Hayes	Norcross, GA	770/840-9200	800/429-3739	2 yr.	
Megahertz	Skokie, IL	800/527-8677	800/527-8677	5 yr.	
Microcom	Norwood, MA	800/822-8224	800/285-2802	5 yr.	
Motorola	Schaumburg, IL	800/668-6765	800/221-4380	5 yr.	●
Multi-tech	Mounds View, MN	800/328-9717	612/717-5888	2-10 yr.	●
Practical Peripherals	Norcross, GA	770/840-9966	800/225-4774	lifetime	
Supra	Albany, OR	800/774-4965	541/967-0072	5 yr.	
Telebit	Chelmsford, MA	800/835-3248	NA	2 yr.	●
U.S. Robotics-Corporate	Skokie, IL	800/877-2677	800/762-6163	5 yr.	●
U.S. Robotics-Personal	Skokie, IL	800/342-5877	800/762-6163	5 yr.	●
Xircom	Thousand Oaks, CA	800/438-4526	800/775-0400	lifetime	
Zoom	Boston, MA	800/631-3116	617/423-4651	7 yr.	

Buying points

Uses for modems

Modems are rapidly becoming a critical accessory for almost all computers. Businesses commonly use modems to share files and data with other offices or to allow employees using notebook computers on the road to log into the office network.

Even if you never leave the office, modems can be used to access commercial online services or the Internet. With a modem, users can also send or receive e-mail, download data or search online databases.

Types of modems

The oldest type of modem, called an acoustic modem, broadcasts and receives tones through a telephone handset. Although relatively uncommon today, acoustic modems are still used by travelers who need to connect from places (such as a pay phone) where no phone jack is available.

External modems are housed in a small box outside the computer. This design tends to be easy to set up, but occupies a serial port on the computer, reducing your ability to add other components. In addition, high-speed modems often have trouble maintaining a fast transfer rate on computers with older serial ports. To avoid this, make sure the computer has a UART 16550 chip controlling the serial port.

Internal modems are designed to fit into an expansion slot inside the computer. They can be somewhat difficult to set up, but are less expensive than external models and sit conveniently out of the way once installed. Most do not work with notebook computers, although a few internal modems are available for specific notebook designs.

PC Card (also called PCMCIA) modems slip into a small slot found on the side of most notebook computers. PC Card modems are very small and lightweight, and do not require their own source of power. Despite their small size, PC Card modems are just as fast as full-sized modems, although they tend to be a bit more fragile.

ISDN "modems" use digital ISDN lines to send and receive data. These can operate about five times as fast as a regular modem, but require ISDN phone service in order to work.

Other technologies currently being developed use cable television wires or satellite transmission to send and receive data. Although these technologies are still in the testing phases, they promise much faster modem speeds in the future.

Using modems with cellular phones

As telecommunications have expanded to encompass more than phone lines, so have modem technologies.

The wireless modem is a relatively new, but expensive, type of modem that operates via radio waves. Some wireless modems use cellular frequencies, while others utilize the new PCS band for wireless communication. If you occasionally need to send data over the airways, many regular modems can be connected to a cellular phone for wireless communication.

Compatibility among different brands

Modem communication standards are set by the International Telecommunication Union (ITU), and are backed by virtually all industry manufacturers. Virtually all current modems adhere to at least some of the ITU standards.

Modems can transmit at speeds ranging from 300 to 33,600 bits per second (bps). When modems first connect they automatically identify and work at the fastest protocol that both modems can understand.

Currently, the fastest ITU protocol is called V.34. This protocol offers 28,800 bps sending and receiving. A 33,600 bps protocol is expected to be approved in the near future.

Faxmodems

Adding fax capabilities to a modem costs only a few dollars. As a result, most modems sold today come with built-in fax capabilities.

However, most faxmodems are not very well suited for frequent faxing. Because fax capability is considered an extra, most manufacturers do not test their faxmodems extensively with other fax machines. It is estimated that faxmodems have trouble connecting to about 10% of all standalone fax machines due to minor incompatibilities. Dedicated fax servers have much better success rates, but cost a minimum of $700.

Even if you have better success with your faxmodem, you may still need to have a standalone fax machine in the office. While computer-generated documents can easily be sent from a faxmodem, other items must be scanned into the computer before sending, which can be a cumbersome process.

Pricing

Since data has a way of rapidly expanding, it generally makes sense to invest in a very fast modem. If you expect to send large files or access information on the World Wide Web, get a 28,800 bps modem. These cost about $200 currently, but give you the fastest speeds possible over standard telephone lines.

Modems that run at 14,400 bps cost under $100, and offer decent speed for most files.

Although they may be quite inexpensive, avoid modems that operate at speeds of 9,600 bps or less, as they are much too slow. In most cases, you will not even save very much money.

Terms

Bits The fundamental unit used by a computer to store data. Bits are expressed as a 1 or 0. A modem's speed is expressed in terms of how many bits can be transferred per second.

Modulation The process by which modem changes the digital signals from a computer into analog sound waves. Regular phone lines are incapable of conveying digital signals, which means that a modem is needed

Modems

to convert signals to analog waves and then, on the receiving end, reconvert them to digital signals. The word modem derives from this process of MOdulation and DEModulation.

Proprietary protocols Sending and receiving protocols that are not approved by the ITU. Modems using these protocols often cannot communicate with most other modems at high speed. "Dual standard" modems are equipped with both proprietary and ITU protocols.

Throughput The total amount of data that can be transferred per second when factoring in the effects of data compression. Few modems can achieve their maximum throughput, since telephone lines and file density limit the speed and degree of compression. Most V.34 modems promise throughput of 115,200 bps, although a few manufacturers claim rates of more than twice as much using proprietary compression techniques. In practice, you are quite unlikely to hit even the 115,200 bps threshold.

Special tips

Avoid modems that communicate at 28,800 bps, but are not "true" V.34 modems. These models use the older V.FC protocol, which differs slightly from the V.34 standard. Because many modems do not recognize V.FC, you may fail to connect at speeds of more than 14,400 bps.

To operate a modem, you must have communication software. Most modems come packaged with software, but you may want to consider other programs to take advantage of easier-to-use menus and features. Also, most online services will send you free software that allows you to use their service more efficiently.

Avoid unknown modem manufacturers. Inexpensive no-name models may not have been thoroughly tested with your software and computer, which can lead to compatibility problems. In most cases, name brand vendors offer very competitive prices on their low-end modems.

Most modems come with two-year to lifetime warranties. However, modems are very unlikely to break. Most of your problems will arise from software incompatibility issues.

If you use a modem to receive faxes, make sure to regularly delete your unwanted files. Fax files can take up a tremendous amount of hard drive space.

See also
Desktop Computers, E-mail Services, Fax Machines, Internet Service Providers, ISDN, Notebook Computers, Video Conferencing Services, World Wide Web Site Setup

Monitors

*I*n the old days of text-based programs, monitors were not a particularly important purchase. Most computer users could be adequately served by a 12-inch monochrome monitor, like those sold with most early IBM PCs.

However, the emergence of graphical operating systems such as Microsoft Windows has created a demand for bigger color monitors. Larger monitors can dramatically improve productivity by allowing the user to view more on the screen at one time. As a result, many firms are finding it worthwhile to upgrade their monitors.

Company	Headquarters	Phone number	Mac	PC
ADI	San Jose, CA	408/944-0100		•
AOC	Milpitas, CA	800/343-5777		•
CTX	Walnut, CA	800/888-2120		•
Goldstar	Englewood, NJ	201/816-2000		•
MAG InnoVision	Santa Ana, CA	800/827-3998	•	•
Mitsubishi	Cypress, CA	800/843-2515	•	•
Nanao (Eizo)	Torrance, CA	310/325-5202	•	•
NEC	Boxborough, MA	800/NEC-INFO	•	•
Panasonic	Secaucus, NJ	800/742-8086	•	•
Philips/Magnavox	Knoxville, TN	800/835-3506	•	•
Radius	Sunnyvale, CA	800/227-2795	•	
Samsung	Ridgefield Park, NJ	800/SAMSUNG	•	•
Samtron	Ridgefield, NJ	800/SAMTRON		•
Sony	Paramus, NJ	800/352-7669	•	•
ViewSonic	Walnut, CA	800/888-8583	•	•

Buying points

Sizes of monitors

Monitor size generally refers to the diagonal measurement of the screen. Screens are typically grouped into five categories: 14 inch, 15 inch, 17 inch, 19 inch, and 20/21 inch screens.

Unfortunately, this diagonal measurement does not translate to the size of the image you actually see. A significant amount of the screen is hidden behind the monitor's plastic frame, or bezel. If you actually measure the exposed glass, it is usually about 0.5 to 1 inch less than the advertised size.

In addition, most manufacturers set the display so it does not reach the very edge of the exposed glass. This is because it is technically difficult to obtain a sharp picture in the corners. The resulting black border takes up additional screen space, often reducing the picture size by as much as two inches when compared to the listed screen size.

How resolution affects what is seen

To get a true understanding of what you will actually be able to see on the monitor, you need to know about the resolutions the monitor can display. The resolution refers to the amount of an image you can see on a screen without scrolling. It is measured in pixels, which are the individual dots of light making up the picture.

Virtually all monitors can show VGA resolution. This is the most common standard for video cards, offering a picture that consists of 640 pixels horizontally and 480 pixels vertically. While VGA offers adequate resolution for basic word processing, it falls short for users who work with multiple windows, complex spreadsheets or large graphics.

To accommodate the need to view more information on a screen, manufacturers have developed so-called "super-VGA" video standards. These show resolutions ranging anywhere from 800 x 600 up to 1600 x 1280 pixels. With super-VGA standards, users can see dozens of additional spreadsheet rows, or as many as two full pages displayed simultaneously. Most of today's monitors are capable of displaying VGA and at least one super-VGA resolution, with larger monitors capable of supporting higher resolutions.

Types of screens

There are three types of screens on the market: spheroid, flat-square, and cylindrical.

Spheroid screens place all points an equal distance from the electron gun. The tubes are inexpensive, but are difficult to view up close, since the middle of the screen bulges noticeably.

Flat-square screens have become the dominant design for higher-end monitors. These screens are not really flat, but are based on a design that greatly reduces the amount of screen curvature.

The cylindrical design shapes the screen as a section of a cylinder. This results in a screen that curves left to right, but does not curve up and down.

The advantage of this design is that it tends to have less of a problem with glare, since most light comes from overhead. Trinitron and Diamondtron are the most common brand names for cylindrical screens.

Available features
No matter what monitor you choose, you want to make sure you have enough controls to properly adjust the picture.

Among the most basic controls are contrast and brightness. These adjust the intensity of the displayed image, and can be useful for adapting the monitor for viewing in well-lit or dark rooms.

Other critical controls include adjustments for horizontal and vertical centering and size. These are needed to ensure that your picture is centered and has the appropriate horizontal and vertical proportions.

Less critical controls include pincushion controls, which allow you to modify the width of the center of the screen versus the top and bottom; trapezoid controls, which tilt the left and right edges in and out; parallelogram and rotation controls, which minimize the distortion of the entire image; convergence controls, which sharpen the focus by making sure the electron beams line up correctly for each dot; and complex color controls, which adjust the appearance of colors on the screen.

Purchasing a monitor
There are dozens of vendors you can turn to for a monitor. The market includes a relatively confusing mix of familiar brands and unfamiliar suppliers. Many of the best selling brands of monitors are sold by computer firms such as IBM, Dell, Gateway, and Compaq. Although some computer vendors make their own monitors, most reliable monitors from less well-known sources. In fact, a list of major monitor manufacturers includes relatively unfamiliar names such as CTX, MAG, Radius, and ViewSonic.

Monitors are sold via computer stores, office equipment stores, mail order, and value added resellers.

Monitor compatibility
Monitors must be compatible with the video card (or video output) used in your computer. Most modern monitors are multifrequency models, meaning that they can accept signals from many different video cards. As a result, you will rarely run into incompatibility problems. Older, single frequency monitors can only handle a specific video signal, and are unlikely to work with most video cards.

Macintosh computers use different video signals than most Windows PCs. As a result, you should check that the monitor is compatible with Macintosh video before purchasing. You may also need to buy an adapter for the plug, since Macs and PCs use different video connectors.

Pricing
Decent 14-inch monitors start at about $300, while 15-inch equivalents are about $50 more. Seventeen-inch monitors are significantly more expensive than 15-inch models, starting at about

$600. Larger 19- to 21-inch screens have street prices ranging from about $1,300 to $2,500.

Terms

Aperture grill   A metal mask found inside a monitor that determines the spacing between the dots of light on a screen. Many less expensive monitors use an iron aperture grill, which tends to heat up and distort the image. A newer type of aperture grill, the Invar shadow mask, does not distort upon heating.

Cathode ray tube (CRT)   A glass tube which is the main component of a monitor. One end of the CRT serves as the monitor screen. At the back end of the CRT is an electron gun which fires a beam of electrons at the screen to display images.

Dot pitch   The unit of measurement indicating how closely dots of the same color are spaced on the screen. A smaller dot pitch gives a sharper appearance, while a larger figure will result in a fairly fuzzy picture. Most monitors have a dot pitch of 0.28 millimeters.

Vertical refresh rate   The rate at which the full screen is redrawn, in cycles per second or hertz (Hz). When a monitor has a low refresh rate, the image appears to flicker. Anything over 72 Hz is considered fine, with 75 or 80 Hz considered quite good.

Special tips

Ignore the high refresh rates promised by interlaced displays. These rates are accomplished by refreshing every other line on each pass, rather than each line. This results in dramatic flickering and rapid "jumping" of thin horizontal lines.

Regardless of the monitor size you select, look for a cylindrical screen or a flat-square screen with Invar shadow mask, a dot pitch of 0.28 mm or better, and a minimum 72 Hz vertical refresh rate in every resolution you expect to use. For large 20- or 21-inch monitors, a dot pitch of 0.30 or 0.31 is acceptable.

Make sure to examine the model you are considering back in your office, as lighting and magnetic fields can have a profound effect on the appearance of the screen.

Although a warranty might provide a long term of coverage, it may take weeks for a monitor to be repaired. Ideally, the warranty will provide for a replacement unit or a full exchange in the event of a breakdown.

One new alternative to traditional monitors are flat screens similar to those found on a notebook computer. Flat screens are currently more than $4,000, but offer very high resolution and refresh rates.

See also
Desktop Computers, Notebook Computers

Multifunctional Devices

*M*ultifunctional devices combine the functionality of several different pieces of office equipment into a single machine. Instead of purchasing a separate fax, copier, scanner, and printer, offices can buy a single machine to perform all these functions.

VENDORS

Company	Headquarters	Phone number	Ink-jet	Laser/ LED	Thermal transfer	PC	Mac
Brother	Somerset, NJ	800/284-4329		●		●	●
Canon	Costa Mesa, CA	800/848-4123	●			●	
Hewlett-Packard	Palo Alto, CA	800/752-0900	●			●	●
JetFax	Menlo Park, CA	800/753-8329		●		●	
Kodak	Rochester, NY	800/255-3434		●		●	●
Konica	Windsor, CT	800/256-6422		●		●	●
Lanier	Atlanta, GA	800/708-7088		●		●	●
Minolta	Ramsey, NJ	800/9-MINOLTA		●		●	●
Mita	Fairfield, NJ	800/ABC-MITA		●		●	
Panasonic	Secaucus, NJ	800/742-8086		●		●	
Ricoh	West Caldwell, NJ	201/637-4264	●	●		●	
Savin	Stamford, CT	203/967-5000		●		●	
Sharp	Mahwah, NJ	800/237-4277		●		●	
Toshiba	Irvine, CA	800-GO-TOSHIBA		●	●	●	
Xerox	Rochester, NY	800/TEAM-XRX	●	●		●	●

Buying points

How MFDs work

Multifunctional devices (MFDs) combine several core technologies, including image scanning, document printing, and fax signaling, into a single unit. Depending on how the technologies are combined, a multifunctional device can perform a variety of functions. For example, connecting the MFD to a computer allows you to scan and print. If you scan a document and then print the resulting digital image, the MFD acts as a copier. And by scanning, printing, and using fax hardware, the MFD can serve as a fax machine.

Different categories of MFDs

Multifunctional devices fall into three categories. Low-end devices are generally designed for small offices and home offices. These machines are typically built around a fax machine, but connect to a computer for scanning and printing. They can also be used as a convenience copier for items that can feed through the fax scanner.

Mid-range MFDs are based around a small copier. These machines include a book platen for copying magazines, books, or other three-dimensional items. They also connect to a computer for printing and scanning, and can send and receive faxes if attached to a phone line. These units are ideal for small workgroups, where workers can reduce the time needed to walk to larger office machines.

High-end MFDs combine copying and printing functions into a single unit. These units offer extremely fast printing, plus sorting and finishing options (such as stapling) normally not found on printers. The idea behind these machines is to provide copier-like functionality from a desktop computer, reducing the need for people to print a document and then walk it over to the copier to make multiple sets.

MFD vs. standalone machines

There are many reasons to purchase a multifunctional device. First, MFDs are less expensive than many separate pieces of office equipment. With fewer machines, you benefit from lower supply and maintenance costs because fewer consumables and service plans are needed.

On the downside, MFDs are not always able to match the performance of their standalone competitors. For example, MFD printers are not always able to handle envelopes and labels as well as a standalone printer. They also typically lack the variety of paper trays you might expect from a similar printer model.

In terms of copying, most low-end MFDs lack basic copier features such as sorters and zoom. In addition, the image quality does not tend to be as good as that from standalone copiers, since most fax-based scanners only capture about 200 dots of information per inch.

As scanners, MFDs typically do not offer the resolution you would expect from a standalone model. Scans tend to be adequate for simple images and text, but poor for photos and other detailed images.

MFDs function quite well as fax machines. However, you should check the transmission speed and memory levels.

Where to purchase an MFD
MFDs can be purchased from mail order vendors, superstores, warehouse clubs or dealers.

In general, you will only find low-end MFDs from mail order vendors and superstores. MFDs with book platen copying are typically only found through office equipment dealers.

Pricing
Low-end MFDs cost anywhere from $600 for a basic ink-jet model to about $4,000 for a fast model based around a laser printer engine. Mid-range MFDs cost anywhere from $2,500 to $7,000. High-end MFDs, consisting of digital copier/printers, cost anywhere from $20,000 to $60,000.

Terms

Book platen The flat area of glass found on the top of photocopiers through which images are copied. A book platen allows users to copy items that are thicker than a sheet of paper. Many MFDs do not have a book platen, requiring items to go through a sheet feeder to be copied.

OCR (optical character recognition) software Software that is designed to read text from a scanned image. With OCR software, users can convert paper documents into word processor files and avoid having to retype the entire document.

PC-based faxing A type of faxing that allows users to fax documents directly from the desktop. PC-based faxing saves the effort of printing and then walking to the fax machine to send a document.

Pixels per inch (ppi) A measurement used to indicate the resolution of a scanner. Most MFDs scan at 200 ppi to 600 ppi.

Special tips

For faxing, be sure the MFD is equipped with at least 0.5 megabytes (MB) of standard memory. This is enough to hold about 25 pages.

One quick way to assess copy quality is by looking at the MFD's copy resolution. A copying resolution of 400 dpi should be reasonable, while 200 dpi copies will be relatively poor. Also make sure to try copying a few documents, paying particular attention to how large dark objects and fine lines are reproduced.

The most popular OCR programs include Xerox TextBridge (800/248-6550) and Caere OmniPage (800/535-7226). If neither is included with the MFD, you should check that one of these programs will work with the unit.

If you are looking for color printing capabilities, some low-end ink-jet models offer color printing at a very low price premium.

See also
Color Printers, Fax Machines, Ink-jet Printers, Laser Printers, Modems, Scanners

For more information, visit
BuyersZone
http://www.buyerszone.com/

Music on Hold Systems

*T*he message/music on hold (MOH) industry began in 1979 with the goal of decreasing the number of callers that hang up on a firm while on hold. MOH systems are a good way to keep buyers on the line during busy periods, and can even be an effective way to promote your products or services.

VENDORS				
Company	Headquarters	Phone number	Digital	Tape
Audiomax	Blue Bell, PA	800/284-HOLD	●	
Creative Audio Network	Ashville, NC	800/467-9552	●	
Custom On-Hold Services	Bothell, WA	800/950-8996		●
GM Productions	Atlanta, GA	800/827-DEMO	●	
Marketing Messages	Newton, MA	800/4-VOICES	●	
Muzak	Seattle, WA	800/331-3340		●
On-Hold America	Ocala, FL	800/860-2863	●	
Speak-EZ Productions	Sherman Oaks, CA	800/723-4272	●	●
Telecorp Systems	Roswell, GA	800/347-9907	●	
Telephonetics	Miami, FL	800/4-HOLD-ON	●	
Thank You For Holding	Los Angeles, CA	800/345-5060		●

Buying points

Phone system compatibility
Message on hold (MOH) systems are designed to work with phone systems that have a MOH port. This means that virtually all PBX and key phone systems can accept an MOH system. MOH ports are less common with smaller KSU-less phone systems and are not available with regular telephones.

There are adapters available that can connect an MOH system to a phone system without a suitable port. However, these work with varying levels of success.

Differences in technology
MOH systems can be broadly grouped as using either analog or digital recording technology.

Analog tape players comprise the oldest type of MOH equipment. These systems use endless loop tapes to play messages. Although these systems are generally inexpensive, they do suffer from lower-quality sound, particularly as tapes wear from repeated use. As a result, few vendors continue to sell analog systems.

Digital systems play music that is digitally recorded onto a hard drive or encoded into memory. Since the recorded information is not susceptible to mechanical wear, the sound quality does not degrade after repeated playback.

Digital systems also provide more flexibility in acquiring new programs. These models can play prerecorded CDs, download programs over the phone, or load music into memory from a cassette tape.

When comparing digital systems, make sure to check the sampling rate used to record programs. The sampling rate directly impacts the quality of the resulting playback, with a higher sampling rate resulting in better sound quality. Look for a system which records at a minimum rate of 64 kilobytes per second (Kbps).

Messaging options
Firms using MOH systems can choose to play music, messages, or a combination of both to waiting callers. Programs are generally 4 to 6 minutes in length, although large call centers may choose programs as long as 32 minutes in length.

Prerecorded programs and music are generally the least expensive way to entertain callers. Customized recordings carry a higher price tag, but can be recorded to include information about your firm's current offerings.

When playing music, it is critical that all copyright licenses are secured. Otherwise, you risk being subject to fines for illegally broadcasting music without a license. Fines for copyright infringement range from $500 to $100,000 per musical piece.

Most MOH companies will take care of any licensing issues for prerecorded programs. They are less likely to help in securing a license to play a radio station since much of their revenues are derived from producing programs.

BMI (615/401-2000) and ASCAP (212/621-6400) represent the music industry and can provide information about licensing requirements.

Obtaining programs

Over time, the cost of new programs often exceeds the initial cost of the MOH unit. As a result, you should be sure that the firm you use can provide music or messages that you find useful.

One way to increase your MOH options is to choose a system based on open standards. This means that the system can use programs from many different vendors. Although proprietary systems are not necessarily any worse, they significantly limit the range of choices you have when buying new programs.

You should also examine the programming capabilities of the MOH vendor. Do they allow you to choose specific songs or voice talents? Do they have in-house recording studios to record your customized messages?

Also ask about the policies for purchasing programs. Some vendors require you to sign yearly contracts that may provide more programs than your firm actually needs. Find out how flexible the firm is with program contracts, including provisions for future pricing levels.

Pricing

MOH systems cost anywhere from a few hundred dollars to about a thousand dollars. In addition, you will need to pay for programming. The frequency and level of customization desired will affect programming costs. Costs for each program can range from $75 to a few hundred dollars.

Special tips

Do not assume the MOH vendor will be responsible for clearing licenses for the programs they produce—make sure to ask. If the firm clears licensing issues, make sure this responsibility is stated in the contract so you can avoid liability in the event problems do arise.

Before you begin playing a radio station on your MOH system, check that your competitors do not advertise on the station. You do not want to provide any unintended advertising benefits for your competitors.

If you sign up for a package of multiple programs, make sure to keep track of the commitment. Some vendors do not issue updates until they are prompted to do so.

Ask to hear samples of the professional voices that an MOH vendor utilizes before signing up. You should be satisfied with these choices or risk paying extra to hire outside help.

Avoid using music behind your voice tracks. It can distract your customers, and they may miss instructions or the message you wish to convey.

See also
Telephone Systems, Voice Mail Systems

NOTEBOOK COMPUTERS

Notebook computers have become a virtual necessity for anyone who travels on business. A notebook computer can easily fit in a briefcase, allowing you to take presentations, documents or spreadsheets on the road. Notebook computers can also serve as a mobile communication center, sending faxes and e-mail from almost any phone jack.

In fact, notebook computers are getting to be so powerful that they are frequently being used in place of full-sized desktop computers in the office. Improved keyboards and screens mean that users now give up very little in comfort, while the small size and portability of notebook PCs means that businesspeople can easily take their work home with them.

VENDORS

Company	Headquarters	Phone number	Fax back number
Apple	Cupertino, CA	800/776-2333	800/462-4396
AST	Irvine, CA	800/876-4AST	800/876-4AST
Canon	Costa Mesa, CA	800/848-4123	800/526-4345
Compaq	Houston, TX	800/345-1518	800/345-1518
Dell	Austin, TX	800/986-3355	800/950-1329
Digital	Maynard, MA	800/DIGITAL	800/388-3228
Gateway 2000	N. Sioux City, SD	800/846-2410	800/846-4526
Hewlett-Packard	Palo Alto, CA	800/443-1254	800/443-1254
IBM	Somers, NY	800/426-2968	800/IBM-4FAX
NEC	Irving, TX	800/NEC-INFO	800/366-0476
Sharp	Mahwah, NJ	800/237-4277	NA
Texas Instruments	Austin, TX	800/848-3927	800/TI-TEXAS
Toshiba	Irvine, CA	800/457-7777	714/583-3800

Buying points

Performance

One of the most critical aspects of a notebook computer to check is how fast it will work. The primary contributors to fast performance in a notebook computer are the processor and the memory.

The processor, or central processing unit (CPU), is the command center for the computer. The type of chip used determines how fast the computer can operate.

Currently, most notebook computers use Intel's Pentium processor. This chip is the same as that used on most desktop models, although notebooks typically use a version that requires less power. The only major competitor to the Pentium is the PowerPC chip which is used in Apple PowerBook computers.

When comparing Pentium chips, focus on the clock speed. This measures how many instructions the computer can complete per second. Faster clock speeds allow for faster processing, but raise the price of the chip and use more power.

The amount of memory used in a notebook computer can also greatly affect performance. Random access memory (RAM) is the amount of data your computer can work with at one time. It is measured in megabytes (MB). Most users will want a minimum of 8 MB of RAM, with 16 MB preferable if multiple applications will be opened at once. Most notebooks can be equipped with additional memory later on if the original amount proves insufficient.

Memory usually must be added by the dealer, and costs about $20 per MB.

Notebook screens

The screen of a notebook computer is one of the most important components. Screens must be small and light, yet easy to read, a combination that is not very easy to achieve. While notebook screens have improved dramatically in the past few years, they are still one of the primary factors distinguishing top-of-the-line models from cheaper designs.

Screens range in size from 8.4 inch (diagonal) on older models to nearly 13 inch on the newest notebooks. Larger screens are easier to read, and can sometimes display a higher resolution image. We recommend models with a screen size of at least 10.4 inches.

A second difference concerns the technology used to produce the image. Active matrix color screens (sometimes called TFT screens) are fairly expensive, but provide bright images viewable from any angle. Less expensive models often use dual scan (or STN) screens. These are fine for use by individuals, but can be too dim for presentation purposes.

Most notebook computers offer a color display, although a few monochrome models are still on the market.

Other components

Other components to examine when choosing a computer include the hard drive, keyboard, and pointing device.

A hard drive is used to store applications and files on the computer. Because hard drives have dropped dramatically in price over the past few years, you should not settle for a small capacity drive. We recommend choosing at least a 700 MB hard drive.

When examining the keyboard, make sure it has full-sized keys, a logical key arrangement, and is comfortable to the touch. A good keyboard will include cursor arrows in an inverse "T", two shift buttons, a tab key, caps lock key, and a delete key. These should be arranged in a way so that they can be easily accessed, without being so small that you unintentionally hit certain keys. For daily use, you may also want to buy a bigger keyboard designed for desktop computers.

Notebook computers substitute compact pointing devices for the computer mouse. Track balls and eraser-like joysticks are the most common types of pointing devices. Some models use a touch pad that directs the cursor by sensing the movement of your finger along the pad. Most people prefer one design over the others, so you may want to try all three before making a selection.

Battery life

If you expect to use a notebook while traveling, there will probably be times that you need to run off battery power. Notebook computers can last anywhere from one to eight hours when running on batteries. Battery life depends on a number of factors, including the type of battery, the computer components, and the type of power management features used.

There are currently three types of batteries on the market. Lithium ion (Li) batteries offer the most power for their size. Their primary disadvantage is that they can take somewhat longer to recharge. Nickel Metal Hydride (NiMH) batteries also offer long life, with quick recharge times. Older Nickel Cadmium batteries (NiCad) offer decent performance, but can suffer from shortened battery life if they are not fully discharged before recharging.

Computer components can have a significant effect on battery life. While faster processors can improve notebook performance, they can actually reduce battery life. Other components such as CD-ROM drives or modems can also quickly drain a battery. As a result, you may want to look for a computer that allows you to remove unneeded components.

In terms of power management, make sure the notebook comes equipped with a wide range of sleep functions. These functions put the computer in a state of hibernation when no data processing is occurring. Good power management can dramatically increase battery life, reducing the draw of power-hungry components such as the hard drive.

Service and support

Service is a fairly critical issue, since notebooks are susceptible to damage from being dropped, sat upon, or scratched. It has been reported that more than 50% of purchased models need service within the first two years. Because the market changes so much, make sure that you buy from a dealer that can act as a long-term source of parts and service.

Most manufacturers offer one- to three-year warranties covering parts and labor, but not damage from misuse or accidents.

Because it is quite likely that your computer will break while you are on the road, you may want to look for a company that offers next-day, nationwide service.

How much will it cost?
Notebook computer prices range from under $1,500 for low-end models to nearly $6,000 for computers with huge screens and fast processors. Models with active matrix screens generally cost about $800 more than ones with dual scan screens. The fastest chips can command price premiums on the order of $1,000.

Terms

Clock speed The number of instructions a processor can execute per second. Clock speed is measured in millions of instructions per second (megahertz, or MHz). It is a good indicator of performance only when comparing the same type of chip.

Resolution The number of dots of light that appear on a screen. Higher resolution mean that more dots appear on the screen, allowing a larger image to be displayed. Most notebooks offer a resolution of 640 x 480 dots, but a few models can show 800 x 600 dot images.

PC Cards A slim, credit-card sized peripheral that can be used with many notebook computers. PC Card designs are available for modems, flash memory, network attachments, and hard drives. Also known as PCMCIA cards.

Special tips

Try before you buy. A buyer's happiness with a notebook computer will greatly depend on how the system is designed. As a result, see if you can test the notebook before purchase, or buy one with a money-back guarantee.

Check all of the connections to make sure they are easy to use and durable. The cover clasp, screen hinges, battery cover, and back panel are most likely to break.

Modular, removable hard drives allow you to keep your data on hand when your unit needs servicing. However, they require more connections, which increases their weight and the chance for damage.

If you are interested in hooking up a notebook computer to a monitor for in-office use, check the maximum size resolution the notebook can support. Not all notebooks are capable of adequately powering a 17-inch monitor.

See also
Desktop Computers, Ink-jet Printers, Keyboards, Laser Printers, LCD Systems, Modems, Monitors, Pointing Devices, Portable Printers

---

For more information, visit
BuyersZone
http://www.buyerszone.com/

Did you know?

The limited viewing angles of a dual scan (STN) screen can actually be an advantage on an airplane, since this means that your seatmate will not be able to see confidential materials displayed on your computer.

Off-site Storage

*O*ff-site storage facilities are designed to provide an inexpensive yet accessible storage area for company records and old files. Off-site storage is generally much less expensive than filling office space with old records, and provides a low-maintenance means of keeping these files accessible, yet out of the way.

PRICING

Services	Price
Boxes—indexing, shelving, & refiling	$1/box
Boxes—retrieval	$1.10-$1.50/box
Folders—indexing	$0.25/file
Folders—retrieval & refile	$1.50-$2/file
Documents—retrieval & refile	$1.50-$2/document
Documents—file updating	$0.50/document
Regular delivery/pickups	$2/box or file ($6 minimum)
Rush delivery/pickups (M-F 8-4)	additional $25/delivery
After 4pm and weekends	additional $50/delivery
Destruction	$2.75/cubic foot
Faxes	$1/page
Copies	$0.08/copy

Source: Oneil Product Development (Pricing reflects East Coast prices; expect West Coast prices to be slightly higher.)

VENDORS

Company	Headquarters	Phone number
Arcus	Pleasanton, CA	510/485-6620
Brambles	Chicago, IL	312/836-0200
Database	Bellevue, WA	206/462-7212
Iron Mountain	Boston, MA	617/357-4455
Pierce Leahy	King of Prussia, PA	800/FAST-FILE
RMS	Chicago, IL	312/733-8078
Safesite	Billerica, MA	508/667-9999

Buying points

How off-site storage works
Facilities that specialize in the storage of records generally offer services that go beyond renting space. A full-service provider will essentially create a document management system for your files. This typically involves bar coding every file, entering information about the record into a database, and storing it in secure boxes. This organization should allow for the immediate retrieval of even the most deeply buried records.

Many storage facilities allow you to search for files on-line and have them delivered to your office. Alternatively, you can schedule a time to access the files in the center's reading room.

Rationale
Off-site storage makes the most sense for companies that are tight on space. If you are considering moving to a larger office space, analyze why the move is being made. Relocating files to an off-site center can often help alleviate the need for a move, or reduce the amount of space you need.

Moving records off-site typically makes the most sense for files that are more than a year or two old, but not old enough to be discarded. If files need to be accessed on a weekly basis, an off-site solution is not likely to be right for you.

Many off-site storage facilities also store media, providing a secure location for computer data and other recordings. Magnetic media that can be stored includes reel-to-reel, cartridges, diskettes, video tapes, audio tapes, microfilm, and microfiche.

Choosing a records storage facility
Before choosing a storage facility, you will need to determine whether you will be storing paper records, computer media or both. Although both types of records are sensitive to storage conditions, computer media generally require more care.

Second, you should get a sense for how often you expect to retrieve materials. This will help you decide whether to consider a facility that is close enough to easily deliver materials versus one that is distant enough to provide the lowest storage costs.

Another aspect to consider concerns delivery time and hours of operation. The facility should offer delivery schedules that vary according to the urgency of the request. You should also look for a facility that is open during all the hours that employees work to ensure access to necessary files.

A final consideration concerns the facility itself. All facilities should have advanced surveillance systems, climate control systems, and restricted access to help keep the records secure. The facility should also be adequately insured to cover loss due to flooding or theft.

Pricing
Pricing for business records management varies considerably based on geographic location. Most facilities

will charge you for each box stored, plus a premium for services rendered.

For the equivalent of a 4-drawer file cabinet, expect to pay in the range of $45 per year. Individual boxes range in price from 50¢ to $5 depending on their size.

Round-trip pickup and delivery charges generally hover around $20, with faster services adding a premium to those charges. Labor associated with any other services will also be added to your bill.

Special tips

Make sure you are making an apples-to-apples comparison when evaluating services. Some records centers offer pricing by the square foot, while others price the storage space by the cubic foot.

Carefully organize your records before they are brought to the storage center. Most facilities will charge a fee to search for a file even if it is not found.

Ask about the hiring practices of the records centers. Employees who will be handling your sensitive data should be thoroughly investigated before being hired.

Avoid having the commercial records center list your company in its list of current clients. Your clients may worry about the security of their records if they have doubts about off-site storage.

The Association of Commercial Records Centers (800/336-9793) offers guidelines to assist in the selection an off-site records center. They can also offer referrals to local members.

See also

Accountants, Computer Backup Systems, File Cabinets

OFFICE SUPPLIES

*E*ach year, businesses spend billions of dollars on office supplies such as pens, paper, toner, paper clips, and notepads. Since most purchases consist of many inexpensive items, it can be difficult to get a sense for whether you are paying a fair price for these supplies. However, with a bit of comparison shopping, businesses can save as much as 10% to 20% per year on office supplies.

VENDORS

Company	Headquarters	Phone number	Sales channels: Contract stationer	Sales channels: Mail order	Sales channels: Super store	Minimum order	Delivery included
Boise Cascade	Itasca, IL	800/47-BOISE	●			varies	●
BT Office Products Int'l.	Buffalo Grove, IL	847/793-7500	●			varies	●
Corporate Express	Broomfield, CO	303/373-2800	●			varies	●
Global	Port Washington, NY	800/8-GLOBAL		●			
Office Depot	Delray Beach, FL	800/685-8800	●	●	●	varies	●
OfficeMax	Shaker Heights, OH	800/788-8080	●	●	●	varies	●
Penny Wise	Bowie, MD	800/942-3311		●		$25	●
Quill	Lincolnshire, IL	800/789-1331		●		$45	●
Reliable	Schaumburg, IL	800/735-4000		●		$25	
Staples	Framingham, MA	800/333-3330	●	●	●	$50	●
U.S. Office Products	Washington, DC	202/628-9500	●			varies	●
Viking	Los Angeles, CA	800/421-1222		●		$25	●
Wholesale Supply	Nashville, TN	800/962-9162		●		$25	

Buying points

Sources of supplies

Office supplies can be purchased from office superstores, mail order companies, local independent dealers or through a contract stationer.

Office superstores combine outstanding marketing with tight cost controls to attract customers. Suburban locations and warehouse-like stocking helps keep overhead low, while their enormous sales volume allows superstores to obtain deep discounts from manufacturers.

Mail order vendors cater to the same small businesses as office superstores, but tend to also appeal to larger companies. These vendors rely on catalogs for their marketing efforts, offering toll free order lines and inexpensive shipping charges to compete with local firms. With distribution centers strategically located, mail order vendors typically offer delivery within 1 to 3 days of an order.

Before the advent of superstores and mail order, the local office supply dealer was the primary source of supplies for most businesses. These dealers usually offer the broadest product selection, making them a good resource for hard-to-find items. Today, office supply dealers are a dying breed, with more than half exiting the market in the past ten years.

Contract stationers primarily target businesses of 75 or more employees. These vendors offer a very broad product line, custom pricing, and full service offerings to attract larger businesses.

Breadth of selection

When it comes to product selection, contract stationers and office supply dealers are the hands-down winners. Contract stationers and office supply dealers typically carry around 25,000 different products, or approximately five times as many items as an office superstore. Office superstores and mail order vendors usually supplement their basic catalog with a stationer's catalog to offer comparable depth. However, these goods will not be immediately available for purchase.

Lowest prices

When buying in small quantities, you will often find superstores and mail order vendor prices offering the lowest prices because of their ability to buy in bulk quantities. Both channels commonly sell popular items priced at or below cost to attract customers. These losses are made up for by strategically placing higher margin generic items and over-priced impulse items.

Firms that purchase office supplies in large volume will often do much better negotiating prices with a contract stationer for frequently ordered items.

Because contract stationers know you will compare prices on the most commonly purchased items, they tend to offer very competitive prices for everything on your list of commonly purchased items. By including an accurate assessment of the items you expect to order, you can minimize the higher amount you will be charged for items not on your price sheet.

In addition to securing pricing for your most often purchased items, you may want to guarantee the prices for other items. See if the company produces an in-house sales catalog against which you can check pricing. In addition, it makes sense to agree upon a discount (typically 35% to 40%) on items ordered through the full-line catalog.

Service

Selection and price are not the only concerns when choosing an office supply vendor. You should also consider service aspects such as ordering, delivery, and reporting.

Ordering options vary quite extensively from one vendor to the next. In some ways, mail order vendors offer the easiest ordering, with most providing extended hours or 24-hour service. Most also offer some sort of ordering via fax or online services.

For larger clients, contract stationers are often more convenient, offering bulletin board and advanced EDI (electronic data interchange) systems for automatic restocking and billing. In some cases, contract stationers will even come to your office and take inventory to identify which items you need.

Delivery practices tend to be quite similar across vendors. Most offer free delivery, although some have a minimum order size for free delivery. Mail order vendors are the most likely to charge for delivery, while office superstores and office supply stores often limit deliveries to businesses within a certain radius.

Reporting is one office supply service that can be very helpful, especially for larger firms that want to identify where money is being spent. Contract stationers usually offer the most comprehensive management reports, breaking down orders by department or product type.

Pricing

Your office probably spends more on office supplies than you think. The typical business spends $500 to $800 per employee on office supplies per year, an amount that greatly exceeds many other office expenses.

Special tips

Although vendors may advertise very low prices for certain goods, do not automatically assume other products for sale are also equally good bargains. This holds particularly true when buying non-essential office supplies such as shipping materials or computer accessories.

To obtain the most favorable pricing from prospective vendors, draw up a list of the twenty products that are used most frequently in your office. Then, ask for price quotes for this list with a couple of contract stationers in your area and compare these prices to those of the same products at your local superstore.

Warehouse clubs are a good option for discount pricing on many common office supplies. After paying an upfront membership fee, customers can take advantage of the bulk buying power and exceptionally low overhead of the warehouse format. The greatest drawback is that warehouse clubs tend to have a very limited, varied selection, which will be a problem for all but the most flexible consumers.

When comparing contract stationers, make sure to evaluate the services that you require. Although contract stationers do not explicitly raise your prices depending on the level of service you receive, it is certainly factored into future rate increases. You should ask only for the services that will help your business function more efficiently. Do not include services in your agreement just because they are "free."

Some contract stationers offer a 1% to 2% rebate if your total buying over a given year exceeds a certain level. In most cases, you should expect to spend at least $10,000 per year to qualify for rebates.

See also
Beverage Services, Copy Paper, Recycling, Toner Supplies

For more information, visit
BuyersZone
http://www.buyerszone.com/

Overhead Projectors

*O*riginally designed for use in the classroom, the overhead projector is now an essential tool for many business presentations. Overhead projectors can be used with transparencies to show graphs and charts, or with an LCD panel to project presentations from a computer.

VENDORS

Company	Headquarters	Phone number	Projector design Transmissive	Reflective
3M	Austin, TX	800/952-4059	●	●
Apollo	Ronkonkoma, NY	516/467-8033	●	●
Buhl	Fairlawn, NJ	800/526-7473	●	●
Dukane	St. Charles, IL	708/584-2300	●	●
Eiki	Lake Forest, CA	714/457-0200	●	
Elmo	New Hyde Park, NY	516/775-3200	●	

Buying points

Overhead projectors vs. slide projectors

Overhead projectors offer several advantages over slide projectors. First, transparencies are easier to produce—all you need is a laser printer or copier. Slides, by contrast, require more lead time and help from a developer.

Second, overhead projectors offer more flexibility. Transparencies can be easily shuffled to change the order during a presentation. Slides, by contrast, are usually shown from a fixed carousel, which limits your ability to change the tone or message in the middle of a presentation.

Finally, transparencies allow the presenter to write or highlight areas of the image for added emphasis during the presentation. A simple transparency marker allows you to write notes, point out areas of emphasis, or even modify the image. Slides usually cannot be written on without causing damage.

The primary disadvantage of transparencies is appearance. Slides typically offer brighter colors and allow more complex images to be displayed.

Types of overhead projectors

Overhead projectors primarily differ from each other in where they place the light source used to project the image on the screen.

Reflective projectors house the light in the head of the unit. Light is projected down onto the base, bounced off a reflector, and then back through the head onto the screen. The advantage of the reflective projector is portability, since the base is much smaller.

Transmissive projectors house the light source in the base of the machine. Because light is projected directly from the base, a transmissive projector can light large or very bright rooms quite effectively.

If you expect to use the overhead projector with an LCD panel, you will need to use a transmissive projector. A reflective projector will generally not produce a light strong enough to project an adequate image through the LCD panel.

Factors affecting image quality

The key to obtaining a good image is to use a lens that combines the proper focal length with high-quality optics.

The focal length of the lens determines the optimum distance between the screen and the projector. For example, a lens with a focal length of 14 inches is designed to be placed 8 to 10 feet from the screen. A wide angle lens, with a focal length of 11.5 inches, is best for a projector that will sit 3 to 4 feet from the screen.

High-quality lenses are quite expensive. As a result, many manufacturers combine multiple, lower-quality lenses to obtain an accurate image at a lower cost. Additional lenses correct distortions produced by the first lens.

Overhead Projectors

Life of an overhead projector
An overhead projector will last at least five to ten years with proper maintenance and cleaning. Most breakdowns occur soon after purchase, and are covered by the warranty. Overhead projectors have few mechanical parts, so they should need minimal repairs.

Types of light bulbs
Halogen bulbs provide light for most overhead projectors. Inexpensive and easy to obtain, halogen bulbs will typically last 50 to 75 hours before burning out, and cost $25 to $45 to replace.

Metal halide bulbs are the main alternative to halogen bulbs. Metal halide bulbs are brighter than halogen bulbs and last nearly 750 hours. However, they cost $200 to $500 and are difficult to replace.

Other options
Some of the most useful options for overhead projectors include: an automatic document feeder which will switch transparencies on cue, a second bulb that can be turned on with the flip of a switch if the first burns out, and glare shields which reduce the amount of light that shines into the presenter's eyes.

Pricing
Depending on the lens and bulb, overhead projector prices vary considerably. Most transmissive overhead projectors cost anywhere from $200 to $1,500, depending on the number of lenses and their quality, the type of bulb used, and the portability of the unit. Reflective units tend to be a bit less expensive.

Terms

Aperture The opening in the stage through which light is transmitted.

Focal length The point between the lens and the screen at which the image will appear right-side up on the screen. A larger focal length indicates a projector that should be farther from the screen for optimal viewing.

Keystoning Projected images that are larger at one end than another due to misalignment of the lenses with the stage or screen.

Lumens A measurement of light output. There is no universal standard of measurement for overhead projectors, so this figure should only be used to compare machines made by the same company.

Stage The area on which the transparency sits. The stage is available in different levels of opacity depending on its use. For use with LCD panels, you will want a clear stage for maximum brightness.

Varifocal lenses Lenses that can be adjusted to manipulate the focal length, and therefore the size of the image, without moving the overhead projector.

Special tips

When you evaluate an overhead projector, bring some transparencies, including one that is quite dark and another that has a fine image, to check the image quality. Also make sure to check the projector under the placement and lighting conditions in which you expect to use it.

Overhead projectors require brighter output when used with LCD panels. Be sure the unit has both a high and low brightness setting if you intend to use LCD panels.

If overhead transparencies remain on a bright base for too long, they can melt or curl. Look for units with a fan cooling system and an automatic overheat shut-off to prevent disasters during a presentation.

Avoid moving an overhead projector by its arm. This can cause the unit's optics to become skewed.

Most overhead projectors weigh 18 to 30 pounds, but there are some "portable" units which weigh much less. Avoid collapsible units which leave the lens unprotected.

See also
Laser Pointers, LCD Systems, Slide Projectors

Did you know?

Research shows people retain only 10 percent of what they hear, but 50 percent of what they hear and see, according to *Incentive* magazine.

OVERNIGHT DELIVERY SERVICES

*O*vernight delivery services help businesses meet tight deadlines, conduct business rapidly, and stay in touch over long distances. Although still a relatively recent innovation, overnight delivery is now virtually taken for granted, with businesses expecting delivery the next morning for anything of even slight importance.

PRICING

Shipment type	Next day	2-3 day
Letter	$10-$16	$5-$13
5-lbs.	$18-$33	$7-$17
25-lbs.	$33-$65	$16-$37

VENDORS

Company	Headquarters	Phone number	Next AM	Next PM	2-3 day
Airborne	Seattle, WA	800/AIRBORNE	•	•	•
Burlington	Irvine, CA	800/CALL-BAX	•	•	•
DHL	Redwood City, CA	800/CALL-DHL	•	•	
Emery	Palo Alto, CA	800/HI-EMERY	•	•	•
Federal Express	Memphis, TN	800/GO-FEDEX	•	•	•
RPS	Pittsburgh, PA	800/ROAD-PAK			•
TNT	Garden City, NY	800/558-5555	(via Airborne)		
UPS	Atlanta, GA	800/PICK-UPS	•		•
U.S. Postal Service	Washington, DC	800/222-1811	•		•

Buying points

Types of delivery services

Over the past several years, the national overnight carriers have greatly expanded their menu of shipping options. Now, businesses can choose among as many as four different guaranteed delivery times when sending packages.

The fastest services promise delivery to major metropolitan areas by 8:00 or 8:30 A.M. These programs carry a hefty premium of $30 or more over other services and are primarily offered by UPS and Federal Express.

Traditional morning delivery services promise delivery by 10:30 A.M. or 12:00 noon to most locations. These remain among the most popular overnight services, since they deliver packages in time for a thorough review and response.

Afternoon delivery services are designed for slightly less urgent packages. These programs promise delivery by 3:00 or 5:00 P.M., and cost a few dollars less than morning delivery.

Most overnight delivery services also offer options for two-day delivery. Two-day delivery tends to cost about 40% less than next-morning delivery, with delivery guaranteed by the afternoon of the second day.

Tracking down packages

A few years ago, only Federal Express was capable of tracking packages while they were in transit. Now all companies have similar systems in place. The main difference is how rapidly each carrier can notify you of a package's status, with response times varying from half an hour to a full day depending on the carrier.

For the high-volume shippers who use tracking on a frequent basis, a more important consideration is the availability of computer tracking software. This allows you to access shipping information easily and quickly from a PC, so you spend less time on the phone or searching through reference books. Most firms offer software that is easy to install, with access to tracking computers via dial-up lines or the Internet.

Sending strategies for low-volume shippers

If you ship fewer than 3 overnight packages per week, generous discounts will generally be unavailable to your firm. To get the best deal, you should use whichever carrier is best suited for each particular package. To do this, first open an account with each carrier and obtain rates for different weights and destinations. Then, before you ship, choose which carrier offers the best deal for that particular package.

Another way for small businesses to obtain lower rates is to work with a shipping consolidator. By combining shipping volumes from many firms, consolidators can negotiate lower rates. Although packages may be shipped via several different carriers, firms need only place one call to the consolidator for pickup.

High-volume shipping strategies

For firms that send numerous overnight packages each week, the best way to save money is to find a carrier that best fits your needs and then negotiate customized discounts. To start, first estimate your monthly shipping volume. Be generous in your estimates, since rates can later be adjusted to reflect your actual traffic. Then approach carriers that best match your shipping patterns.

Airborne, Federal Express, and UPS specialize in letter-sized packages. UPS recently switched to a distance-based pricing structure, which may make it particularly attractive if you often ship to nearby locations. Burlington and Emery do not offer as competitive rates for letters, but are much more competitive for businesses sending large packages.

Regional overnight carriers

In addition to the major national carriers, there are a number of regional overnight carriers in the market. These companies specialize in the expedited delivery of packages within a defined geographic region.

Smaller shippers that have special shipping needs but find they are too small to warrant much attention from the national providers may want to consult a regional carrier. Regional carriers are often quite flexible in accommodating specific needs and concerns.

Generally, a company should be shipping about five packages a week to consider working with a regional carrier. Pricing from these carriers at such shipping volumes can be quite competitive with the larger players.

Special tips

The Postal Service's Express Mail is the only standard program that delivers on Sundays and holidays. Express Mail does not even have a surcharge for this service.

Emery uses a different pricing system than other companies. Prices are quoted for each package based on the firm's current traffic and shipping loads.

When sending a package, make sure to ask when in the day the recipient needs to receive it. Next afternoon delivery is significantly less expensive than morning delivery.

Some carriers offer heavily discounted overnight shipping envelopes to companies willing to pre-pay for shipping.

Check when packages arrive. You may not have to pay for packages that arrive after their guaranteed time. While some carriers will refund the full price of a shipment that does not meet its deadline, others will only discount the cost to reflect the level of service that was provided.

See also
Ground Shipping, International Expedited Delivery, LTL Shipping, Same Day Delivery Services

For more information, visit
BuyersZone
http://www.buyerszone.com/

PAGERS

*P*agers are small wireless devices that allow you to stay in touch with coworkers, clients or suppliers. The units contain a small display that shows a phone number or a text message from the person trying to reach you.

EQUIPMENT VENDORS

Company	Headquarters	Phone number	2-way
Motorola	Libertyville, IL	800/548-9954	●
NEC	Irving, TX	800/CALL-NMI	
Panasonic	Secaucus, NJ	800/545-2672	
Samsung	Deerfield Beach, FL	800/631-4782	●
Uniden	Fort Worth, TX	800/364-1931	

SERVICE VENDORS

Paging service provider	Headquarters	Phone number	Coverage area
AirTouch	Dallas, TX	800/6-AIRTOUCH	most of U.S.
American Paging	Minneapolis, MN	800/822-5554	most of U.S.
Ameritech	Hoffman Estates, IL	800/MOBILE-1	Chicago/NW Indiana area
Arch	Westborough, MA	508/898-0962	most of U.S.
AT&T	New York, NY	800/462-4463	most of U.S.
MCI	Washington, DC	800/888-7737	most of U.S.
Metrocall	Alexandria, VA	804/355-7333	most of U.S.
Mobilecom	Ridgefield Park, NJ	201/440-8400	most of U.S.
PageMart	Dallas, TX	214/750-5809	most of U.S.
PageNet	Plano, TX	214/985-4100	most of U.S.
SkyTel	Jackson, MS	800/759-8737	most of U.S.

Buying points

Types of pagers
There are three types of pagers currently on the market. The simplest and most prevalent pagers are numeric models. These display numbers entered by a caller from a touch-tone phone. They can indicate a phone number to call, or a code for a specific pre-planned message (e.g., "11" means you have a voice mail message, "22" means call the office).

Alphanumeric pagers offer the same capabilities as numeric pagers plus the ability to display short written messages. This can save time, since a text message often eliminates the need for a return call. While nowhere near as common as numeric pagers, alphanumeric pagers have recently grown to claim nearly 10% of the market. A related type of pager is the voice pager, which can display a phone number and play a short voice message.

The newest type of pager is a two-way pager. These models not only display a message, but also allow the recipient to send back a reply. In many cases, this completely eliminates the need for a phone call, saving time and money. Two-way paging is still very rare, with service currently offered in only a few metropolitan areas.

How a pager works
Numeric pages are the simplest to use. Using a touch-tone phone, the caller dials a paging service, punches in the account number, and then enters the numeric code that will appear on the pager (typically the return phone number). The paging service then sends a signal to the local paging terminal, which transmits the message via radio waves over the entire coverage area. Only the pager with the relevant account will display the signal.

Alphanumeric pagers work in much the same way, but require some extra steps for the transmission of text. The most common method is to call the carrier operator, who then transcribes the message to be sent to the pager. Other ways to send text include using specialized software to transmit text via modem or purchasing a dedicated alpha entry terminal. The dedicated terminal is used primarily by companies that need to send text messages to numerous pagers at once.

Two-way pagers use the PCS (Personal Communications Services) band recently auctioned by the FCC. PCS uses low-power signals that are conveyed by many small signal towers within a given region. Even a small pager can contain all the necessary PCS technology to receive and send messages.

In most cases, a two-way pager is equipped with a few small buttons to send specific responses. Future models may be integrated into notebook computers for more customized replies.

Features
One of the most common paging features is the ability to change how the pager alerts the user. The standard method is to play a series of beeps; however, many models can be set to silently vibrate when a message

arrives. The vibrating setting is ideal for use in a quiet setting when you do not want to disturb those around you.

Expanded memory is another useful feature. Depending on the type of pager, expanded memory allows you to store anywhere from 10 to 30 messages in the pager. This allows users to store phone numbers in memory for future reference. Some pagers will even retain messages in memory when the battery is removed.

A time and date stamp feature tells you exactly when a message arrived. This can be quite useful if calls will not be returned until later.

Voice mail is a service offered with some paging plans. In such cases, the caller is given the option of sending a page or leaving a voice mail message. Voice mail allows callers to leave messages without waiting for a return call. Alternately, many voice mail systems can be programmed to offer pager notification of newly arrived voice mail messages.

Coverage area

Depending on where you expect to receive pages, there are services that offer local, regional or national coverage. Larger coverage areas tend to be more expensive, but ensure that you can be reached no matter where you travel.

Pricing

The paging market is very similar to the cellular phone market. The equipment has become more and more of a commodity over time, with service increasingly becoming the differentiating factor. Many dealers waive the pager activation fee or sell the units at a loss to attract new customers.

Depending on the plan, monthly service fees can range from $10 to $40 per month, with payment on a quarterly or annual basis. Service fees will also vary depending on whether you currently own a pager.

If you will be buying a pager, expect to pay $30 to $150 depending on the type of pager and accompanying features. Pagers can also be leased for a minimal monthly fee.

The coverage area will significantly affect the monthly service charge. Local service starts at less than $10 per month, while national service is priced closer to $30 per month.

Special tips

Most cellular telephone companies now offer paging services as well. If you already have cellular service or are considering it, you may want to try to bundle the two purchases together to qualify for a better deal.

Not all pagers work with all service providers, but most pagers can be "recrystallized" to operate with a different provider. However, recrystallization may cost as much or more than simply purchasing a new pager.

See also
Cellular Service, Cellular Telephones, PDAs, Telephone Systems

Paper Shredders

*P*aper shredders are used to destroy confidential documents. Shredders cut pages into small pieces before disposal so they cannot easily be read if found in the trash. Although company documents may not be a matter of national security, many firms use shredders to ensure that sensitive documents do not become public knowledge.

PRICING

Type of shredder	Price range
Personal strip	$149-$749
Personal cross-cut	$499-$1,599
Office strip	$1,099-$2,195
Office cross-cut	$1,885-$2,995
Wide paper strip	$1,252-$2,995
Wide paper cross-cut	$2,150-$4,599

VENDORS

Company	Headquarters	Phone Number
Allegheny	Delmont, PA	800/245-2497
Ameri-Shred	Monroeville, PA	800/634-8981
Cummins-Allison	Mt. Prospect, IL	800/621-5528
Dahle	Peterborough, NH	603/924-0003
Datatech	W. Conshohocken, PA	800/523-0320
Destroyit	N. Charleston, SC	800/223-2508
EBA	New York, NY	800/682-3226
Fellowes	Itasca, IL	800/955-0959
GBC	Northbrook, IL	800/477-9900
Intimus	Sanford, NC	800/344-5162
Olympia	Dallas, TX	800/832-4727
Oztec	Port Washington, NY	800/223-0328
SEM	Westborough, MA	800/225-9293
Shredex	Shirley, NY	516/345-0300
Wilson Jones (Acco USA)	Wheeling, IL	800/222-6462

Buying points

How a paper shredder works
Paper shredders consist of a pair of rotating cutting blades, a paper comber, and a motor that drives this assembly. Paper is fed between the two intermeshing blades and is split into many small strips by the force of the blades.

Types of shredders
Shredders vary according to how they are used and the types of materials that will be destroyed.

Personal shredders are designed for infrequent use by one person. These models typically require a strict diet of just paper in order to avoid jams and breakdowns.

Commercial grade shredders are much larger units, designed for shredding documents from many people in an office. Commercial shredders can handle large amounts of documents and the occasional paper clip.

Purchasing considerations
The three main considerations when buying a shredder are the types of materials you will be shredding, the volume of shredding the machine will be handling, and the security level your company needs.

Most commercial shredders are designed to handle paper, with the occasional paper clip or staple thrown in. However, some models are designed for larger objects, including items such as videocassettes and computer diskettes. Other shredders are equipped with a wide feeding mouth to allow wide computer printouts to be fed directly into the machine.

The volume of paper the shredder will be handling is a second major purchase consideration. This is a function of the unit's paper capacity, or how much paper can be fed at once, as well as its shredding speed. In order to make sure you do not quickly outgrow a shredder, be sure to carefully estimate your usage, and build in room for company growth.

In terms of security, most businesses find a basic strip-cut shredder adequate. These machines cut paper into ribbon-like strips, varying in width from $1/12$ inch to 1 inch. However, for more confidential documents, cross-cut shredders are preferred. These machines cut both lengthwise and widthwise, turning a page into 500 to 800 confetti-like pieces of paper. For the highest security requirements (such as military contractors), there are even shredders that add chemicals to reduce paper to a pulpy mass.

Maintenance concerns
Aside from the very low-end models, shredders are designed to last seven to ten years. Ongoing maintenance of these units typically includes oiling the cutting assembly and replacing bags as they fill.

Terms

Auto reverse An essential feature for all but the most basic shredder users. This feature means that the shredder will automatically reverse the cutting process when jams occur. This can prevent the cutter blades from bending or breaking.

Cross-cut shredders Shredders that cut paper both lengthwise and widthwise. These machines insure that pages cannot be pieced together by a determined reader.

Sheets per pass The number of sheets that can be fed into the machine at a time.

Strip-cut shredders Shredders that reduce papers into long thin strips.

Throat width A measurement of how wide a sheet can be fed into the shredder.

Special tips

Replacement bags can be purchased from the shredder manufacturer. However this can be very costly, with prices often more than 50¢ per bag. A better alternative is to contact a plastic bag manufacturer and order bags with similar dimensions.

Office equipment dealers that specialize in the sale of shredders often provide the best selection of models. However, if you are simply looking for a shredder for infrequent personal use, an office superstore's offerings should be fine.

A bin full indicator can be a very useful feature, particularly for shredders that are housed in a cabinet. Overflowing bags of shredded paper are one of the most common causes of paper jams.

Watch out for dangling objects, like neckties, that can accidentally feed into a shredder when it is in use. For safety reasons, the on/off switch should be in easy reach of the user.

See also
Business Forms, Checks, Copy Paper, Photocopiers, Safes

Did you know?

Although an ethically questionable tactic, plucking information from garbage left in a public place is not illegal. In fact, in 1988, the Supreme Court ruled that garbage left for pickup can be taken by the government without a search warrant.

PAYROLL SERVICES

*P*ayroll services help businesses keep track of and manage payroll. These firms calculate the amount owed each employee, and provide payroll checks according to your payroll schedule.

VENDORS

Company	Headquarters	Phone number	States served
Advantage	Auburn, ME	800/876-0178	17 states
Allied Payroll Service	Rock Hill, SC	800/868-5852	NC, SC
Automatic Data Processing	Roseland, NJ	800/225-5237	48 states
Ceridian	Minneapolis, MN	800/729-7655	26 states
Comprehensive	Mission Viejo, CA	800/323-9009	36 states
Compupay	Miami, FL	305/591-8627	AZ, FL, WA
Computing Resources, Inc.	Reno, NV	800/422-8800	CA, NV
Datarite Payroll Service	Manchester, NH	603/625-5399	11 states
Dial A Check	San Antonio, TX	210/366-9511	10 states
Interpay	Mansfield, MA	800/448-9847	12 states
Minidata	Pine Brook, NJ	800/537-9448	NJ, NY, PA
Paychex	Rochester, NY	800/322-7292	35 states
Payroll 1	Royal Oak, MI	810/691-2550	16 states

Buying points

Outsourcing rationale
While the majority of U.S. businesses process paychecks internally, this is not always a cost-effective process. At minimum, internal payroll processing requires the purchase of a computer or manual accounting program and training to use it. In addition, businesses need to keep up to date on changes in personnel, deadlines, and tax requirements on an ongoing basis.

Using a payroll service generally makes sense if your payroll changes with each pay period. If your company has employees working varying amounts of hours each week or has a significant turnover rate, a payroll service can be a time and cost efficient alternative to internal processing. Using a payroll service can also be helpful if you have to deal with paying payroll taxes for multiple states.

On the other hand, if your payroll expenses are quite stable, you may find handling payroll internally to be more cost-effective.

Services provided
A payroll company's basic services include calculating payroll and tax obligations for each employee, printing and delivering checks, and providing management reports. Paychecks can be issued on a weekly, bi-weekly, monthly, semi-monthly, or yearly payroll basis.

Some services offer tie-ins with 401(k) and Section 125 mutual fund plans, allowing employees to designate automatic deductions from their paychecks. In addition, payroll firms can offer services such as automatic check signatures, envelope stuffing and direct deposit of checks. Payroll firms also issue W-2 forms for an additional fee of about $1 per form.

Choosing the right payroll service
In addition to offering the services you require, a payroll service should offer a high level of customer service. Unlike some other business services, you will need to communicate regularly with your payroll provider. If your sales representative will not be handling your account, make sure to speak with the customer service reps and references to ensure that you will be satisfied.

You should look for a service that is within reasonable driving distance, allowing you to pick up checks in case of an emergency. Also check that the company is bonded to ensure your company will not suffer from any potential financial mishandling.

Filing payroll taxes
Many payroll services offer the option of filing state and federal payroll taxes. Typically, this service is offered at little or no cost. This is because the payroll provider will impound the tax due at the time paychecks are issued, earning interest on the funds until the money needs to be handed over to the government. Most services assume responsibility for penalties resulting

from incorrect filing; however, your company may be liable for any interest charges.

Keep in mind that many companies will not calculate local or city payroll taxes. Make sure to inquire about this if it is a significant issue for you.

Relaying payroll information to the service

Each pay period, payroll data has to be "called in" to the service provider. This can be done via telephone, fax or computer.

The telephone is the traditional way of communicating information. The biggest problem is typically finding a mutually agreeable time for both people to be on the phone.

The fax machine eliminates scheduling conflicts and miscommunicated facts, but can bring up security risks concerning who receives the faxes and who will oversee the fax being sent.

Communicating payroll by modem is often the most efficient method, with the only real problem being the potential difficulty in setting up a connection.

Pricing

The market for payroll is competitive and reflects local market conditions. The basic service costs between $0.70 and $2.00 per check, plus a base account fee. The amount of the base fee depends on the pay period, with the less frequent payroll periods costing more. Over a year, however, less frequent payroll periods will cost less to maintain.

In addition, there can be fees for adding or dropping employees, adjusting employee information, or setting up your account. Fees can differ dramatically across services; it is important to check them out before signing up for a service.

Terms

Certified Payroll Professional (C.P.P.) This is a certification given by the American Payroll Association to payroll personnel that pass a standardized examination.

FICA/FUTA Taxes paid to the federal government that support Medicare, Social Security, and unemployment funds. While the costs of Medicare and Social Security are shared equally between the employee and the company, FUTA taxes are borne by the company alone.

Float The interest income that is accrued between the time the payroll service transfers funds into its account, and the time when payroll checks and taxes are actually paid. Firms with large payrolls should carefully calculate the lost revenue due to float when choosing a provider.

Special tips

If a firm's only business is payroll, make sure to check the number of clients it supports. To ensure stability, a payroll service should ideally maintain at least 500 clients.

Transitioning to a new payroll firm rarely occurs without glitches. Be especially thorough in reviewing the first paychecks issued through the service, and the money paid to cover tax obligations.

Do not be swayed by services that waive charges upon sign-up. Often rates go up or charges start accruing after six months to a year of service.

See also
401(k) Plans, Accountants, Pension Plans

For more information, visit
BuyersZone
http://www.buyerszone.com/

Did you know?

The Internal Revenue Service reports that one out of every three employers is charged with payroll mistakes, with penalties totaling in the billions of dollars.

PDAs

*P*ersonal digital assistants (PDAs) are handheld computers designed to help businesspeople schedule, communicate, and organize their thoughts.

VENDORS

Company	Headquarters	Phone number	Type	Pen input	Fax/ E-mail	Weight (oz.)
Apple	Cupertino, CA	800/SOS-APPL	Traditional	●	●	12.0
Hewlett-Packard	Palo Alto, CA	800/443-1254	Traditional	●		11.5
Motorola	Schaumburg, IL	800/934-4721	Traditional	●	●	28.8
Psion	Concord, MA	508/371-0310	Palmtop		opt.	9.7
Sharp	Mahwah, NJ	800/BE-SHARP	Traditional	●	●	13.6
Sony	San Jose, CA	800/55-MAGIC	Traditional	●	●	12.0
U.S. Robotics	Los Altos, CA	800/881-7256	Palmtop	●		5.7

Buying points

Role of a PDA
A personal digital assistant is a small computer designed for travel. PDAs are smaller than even the tiniest subnotebook computers, weighing about one pound and easily fitting in your hand. They also are more powerful than electronic organizers, with an open architecture that allows third-party development of PDA applications. This typically gives PDAs a wider range of available software than proprietary electronic organizers.

Uses for a PDA
PDAs can accomplish a wide range of tasks depending on what software is installed.

One of the most common uses of a PDA is as an organizer. PDAs can store addresses and phone numbers, and keep track of daily appointments.

A second use is for communication. Most PDAs can be equipped with a fax and modem for communicating with other computers. You can pick up or send e-mail with a PDA, or even send basic fax messages. A few systems will even work with commercial on-line services, allowing you to browse news or data.

PDAs can also run computer programs such as word processors and spreadsheets. Although PDAs tend to be too small for intensive work, they can be used to make final edits on a document or recall numbers for a presentation.

Other uses of PDAs tend to be more specialized. Some applications are designed for specific industries, such as a physician PDA program that tracks drug prescriptions and diagnoses. PDAs are often well-suited to industries where tracking data is important, but a traditional portable computer would be too bulky.

How PDAs differ
The biggest differences among PDAs concern how data is entered into the system.

Many PDAs, including the Apple Newton and Sony MagicLink, are pen-based models. This means that an electronic "pen" is used to draw on the screen and operate the PDA. Pen entry means that users do not have to push tiny keys, but requires a more sophisticated processor and some adaptation on the part of the user.

Most pen-based systems offer the ability to convert handwriting directly into editable text. Although this feature was initially the target of many jokes, handwriting recognition has dramatically improved since the first generation of PDAs. Most systems now use a special alphabet of letters to improve comprehension. Using the alphabet takes a bit of adjustment, but makes handwriting recognition a much more practical function.

Other PDAs, such as the Psion Series 3a and U.S. Robotics Pilot, use a small keyboard to enter information. This approach eliminates the need to learn specific characters, but can be a bit tedious to use on such a small unit. Sharp's Zaurus system combines the two approaches, offering handwriting recognition and a keyboard.

Connecting to a computer

Since PDAs do not have a disk drive, they must be connected to a computer to upload or download documents. Many PDA users rely on a regular computer for data entry, downloading files to the PDA for easy retrieval.

The most common way to connect a PDA to a computer is to use a serial cable and special software. The software configures data in such a way so as to easily send it to the PDA.

A few PDAs use an infrared port to transfer data to a computer (or another PDA) using an infrared beam of light. The infrared port works about as well as a serial cable, although you will need an infrared attachment for your PC to use this method.

Available PDA accessories

As with computers, there are many PDA accessories to increase the capabilities (and the cost) of a system.

One of the most useful accessories is a modem. This can be used with the PDA to send and receive e-mails and faxes. Make sure available modems operate at sufficiently high speeds; many PDAs will not work with modems that send or receive at more than 9,600 bits per second.

For connectivity from any location, some PDAs can be equipped with wireless modems. These use cellular or other signals to radio data to local transmitters. This data is then switched onto the public phone network. Wireless modems are technologically impressive, but often cost as much as the PDA itself.

Most PDAs can also be equipped to print from any standard PC printer. This typically requires printing software and a special cable.

One popular device for increasing the capabilities of a PDA is to equip the unit with a PC Card slot. These slots are the same as those found on notebook computers, and allow users to easily add modems, memory or storage devices to the PDA.

Batteries

Unlike notebook computers, PDAs generally offer very long battery life. Most run off a few standard AA alkaline batteries, and can operate 50 or more hours at a time.

Rechargeable batteries are often a good investment if you expect to frequently use the PDA. Many models can be equipped with NiCad or NiMH batteries as an option.

Pricing

The PDA market is remarkably competitive at present. There is not a large demand for most products, so manufacturers are eager to offer new and useful features at attractive prices to entice buyers. Keyboard PDAs generally cost about $300, while pen-based PDAs cost between $700 and $1,000.

Terms

Connectivity   The ability to transfer files between a PC and a PDA. This file transfer allows PDA files to be easily converted to common word processing, spreadsheet, database, and agenda file formats.

PC Card   A standard type of peripheral originally designed for notebook PCs. PC Cards are about the size of a credit card, and slip into a small slot on the side of a computer or PDA. There are many different PC Cards on the market, including modems, hard drives, and memory cards. Also known as PCMCIA cards.

Special tips

Make sure the PDA is expandable via software updates, so that the equipment will not become obsolete when new software is released.

Make sure the PDA is easy to use in conjunction with your PC. Some units will not work with Macintosh computers or other operating systems.

Battery life can vary considerably from one PDA to the next. Some units run on two AA batteries for months, while others can drain the batteries in just a matter of weeks.

See also
Modems, Notebook Computers, Portable Printers

Pension Plans

*P*ension plans provide a long-term source of income for employees after retirement. These plans are often very effective at helping to attract and retain employees. In addition, due to tax benefits, pension plans are often more cost-effective than other forms of compensation.

Buying points

How they work
A pension plan is a company-sponsored retirement savings plan. Tax-free contributions to a pension fund are made by the firm, employees or both parties. This fund can be invested in a number of different ways, with the resulting money paid out to the employee upon retirement.

Taxes are accrued when the retiree actually receives the money; this typically offers the advantage of having the money taxed at a lower rate. In addition, since the funds are contributed before taxes, one dollar invested in a pension plan is worth more than a dollar paid to the employee. Through these tax breaks, the federal government ends up paying for about one third of pension benefits.

What a company gains
Pension plans can help boost employee satisfaction and dedication. They can help attract employees and act as a reward for loyal service. In some cases, plans that are structured to provide more benefits with increasing terms of employment can even encourage employees to continue working for the firm. For long-term employees, pension plans can even help decrease health care costs, by giving older employees more of an incentive to retire.

Pension plan vs. cash bonus
Whether to offer a pension plan or simply a cash bonus will depend on the type of people you employ and your expectations of them. Firms with a very stable, older workforce would do well to consider a pension plan. With retirement looming nearer, such employees are more likely to

appreciate funds that will help them comfortably retire.

On the other hand, firms that tend to employ many young people or have a fairly transient workforce may find it more motivating to pay employees directly. Such employees typically place less value on long-term benefits and may not be around long enough to attain (or appreciate) full vesting into a pension plan.

Types of plans

There are two main types of pension plans: defined benefit plans and defined contribution plans.

Defined benefit plans promise a specific monthly payment at retirement, based on factors such as the employee's average salary and time spent with the firm. The company does not need to contribute a set amount each year, but does need to invest the money in such a way as to cover the promised benefits.

Defined contribution plans promise a specific yearly contribution to the pension plan, usually based on salary, but do not offer any fixed benefit. Depending on the success of the pension investments, the actual payout to retirees can vary significantly.

Defined benefit plans are generally considered to offer more security than defined contribution plans, since the government guarantees all defined benefit plans in the case of bankruptcy. However, this guarantee is costly, with businesses paying a premium on each defined benefit plan to support the government's guarantee program. As a result, businesses have moved away from defined benefit plans in recent years; 82% of pension plans are now of the defined contribution variety.

An intermediate option is the target-benefit plan, which offers the advantages of a defined benefit plan with the simpler administration of a defined contribution plan. Essentially, these plans specify a defined yearly contribution, but weigh the contribution by the age of the employee to achieve similar end benefits no matter when the employee enters the plan. As a result, yearly contributions for older employees will be greater than those for younger employees.

Unlike defined benefit plans, however, target benefit plans are not committed to a set rate of return. Employees assume the risk of poor investments, with pension benefits falling below the target if contributions fail to achieve expected returns.

Non-qualified plans

Most pension plans are qualified, meaning that the Internal Revenue Service (IRS) specifically approves the plan structure, allowing it to qualify for many tax benefits. However, non-qualified plans are often a better choice for smaller firms, where the added expense of designing a qualified plan is not worth the tax savings.

Currently there are two types of non-qualified pension plans, called the simplified employee pension (SEP) and the salary-reduction simplified employee pension (SAR-SEP).

SEPs are essentially individual retirement accounts (IRA) that are established by the company for each employee. Funding is contributed by the employer and is tax deductible. However, SEPs require much less documentation than a standard defined contribution plan, with businesses needing only to fill out a single IRS form (5305-SEP).

SAR-SEPs are essentially a SEP that is funded by employee-selected salary reductions. These plans were first allowed in 1986, with the aim of providing 401(k)-like benefits to smaller firms. Firms must have fewer than 25 employees to set up a SAR-SEP, and all contributions must be within a specified percentage of salary.

How to set up a pension plan

Choosing the right pension plan administrator will determine how easy your plan is to use and can even affect how well your investment grows. Insurance firms, mutual fund companies, and third party administrators (TPAs) are the primary managers of most pension plans.

Insurance companies will usually work very closely with companies to design a plan. They are often a good choice for target benefit and age-weighted plans, which may need to be customized to fit your particular business needs.

Mutual fund companies typically offer prototype plans that can be adjusted to fit specific needs. They typically offer low start-up and yearly costs, which makes them well suited for small- and medium-size businesses looking for simpler plans.

TPAs specialize in developing and administering pension plans. Their small size and focus makes them well suited for working with smaller companies, even those with fewer than 25 employees. TPAs often offer more investment options and flexibility than mutual funds and insurance agents, and can design a wide range of different plans.

Budgeting total contributions

Most pension planners figure that employees should retire with yearly benefits equal to 60% to 70% of their salary. The age of the employee and the expected return on investment should help you calculate the yearly expense of the program. Once a plan is established, it is very difficult to lower benefits. As a result, you should make sure that the necessary yearly investment in the plan stays below a level that would cause real hardship for your company.

Pricing

The cost of a pension plan depends on the level of benefits and the ongoing administrative costs. In some cases, setting up a basic pension plan may cost no more than $10 per person to complete the proper forms. On the other hand, even a semi-customized target benefit plan can easily run thousands of dollars in set-up costs. Similarly, the high cost of administering defined benefit plans make them usually only suitable for companies of 100 or more people.

Low-ball proposals from pension plan administrators may exclude provisions that will decrease your funding costs over time. As a result, make sure to get a sense for how each plan will become more or less costly in the future as employees join and leave the firm.

Terms

401(k) plans Pension plans funded by salary deductions. Employers only pay administrative and set-up costs, although some firms may elect to match 401(k) contributions.

Cash balance plans A type of defined benefit plan for which the company contributes a set monthly amount and promises a minimum guaranteed interest rate. However, a cash balance plan does not promise a specific level of benefits upon retirement.

Pension Benefit Guarantee Corporation (PBGC) The government's fund that guarantees pension plans. It is supported by premiums paid on defined benefit plans.

Qualification The process through which firms become authorized to establish a pension plan. This process requires extensive filing with the IRS, plus annual updates. Qualified plans are those meeting all IRS requirements, thereby making the firm eligible for numerous tax benefits.

Vesting schedule A timeline that indicates the level of benefits an employee accrues according to his or her length of employment. Vesting is designed to reward long-term employees.

Special tips

Firms of more than ten people will usually be better off establishing a qualified pension plan. Although set up costs are often higher, this premium tends to be outweighed by tax benefits for firms of 10 or more people.

Non-profit organizations that are tax exempt under section 501(c)(3) can offer 403(b) plans. This is essentially a 401(k) plan for a non-profit organization. Costs for the organization are limited to the price of setting up and administering the fund.

For more information on pension plans, call the Employees Benefit Research Institute (202/659-0670) or the National Underwriters Co. (800/543-0874).

Many providers offer "prototype" plans to cut the cost for small firms developing a plan. Prototype plans are designed for immediate IRS approval.

See also
401(k) Plans, Accountants, Health Insurance, Payroll Services

Did you know?

Forty-six percent of employees prefer pension benefits to cash compensation or a share in the company, according to a survey by the Employee Benefits Research Institute.

PHOTOCOPIER CONTROLS

*P*hotocopier controls are systems that track copier usage by requiring users to enter a specific billing code prior to copying. Used primarily by law firms, insurance companies, and accounting firms, copier controls offer a way to bill specific departments, individuals, or clients for copies that are made.

VENDORS

Company	Headquarters	Phone number	Sales channel Dealers	Direct
Abaddon	North Palm Beach, FL	800/226-3440	●	●
Accountor Systems	Westchester, IL	708/343-2522	●	●
Atrix	Minneapolis, MN	800/222-6154	●	●
Copy Guard	Miami, FL	800/755-9511	●	
Danyl	Moorestown, NJ	609/234-8000	●	●
Equitrac	Coral Gables, FL	800/327-0183	●	
Hecon	Eatontown, NJ	800/524-1669	●	●
Pitney Bowes	Stamford, CT	800/MR-BOWES	●	●

Buying points

Uses
Photocopier controls allow a firm to accurately track and monitor copier usage. This data can be used to set departmental budgets, find inefficiencies in the office, or bill clients. Copier controls can also be used to improve the efficiency of scheduling maintenance and purchasing supplies.

Types of systems
Copier control systems can be installed in one of three ways: standalone systems, local area network (LAN) installation, and wide area network (WAN) installation.

Most small offices will want to install a standalone system. This means that a copier control unit is mounted on each copier in the firm. To collect data, someone in the office must walk to each computer and download the data onto a notebook computer or disk.

In larger offices, this task can be very time consuming. As a result, some firms link all their photocopiers to a centralized PC. This networking allows data to be directly exchanged between the PC and each copier. However, setting up a LAN copier control system requires wiring each photocopier to the network, which can be fairly costly.

For offices that wish to network photocopiers at multiple locations, a wide area network installation may be most appropriate. In this case, each control unit is fitted with a modem that calls information into a central location. A WAN control unit can be programmed to make calls at night when calling rates are lower, and can share an outside line with other telecommunications equipment.

Tracking usage
User activity can be tracked via PIN (personal identification numbers) codes, magnetic cards, or "intelligent" cards using embedded silicon chips. PINs do not require employees to carry cards, but do require each person to remember one or more codes. Cards are easier to use, but can be lost and may be expensive to reprogram for new clients or projects.

Programming usage limits
Control systems allow you to place limits on the number of copies made by each group or user, the total run length, or even the total volume copied by a machine. To get around these limits, authorized users can be given access to an override feature.

Types of management reports
Most copier control units offer management reports that track usage for each user, department or project, as well as total usage, usage per transaction, usage per day, and even usage per hour. If all photocopiers are linked to a centralized computer, usage reports can be generated for all networked photocopiers to determine the best ways to configure resources for the entire office.

An important consideration when selecting a vendor is the type of software available for managing the collected data. You should make sure that data can be easily downloaded to your current computers, and can be imported into a spreadsheet or database program if desired.

Add-on vs. built-in units
Many new copiers offer built-in account code functions. These do not require an additional control system investment and are often easier to set up than a third party system. For basic tracking needs, they can be a cost-effective alternative.

The disadvantage of integrated systems is that they usually do not offer the flexibility of add-on units. Most offer only one way to upload data to a PC, which may not fit with the data analysis needs of your firm. In addition, integrated systems are often not capable of working together in a LAN or WAN environment.

Other access controls
Access controls are available for other types of office equipment, including fax machines, mailing equipment, and laser printers. However, photocopiers tend to be the most popular application for these devices, since maintenance and supply costs are so much higher for a photocopier than most other types of equipment.

Pricing
Copier control systems vary in cost depending on the type of control system, and whether it is standalone or networked. Basic standalone units start at approximately $400, while LAN/WAN units cost as much as $1,000 each. Software for managing the downloaded data will usually cost an additional $1,000 to $1,500.

If the system is not accessed via PIN codes, you will need to purchase access cards. Disposable cards tend to be the least expensive, while "intelligent" cards with a programmable chip are by far the most expensive.

When comparing pricing from one vendor to the next, keep in mind that the control system price alone may not be an accurate figure for comparison. Components such as an installation kit and cables may significantly influence the cost. When asking for a bid, be sure to specify that all anticipated costs be included so that competing bids can easily be compared.

Special tips
Large display monitors on a control system can help make the unit much easier to use. Users will not have to read many awkward abbreviations if the system has a larger display.

Avoid systems with an integrated printer, monitor and keyboard. Separate components allow you to replace just the component needing repair in the event of breakdown.

Determine the number of accounts you will need at any one time before beginning your search. This will help you determine the total number of account codes a system will need to support.

If you only need a system that records the number of copies being made (such as in a copy shop setting), the least expensive alternative is a counter that can be reset with each new customer.

If you expect individuals to make personal copies on the photocopier (in a library or school setting), you may want to install an unattended vending system. This allows infrequent users to purchase a card that is preprogrammed with a specific number of copies or dollar value.

See also
Copy Paper, Photocopiers

> **Did you know?**
>
> It is estimated that nearly a quarter of the 600 billion copies made each year are deemed wasteful or unnecessary, according to *Government Executive*.

PHOTOCOPIERS

Photocopiers allow firms to reproduce documents, receipts, forms, and written work for distribution or record-keeping. Few offices can operate without a photocopier, making these machines among the most heavily-used pieces of equipment in many firms.

PRICING

Photocopier type	Price range
Featherweight copier (up to 4,000 copies per month)	$1,500-$5,800
Lightweight copier (4,000-15,000 copies per month)	$4,300-$11,700
Middleweight copier (15,000-30,000 copies per month)	$6,600-$22,000
Heavyweight copier (30,000-75,000 copies per month)	$16,600-$56,100

VENDORS

Company	Headquarters	Phone number	< 10	10-19	20-35	36-80	80+
Canon	Lake Success, NY	800/OK-CANON	•	•	•	•	•
Gestetner	Greenwich, CT	800/765-7746		•	•	•	•
Kodak	Rochester, NY	800/255-3434			•	•	•
Konica	Windsor, CT	800/2-KONICA		•	•	•	•
Lanier	Atlanta, GA	800/852-2679	•	•	•	•	•
Minolta	Ramsey, NJ	800/9-MINOLTA		•	•	•	•
Mita	Fairfield, NJ	800/ABC-MITA		•	•	•	•
Monroe	Morris Plains, NJ	201/993-2000		•	•	•	•
Nashuatec	Greenwich, CT	800/595-1599		•	•	•	
Oce	Chicago, IL	312/714-8500				•	•
Panasonic	Secaucus, NJ	800/843-0080	•	•	•	•	•
Pitney Bowes	Stamford, CT	800/MR-BOWES		•	•	•	•
Ricoh	West Caldwell, NJ	800/63-RICOH		•	•	•	•
Royal Copystar	Fairfield, NJ	800/824-STAR		•	•	•	
Savin	Stamford, CT	203/967-5000		•	•	•	
Sharp	Mahwah, NJ	800/237-4277	•	•		•	•
Toshiba	Irvine, CA	714/583-3000		•	•	•	•
Xerox	Rochester, NY	800/TEAM-XRX	•	•	•	•	•

Buying points

Usage
When buying a copier, the first thing you need to determine is what "strength" machine you require. This is usually indicated by the number of copies you expect to make.

If you already have a copier, start by checking how many copies you currently make per month. All machines have a counter, usually under the platen glass.

In your calculations, take into account the fact that you will experience increased usage with a new copier. To start, businesses can expect to see usage increase 10% with any new model. In addition, if you expect the firm to grow, inflate your usage expectations by the appropriate amount.

The final step is to compare this figure with the monthly copy volume figures for various copiers. These tend to be heavily inflated, so make sure you will not exceed 60% to 70% of the rated maximum. If you expect usage to increase fairly significantly, you may want to look at models that offer monthly volumes twice your current usage.

Copy speed
Copy speed and monthly volume tend to go hand-in-hand, with faster machines usually offering higher monthly volumes. However, make sure the copy speed is well suited for the type of use the copier will receive. If your firm normally makes many single copies, look for a copier with a fast first copy speed. On the other hand, firms that usually copy multi-page documents can give up something in first copy speed in exchange for faster overall copy speeds.

Copier options
Copiers can be equipped with a wide range of options. For most businesses, the really useful options are the ones that improve the machine's productivity.

One of the most useful options is a feeder. Feeders are designed to automatically feed original documents onto the copying surface. They reduce the time needed to make copies, particularly for multi-page documents.

Sorters and sorter staplers are designed to collate and finish multi-page documents as they exit the machine. These options consist of several horizontal bins into which copies are placed. Sorter staplers include a built-in stapler to bind the collated documents.

Duplexing units allow a copier to copy onto both sides of a page. They usually consist of a storage tray in the machine, which stores pages printed on one side until they are ready to receive an image on the back side.

Differences among feeders
There are several different types of feeders on the market.

An ADF, or automatic document feeder, takes each sheet and moves it across the copying glass. These feeders are fine for a single-sided document, but cannot automatically make copies of the reverse side of an original.

A "recirculating" feeder, or RADF, is able to make copies of the back side of a sheet by flipping the page within the feeder. RADFs tend to be more expensive than ADFs, but are often the only option for larger machines.

A third type of feeder is a recirculating document handler, or RDH. An RDH can copy both sides of a sheet just like an RADF, but operates in a somewhat different manner when producing multiple sets. An RADF makes as many copies as is necessary of each page before moving on to the next page. In contrast, an RDH makes only one copy of each page, recirculating the originals as many times as is necessary to make the required number of copies.

Although RADFs and RDHs sound similar, this detail results in substantial differences when outputting pages. RADF pages emerge uncollated, requiring multiple sorter bins to create collated documents. In contrast, copiers with RDH feeders automatically produce collated documents. In fact, most RDH copiers do not use sorter bins at all, instead simply offsetting each document slightly on the output tray. With sorters typically costing thousands of dollars, this slight difference can make a big difference in the cost of the machine.

Minimizing break downs
Anyone who has ever worked in an office knows that copiers break down. However, most problems occur because of over-use or human carelessness, not because of significant differences between brands or specific models. As a result, the best way to make sure a machine keeps working is to carefully scrutinize warranties and service contracts.

The best warranty is one that promises replacement of the copier if you are dissatisfied. Less attractive are extended customer satisfaction guarantees, which offer free replacements at the dealer's discretion for unrepairable models. This sounds promising, but does not give you a great deal of flexibility if a copier requires frequent repairs. You will find 90 day parts and labor warranties of little value, since most copiers perform well in the first six months.

Copiers require anywhere from 8 to 20 service visits a year, with even a top-performing model needing three or four per year. It is important to obtain a service agreement that outlines prices for labor and/or parts when buying a copier.

Choosing the right service agreement
Almost all service agreements cover the cost of replaceable parts. This includes parts that break or malfunction during use, or those that require regular replacement such as fuser, oil rollers, and cleaning blades.

Consumables such as toner, developer, and paper are typically excluded from service agreements. The photoconductor, or drum, is alternately classified as a consumable or a replacement part. This can drastically change a contract's pricing because of its high replacement cost.

To find the best service agreement, solicit bids on an agreement that you, not the dealer, have outlined. Include expectations for coverage of emergency repairs and response time, routine maintenance, and the rate of increase of future service costs.

Pricing

Copier prices reflect the overall speed and copy volume of the machine. Personal copiers can be found for less than $1,000, low end (10 cpm) machines start at about $2,000, and high-end models (80 cpm) cost $30,000 or more.

Few copiers are sold at list price. You should expect discounts of 10% to 25%, depending on the age of the design and competition in the market segment.

Renting or leasing a copier is often an attractive alternative to buying, particularly for startup firms. Some leases charge by the monthly copy volume and require trade-ups as your volume rises.

The price of a service agreement accounts for anticipated copy volume, age and type of unit, and the distance from the dealer. In total, it should cost 5% to 8% of the original copier purchase price.

You may be able to save 15% to 20% on supplies by buying them through an alternate source. Remember that you do not have to buy a copier, a service agreement, and toner from the same dealer.

Terms

Bypass tray A device designed to handle thicker materials such as acetates or card stock. The bypass tray uses a shorter, straighter paper path to reduce the risk of jamming.

Copies per minute (CPM) Indicates the number of 8.5 x 11 inch pages the copier can output per minute. In some cases, the automatic feeder may not be fast enough to keep up with the copier; this will reduce your effective cpm.

Duplex printing The ability to automatically print on both sides of a page. This can be a useful feature, but it tends to be prone to paper jams. If you want duplex printing, you will also want a document feeder that can handle two-sided originals.

Remote diagnostics A system that connects to a phone line and automatically calls the dealer if a problem arises. Such a system can speed repair time and help ensure that maintenance schedules are accurately followed.

Special tips

Most copiers reach the end of their useful life after approximately five years. You will usually save money by purchasing a new copier rather than trying to maintain an old model.

If you are purchasing copiers for multiple locations, it may be best to buy through a direct sales agent. Unlike most dealers, direct sales agents can handle sales to multiple locations, with an associated team of technicians available for servicing.

Consider buying fewer, larger copiers to replace many smaller ones. This is almost always more cost effective in terms of purchase price and maintenance costs, but may be less efficient if it requires employees to walk farther and wait longer to use a copier.

A pay-as-you-go service plan for copiers equipped with feeders, sorters or duplexing will usually be quite expensive. These components tend to break down much more than the copier mechanism itself.

The dealer should have technicians specifically trained to repair your model. If not, be very wary of entering an agreement with that dealer.

See also
Copy Paper, Multifunctional Devices, Photocopier Controls, Recycling, Toner Supplies

For more information, visit
BuyersZone
http://www.buyerszone.com/

Pointing Devices

*A*lmost all computers now require a mouse (of the electronic rather than furry variety) to maneuver around the system's desktop. However, the mouse that is sold with a computer system is not necessarily the best choice for the end user. Aftermarket pointing devices offer additional features and capabilities, and may even be able to reduce the likelihood of repetitive stress injuries.

PRICING

Type of pointing device	Price range
Mouse	$20-$100
Trackball	$50-$115
Touchpad	$50-$120
Cordless	$80-$450

VENDORS

Company	Headquarters	Phone number	Mouse	Trackball	Touchpad	Cordless	PC	Mac
Alps	San Jose, CA	408/432-6000	•		•		•	•
Apple	Cupertino, CA	800/776-2333	•	•	•			•
Cirque	Salt Lake City, UT	800/454-3375			•		•	•
Gyration	Saratoga, CA	800/316-5432	•			•	•	•
Interlink	Camarillo, CA	800/340-1331	•			•	•	•
Itac Systems	Garland, TX	214/494-3073		•			•	•
Kensington	San Mateo, CA	800/535-4242	•	•			•	•
Logitech	Fremont, CA	800/231-7717	•	•		•	•	•
Microsoft	Redmond, WA	800/426-9400	•			•		
MicroSpeed	Fremont, CA	510/490-1403	•	•			•	•
Mindpath	Dallas, TX	214/233-9296	•			•	•	•

Buying points

Types of pointing devices

The four most common pointing devices are mice, trackballs, touchpads, and pointing sticks.

Mice, the most common of the four, are small, handheld "boxes" with a ball on the bottom. As the mouse is dragged across a surface, the cursor on the screen moves in the same direction. Mice come in all shapes and sizes, and have anywhere from one to five buttons, with each button performing a different function.

A trackball is essentially an upside-down mouse, with the ball appearing on the top of the unit. Instead of moving the entire assembly, you simply roll the ball in the desired direction. Trackballs also come in many different shapes and sizes, with single or multiple buttons.

A touchpad is small electronic pads that move the pointer as you drag a finger across the pad. Touchpads work by sensing the electrical capacitance from a finger, and translating this into movement on the screen. Buttons can be located below the touchpad, or the unit can be programmed to treat a "tap" on the touchpad like a click on a mouse button.

A pointing stick is a small eraser-shaped knob that is commonly found on notebook computers. Pointing sticks move the pointer by responding to directional pressure on the knob. Buttons are normally located on the keyboard below the pointing stick.

Advantages and disadvantages of each design

Mice are generally the least expensive type of pointing device, with basic models available for less than $10. They also tend to be among the easiest to use, and are well suited to handle both rapid movement and fine detail work. On the downside, a mouse must be cleaned regularly, takes up a significant amount of desk space, and requires the user to take at least one hand off the keyboard.

Trackballs use less desk space than mice and can be integrated into a keyboard. While they do require less arm and hand movement than a mouse, trackballs require more wrist and finger movement.

Touchpads take up less space than trackballs, and are virtually immune to dust and damage. However, touchpads place more stress on the index finger. It can also be difficult to achieve precise cursor control when working.

Pointing sticks are the smallest of all the pointing devices, requiring no more space than a small gap between keys on the keyboard. They do not need cleaning, and are almost immune to damage. However, they are not especially good for rapid movement or detailed work, and place a great deal of stress on the index finger.

Differences across models

Pointing devices are available at a wide range of price points. Low-end models often do not provide very precise cursor movement, which can be frustrating for some types of work. High-end models often add software that allows you to program customized actions into buttons found on the device. Software features may also allow you to control the sensitivity and action of the pointing device for the different applications you use.

Preventing repetitive stress injuries
You can reduce the risk of repetitive stress injuries by alternating your pointing devices on a weekly basis (or at least alternating hands), keeping your wrists straight, and taking frequent breaks. The more time you spend at a keyboard, the greater your risk of injury.

Terms

Button lock A feature that "holds" a button down by simply clicking an alternate button. This allows you to highlight or drag objects without keeping a button manually depressed.

Carpal tunnel syndrome (CTS) One of the most common repetitive stress injuries. It occurs when nerves passing through the wrist are restricted due to an unnatural typing position.

Repetitive stress injury (RSI) An injury that arises from repeated movements that place unusual stress on a body part. While carpal tunnel syndrome is the most highly publicized ailment, bursitis, tendinitis, and tenosynovitis are also quite common.

Special tips

PC-compatible pointing devices can be used on Macintosh-compatible computers by using an adapter available from the Silicon Valley Bus Company (408/623-2300).

Windows users should purchase a mouse with at least two buttons. The second mouse button is increasingly being used for important functions in Windows 95-compatible programs. Macintosh users do not need a second button, although it can be a useful feature.

Cordless pointing devices are often very useful if you need to operate a computer during a presentation. Infrared pointing devices require you to point the device directly at a receiver attached to the computer, while those using radio waves can operate anywhere within a specific range.

Look for a pointing device model that offers a 90-day trial period. It usually takes some time to get used to a new design, so you should make sure you can return a pointing device that does not feel good to use.

Computer users who need pinpoint control may want to consider pen pointing devices. Like a touchpad, a pen pointer moves a cursor according to how the pen moves across the tablet.

See also
Desktop Computers, Keyboards, Notebook Computers

Portable Printers

*P*ortable printers are small, battery-powered printers designed for computer users on the go. Barely wider than the paper on which they print, portable printers can easily fit in a briefcase alongside a notebook computer. These units can weigh about one pound, and are capable of printing documents, envelopes, or acetates.

· VENDORS

Company	Headquarters	Phone number	Mac	PC	Ink-jet	Thermal	Thermal transfer
Apple	Cupertino, CA	408/996-1010	●		●		
Canon	Costa Mesa, CA	800/848-4123		●	●		
Citizen	Santa Monica, CA	800/4-PRINTERS	●	●			●
Digital	Maynard, MA	800/777-4343		●	●		
Hewlett-Packard	Palo Alto, CA	800/752-0900	●	●	●		
Mannesmann Tally	Kent, WA	206/251-5500	●	●	●		●
Olivetti	Bridgewater, NJ	908/526-8200		●	●		
Pentax	Broomfield, CO	800/543-6144		●		●	

Buying points

Types of portable printers
Portable printers work in one of three ways. Thermal transfer printers work much like a typewriter, using heat and pressure to transfer images from a ribbon to the page.

Ink-jet printers use small cartridges of liquid ink, spraying very fine drops through a nozzle to create images.

Thermal printers operate like older fax machines. These models use heat-sensitive paper, which is marked with a small heating device to produce images.

Advantages and disadvantages
The main advantage of thermal and thermal transfer printers is that they can be very small. The smallest thermal printer weighs only 14 ounces, while the smallest thermal transfer printer weighs only 1.1 pounds. In contrast, ink-jet printers start at about 2.4 pounds.

On the other hand, ink-jets generally produce much better output than thermal transfer and thermal models. Ink-jets can produce decent images, particularly if very smooth paper is used. Thermal transfer machines often print horizontal bands on dark images and thermal printers require a special type of paper that can be unpleasant to use.

Compatibility with computers
Most portable printers come with drivers to work with DOS or Windows applications. In most cases, you will have no trouble printing as long as your notebook computer has a serial or parallel port. However, only a few portable printers work with Macintosh Powerbook computers. In most cases, you will need to purchase a Mac-compatible cable.

Resolution
Resolution refers to the number of dots produced per inch by the printer. Most portable printers offer a printing resolution of 300 dots per inch (dpi). This produces enough detail for excellent text and adequate graphics. For higher resolution images, a few portable printers can produce 600 x 300 or 720 x 360 dpi output. This results in slightly better looking output, but does not match the true 600 x 600 resolution of most laser printers.

Color
Manufacturers of thermal transfer and ink-jet printers now offer color ribbons/ink for color printing. By replacing the black ribbon or cartridge with a three-color model, some printers can produce full-color output.

For ink-jet printers, color tends to be quite acceptable. You will find that color cartridges do not last very long, but portable models are acceptable for creating a few color pages.

Color printing from thermal transfer printers tends to be less useful. Most color ribbons have difficulty lasting even a full page. Even worse, color images tend to be quite unimpressive.

Thermal printers cannot offer color output since the print technology does not allow for such differentiation.

Printing speed

For black and white printing, most portable models can print a maximum of four pages per minute. In practice, many print at closer to one page per minute. For color or more complicated graphics, some printers will require as long as 45 minutes to churn out a full-color image.

If you expect to print multiple pages at a time, you should pay extra attention to the sheet feeder and battery performance.

Sheet feeders can hold anywhere from 5 to 80 pages. They allow you to avoid the hassle of manually feeding paper one sheet at a time. When examining a feeder, make sure you can feed more than just full-sized sheets. The best feeders will also handle envelopes or transparencies.

The performance of the printer's battery also plays a critical role in the usability of the printer. Most printers use Nickel-Cadmium (NiCad) batteries. These batteries can print up to 90 pages, and can typically be recharged while still in the printer. A few models use Nickel Metal Hydride (NiMH) batteries, which can print as many as 250 pages but take more time to recharge. In some cases, you may need to buy an external fast charger to effectively use an NiMH battery.

Pricing

Portable printers tend to be fairly inexpensive. Models range from a low of $200 for non-color thermal transfer printers to a high of $350 for a color ink-jet model.

Since portable printers tend to use very small cartridges or ribbons, they cost more per page to print. You can expect to pay 5¢ per page for thermal transfer printers, and as much as 11¢ per page for some ink-jet printers. Color printer costs are even higher, hovering around 70¢ per page.

A car-lighter adapter, quick charger, and additional battery are all options you may want to purchase. Batteries cost $60 to $80, while the car-lighter adapter and charger can easily add another $100 to the price of a model.

Terms

Ink-jet printers These printers spray small droplets of ink to form images on a page. Canon has a patented ink-jet process called Bubblejet printing.

Resolution The level of detail that can be printed by a printer, indicated by dots per inch (dpi). Most businesses use 300 or 600 dpi printers.

Thermal transfer A printing technique that uses heat to transfer images from a ribbon. Thermal transfer printing, sometimes called thermal fusion printing, does not require special paper.

Thermal printing A printing technology that uses heat to mark special, heat-sensitive paper. No ink or ribbons are required.

Special tips

Watch out for models that use an external paper feeder. These feeders can substantially add to the size and weight of the unit.

There are alternatives to lugging around a portable printer. One of the best techniques for printing is to use a faxmodem with your notebook computer. If you need a page printed, you can usually fax it to a hotel's fax machine. Make sure to set the fax transmission on high quality, and try to send to a plain paper fax machine.

See also
Color Printers, Dot Matrix Printers, Ink-jet Printers, Laser Printers, Notebook Computers, PDAs

For more information, visit
BuyersZone
http://www.buyerszone.com/

POSTAGE METERS

Companies that conduct a significant amount of business via mail will find a postage meter system to be a very useful piece of equipment. By eliminating the cluttered look of letters with many stamps, postage meters give mailings a "big company" look. More practically, a postage meter can save trips to the post office and reduce the time needed to prepare mail. Meters also provide an easy way to keep track of how much money is spent on mailings.

PRICING

Type of base	Price range
Manual feeder only	$800-$1,500
With semi-automatic feeder	$800-$6,000
With automatic feeder	$2,300-$11,500

VENDORS

Company	Headquarters	Phone number	Sales channels		Market share
			Dealers	Direct	
Ascom Hasler	Shelton, CT	800/243-6275	●	●	7%
Francotyp-Postalia	Lisle, IL	800/95-NO-INK	●		1%
Neopost	Hayward, CA	800/624-7892	●	●	6%
Pitney Bowes	Stamford, CT	800/MR-BOWES		●	85%

Buying points

Postage meter system
A postage meter consists of two parts: the meter and the base. The meter keeps track of the postage that has been used and stamps each outgoing piece of mail. The base feeds envelopes through the meter. The reason for this distinction is that meters cannot be purchased—they must be rented from the manufacturer. Bases can be purchased, although many businesses choose to rent or lease the units.

Differences among meters
The primary difference among meters concerns how postage is stored. Older meters are mechanical, meaning that postage is tracked on counters within the machine. Newer models are electronic, using digital memory to record postage usage.

The Postal Service prefers electronic meters because they are difficult or impossible to tamper with, which helps reduce postage fraud. Mechanical meters will be phased out beginning March 1997, with all units scheduled for replacement by March 1999.

For end users, mechanical meters continue to offer some advantages over newer electronic models. They are less expensive to rent and can often be used with older, less expensive bases. As a result, while they remain available, mechanical meters may be a better choice for many users.

Differences among bases
Bases differ primarily in how enve-lopes are handled. The least expensive bases are manual, requiring the user to place each letter onto the rollers and guide it through the meter.

A more expensive design includes a semiautomatic feeder, which grabs letters one after another, feeding them in a nearly continuous stream through the machine.

The fastest bases have fully automatic feeders. These will automatically stamp a stack of letters without requiring human supervision. Automatic feeders cost at least $1,000 more than semiautomatic feeders, but can greatly speed the mailing process for high-volume mailers.

Additional features
Most bases can be equipped with additional features such as stackers and sealers to speed the mailing process.

A sealer wets and seals each envelope as it passes through the base. On most systems, the sealer can be used independently of the meter to seal items such as paycheck envelopes.

After mail is sealed and stamped, it must be cleared from the machine. This requires a stacker. Basic stackers are nothing more than a plastic tray to catch letters exiting the machine. They tend to fill up after only a few dozen letters. Power stackers can stack more envelopes by using a mechanized wheel to push letters farther from the meter. These cost about $1,000.

Stamping larger packages
Larger packages or colored envelopes can be postmarked by using a stamped strip of adhesive paper called tape. Tape can be difficult to accurately

feed through the machine by hand. In some cases, the meter may miss the strip entirely and waste postage.

As a result, businesses that send many large packages should look for a base equipped with an automatic tape dispenser. These are available in two varieties. Pre-cut dispensers pull single pieces of tape from a bin on top of the machine. Roll dispensers use a continuous roll of tape inside the base, cutting it to the proper length after stamping. Businesses sending many packages will find that roll tape is less expensive to use over time, even though a roll dispenser may cost an extra $100 to $650.

Refilling the postage meter
Most postage meters must be "filled" by the post office. This involves prepaying a certain amount of postage at the local post office. The post office sets internal counters on the meter and the postage used is automatically subtracted from this fund as letters are stamped.

These days, many meters can be refilled by phone. With this method, you typically send a check to your vendor for postage. When you need a refill, the vendor transfers the funds via telephone into the meter. In most cases, you will need an electronic meter to utilize this feature, which typically costs around $8 per refill.

Servicing your postage meter
Buyers will find that as their system become more complex, so will their need for service. Service for a postage meter system can be confusing because of differences in ownership of the meter and the base. Because the meter is rented, the manufacturer is responsible for repairs on the unit. There is no service contract, but you should inquire about how long it will take to get repairs or a replacement unit.

Because the base is usually owned, a service contract may be necessary on this component. Most low-end systems are fairly simple and do not require a service agreement. However, a service contract becomes more critical as you add options such as sealers and power stackers. In addition, any base that uses a lot of electronics should be covered by a service contract, since these parts tend to be very expensive to replace.

A service contract typically costs 10% of the purchase price, with rates increasing 5% to 8% per year.

Getting a good deal
The postage meter industry has not grown much in recent years, meaning that sales representatives may be quite aggressive when trying to win business.

First, make sure to ask about purchasing a base instead of leasing or renting an entire system. Leasing or renting a postage meter system can be as much as 75% more costly than buying the base and renting the meter separately over a two- or three-year period.

Also watch out for package deals that include a meter, base, and scale. These are often a bad bargain, giving you more equipment than you really need. Instead, price items separately, only agreeing to a bundle if each component makes sense.

Bases and meters are incompatible across vendors, so sales reps have a great incentive to lock up customers when they first look for postage meters. Watch out for sales reps who offer very inexpensive systems. In many cases, you will quickly outgrow the first model and be forced to pay much more for a better-equipped system.

Pricing

Meter rental fees range from $200 to $900 a year. Rates usually vary according to postage usage, with higher levels of usage translating to higher rental charges. In addition, rates for many meter rentals are designed to increase during each year of the agreement. Investigate how big an increase you will face in upcoming years before agreeing to any multi-year deal.

Prices for bases start at $600. Feeders cost an additional $300 to $1,700. You should aim for discounts of about 10% off list price. Before buying any add-ons, consider which are absolutely necessary because they are costly and rarely save enough time to pay for themselves.

Terms

Accounting codes These codes allow you to assign the cost of postage to different departments or clients.

Auto postage reset This feature prevents users from accidentally printing large denominations of postage. Meters accomplish this by resetting to 32¢ after each use, or by requiring a safety button to be pushed if the amount is over $1.00. Either method is useful, especially if more than one person will use the machine.

Decimal or bulk mail meters These meters are able to print postage in fractional amounts. Bulk mailings typically require postage to three decimal places, such as $0.198.

Indicia Marking that indicates the amount of postage used on the envelope, as well as the date and meter number.

Meter setting The maximum postage the meter is able to postmark. Machines have a set maximum, usually $99.99, $9.99, or 99¢.

Postage capacity The maximum amount to which the meter can be filled. Most meters go to $9,999, while a few run as high as $99,999.

Special tips

If you send fewer than 30 letters per day, stamps probably should remain your low-tech postage meter. Stamps can even be more effective than a meter for convincing people to open your mail.

If your mail volume is erratic or has certain days with much higher volume, consider subcontracting large mailings to a mailing house. Mailing houses can stuff, seal and meter large quantities (500 letters or more) much more efficiently than an in-house meter. Mailing houses charge 1 to 3 cents per piece, depending on the task.

The most effective way to obtain a discount on a system is to let the rep know you are considering models from another vendor. Just mentioning an interest in other manufacturers can often lead to substantial discounts or months of free meter rentals.

Used bases typically sell for 30% to 50% less than comparable new models, with virtually no difference in performance. The largest and best known vendor of used bases is Evcor (800/873-8267). This company has 20 offices nationwide and sells more than $20 million in used bases each year.

See also
Ground Shipping, International Expedited Delivery, Letter Folding Equipment, Letter Opening, Equipment, LTL Shipping, Overnight Delivery Services, Postal Scales, Same Day Delivery Services

For more information, visit
BuyersZone
http://www.buyerszone.com/

Postal Scales

*P*ostal scales are designed to increase mailing efficiency by reducing overpayment on outgoing mail. By obtaining a good scale, the typical business will save 10% to 15% on postage.

PRICING

Electronic scale	Price range
2-5 lbs.	$119-$1,295
10-30 lbs.	$249-$1,795
100+ lbs.	$169-$4,995

VENDORS

			Can be interfaced with postage meter from			
Company	Headquarters	Phone number	Ascom Hasler	Francotyp-Postalia	Neopost	Pitney Bowes
Ascom Hasler	Shelton, CT	800/243-6275	●			●
Detecto	Webb City, MO	800/822-2260	●			●
Micro General	Santa Ana, CA	714/667-0557	●		●	●
Neopost	Hayward, CA	800/624-7892			●	
Pelouze	Bridgeview, IL	800/654-8330				
Pitney Bowes	Norfolk, VA	800/MR-BOWES				●

Buying points

Types of scales
Postage scales come in both manual and electronic versions. Manual scales use a balance or a spring to weigh envelopes, while electronic scales use a pressure-sensing microprocessor.

Manual scales can be very accurate, but usually require users to accurately read the weight from a mechanical needle, which increases the chances for human error.

In contrast, electronic scales provide a clear, unambiguous digital readout, which is unlikely to cause any confusion. To reduce human error even more, many digital scales can be interfaced with a postage meter to automatically set the meter to the appropriate amount.

Postage meter interface
If you do not need a scale that can automatically set postage on the meter, you can buy any scale you desire. There is no need to buy a scale from the meter manufacturer, since there are no compatibility issues between the two pieces of equipment.

Your choices are generally more limited if you want the scale to automatically set the correct postage on the meter. Almost all the postage meter manufacturers offer scales that interface with their mid- and high-end meters. There are also third-party scales that can be interfaced with postage meters. These often require a special interface in order to work.

Incorporating postage rate increases
Since scales convert weight into postage, they must be adjusted each time postal rates change.

Most electronic scales use a microchip encoded with rate information. When rates change, you can purchase a new microchip to incorporate the new rates.

Be sure to ask about the charges for a new microchip. Some scale manufacturers charge very high rates for each new chip. Others charge less per chip but store rate information across several chips that must all be individually replaced.

A few manufacturers offer extended coverage programs that allow for rate updates at no additional charge.

Features
One of the most useful scale features is a "comparison shopping" option. This enables you to determine the most economical rate among the different classes of mail. Most scales incorporate First Class and Standard Class rates from the U.S. Postal Service, with some scales adding pricing for alternative package carriers such as DHL, FedEx, RPS, and UPS. Fancier scales will even include the cost of postal services such as certified or registered mail.

Handling oversized envelopes
If you primarily send small documents weighing less than 2 lbs., almost any scale will be able to handle your needs. However, if you anticipate a more diverse mix of

outgoing documents, then you will need to make sure that the scale can handle oversized packages and heavier weights.

When evaluating scales, look at the size of the weighing platform, as well as the maximum weight that the unit can measure. An automatic lock feature that stores the weight reading can be very useful for large packages that block the display from view.

Other considerations

Another important consideration is ease of use. Since many different people may be using the scale, you want to find one that is relatively intuitive to use. Look for scales that have an easy-to-read keypad or user prompts for simplified entry.

Pricing

Basic manual scales cost less than $10. Electronic scales typically start at about $75, and rise to several hundred dollars for scales that can handle alternate carriers or heavier weights.

If you expect to interface the scale with a postage meter, be sure to find out how much the interface will cost. A postage meter interface typically adds a few hundred dollars to the price.

Terms

Postage meter interface An accessory that allows some scales to automatically enter the appropriate amount of postage at the postage meter.

Zip-to-zone conversion A feature that automatically converts a ZIP code to the proper zone for calculating zone-dependent rates for carriers like RPS and UPS.

Special tips

If you are concerned about unauthorized use of the interfaced scale and meter, you may want to consider purchasing a scale with a password feature.

Accounting features allow you to charge postage and other handling charges to individual clients or departments. In many cases, it is less expensive to obtain management reports from the scale than from the postage meter.

For shipments that exceed the weight capacity of the scale, look for a scale that allows you to manually enter the weight for rate calculation.

Companies will generally pay less to purchase a scale from a third party vendor than from a postage meter vendor.

See also
Ground Shipping, International Expedited Delivery, Letter Opening Equipment, LTL Shipping, Overnight Delivery Services, Postage Meters, Same Day Delivery Services

PPOs

A preferred provider organization, or PPO, is a collection of physicians and hospitals that agrees to provide health care at a reduced cost to its members. These organizations have become very popular in recent years as a way to limit health care costs without the restrictions of a health maintenance organization, or HMO.

Buying points

PPO basics
Most PPOs are quite similar to health insurance policies with the exception that there are two different levels of coverage depending on the type of providers you use. For visits to doctors and hospitals that are affiliated with the PPO, patients pay a low deductible and little or no co-insurance. Visits to doctors and hospitals outside the network are not as fully covered, requiring higher payments from the patient.

This structure is designed to encourage PPO members to use specific doctors and hospitals that have been designated by the organization as "preferred providers." These doctors and hospitals agree to provide health care to PPO members at lower rates, which allows the PPO to reduce overall health care costs.

PPO network differences
Unlike HMOs, PPO networks are not as tightly regulated. As a result, networks can range from very loose discounting agreements to fairly rigid networks with specific policies and oversight.

The type of network structure can significantly affect the benefits and drawbacks of joining a PPO. Loosely organized networks tend to offer the greatest choice for patients, with few treatment restrictions. On the downside, these networks are often not much better at controlling costs than traditional health insurance, which can result in higher premiums over time.

Tightly structured PPOs are often much better at controlling overall costs. By requiring patients to obtain referrals and second opinions before getting treatment, these networks can often reduce the overuse of health care. However, this often comes at the expense of the patients' ability to manage their own health care treatment.

Evaluating PPO networks

To evaluate a PPO network, buyers should take a close look at the quality of both the doctors and hospitals in the network.

First, inquire about what screening process the company uses when signing up physicians. A screening process should ideally include checks of the doctor's background, including analysis of any previous malpractice issues.

Also ask how many physicians have been certified by the American Board of Medical Specialties. In order to be certified, the physician must demonstrate competency in a specialty by passing tests or meeting training requirements. Ideally, 85% or more of the physicians should be board certified.

Some plans sign up doctors simply to boost their numbers. To get a better sense of the availability of doctors in the network, ask what percentage of the doctors are actually accepting new patients.

Also examine how second opinions are handled and how disputes in treatment are settled. PPOs should have a set procedure in place for disagreements to be aired before a grievance board.

Checking out-of-network care

The ability to opt out of the network often lulls PPO members into a sense of false security. If the network is not up to snuff, people feel they can simply go outside the network for care.

In practice, however, many PPOs make it impractical to obtain care outside the network. By setting high deductibles and co-insurance, plans can make visits outside the network prohibitively expensive.

As a result, health care buyers need to carefully examine the details of a PPO policy before signing up for a program. The evaluation should consider not only the quality of the health care network, but also the costs of, and restrictions on, receiving care outside the network.

Examining the policy

Prospective PPO members should also make sure to carefully scrutinize policy details, particularly those that deal with receiving treatment outside the network.

To start, make sure that deductibles and co-insurance do not drastically exceed what you would pay with a traditional insurance policy. Be wary of policies that require patients to co-insure more than 25% of the cost of treatment, or that continue to charge co-insurance for costs in excess of $5,000.

Next, check what types of conditions are covered. Some policies limit out-of-network coverage to specific conditions, or set artificially low limits on the maximum payment. As with any health insurance policy, you should look for coverage with at least a $1 million maximum payout.

Also watch out for low reimbursement levels. Some programs pay a set maximum per procedure, which may be far less than what a physician or doctor actually charges. If the reimbursement level is too low, the patient can be left paying the difference. To avoid this, check with a physician to see if reimbursement levels from the PPO are within the normal billing range.

Finally, look for a plan that offers a specified mechanism for handling member disputes. A clearly outlined appeals process will give members a way to protest unfair reimbursement levels or other problems. Consulting the state department of insurance, which keeps records of patient complaints, may also shed some light regarding patient satisfaction.

Pricing

PPOs cost an average of $3,386 per employee per year, according to the "1994 National Survey of Employer-Sponsored Health Plans" by Foster Higgins.

In terms of patient out-of-pocket costs, PPOs can vary tremendously. Some networks require members to pay only a small deductible with each visit, much like an HMO. Others keep deductibles and co-insurance in place, but provide discounts off regular doctor and hospital charges.

Terms

Co-insurance The part of a health care bill that is shared between the insurer and the patient. For example, co-insurance often requires the patient to pay 20% of the first $5,000 of health care costs for the year. This means that a patient may owe as much as $1,000 towards the cost of treatment. Most PPOs use co-insurance, although some waive the charge for treatment within the network.

Deductible The fee that a patient pays for health care. Deductibles can be fixed on a per-visit basis, such as $25 per visit, or can be fixed on a yearly basis, such as the first $500 of health care costs per year.

Health maintenance organization (HMO) An alternate type of managed care network. HMOs are governed by more regulations than PPOs, which makes them usually more rigid in terms of network rules and structure.

Managed care A term that describes all programs that try to control health costs by limiting the use of unnecessary treatments. HMOs, PPOs, point of service plans, and utilization review are all forms of managed care.

Special tips

The decision whether to join a PPO is often significantly affected by what types of health care networks are popular in your geographic area. If HMOs are much more common, PPOs may have difficulty signing up the best doctors and hospitals as preferred providers. On the other hand, you may find almost all doctors signed up with a PPO in areas dominated by these organizations.

If your firm is very small, you may want to consider joining a multiple employer welfare association (MEWA). MEWAs are groups assembled to provide employee benefits to more than one business. Health coverage offered by chambers of commerce and professional associations are some of the most common examples of MEWAs. However, be very careful to check the credentials of any MEWA you use; industry experts estimate 1% to 2% of MEWAs are actually fraudulent operations.

Purchasing health care is a decision that often requires extensive knowledge of local markets. While it is possible to learn about the market on your own, it can be easier to pool information about the quality of care offered by local health care providers. The National Business Coalition on Health (202/775-9300) represents about 90 of these purchasing coalitions.

See also

Business Insurance, Health Insurance, HMOs, Workers Compensation Insurance

For more information, visit
BuyersZone
http://www.buyerszone.com/

Prepaid Phone Cards

*I*n Europe, the majority of payphone calls are made with prepaid phone cards. These cards are programmed with a set amount of money, from which amounts are electronically deducted as calls are placed.

In the past few years, this concept has been exported to the U.S., but with a twist. In Europe, prepaid phone cards are used with payphones equipped with magnetic readers, into which the cards are inserted. Since these specially-equipped phones are not widely available in the U.S., prepaid phone cards in the U.S. require the user to first call a toll free number, and then enter the card number, before they can place a call.

Company	Headquarters	Phone number	Denominations
VENDORS			
AT&T	Basking Ridge, NJ	800/462-1818	$15, 25, 50
Frontier	Rochester, NY	800/783-2020	$10, 20, 50
LCI	McLean, VA	800/800-8285	$10, 30, 60, 120
MCI	Washington, DC	800/652-4613	$5, 10, 15, 20
NTC	Irvine, CA	800/569-4682	$25, 50, 75, 100
Sprint	Overland Park, KS	800/366-0707	$5, 10, 20, 50
TeleDebit	Sarasota, FL	800/864-1313	$30
Western Union	Bridgeton, MO	800/374-0909	$10, 20, 50
World Telecom	Mountain View, CA	800/827-6299	$20+

Buying points

How a prepaid phone card works
Prepaid phone cards can be purchased in various denominations, measured in dollars or total minutes. Once the card is purchased, the caller can place a call from any phone by dialing the toll free number listed on the back of the card and then entering the card number. After being notified about how many minutes of calling time remain on the card, the caller can then dial the desired phone number.

Denominations
Some prepaid phone cards can be programmed with any amount of money, while others come in specific denominations ranging from $1 to $100. Some prepaid phone cards can be refilled over the phone using a major credit card. Other cards simply expire when they run out of calling time and must be discarded.

Advantages and disadvantages of prepaid phone cards
The greatest disadvantage of prepaid phone cards is that you pay for the calls ahead of time. This means that if you lose a card, you lose the value remaining on the card. Prepaid phone card spending is also more difficult for a business to track because calls placed with the card do not appear on any bill or statement.

The primary advantage of having a prepaid phone card is that liability is limited in case of misuse or theft. This is appealing for businesses that are located in high-theft areas, or firms that must issue cards to many short-term employees.

The real advantage of these phone cards is for the card vendor. Prepaid phone cards have none of the billing complexity of calling cards, so calls can be processed more cost-effectively.

Features
Prepaid phone cards are available with some of the same features as calling cards. A voice mail option allows the prepaid phone card holder to distribute a toll free number to callers. The card holder can then check this mailbox from the road.

Prepaid phone cards can also be given to others as promotional devices. Such cards can be programmed to play custom audio messages, offer interactive market research tools, and provide for automatic fax-back services.

Certain cards can be programmed to pay only for calls to a specific number. This feature can be used to limit the use of the prepaid phone card to calls to the office.

Pricing
Prepaid phone cards usually vary in price from 25¢ to 60¢ per minute. Some cards offer volume discounts, which can result in lower rates for subsequent refills.

Terms

Access number A toll free number that the user calls to connect to the prepaid phone card network. Once connected, the user can make calls to any other phone.

Call rounding Measures how the length of each call is calculated. The minimum call length indicates the minimum time deducted from the card for each call, while the billing increment indicates the time increment used for billing calls extending beyond the minimum length.

Special tips

If you have any problems or questions regarding your prepaid phone card, contact the United States Telecard Association's Consumer Hotline (800/333-3513).

Some prepaid phone cards can only be used with touch tone telephones.

If you encounter a rotary phone, you may want to purchase a touch tone generator from an electronics store such as Radio Shack.

Prepaid phone cards are not always the most cost-effective option for calling from the road. Buyers should make sure to compare them to alternative calling methods such as calling cards or toll free services.

See also
Calling Cards, Cellular Service, International Callback, Long Distance Service, Toll Free Service

Public Relations Firms

*M*ovie stars aren't the only ones who need good press. Public relations firms can help a company publicize its initiatives and respond to media inquiries. Used effectively, public relations can be a powerful component of a company's marketing strategy.

Buying points

What they do
Public relations (PR) firms can provide a variety of services. They can help a business communicate its message to the whole world, or to a more limited audience. They can help define an appropriate corporate image, manage a company's interactions with particular groups, and craft public responses to a crisis or opportunity. On an ongoing basis, PR firms can help a company keep in touch with the press, answer media inquiries, and draft press releases or speeches for corporate announcements.

Outsourcing vs. in-house
Public relations can be handled either internally or externally. The main advantage of working with in-house staff is convenience. It can be much easier to coordinate communication efforts and keep a PR person informed when this person works for your company.

However, tapping an outsider for help can be useful, giving your firm a more detached perspective on the importance or angle of announcements. In addition, outside PR specialists may offer better contacts.

Checking experience
One of the most important things to check when considering PR firms is their experience. You should consider not only a firm's years of experience, but also the types of projects a firm has handled.

Ideally, the firm will have experience in your industry. That way, the PR firm will be knowledgeable about your industry and will have a good set of press contacts already developed. Ask for a client list to get a sense for the firm's areas of expertise. It can also be useful to learn if the person who handles similar clients would be available to handle your account.

Press clippings can be a good indicator of the firm's past success in generating coverage. Take a look at the type of clips displayed, paying special attention to whether the coverage was generated within the industry or in the general press. Generally, it is more difficult to obtain coverage in broad-interest newspapers or magazines than in trade publications.

Also check a PR firm's portfolio. Take the time to review press releases and other written materials. These materials should not only be well-written, but should also be compelling. For a few of these clips, learn how they were distributed and whether they were picked up by any media outlets.

Interviewing prospective liaisons

Your satisfaction with a PR firm will be most influenced by the person handling your account. As a result, it is critical that you find the person not only pleasant to work with, but also a plentiful source for fresh ideas.

The PR contact should have a natural aptitude for your industry. It is important that the person be capable of handling fairly sophisticated questions from the press. Otherwise, the PR firm will simply serve to funnel requests to your office.

Ideally, you should interview the key people who will be handling your account. Get a sense for how long it will take to bring these people up to speed on your company's offerings, judge the intelligence of their questions, and see how inventive they are in generating PR ideas. It can even be useful to make up a potential PR scenario and ask them to suggest attention-getting angles.

How billing works

PR firms generally bill companies on an hourly basis, plus expenses. To avoid any unpleasant shocks, it is important to understand the hourly rate and what might be included as expenses.

Firms that use PR firms on an ongoing basis will typically work on a monthly retainer. This is a monthly payment made to the PR firm from which charges for the PR firm's services are deducted. The client is typically billed on a monthly basis for any services rendered that exceed the amount of the retainer.

Some PR agencies will charge a flat fee for specific projects such as a store opening, trade show or publicity campaign. This can be a good alternative for firms interested in working within a fixed budget.

Pricing

The hourly rates for a PR firm can vary from $100 to $500 per hour. This will depend primarily on the experience of the individuals assigned to your account.

Special tips

Contact the Public Relations Society of America (212/826-1750) for the names of member firms in your area, or J. R. O'Dwyer Company (212/679-2471) for their national or regional public relations directories.

Inquire about the resources a PR firm has in-house. Firms already familiar with your industry should have the various industry directories and newsletters in their libraries. Otherwise, your fees may be paying for these investments.

When screening firms, make sure to ask about any minimum billing requirements. This should allow you to find out which companies only work with very large accounts.

Firms using a PR firm on an ongoing basis should schedule yearly reviews. A yearly meeting can be a good way to review the effectiveness of the PR firm and decide upon future PR strategies.

See also

Advertising Agencies, Clipping Services, Fax Broadcasting Services, Graphic Designers, Stock Photography, Trade Show Displays

Recordable CD Drives

*R*ecordable CD drives are a special type of CD-ROM drive that can not only read a compact disc, but also write information on to a blank CD. Also called CD-R drives, these drives allow businesses to make permanent CD archives of frequently-used information. CDs created in a CD-R drive have the durability of a standard CD, and can be used in any computer with a standard CD-ROM drive.

PRICING

Drive type	Price range
4X-read/2X-write	$800-$1,200
4X-read/4X-write	$1,000-$1,800

VENDORS

Company	Headquarters	Phone number	Includes software	Warranty
Dynatek	Bedford, Nova Scotia	800/267-6007		1 yr.
Hewlett-Packard	Loveland, CO	800/810-0134	●	2 yrs.
JVC	Irvine, CA	714/261-1292	●	1 yr.
Olympus	Melville, NY	800/347-4027	●	1 yr.
Philips	San Jose, CA	800/235-7373	●	2 yrs.
Pinnacle Micro	Irvine, CA	800/553-7070	●	1 yr.
Pioneer	Long Beach, CA	800/444-6784	●	1 yr.
Ricoh	San Jose, CA	800/955-3453		1 yr.
Smart and Friendly	Chatsworth, CA	818/772-8001		1 yr.
Sony	San Jose, CA	800/352-7669	●	1 yr.
Yamaha	San Jose, CA	408/467-2300		1 yr.

Buying points

CD-R technology

Recordable CD drives are a new variation of the compact disc players first introduced in the early 1980s. The CD-R uses a high-powered laser to "burn" the appropriate coding into a blank CD. This disc can then be read like any mass-produced CD-ROM.

CD-R technology does have some limitations compared to other forms of data recording. First, CD-R can only record on blank areas of a CD. This means that once information is recorded, that part of the disc cannot be reused. CD-R recording is also more time consuming than some types of data recording, with individual CDs taking anywhere from 30 to 90 minutes to prepare and record. Finally, recordable CD drives are very sensitive to problems during the recording process. Even a small processing delay from another application can ruin a recording session.

CD-R applications

CD-R drives have many applications for businesses. The most popular application is to use CD-R to archive important files. For example, a business could store thousands of old tax records or invoices on a single CD-R. The data would be secure from most kinds of damage, yet would be easily accessible on almost any computer. It would also be much cheaper to store the data on CD than on paper, floppy disks or a hard drive.

CD-R can also be used to distribute data and applications. For example, complete inventory databases could be sent on CD to branch offices. This would provide employees with immediate access to critical data, saving money by avoiding the need to retrieve the information over phone lines.

A third use of CD-R is for multimedia presentations. Modern computer presentations with video, audio, and graphics are often far too large to fit onto individual floppy disks or even some hard drives. A CD version allows travelers to carry a small disc that is compatible with almost any computer system.

Recordable CD drives are not a very good solution for storing data that changes on a frequent basis. For example, CD-R is not good for daily backups, since each CD cannot be reused once it has been recorded. A better choice in these instances would be tape drives, which can be re-recorded many times before wearing out.

Speed

The first generation of CD-ROM drives rotated fast enough to transfer 150 kilobytes per second (Kbps). This is now referred to as a single speed drive. Most modern drives now rotate several times as fast as the old single speed drives. Double speed (2X) drives transfer 300 Kbps, while quadruple speed (4X) drives transfer 600 Kbps. The fastest CD-ROM drives currently available are 10X speed drives.

Similar speed measurements are used for CD-R drives. However, the speed figure for CD-R drives is typically expressed in terms of both read and write speeds. The read speed describes how fast the drive can play a CD, while the write speed describes how quickly a CD can be recorded.

Most CD-R drives currently on the market read at 4X speed, but write at 2X speed. This is acceptable if you can devote about 37 minutes to writing a CD. A few models read and write at 4X speed, which results in recording times of about 19 minutes.

Keep in mind that rotation speed is not the only factor that determines how fast you can record a CD. The speed of your computer, the type of software used, and the technical specifications of the drive can also have a significant impact.

Recording software

To record onto a CD, you will need premastering software. This software manages the process of recording data onto the CD, including the process of converting data to the appropriate format.

Most CD-R drives come bundled with a "lite" premastering software package. This means that the software is a scaled-down version of the complete product. To produce some types of CDs, you may have to purchase a full blown version of the premastering software, which can add an additional $350 to $1,000 to the total cost. Common premastering software titles include Astarté Toast (612/483-5338), Corel CD Creator (800/772-6735), and JVC Personal RomMaker (714/261-1292).

Since premastering is very complex, you should actually try out the software before choosing a drive. Some programs make the process very simple, using a series of questions to configure the appropriate formats and recording parameters. Others are designed for experienced users, requiring you to understand exactly what formats you want before you start.

CD formats

As CDs have become increasingly popular, many formats have been introduced for storing data. Most drives support all formats, but you must be certain that your premastering software supports the format that is best for the CD applications you wish to create.

Yellow Book is the most basic CD-ROM format. CDs recorded in this format can be played in every CD-ROM drive, including the slowest single speed models.

Another popular CD format is called CD-ROM XA. This goes beyond the basic Yellow Book Standard, allowing CDs to interweave audio and data for multimedia applications.

Other CD formats tend to be infrequently used on PCs. These include the Enhanced CD format, which allows music CDs to include data and graphics, and the Green Book Format, which is used for the CD-Interactive (CD-I) format that was developed for some home entertainment systems.

Recording sessions

Another issue concerns the number of recording sessions supported by the software. Some CD-R drives allow you to write only one time per CD. This means that the CD cannot be reused, even if there are blank areas remaining on the disk.

If you will want to add data to blank areas of a CD over several recording sessions, you will need software that supports multisession recording. Look for software that uses a single table of contents for all recorded data. That way, information appears on the CD under a single icon. A less popular alternative creates separate directories for each recording session.

Pricing

Just a few years ago, CD-R drives sold for close to $10,000, and blank, recordable CDs were nearly $30 per disc. Today, CD-R drives start at less than $600, although high speed models can still fetch more than $3,500. The factors that affect price the most are the speed of the drive, the recording software, the CD-ROM formats supported, and the type of warranty available from the vendors. Blank CDs can be purchased in bulk for about $6 per disc.

Low-end packages typically include a 2X-write/4X-read drive, with a "lite" software package and limited support. However, with the price of CD-R drives falling monthly, you can expect 4X read/write models to soon be available for less than $1,000.

Terms

CD-ROM XA format An extended architecture that allows interweaving of audio and video to produce full motion video and synchronized sound.

Digital video disc (DVD) A new format standard that allows for increased storage capacity on CDs, as much as 25 times that of traditional CD-ROM discs. DVD cannot be read by CD-ROM or CD-R drives, but DVD drives will be able to read regular CD-ROMs. DVD is expected to launch by early 1997.

ISO 9660 A file format used on most CD-ROMs. ISO 9660 files can be read on a wide range of computer platforms.

Multisession recording A format that allows a CD to be created over several sessions rather than all at once. Multisession recording allows users to record until all the blank areas of the CD are filled.

Special tips

The new DVD standard allows a single disc to hold up to 17 gigabytes of data—considerably more than the 650 megabytes of space available on a CD. This will allow large programs that are currently sold on multiple CDs to be consolidated onto one DVD disc. It is anticipated that a DVD-R (DVD recordable) drive and DVD-E (DVD erasable) drive will eventually be developed, but they are still a few years away from reaching the market.

To record onto a CD, you will need at least 650 megabytes of space on a hard drive. We recommend at least a 1 gigabyte drive to allow room for temporary files. You will also need an "AV" drive, which ensures that data is transferred at a consistent rate over time. Regular drives often pause momentarily to recalibrate their settings, which can easily crash a recording session.

Although CDs last a very long time, you cannot be sure that data will be saved forever. Archived data on CD is currently certified to last 10 years.

See also
CD-ROM Drives, Computer Backup Systems, Desktop Computers, Notebook Computers

Recycling

*B*usinesses typically produce a large amount of trash. On average, each office employee generates about three pounds of garbage every day.

Fortunately, about two-thirds of office trash can be recycled. By recycling, firms can not only help the environment, but also help reduce disposal costs.

RECYCLED PAPER VENDORS			
Company	Photocopier	Laser printer	Bond
Badger Paper Mills Co.	•	•	•
Boise Cascade Business Papers	•	•	•
Hammermill Papers	•	•	•
International Paper	•		
James River Corp.	•	•	•
Nationwide Papers		•	•
Union Camp Corp.	•	•	
Wausau Paper Mills Co.			•
Weyerhauser Corp.	•	•	•
Xerox Corp.	•		

Source: National Office Paper Recycling Project, *Guide to Recycled Office and Business Paper Containing 20% Post Consumer Fiber*

Buying points

What can be recycled
In an office setting, the most commonly recycled item is paper. The most valuable paper is typically fanfold computer printout. Because sheets are large and unbroken, there are many long paper fibers well suited for recycling.

White paper and manila file folders are also highly desirable for recycling. Many recyclers will pay for these materials if they are carefully sorted.

Other paper types are usually less valuable. Colored paper, corrugated boxes, and newspapers can be sold for profit, but are often worth next to nothing when there is a glut on the market.

Unsorted paper is worth the least, with few vendors willing to pay for a mix of paper types. However, even unsorted paper has value and can be less expensive to haul away than regular trash.

Recycling other items
Offices can recycle metal, glass, and plastic in addition to paper. However, many offices do not use these items in large enough quantities to justify a full-fledged recycling program. In these cases, it is often worth joining with city programs or other businesses to collect enough of these materials for a recycler to buy. Another option is to simply reuse materials to avoid the hassle of recycling.

If you do use a lot of metal, glass or plastic in your company, it is often very economical to contact a recycler. Metal attracts very high prices, even for relatively small quantities, and glass and plastic items are both valuable as long as they are kept well sorted.

Computer components, particularly toner cartridges, ribbon cartridges, and computer disks, are also part of a very active recycling market. You will usually need to contact a different type of recycler than the one you would use for paper recycling, but all of these items can attract reasonably high prices.

Cleaning up your trash
Purity is a major factor affecting the value of recycled materials. Foreign objects require the recycling company to further sort the material, or settle for a lower-quality recycled product. As a result, recyclers are very demanding when paying for sorted materials.

In most cases, metal objects such as staples and paper clips are not a big concern for paper recycling, since they can easily be sorted out during the recycling process. Colored paper is a much bigger concern, since it can be difficult to detect and can significantly lower the quality of the batch. Glues and plastics can also be serious contaminants, particularly in large quantities.

Who offers recycling
The first thing to do when looking for a collector of recycled goods is to check with your current waste hauler. If your waste hauler does not provide recycling services, you can at

least obtain information about your current disposal costs and ask to be referred to collectors that service your area. Ideally, a recycler will be interested in taking away all of the recyclables you produce.

In addition, each state has a recycling department. These departments can serve as clearinghouses of information, pointing you to local recyclers and providing tips for starting a program.

Setting up a recycling program

Setting up a recycling program can be as easy as placing a container in a room and posting a note indicating what can and cannot be thrown into it.

You will need to understand the types and volume of recyclables generated in your office. Determining the value of these recyclables and the effort required by employees to recycle them should affect the type of program you create.

One person in the office should be designated as the primary coordinator of the recycling program. This person can assume responsibility for developing and implementing the program and can act as the liaison between the recycler and the company.

As the recycling program gets underway, be sure to keep both employees and management informed of its progress so the program does not lose momentum.

Pricing

Recycling prices vary tremendously depending on the area of the country and the current supply and demand for recycled goods. In general, high quality computer printouts are the most valuable papers, fetching as much as $100 per ton when in demand. Most other grades fetch $10 to $70 per ton, although paper gluts can reduce the price paid for newspapers or mixed grades.

Companies that do not generate large amounts of recyclables may find that recyclers will charge a monthly fee for clearing bins. To get a true sense for the costs of such a service, you should compare these charges to the price you would otherwise pay for waste disposal.

Special tips

If you are starting a recycling program, consider a kick-off event on Earth Day (April 22).

Avoid overwhelming employees with recycling initiatives when starting a program. It is generally more effective to start a program by recycling one or two items and then expand slowly.

To make it easy to recycle, give each employee a recycling bin right by his or her desk. These bins can then be dumped into an intermediary container in a common area, like the copy room or supply area.

The National Office Paper Recycling Project (202/223-3088) offers many recycling suggestions in two inexpensive titles: *Office Paper Recycling Guide* and *Recycling at Work: Guide for Building Managers*.

Recycling does not work unless someone buys recycled products. For more information about buying recycled products, the Business Products Industry Association (800/542-6672) has published the *Resource Guide to Business Products Manufacturers' Recycling Products and Programs* and the American Plastics Council (800/2-HELP-90) has published *Purchasing Recycled Plastic Products* and *Recycled Plastic Products Source Book*.

If you decide not to recycle, an effective way to cut costs anyway is to pack your trash more tightly. Trash haulers charge businesses by volume, but pay for disposal by the ton. Therefore, if you pack your trash into a smaller volume, you will not have to pay as much.

Another way to recycle paper is through reuse. For example, companies can collect printed papers and use the back sides for notes and messages. Similarly, many printers can print the back side of printed paper without jamming.

See also
Copy Paper, Off-site Storage, Office Supplies, Paper Shredders, Photocopiers, Toner Supplies

Did you know?

More than 12 million tons of office paper is generated each year in the U.S. by office workers, according to the National Office Paper Recycling Project. A typical company with 65 employees will produce 500 lbs. of waste paper in six working days.

SAFES

*A*lthough a simple locking cabinet can secure your valuable papers from prying eyes, it will do little to protect them from theft or damage from fire. Safes provide an extra level of protection for documents, computer data, and other items that your company would be hard pressed to duplicate if lost.

VENDORS							
				Types of safes		Sales channel	
Company	Headquarters	Phone Number	Media	Wall/ Floor	Record	Direct	Retail
Amsec	Fontana, CA	909/685-9680	●	●	●	●	●
Fort Knox	Orem, UT	800/821-5216				●	●
Gardall	Syracuse, NY	800/722-7233		●	●	●	●
Meilink	New Albany, IN	800/MEILINK	●		●		●
Schwab	Lafayette, IN	317/447-9470	●		●		●
Sentry	Rochester, NY	800/828-1438	●	●	●		●
Sisco	Carson, CA	800/223-8566	●	●	●		●

Buying points

Differences between safes

Safes offer varying levels of fire and burglar resistance. The Underwriters Laboratory (UL) tests and labels safes and locks for their level of heat resistance and durability.

To test safes for theft resistance, the UL subjects them to picks and blow torches. The UL uses the TL15 and TL30 designations to indicate safes that can withstand 15 and 30 minutes of drilling, respectively.

The UL also tests safes to see how secure they are in a fire. Testers heat safes in a furnace for half an hour or more to see how the contents fare. Safes that pass this test can maintain an interior temperature of less than 350°F (degrees Fahrenheit). Designated-record safes, these models will protect paper documents from 1,700°F heat for up to four hours.

You may also want to see how a safe will fare if it is dropped. In a fire, a safe may fall through the floor, break open, and spill the contents you are seeking to protect. The UL also indicates whether a safe can survive a 30-foot impact, which simulates a fall of 3 stories.

Size

Since safes are a long-term investment, it is important to get a sense for what you will need to protect, both now and in the future, before you choose a model.

Make sure to consider both the internal and the external dimensions. You want to make sure that the safe will fit into its designated space, but you also want enough internal space to store your valuables. It can be helpful to measure the largest item you will place in the safe to get a sense for the minimum dimensions you can accept.

Keep in mind that a larger safe does not necessarily insure greater security. Although large safes cannot be removed as easily by a burglar, they also cannot be removed by you in case of fire.

Protecting computer software

Media safes are designed to protect disks and other audio/visual equipment such as video and cassette tapes from fire. These materials have special requirements because they are more fragile than paper documents. Diskettes, for example, can be ruined at temperatures far below the 350°F maximum specified for papers. Diskettes also require humidity below a certain level.

Due to these requirements, media safes tend to be very expensive, often costing thousands of dollars. In most cases, a more cost-effective approach is to purchase a separate media chest or media drawer for computer disks. If stored in a fireproof file cabinet or safe, this container will provide adequate protection for only $100 to $350.

Installing a safe

For the greatest level of security, safes should be installed into the wall or the floor. Installation charges will vary according to what is underneath the safe. If placed in concrete, the safes will not only be highly burglar resistant but will also be beyond the reach of most fires. Unfortunately, installation in these cases can be quite costly, often exceeding $600.

A less expensive solution is to bolt a safe to the floor. However, this does not provide any extra protection from fire.

Locks

Most low-end safes come with old-fashioned combination locks or a key lock. These are not particularly effective against an experienced burglar, but cost less than $100.

For those requiring greater security, the UL has approved electronic and digital locks that cost up to $350. Some are X-ray- and manipulation-proof, making the codes nearly impossible to crack. Other safes can only be accessed by swiping your credit card. You can even attach an electronic control device that regulates the times when a safe can be opened.

For additional protection, a drill-resistant hard plate can be placed over the lock and a steel bar along the interior to prevent the door from being removed.

Pricing

Three factors affect the cost of a safe: size, resistance, and the type of lock. A small fireproof money chest will cost less than $100. On the other end, a large record safe capable of resisting a four-hour fire can cost nearly $7,000.

Terms

Composite safe Type of safe in which a layer of concrete is poured between the outer and inner walls of the safe for increased protection from fire.

Depository safe Safe equipped with a slot to deposit money throughout the day without having to open the safe each time.

Media safe Type of safe designed for sensitive computer disks or audio/visual tape. These safes maintain an interior temperature of less than 125°F. In addition, humidity levels in media safes remain below 80% when the container is subjected to 1,550 to 1,700°F heat.

Record safe Type of safe that can withstand temperatures of up to 1,700°F while maintaining an interior temperature of 350°F or less. These safes will typically have compartments and shelves to store books and binders.

See also
File Cabinets, Off-site Storage, Paper Shredders

Did you know?

Paper begins to char at approximately 400°F to 420°F, and will burn at 450°F to 470°F.

Same Day Delivery Services

Sometimes, overnight delivery is just not quick enough. Maybe you need emergency replacement parts, or maybe a contract needs to be signed by the end of the day. For these situations, businesses can turn to same day delivery services for help.

VENDORS

Company	Headquarters	Phone number	Airport-to-airport	Door-to-door
Airborne Sky Courier	Reston, VA	800/336-3344		●
Consolidated Delivery & Logistics	Paramus, NJ	201/291-1900		●
DHL Same Day (Midnite Express)	Los Angeles, CA	800/DHL-ASAP		●
Dynamex	Toronto, Ontario	800/461-9458		●
FedEx (Network Courier)	Memphis, TN	800/GO-FEDEX		●
Northwest VIP Same Day	Minneapolis, MN	800/638-7337	●	●
Southwest Airlines Cargo	Dallas, TX	800/533-1222	●	
TNT	Garden City, NY	800/677-4444		●
Transport Network	Livingston, NJ	800/784-7874		●
U.S. Delivery Systems	Houston, TX	800/293-1200		●
UPS SonicAir	Scottsdale, AZ	800/451-4550		●

Buying points

Types of services
Same day delivery service providers include messenger couriers and air couriers. Messenger couriers operate on a local or regional basis, using fleets of vans or bikes to deliver packages within a specific area. Messenger couriers also typically have agreements with other courier firms, allowing them to hand off deliveries going outside their area.

Air couriers handle packages going between cities or out of the country. Air couriers arrange for packages to be included on outgoing flights, and arrange for drop off and pickup at each end of the trip.

Airline programs
While all air couriers offer door-to-door delivery, only a few airlines offer this service. With the basic airline service, you must deliver the package to the airport at least 30 minutes prior to the scheduled flight time and then arrange for another party to pick it up at the destination airport. This can be as quick as a courier service, but is certainly not as convenient.

Airlines that do offer door-to-door delivery typically use local courier services at both ends of the flight route.

Speed
Local couriers will generally offer several levels of service, depending on how quickly the package must be delivered. If necessary, deliveries can be made as quickly as a courier can bike or drive.

Air courier delivery times depend on the origin and destination, as well as commercial flight schedules. Most U.S. flights take no more than six hours, with final delivery to local areas within an hour of landing.

Pricing
Within a metropolitan area, messenger couriers generally have set published rates based on the delivery route. Charges usually start at $15, going up to about $50 for small packages within the metropolitan area.

Charges vary depending on whether the pickup is scheduled ahead of time, and the size and weight of the shipment. Once outside the metropolitan area, the charges increase according to size, distance, and route traveled.

With air courier rates, there are many more variables affecting price. Deliveries start at around $150 for a package of approximately 20 pounds. The size of the package, the route traveled, and timing will all affect the charges. International same day delivery is even more expensive, with a typical charge of more than $300 for the first ten pounds.

Extra charges can also be assessed if you make the courier wait more than a few minutes, or if you send the package during the weekend or off-hours (i.e., 6 p.m. to 8 a.m.).

Regardless of which method you choose, the volume you ship with a particular carrier will influence the price you pay. Since there is so much competition, discounting is readily available.

Special tips

If you conduct much overnight delivery shipping, consider consolidating your same day service with these carriers to obtain higher total volume discounting.

Some courier services charge extra fees if you exceed certain weight or size requirements, so be sure to review the shipping restrictions.

Before working with any courier for an overseas delivery, it is a good idea to check references from current clients who ship to the same country. This is because you want to avoid being the first customer to need priority shipments to a particular country.

If a courier will be transporting sensitive materials, you may want to check into how employees are hired.

Check that a courier firm is adequately insured in the event your package is lost, stolen or damaged in transit. You may want to check for any limits in compensation for particularly valuable items.

See also
Ground Shipping, International Expedited Delivery, LTL Shipping, Overnight Delivery Services

SCANNERS

A scanner is an optical device that "reads" documents and other paper-based images and transforms them into computer files. Scanners are used to import photos and drawings into a computer, and (with software) can be used to turn printed pages into editable computer files.

BIT DEPTH SCANNING CAPABILITIES

Bit depth	What the scanner can discern	Bit depth	What the scanner can discern
1-bit	Black and white	16-bit	65,000 colors
4-bit	16 grayscales	24-bit	16.7 million colors
8-bit	256 grayscales	30-bit	1.1 billion colors
10-bit	1,024 grayscales	36-bit	69 billion colors
12-bit	4,096 grayscales		

VENDORS

Company	Headquarters	Phone number	Mac	PC	Handheld	Sheetfed	Color flatbed	Slide
Agfa	Wilmington, MA	800/685-4271	●	●			●	
Bell & Howell	Chicago, IL	800/SCAN-494	●	●		●		
Brother	Irvine, CA	800/276-7746		●		●		
Canon	Costa Mesa, CA	800/848-4123	●	●			●	
Epson	Torrance, CA	800/922-8911	●	●			●	
Fujitsu	San Jose, CA	800/626-4686	●	●		●	●	
Hewlett-Packard	Santa Clara, CA	800/722-6538	●	●		●	●	
LaCie	Beaverton, OR	800/999-0143	●			●	●	
Microtek	Redondo Beach, CA	800/654-4160	●	●		●	●	●
Mustek	Irvine, CA	714/250-8855	●	●	●	●	●	
Nikon	Melville, NY	800/526-4566	●	●				●
Panasonic	Secaucus, NJ	800/742-8086		●		●		
Polaroid	Cambridge, MA	800/343-5000	●	●				●
Ricoh	San Jose, CA	800/955-3453	●	●		●	●	
Tamarack	Orange, CA	714/744-3979	●	●			●	
UMAX	Fremont, CA	800/562-0311	●	●	●	●	●	

Buying points

How a scanner works
Scanners work by converting a page into a grid of thousands or millions of tiny dots. An optical reader examines the color or shade of each dot, and records the information in a computer file. By assembling this data, the computer can create a digital record of the original image.

Uses for a scanner
Businesses use scanners in a variety of ways. The most popular use is for graphics design. Although most images are printed and distributed on paper, computers are much more flexible when it comes to altering or manipulating images. Because of this, scanners are often used to capture photos and drawings. These scans can then be modified and placed in presentations, brochures or other documents.

More recently, many businesses have begun to use scanners for data entry. A document can be scanned into the computer, and then analyzed with software designed to "read" letters and numbers. This optical character recognition (OCR) software can convert a document into a standard computer file, such as a word processing document, for editing.

A third use of scanners is for digital storage. Because paper documents are somewhat bulky and fragile, storage costs tend to be quite high. Scanners allow businesses to convert paper documents into digital images, which can be stored on a small hard drive or CD-ROM. With proper cataloging, digital storage can allow businesses to easily search their files and pull up relevant documents in a matter of seconds.

Different types of scanners
There are currently four main types of scanners on the market. Handheld scanners are designed to be dragged across a page by hand. Although cheap, handheld scanners require skill and patience to scan a full page document.

Sheet-fed scanners are just a bit more expensive but much more convenient. These scanners look a bit like a small fax machine, with a paper tray for inputting sheets. The scanner grabs each sheet from the tray and pulls it through the machine.

Flatbed scanners look like the top half of a copier, with a large sheet of glass under a plastic cover. The advantage of these models is that you can scan items such as books, which are too thick to fit through a sheet-fed model. On the downside, flatbed models take up a lot of desk space.

Slide scanners are designed to scan 35 mm slides and negatives. They are very small, with very compact scanning units that can obtain detailed information from small images.

Purchasing considerations
When buying a scanner, the first thing to check is the bit depth of the unit. This refers to the amount of information the scanner can capture. Models that offer one- to eight-bit scanning can only see documents to be

scanned as grayscale images. One- to four-bit models are generally suitable for scanning text, while eight-bit scanners can capture high-quality black and white photos or drawings.

To produce reasonable color scans, you need a 24-bit scanner. These capture the full range of 16.7 million colors visible to the human eye. For super-high quality images, there are even 30- and 36-bit scanners, which capture additional data to ensure that the right colors wind up on screen.

A second buying concern is the resolution of the scanner. This refers to the number of dots that the scanner captures in each inch of a document. Most scanners capture 300 pixels per inch (ppi), which is fine for standard-sized text and most photos. However, if you expect to enlarge images before printing, look for a scanner that offers 600 ppi resolution.

When examining resolution, make sure to compare true or "optical" resolutions. Some scanners advertise higher "interpolated" resolutions, which simply means that the software guesses what the image should look like between scanned dots.

Where to purchase a scanner

Low-end sheet-fed scanners are widely available in computer stores and mail order outlets, as are basic flatbed scanners. Many of the major mail order computer stores offer competitive prices.

High-end flatbed models are often only found at specialized dealers or in catalogs that cater to the design and prepress industry. In terms of catalog vendors, try DTP Direct (800/643-3369). Express Direct (800/925-6777) and PrePRESS Direct (800/443-6600) also have a good selection of these units.

Pricing

Handheld scanners sell for as little as $100. Sheet-fed models sell for as little as $200, although high-speed models can cost many times this price. Flatbed scanners range in price from about $400 to $2,000. Slide scanners start at about $700, although most models cost more than $1,000.

Terms

Bit depth The amount of information the scanner can capture for each dot. A one-bit scanner captures only black or white, while an 8-bit scanner can capture 256 discrete shades. To capture full color, you will need a 24-bit scanner.

Grayscale The number of shades of gray a scanner can capture. A scanner with a higher bit depth will be able to discern more discrete shades of gray from a given image.

Optical character recognition (OCR) software Software that is designed to read text from a scanned image. With OCR software, users can convert paper documents into a word processing file rather than having to retype the entire document.

Pixels per inch (ppi) Indication of the number of discrete dots the scanner will capture in each inch of a document. Higher ppi figures result in more data for enlarging or modifying an image. Some manufacturers use the expression "dots per inch" (dpi) instead of ppi.

Transparency adapter An adapter that allows a flatbed scanner to be used for scanning transparencies, slides or negatives. It is often sold as an option, or included with high-end models.

Special tips

If you expect to use the scanner for data entry, pay attention to the paper handling features and speed at which the unit can scan pages. In general, you should look for a scanner that has or can be equipped with an automatic document feeder. In terms of resolution, you should find 300 ppi resolution and 8-bit gray scale to be sufficient. Finally, make sure the scanner includes name-brand optical character recognition (OCR) software, or be prepared to buy a program such as Caere OmniPage (800/535-7276) or Xerox TextBridge (800/248-6550) on your own.

If you expect to use a scanner to capture graphic images, stick to a flatbed model. These will be much more flexible for scanning from magazines or books and generally offer better quality scans. Businesses producing lower quality output, such as laser printed documents or two-color work can usually use a 24-bit scanner. However, high-quality scanning requires a 30-bit scanner with true 600 x 600 resolution. Keep in mind that quality is not as important if the images are for display on a computer, since screen resolutions are only 72 dpi.

It is not at all uncommon for graphic designers to scan images from magazines or books to create new designs. However, this is often illegal, since copyrighted works cannot generally be scanned and reproduced without permission. Rights and permissions agencies such as BZ/Rights & Permissions (212/580-0615) and Thomson & Thomson (800/356-8630) can help you avoid copyright violations.

See also
Desktop Computers, Fax Machines, Multifunctional Devices, Notebook Computers

For more information, visit
BuyersZone
http://www.buyerszone.com/

SIGNS

*F*or many small businesses, signs are an important means of advertising a company's existence. However, signs are not for public display only. They can also help direct visitors around your office and alert employees to hazardous or off-limit areas.

SAMPLING OF ADA REQUIREMENTS

ADA requirements	Permanent room signs	Directional or informational signs	Suspended or projected overhead signs
Characters should have a width-to-height ratio between 3:5 and 1:1		●	●
Characters shall be 3" minimum in height			●
Characters shall be at least 5/8" in height, but no higher than 2"	●		
Raised and brailled characters	●		
Pictorial symbol signs	●		
Character and background should be eggshell, matte, or other non-glare finish	●	●	●
Character should contrast with their background, either light on black or dark on light	●	●	●
Mounting height to be 60" above the finished floor to the centerline of the sign	●		
Minimal 80" vertical clearance			●

Source: Innerface Architectural Signage

Buying points

Types of signs
Signs can be created for outdoor or indoor use.

Typically, outdoor signs are used for marketing purposes or to direct visitors. They can be found on rooftops, walls, and awnings; standing alone by buildings; hanging as banners; and even displayed on the sides of cars and trucks.

Indoor signs are usually hung from ceilings or attached to walls. These signs are usually created for use in a reception area or to direct visitors. Signs are also often created for trade show displays.

Sign materials
There are many different materials companies can use to make signs. Sign makers typically consider requirements in terms of lettering and substrate materials.

Sign lettering can be as straightforward as adhesive vinyl or as eye-grabbing as neon. Other materials commonly used for lettering include metal, wood, plastic, and foamcore. Lettering can also be engraved. While once quite prevalent, paint is now much less common as a lettering medium.

Buyers also have the choice of many substrates, which serve as the backing for the lettering. Materials used for backing include plastic, paper, cloth, vinyl, wood, foamcore, glass, and aluminum. Mixed substrates are also available.

Since sign materials come in varying levels of quality, you should inquire about their durability when comparing quotes. Accompanying warranties for the materials can also serve as a good proxy for quality.

Designing signs
Buyers need to consider a number of factors to create effective, long-lasting signs.

First, think about the distance the average viewer will be from the sign. In addition, factors such as sign height, lighting, and time of day can affect how easily the sign can be viewed.

Also think about the sign's expected wear and tear, and make sure the appropriate materials are used. Signs can be destroyed not only from weather conditions, but also from travel and general mishandling.

Choosing a sign company
One of the first things to do when choosing a sign company is to find one that specializes in the type of sign materials you desire. Although most companies will not claim any specialties in their advertising, many will in fact be particularly proficient at making a certain type of sign. You will often find faster turnaround, higher quality execution, and better pricing when working with such a company.

Sign companies can also specialize in particular types of projects. For example, some companies have substantial experience in the planning and placement of signs throughout a building. Working with people who are particularly knowledgeable about the issues surrounding a given project can significantly affect the types of signs that are created.

Also consider the capabilities you require. Firms that do not have designers in house may want to assess the portfolios of graphic designers working at the sign company. Alternately, companies that already know what they want implemented should look for a sign company that accepts computer files on disk for direct outputting.

Complying with the ADA

The Americans with Disabilities Act (ADA) requires all commercial facilities (which include any building open to the public) to accommodate the special needs of individuals with disabilities by removing physical and communication barriers. This means that buildings such as hospitals, government buildings, public and private schools, transportation terminals, hotels, restaurants, and manufacturing facilities must meet ADA requirements in terms of signage design and installation.

There are companies familiar with the ADA that can help your firm conform to the regulations. Keep in mind that while there are costs involved with ADA compliance, the government also provides ADA-specific tax refunds for businesses.

About zoning regulations

Many towns have specific regulations about the type or size of outdoor signs businesses may erect. If the zoning laws in your area prevent you from installing the type of sign you desire, you may need to apply for a variance to the existing code. Sign companies should be familiar not only with local regulations, but also with the process for applying for a variance.

Pricing

Sign costs depend on size, material, color, and content. They can range from $8 for a small sign (12 x 6 inch with a basic design) to nearly $100 for a larger sign (30 x 30 inch with more complicated features). Sign costs can easily climb up to the hundreds or even thousands of dollars when using costly materials or producing gigantic signs.

When comparing quotes, remember to add in any delivery charges.

Terms

Backlighting An effect achieved by lighting a sign from behind. Backlighting is often used with trade show displays for greater visibility.

Substrates The material used to form the background of a sign to which lettering is attached. Also known as backing.

Variance A modification to existing zoning regulations granted by a local agency.

Special tips

If you expect signs to change over time, look for a design that is easy to update or change. In many cases, updates can even be made by your staff instead of returning the sign to the signage company.

Although most signs are custom made, it is possible to find pre-made standard signs. You can often find stock signs for use in laboratories, retail stores, and warehouses. Buying stock signs can be much cheaper than having a sign custom-made.

Magnetic signs can be a good alternative for companies seeking to add a sign to cars or trucks. That way, employees who also use the car for personal use can remove the sign after business hours.

Sign companies are generally busiest during the summer. Expect longer turnaround times during this time of the year.

See also
Advertising Agencies, Color Printers, Graphic Designers, Stock Photography, Trade Show Displays

Did you know?

Light emanating from signs can be a major crime deterrent in urban areas. During the energy crisis of the 1970s, reports indicate there was a 30% rise in crime when downtown signs were turned off.

SLIDE PROJECTORS

Slide projectors offer a compact and simple way to share information with a large group of people. By incorporating talking points and charts on standard 35 mm slides, a presenter can convey complex images to a large audience.

Company	Headquarters	Phone number
Elmo	Hyde Park, NY	516/775-3200
Hardware Xenon	South Hackensack, NJ	201/440-0216
Kodak	Rochester, NY	800/242-2424
Navitar	Rochester, NY	800/828-6778
Telex	Minneapolis, MN	800/828-6107

Buying points

How slide projectors are used
Slide projectors are ideal for presentations that remain quite similar over time. Although it can be fairly costly to have slides created, they can easily be stored and reused. In addition, slide projectors tend to be much less bulky than presentation alternatives such as overhead projectors or LCD projectors.

Slide projectors are not as well suited for presentations that frequently change or must be updated over time. They are also less well suited for interactive presentations where slides are unlikely to be viewed in a static order. In these cases, you may want to invest in LCD panels or projectors that allow presentations to be easily modified or rearranged.

About the technology
One of the biggest differences among slide projectors is the brightness of the lamp, or bulb, that is used to project the image. Less expensive projectors typically use a 250 watt bulb, which may not be suitable for large or bright rooms. Brighter bulbs of 300 or more watts allow images to be viewed even in less than ideal conditions.

A second consideration is the life of the lamp. Depending on the type of lamp that is used, bulb life can vary from 15 to 200 hours. Lower life figures are acceptable as long as the lamps are inexpensive and easy to replace.

A third consideration is the lens used by the slide projector. Lenses come in two types: fixed focal and zoom. Fixed focal lenses are best if all presentations are made from a standard distance from the screen. Zoom lenses, while more expensive, are best for slide projectors that are used in a variety of locations. Most zoom lenses can adjust from 100 to 150 millimeters.

Key features
The slide projector is not a particularly fancy piece of equipment. All units should be able to project slides in either a forward or backward order and should be equipped with some type of handheld control.

Unless all of your slides are of the same type—made by a service bureau or taken with a 35 mm camera—the auto focus feature is the most important feature. This feature automatically pulls the image into sharp focus when going through slides in a presentation. Some projectors allow you to turn this feature off if your slides do not require it.

A built-in screen is a convenient feature for those who wish to preview slides or present to a small group without using a full-sized screen. Most units that offer this feature project images on a built-in screen that can be as large as 9 x 9 inch.

People who find they often reorganize slides for various presentations may want to find a projector that can change the presentation order without requiring the slides to be physically rearranged. These models are controlled by computers equipped with special presentation software.

For an additional $350, most projectors will accept an automatic lamp or bulb changer. These high-end units automatically switch lamps if a burnout occurs.

Buying a slide projector

Slide projectors can be purchased from audio visual dealers, as well as office superstores and photographic mail order catalogs.

If the slide projector is only needed for one presentation, renting a projector and any necessary accessories is typically a better alternative.

Pricing

The price of a slide projector is dependent on the lamp, lens, and durability. While projectors for home use can be less expensive, most slide projectors range from $400 to $2,000.

Features such as a built-in screen or auto focus can add $100 to the price of the model.

Terms

Ambient lighting Refers to the lighting of the room. The greater the ambient lighting, the stronger the slide projector lamp will need to be to project visible images.

Dissolve rates This measures the fade rate of slides on the screen. Some accessories allow dissolved images to be "frozen," or superimposed on other images in a multi-projector presentation.

Embossed mount A type of slide mounting that contains a beveled edge around the aperture (or opening) where the slide is held.

Random access This feature allows slides to be accessed out of the order in which they are kept in the slide tray.

Special tips

Avoid projectors built for home use. Most of these models are not designed for the rigors of travel or constant use in a business setting.

Be wary of using slide trays that hold 140 slides. These trays have less clearance between slides than slide trays with just 80 slots. Limited clearance for bent or worn slides can cause frequent performance problems or jams.

Always carry an extra lamp. The lamp filaments can easily break while the projector is in transit, leaving your projector inoperable.

Set up a projector so that the distance from the farthest audience member to the screen is about five times greater than either the height or width (whichever is shorter) of the projected image.

While glass is the most expensive mounting type for slides, it also keeps the slides the flattest. Embossed and non-embossed cardboard and plastic are less durable, but more economical.

See also
LCD Systems, Overhead Projectors

Stock Photography

Stock photographs are used by businesses to add color and excitement to marketing pieces and presentations. Stock photographs allow you to avoid the expense of hiring a photographer, particularly in cases where you cannot easily provide the needed image.

VENDORS

Company	Headquarters	Phone number	Stock photography agency	Digital stock photos
Archive Photos	New York, NY	212/675-0115	●	
Comstock	New York, NY	212/353-8600	●	
Corel	Ottawa, Ontario	800/772-6735		●
Digital Stock	Solana Beach, CA	800/545-4514		●
Form and Function	Portland, OR	800/779-5474		●
FPG International	New York, NY	212/777-4210	●	
Image Bank	Dallas, TX	214/863-4900	●	
PhotoDisc	Seattle, WA	800/528-3472		●
Tony Stone	New York, NY	212/545-8220	●	

Buying points

Sources of stock photos

Stock photos are available from three major sources. The traditional source is a stock photography agency. These agencies keep millions of photos of all types on file. Once you describe your needs, the agency can find a particular image that closely matches your specifications.

A second way of obtaining stock photos is to contact a local photographer. Photographers keep photos from past shoots, and will sell or license these photos for a small fee. Local photographers can be a particularly good source if they specialize in the type of shots you require.

The newest way to obtain stock photos is to purchase digital stock photography. These consist of photograph collections that are stored on CD-ROMs. Digital stock photography can typically be used without paying a royalty.

Which to use

There is no getting around the fact that many more photographs are currently available from stock photography agencies and local photographers than from CD-ROMs. This means that the traditional channels will continue to be a primary source of photos for a long time.

Nevertheless, digital stock photography has a number of advantages. For one, most digital stock photos do not charge a royalty for each use. This means that once you buy the CD, anything on the disc is yours to use.

A second advantage of digital storage is indexing. Although stock agencies may have well-organized files, they cannot let you rummage through them each time you need a photo. In contrast, most CD-ROMs come with a thumbnail viewer, which allows you to quickly scan through small versions of each photo.

The downside of digital stock photography is quality. First, most photos on CDs are not great works of art. Top photographers charge a lot for their work, which makes it impractical for CD-ROM publishers to use the best sources for images. However, they should be more than adequate for most business needs.

A second quality issue is that even CD-ROMs have limited storage capacity. While it is possible to store several hundred high-quality photos on a CD, many contain well over 1,000 images. This means that some CD-ROM images may be insufficient for high quality brochures or presentations.

Finding images

Most stock photo agencies and digital stock photo CDs have catalogs that you can flip through when looking for a particular image. Some even offer interactive catalogs that allow you to sort photos according to a range of preferences.

Pricing

Photos from stock photography firms are typically rented on a per use basis. Most photos cost somewhere between $250 and $1,500. Fees typically depend on the image's distribution, size and placement, and intended use. In addition, buyers are billed for researching requests, the right to change or collate images on your computer, and scanning the image.

Digital stock photos usually do not require royalty fees. Instead, users purchase a CD-ROM at a price that covers the cost of using those images any number of times. Fees range from $10 to $250 per disc, with each CD-ROM holding anywhere from 100 to several thousand images. Additional charges can be incurred when using images for commercial resale.

Special tips

The Picture Agency Council of America lists the specialties of each member stock photography agency in its directory. The directory is free, and can be obtained simply by faxing a request on letterhead to (507/645-7066).

Many digital stock photography agencies also offer reproduction rights to both black and white and color photographs, film footage, illustrations, and other images.

Kodak Picture Exchange (800/235-6325) offers self-service access to a database of more than 30 separate image banks for your perusal. With the convenience of self-service, you can download design proofs to be placed in the layout while you submit an on-line "image request" or order an image directly. Other digital stock photography agencies offer similar services via the World Wide Web.

Before you buy an inexpensive photo CD-ROM, be sure to get a sense for the quality of the images. Expensive discs are usually geared for professional designers, while the less expensive discs are targeted at the general public and may have much lower quality photos.

See also
Advertising Agencies, CD-ROM Drives, Graphic Designers, Signs, Trade Show Displays

---

For more information, visit
BuyersZone
http://www.buyerszone.com/

Did you know?

The beginning of the stock photography industry can be traced back to the Civil War, when an enterprising photographer sold the images he shot on the battlefield.

Systems Furniture

Systems furniture offers companies a way to divide large, noisy office spaces into private work areas. Like a child's Lego set, systems furniture allows you to create virtually endless varieties of configurations by mixing and matching the three main building blocks: panel, worksurface, and storage areas.

				Type of system	
Company	Headquarters	Phone number	Budget	Mid-market	High-end
Allsteel	Aurora, IL	800/764-2535		●	●
Geiger Brickel	Atlanta, GA	800/444-8812			●
GF Office	Canfield, OH	216/533-7799	●	●	●
Haworth	Holland, MI	800/344-2600	●	●	●
Herman Miller	Zeeland, MI	616/654-8600	●	●	●
HON	Muscatine, IA	800/833-3964	●	●	
K. I.	Green Bay, WI	414/468-8100	●	●	●
Kimball Int'l.	Jasper, IN	800/482-1616	●	●	●
Knoll Group	E. Greenville, IN	800/445-5045		●	●
Smed	Calgary, Alberta	403/279-1400	●	●	●
Steelcase	Grand Rapids, MI	800/333-9939	●	●	●

Buying points

Types of systems furniture

Systems furniture is available in two main designs: panel-mounted and freestanding. Panel-mounted designs use wall panels as the basis for the system, mounting components such as desks and file cabinets directly onto the panel sides. Freestanding, or modular, components use freestanding panels that are placed around furniture.

Each design has advantages and disadvantages. Panel-based systems offer greater design flexibility, as units can be assembled to maximize space usage. Panel systems can also be equipped with internal power options, and can be a bit taller to provide greater privacy and noise reduction.

The main advantage of modular systems is that they can be easily installed and reconfigured. This makes them more convenient for firms that will often rearrange or move office space.

Privacy issues

Systems furniture is generally not as soundproof or private as an individual office. However, by choosing the proper components, it is possible to create spaces that feel like separate rooms.

Panel height is usually the key to privacy. Panels range in height from 30 to 80 inches. Thirty-inch partitions allow for communication between desks without standing, and are often used for interactive jobs such as secretaries or assistants. Fifty-inch panels provide greater privacy for phone calls, but allow for conversation while standing. The tallest panels afford enough privacy to hold meetings.

The type of material used in the panel also contribute to privacy. Panels that use more sound-absorbing materials will help reduce noise levels. However, other factors such as the space height, flooring, and ceiling material also affect conversational privacy.

Types of worksurfaces

Worksurfaces typically differ in terms of their shape and construction. While the basic worksurface is rectangular, rectangles can be added together to form an "L" or "U" shape. People who hold conferences in their spaces may find rounded extensions useful.

Worksurfaces are constructed using a number of different materials, including plastic and wood laminates. Generally, plastic laminate will be the less expensive option.

Storage space options

Companies can choose to offer storage above, below or next to the worksurface.

Open shelving and overhead bins offer convenient above-the-desktop access without taking up valuable floor space. These either hang from the panel wall or are placed on top of a worksurface.

Pedestals consist of regular and file drawer units that are placed under the worksurface. To increase mobility, pedestals can be purchased as wheeled units. When adding storage under a worksurface, keep in mind that there should be enough leg space so as not to constrict movement.

Lateral files, bookshelves and credenzas can provide additional storage for a workstation. These can be useful for workers who require a lot of easily accessible filing space.

Allowances for computer users
Offering a healthy typing environment is probably the most critical aspect of designing a workstation for computer users. The key to this is placing the computer keyboard at an appropriate height. Varied or adjustable height worksurfaces and keyboard drawers help address the fact that most people need to type at a lower height than that offered by the typical desk surface.

Allowances should also be made for the additional space (and depth) a computer monitor can take. Planners should make sure that wires can be quickly funneled out of the way to minimize "dead" space. Finally, issues related to powering the computer should also be addressed. High-end systems have more sophisticated internal wiring that can be plugged directly into the building's power grid, thus avoiding the need for extension cords snaking around the office.

Making a final decision
Since systems furniture simply consists of building blocks, you should try to anticipate your future needs. A good system should be able to adapt to different designs as your firm's needs change.

In addition, look into the stability of the manufacturer and the product line. System components are often not interchangeable across vendors. As a result, you should choose carefully since you will want to be able to order additional components for the life of the system.

Finally, check the system's durability. Systems furniture is designed to last many years, with the warranty providing a good indication of the expected life span. Check whether employees will be able to handle some of the repairs, which can decrease the need for expensive service. It also makes sense to assess the availability and cost of parts and service options.

Pricing
Systems furniture can cost anywhere from $750 to $10,000 per workstation. Price depends on the number of units, the amount of furniture in each workstation, the worksurface materials, the height and noise resistance of the panels, and even the color. There should not be large price differences between panel and modular systems if you are outfitting both with the same furniture and electrical requirements. Any bids you receive should include installation fees and hardware expenses per workstation.

Terms

Noise Reduction Coefficient (NRC) Noise absorption measurement, ranging from 0 to 1.00, with 1.00 offering the most absorption. Panels with 0.85 NRC will have very good sound dampening qualities.

Sound Transmission Class (STC) Measurement of sound control from 35 to 60, 60 being the highest. 40+ indicates very reliable sound control.

Worksurface The systems furniture equivalent of a desktop.

Special tips

Begin your search for systems furniture at least a few months in advance. It can take 8 to 12 weeks for delivery if you buy from a high-end manufacturer.

Make sure to use your volume purchasing power. As the size of the purchase increases, your discount should rise to nearly 50% off the original price.

One way to cut costs is to use different sorts of panels in a workstation. For example, you may be able to save by choosing to purchase just one wired panel per workstation.

If employees will have computers at their desk, be careful about installing metal panels that can hold magnets. Magnets can erase a system's hard drive.

See also
Chairs, Desks, File Cabinets

For more information, visit
BuyersZone
http://www.buyerszone.com/

TELEMARKETING SERVICES

*T*elemarketing services make or receive large numbers of calls on a company's behalf. A telemarketing firm can be used to prospect for customers, sell a product, or respond to inquiries via the phone. These services can be a cost-effective alternative to creating an in-house telemarketing group.

PRICING

Average annual wage for TSRs paid by hourly wage only (no commission)

Type of service	Full time	Part-time
Inbound (high)	$22,000	NA
Inbound (low)	$15,600	NA
Inbound (average)	$18,800	NA
Outbound (high)	$18,200	$10,000
Outbound (low)	$18,200	$8,620
Outbound (average)	$18,200	$9,310
Both (high)	$26,400	$16,640
Both (low)	$14,000	$16,640
Both (average)	$20,174	$16,640

Source: *Telemarketing* (June 1995)

VENDORS

Company	Headquarters	Phone number	Minimum size outbound project accepted
Edward Blank Associates	New York, NY	800/ED-BLANK	500 hrs.
FutureCall Telemarketing West	Colorado Springs, CO	800/489-5134	none
ICT Group	Langhorne, PA	800/799-6880	500 hrs.
IntelliSell	Omaha, NE	800/348-4486	200 hrs.
ITI Marketing Services	Omaha, NE	800/562-5000	5,000 calls per month
Market USA	Des Plaines, IL	800/MKT-USA-1	300 hrs.
RMH Teleservices	Bryn Mawr, PA	800/367-5733	500 hrs.
SITEL Corporation	Omaha, NE	800/445-6600	200 hrs.
TeleMark	Portland, OR	800/783-6000	500 hrs.
Zacson Corporation	Pleasanton, CA	800/478-6584	500 hrs.

Buying points

Types of services
Telemarketing services can be broken into two major categories: inbound and outbound. Inbound services provide customer support and product information for consumers who call a firm. Outbound services, on the other hand, provide telephone sales representatives (TSR) who call potential clients with product information and sales pitches.

Reasons to outsource
Setting up a telemarketing department is not easy. To begin with, a large amount of capital expenditure for items such as phone lines, furniture, floor space, computers, and client databases is needed to set up a full-fledged call center. In addition, you will need to go through the effort of hiring and training telephone sales representatives and a management staff.

For companies that do not have a long-term need for telemarketing, outsourcing makes economic sense. Telemarketing services already have the hardware, manpower, and expertise, and economies of scale often allow them to operate at a much lower cost than companies that set up their own in-house operations. Finally, since dedicated telemarketing firms have years of experience, they can help select, design, and test calling lists and scripts.

Choosing a service
When considering a telemarketing firm, first outline your goals for the project and your expectations of the telemarketing firm. You will want to choose a firm with experience in your industry and with similar campaigns. Speak to companies that have worked with the telemarketing firm in the past, and make certain that the company has all the technology and expertise that you require.

The quality of your telemarketing representatives is also tremendously important. Learn about the telemarketing firm's minimum requirements for hiring a TSR. Inquire about the turnover rate and the firm's payment structure. These statistics often reflect the experience and motivation of the TSRs and the company's long-term investment in its employees.

Since most customers assume they are in contact with your company when they reach a TSR, you need to be confident that the philosophy and image of the TSRs are consistent with your own. To check the image the firm conveys, visit the phone centers and monitor actual phone conversations on an unannounced basis.

Finally, make sure your account receives the personal attention it deserves. You should make sure you are a large enough account that TSRs will be knowledgeable about your company and your products when handling calls.

Telemarketing success
The success of a telemarketing campaign depends on many factors. The selling script, the time of the day when calls are generated, the personality of the TSRs, and the list of

potential prospects can all influence the outcome of a campaign.

Often, scripts that direct the TSRs to push for a sale within the first 30 seconds of the conversation tend to result in fruitless calling. Additionally, a too "selective" or too "inclusive" prospect list may yield lower results than expected. Finally, changing the time or the day when calls are made can alter the outcome of the campaign. While a successful sales campaign may often be preceded by failures, your telemarketing firm should be flexible with and receptive to any changes you suggest.

Pricing

When it comes to hiring a telemarketing firm, it is difficult to pinpoint a specific market rate. Costs depend on a myriad of factors, including the type of project, skills and expertise required of TSRs, technologies needed, and even the time and day calls are generated.

Many large telemarketing firms require a minimum work order. These minimum orders can range from 1,000 to 10,000 person hours per project. Most firms charge an hourly rate and bill by the actual time spent on calls. As the number of hours increases, the cost per hour drops. Overall, the number of calls received or generated determines the actual amount of the bill.

The payroll structure of your telemarketer also affects the bill. For companies that do not offer commissions to TSRs, you can expect the base hourly charge to be relatively high. Companies that do pay commission charge relatively less per hour. Depending on the cost of your product and the base salary of TSRs working on your project, commission charges may range from as little as 1% to as high as 10% of the revenue generated.

Terms

Automated call distributor (ACD) A phone system accessory that routes incoming calls among a set of extensions to ensure they are handled efficiently. ACDs are generally used in call centers that process many incoming calls.

Call detail recording (CDR) A reporting mechanism that generates a chronological list of every call leaving the phone system, including the extension that made the call, duration of the call, and other pertinent information.

Call forcing A call distribution feature. It automatically directs a waiting call to the next available agent.

Call sequencer An accessory that allows operators to manually distribute incoming calls based on the amount of time the caller has been waiting. It provides basic management information reports and announcements to callers in overload situations.

Special tips

It can be helpful to work with a firm that pays commissions if you are looking for a firm to sell your company's offerings. Commissions can be more motivating to TSRs than a guaranteed hourly rate.

Industry magazines such as *Telemarketing & Call Center Solutions* (800/243-6002) and *Direct* (203/358-9900) carry information and advertisements from major telemarketing firms.

See also
900 Service, Fax on Demand, Long Distance Service, Telephone Directory Software, Telephone Headsets, Telephone Systems, Toll Free Service, Voice Mail Systems

TELEPHONE DIRECTORY SOFTWARE

Telephone directory software uses the immense storage capacity of a CD-ROM to make the data from hundreds of phone directories available and readily accessible. Users can look up individuals or businesses around the country by name, address, or phone number. In many situations, this software can be an inexpensive alternative to the telephone company's directory assistance service.

VENDORS				
Company	Headquarters	Phone number	Mac	PC
American Business Information (ABI)	Omaha, NE	800/555-5666		●
Digital Directory Assistance (DDA)	Bethesda, MD	800/284-8353	●	●
Pro CD	Danvers, MA	800/992-3766	●	●

PRICING		
Company	Price range for business directories	Price range for residential directories
American Business Information (ABI)	$13-$60	$13-$45
Digital Directory Assistance (DDA)	$25-$159	$30-$159
Pro CD	$28-$180	$35-$180

Buying points

Differences in directories
There are many different types of phone directories. Some include only residences, others only businesses. There are also specialized directories that focus on toll free numbers, international phone numbers or fax numbers.

Phone directories also differ in terms of what data is available. Some include only phone numbers, while others offer full addresses and additional information about the residence or business.

A third difference concerns searching capabilities. Some directories allow you to search based upon any piece of information, while others require the name of the person or business before they can locate the desired information.

Search times
Phone directories are quite fast, although retrieval speed does depend on the speed of your computer and CD-ROM drive. In most cases, searches take less than five seconds.

Accuracy of information
While certainly not 100% accurate, most CD-ROM directories approach the accuracy of phone books at the time of release. You will, however, typically find more typographical mistakes than in phone books.

To keep up with the frequent changes in telephone numbers and addresses, most phone directory software companies offer optional subscriptions to their products, producing updates on a quarterly basis.

Downloading names for mailings
Most phone directories allow a limited number of names to be downloaded for use in direct mailings. This can be an inexpensive way to obtain a basic mailing list. Some manufacturers also sell higher-priced directories that allow for unlimited downloads.

Special tips
Watch for usage limitations. A few programs limit the number of searches you can conduct, requiring you to pay more money when you reach the limit.

Bigger directories are not always better. Databases with lots of information can take up as many as six separate disks. These can be much less convenient to use than smaller databases if you do not need all the included information.

One interesting capability offered by some directories is a "look harder" feature, which can look up names with a similar spelling and address. This capability is very useful if you are searching for names that may be abbreviated or misspelled.

If you expect to frequently use a phone directory for mailings, you should look into purchasing names from a mailing list provider. Although a mailing list may cost more upfront, you will often save money overall through more precise targeting and more up-to-date information.

See also
International Calling, Long Distance Service, Telemarketing Services, Toll Free Service

Telephone Headsets

A telephone headset allows you to talk on the phone while keeping both hands free. They can be used with virtually any kind of office or home phone, and can be installed by simply connecting one or two plugs.

VENDORS

Company	Headquarters	Phone number	Cordless	Warranty
ACS	Scotts Valley, CA	800/995-5500	●	1-2 years
GN Netcom	Eden Prairie, MN	800/826-4656		2 years
Hello Direct	San Jose, CA	800/444-3556	●	1 year-lifetime
JABRA	San Diego, CA	800/327-2230		2 years
Nady	Emeryville, CA	510/652-2411		1 year
Plantronics	Santa Cruz, ,CA	800/544-4660		2 years
Starkey	Eden Prairie, MN	800/262-8611		1 year
UNEX	Nashua, NH	800/345-8639		2 years
VXI	Rollinsford, NH	800/742-8588		1-2 years
WiTec	Westlake, Village, CA	800/347-1420		1 year

Buying points

How phone headsets work
Phone headsets are used in conjunction with existing telephones. Setup simply requires connecting the phone base and headset to a common amplifier.

With most phone systems, you must lift the handset to access a phone line or disconnect a call. You also use the phone to dial, which means that the dial pad must be on the base of the phone, not in the receiver.

Choosing a headset
Your choice of a headset will heavily depend on how you use the telephone. The main factors to consider are comfort, sound quality, and price.

Individuals who spend most of their day talking on the phone will typically want a binaural headset that covers both ears. Binaural headsets provide optimum acoustics and block out noise.

People who spend less time on the phone may be more concerned with aesthetics. Most people want a very inconspicuous headset that can easily be removed. In most cases, a monaural model worn over the ear, in the ear, or behind the head will be the best solution. If you wear eyeglasses, you may want to avoid an over-the-ear headset, since these do not fit well with eyeglass frames.

Features
Noise canceling is a feature that helps to block background noise around the headset user. With noise canceling, the person on the other end will only hear you, not the activity in the office. Noise canceling is becoming more common on headsets, but you will often have to pay extra for it.

A handset/headset switchover feature allows the user to switch between the handset and the headset without switching cords. You should make sure that the feature is well marked and accessible in a hurry; when the phone is ringing, you do not want to guess which unit to pick up.

A quick disconnect feature allows you to disconnect the headset from the rest of the equipment. This means that you do not have to remove the headset if you need to leave your desk. When shopping for a headset, check that the quick disconnect lives up to its name; a few models require a bit of a wrestling match to disconnect the two halves.

Damage to hearing
Headsets are designed to be as safe as your phone.

Your hearing can be harmed by sharp increases in decibel levels, such as the noise heard when you dial to a modem or a fax machine. Most manufacturers offer a feature that protects you from such loud noises. Depending upon the company, this feature is known by different names, such as automatic gain control or tri-level compression.

Pricing
Headset systems, including the amplifier and a headset, cost between $75

and $350. The price differences are more often a result of variations in the amplifier rather than the headsets. For example, headsets with noise canceling will cost more than those without it.

Terms

Amplifier Unit that contains most of the controls and adjustments for headset operation.

Binaural design Model that uses two earpieces to transmit sound.

Boom The microphone that picks up the sounds from a voice. The boom can also refer to the metal or plastic tube that connects the microphone to the rest of the headset.

Monaural design Model that uses one earpiece to transmit sound.

Mute Button that stops transmission of your voice to the person on the other end of the line.

Voice tube A thin plastic tube that channels sound to a microphone positioned near the side of the face. Many users consider voice tubes to be less intrusive than other types of microphones.

Special tips

Make sure that the amplifier you choose is compatible with your phone jack. Certain models may be incompatible if your phone requires a two prong jack instead of a standard modular connector. Most companies sell adapters to connect a standard amplifier to any phone.

If you are considering a wireless system, check how long the battery will last. Some headsets only provide two to four hours of talk time, which may not be enough for some users.

If you are concerned with hygiene issues, you should consider buying headsets with removable earphones or removable ear phone covers. Users can keep their own earphones, which they can attach to any headset at any time.

You should examine headset warranties before purchasing a unit. Headsets are subject to heavy use by a variety of people. Check what parts the warranty actually covers, because repairing a headset is often as expensive as replacing it.

See also
Dictation Equipment, Telemarketing Services, Telephone Systems

Telephone Systems

A telephone system is one of the most difficult of all office purchases. Not only is the equipment tremendously expensive, but the entire purchasing process is fraught with unfamiliar terms and complex technology.

Even worse, the problems associated with buying the wrong system can be tremendous. Choosing the wrong telephone system is not a mistake that can simply be relegated to the dusty corner of the office. Instead, a poorly chosen system will adversely affect the entire office for years.

Company	Headquarters	Phone number	Key	PBX	Hybrid
Comdial	Charlottesville, VA	800/347-1432	●		●
Executone	Milford, CT	800/955-9866	●	●	●
Fujitsu	Phoenix, AZ	800/553-3263		●	
Hitachi	Norcross, VA	770/446-8820		●	
Inter-Tel	Chandler, AZ	602/961-9000	●	●	●
Iwatsu	Carlstadt, NJ	201/935-8580	●	●	●
Lucent Technologies	Basking Ridge, NJ	800/247-7000	●	●	●
Mitel	Kanata, Ontario	800/MITEL-SX		●	
NEC	Melville, NY	800/TEAM-NEC	●	●	●
Nitsuko	Shelton, CT	800/365-1928	●	●	●
Nortel	Richardson, TX	800/4-NORTEL	●	●	●
Panasonic	Secaucus, NJ	800/435-4327	●	●	●
Siemens Rolm	Santa Clara, CA	800/ROLM-123	●	●	●
Tadiran	Clearwater, FL	813/536-3222	●	●	●
Telrad	Woodbury, NY	516/921-8300	●	●	●
Toshiba	Irvine, CA	800/222-5805	●	●	●

Buying points

Types of phone systems
There are two major types of phone systems on the market. Key systems are traditionally used by companies with fewer than 50 employees, while private branch exchanges, or PBXs, handle larger workloads. Key systems are based on the old multi-line phones that used several buttons, or keys, to access an outside line. PBXs are essentially a smaller version of the switching equipment used by the phone company to direct calls.

More recently, the distinctions between key and PBX systems have been blurred. Many key systems now include features that were once available only on PBXs. In addition, some systems operate internally as either a key or a PBX depending on the software that is installed. The term "hybrid" is often used to describe systems that resemble both key and PBX systems.

Digital vs. analog systems
Most newer and more expensive phone systems communicate via digital technology. This means that sound is transmitted as bits of data rather than audio waves.

Theoretically, digital transmission has many advantages over analog transmission. Digital signals are less affected by interference and line degradation, meaning that digital lines have virtually no static or hiss.

However, most businesses make outgoing calls over regular analog lines. This means that even a digital phone system must convert signals back to analog waves whenever a call leaves the office. Because very little sound degradation occurs within the smaller confines of an office, analog systems actually sound about the same as their digital counterparts.

The main reason for buying a digital system is that these systems tend to be better equipped to handle computer telephony, or CTI, applications.

Sizing a phone system
When buying a system, a primary concern is to make sure the unit is the right size for your firm. This means understanding the size constraints of the system.

In the case of key systems, system size is usually indicated as a combination of "lines" and "extensions." Lines indicate the total number of telephone lines used by the company, while extensions refer to every phone within the company. For example, a system might accommodate up to 12 lines and 36 extensions.

In contrast, most PBXs define size in terms of "ports." "Total ports" indicate the maximum number of connections that can be made to the system. This includes outside lines, inside extensions, as well as accessories such as voice mail or automated attendants.

Even if a system can handle your current phone traffic, you also need to check that it will be able to handle your future expansion needs. The ideal system should be able to handle such expansions in a very cost-effective manner. Check which items will need to be purchased or replaced as your needs grow in order to get a good sense for your future costs.

Considering some key features
Systems can be equipped with literally hundreds of features for switching calls and directing traffic. However, dealers estimate that 95% of system features are never used within a company.

Instead of comparing features on a one-to-one basis, you should examine how a phone system will be used in your office. Limit your feature search only to those features that will improve the firm's work flow. This will allow you to focus on the real differences between systems for your office.

Although having the right features is important, even more important is making sure the features are easy to access. Because most employees devote very little time learning how to use a phone system, it is very important that the most common functions be extremely simple and intuitive to use.

Selecting a dealer
Virtually all phone systems require the assistance of a dealer for programming and installation. As a result, finding a good dealer can be the most important part of the purchase, since any phone system you choose needs to be properly installed for optimal performance.

The most important consideration in choosing a dealer is the number of installations completed with your system. A dealer who has installed many of the same systems will be much more familiar with the problems that can occur.

Ideally, the brand you are considering should be the best selling brand sold by the dealer. Knowing that the dealer is committed to the line, you can be assured of a long-term source for service and parts.

You should also inquire about the dealer's specific installation experience. Ask about the size of the companies involved, and what options or features were added. Also make sure to obtain a list of references, including several completed in the past year, so you can ask about their experiences in detail.

Submitting a request for proposal
When you have identified three to five dealers and systems that meet your needs, you are ready to ask for written proposals.

The proposal is a written explanation of the dealer's installation plan. It includes details on the system capabilities and costs, installation time frame, as well as arrangements for future service.

These proposals are obviously much more useful if they follow a similar format and content. This allows you to compare proposals easily across vendors. A simple way to make sure this happens is to write your own request for proposal (RFP). The RFP explains to the dealer the type of proposal you are interested in receiving and should include the information a dealer needs to know about your firm to make appropriate recommendations.

Pricing

While the smallest systems may cost a few thousand dollars to install, the price tag for more complex models can quickly climb to tens of thousands of dollars.

Phone system prices vary based on four factors. The first variable is the price of the central cabinet, which controls and oversees the entire phone system. This price differs between systems, and rises as cards and accessories are added to a system. A small central cabinet can cost as little as $3,000, with the price increasing considerably for larger systems.

The second cost element is the phones themselves. Most systems can be equipped with several different types of phones. The least expensive sets may cost less than $100, but can make accessing features very difficult. On the other end, some "executive phones" sell for many times the standard price. These phones can make using the system slightly easier, but are more often just a significant source of profit for the dealer.

Wiring and installation is the third major cost of a system. It can be very inexpensive to install wires in an unfinished building. However, installing wiring through finished walls can quickly add up.

The fourth pricing variable is everything else. This includes training, programming, service, and future modifications. Pricing is usually based on the time these tasks will require, and can often be the most flexible portion of a bid. Sometimes, it is best to compare the hours that will be spent completing training/programming/service tasks with the price tag for the service.

Terms

Automated attendant A phone system accessory that answers the phone electronically, allowing callers to route themselves through a series of menu prompts (e.g., press 1 for sales) to the appropriate department or extension. Many voice mail systems come equipped with a basic automated attendant system.

Automated call distributor (ACD) A phone system accessory that distributes incoming calls among a set of extensions to ensure they are handled efficiently. ACDs are generally used in call centers that process many incoming calls.

Computer telephony integration (CTI) A term used to describe the broad category of applications that involve connecting a phone system to a computer. CTI makes it possible for a computer to receive data from an incoming call and process it into something useful for your business. The most common example is using caller ID information to bring up the appropriate database file on a computer screen.

Voice mail system An accessory that allows callers to leave personal messages if an extension is not answered. Voice mail systems are generally purchased separately from a phone system, although many phone system manufacturers sell voice mail systems under their same brand name.

Special tips

One good way to save money is to buy used components such as phones or cards. There are more than 300 remarketers, with many offering strong guarantees for their remanufactured products. Some of the larger remarketers include CIS (800/343-5554) and D&S (800/227-8403).

If you expect to use voice mail with your phone system, make sure that any phone system you are considering is capable of working with a wide range of third-party voice mail systems. By keeping your options open, you will minimize the chance of getting stuck with an inferior or overpriced product.

To avoid rewiring down the road, you should request that plenty of wiring be installed when the system is first purchased. A good benchmark is to ask for at least double the wiring you currently need. While this will add to the cost of installation, it will really only be a fraction of the cost you will face if wires need to be added later.

Shop for a dealer's advice at the beginning of the quarter when sales targets have just been set, and make your purchase at the end of the quarter when you can get a much lower price.

Many local phone companies charge different rates for phone lines that connect to a key system versus phone lines that connect to a PBX, even though both have essentially the same functionality. Check rates beforehand to see if this may affect your buying decision.

See also
Answering Machines, Centrex Service, Conference Calling Services, Conferencing Equipment, Cordless Telephones, Fax on Demand, ISDN, KSU-less Phone Systems, Music on Hold Systems, Toll Fraud Prevention, Voice Mail Systems

---

For more information, visit
BuyersZone
http://www.buyerszone.com/

Temporary Help Services

*V*ery often, choosing a temporary help service amounts to nothing more than a last minute phone call to fill an absence or to get help in a crisis. However, taking a more strategic approach to choosing a temp service can actually be very valuable. Not only can costs be reduced, but you may be able to find temporary employees who are far more productive for the tasks at hand.

VENDORS

Company	Headquarters	Phone number	Industrial	Office/ Clerical	Technical/ Professional	Number of offices
Accountemps	Menlo Park, CA	800/803-8367			●	185
Adia	Redwood City, CA	415/610-1000	●	●	●	579
Career Horizons	Woodbury, NY	516/682-1400	●	●	●	510
Express	Oklahoma City, OK	800/652-6400	●	●	●	289
INTERIM	Ft. Lauderdale, FL	305/938-7600	●	●	●	900
Kelly	Troy, MI	810/362-4444	●	●	●	750
Labor World	Boca Raton, FL	407/997-5000	●			107
Manpower	Milwaukee, WI	414/961-1000	●	●	●	1,100
Norrell	Atlanta, GA	404/240-3000	●	●		260
Olsten	Melville, NY	516/844-7800	●	●	●	570
Pro Staff	Minneapolis, MN	612/339-2221	●	●		125
Remedy	San Juan Capistrano, CA	714/661-1211	●	●	●	155
Snelling & Snelling	Dallas, TX	214/239-7575	●	●	●	280
Talent Tree	Houston, TX	713/789-1818	●	●	●	140
Todays	Dallas, TX	214/380-9380		●	●	97
Volt	Orange, CA	714/921-8800	●	●	●	162
Western	Walnut Creek, CA	510/930-5300	●	●	●	350

Buying points

How temps are used
Most commonly, temporary employees are used to address normal fluctuations in a company's work flow. In order to save money, companies keep staff levels low and use temps to handle the excess work. Examples of this include hiring temps for large mailings, unexpected orders, or time-sensitive projects.

A second major use of temps is as contingency workers to fill positions that are temporarily vacant. This helps a firm to avoid overworking permanent employees and can reduce the need to shuffle job responsibilities.

A third use of temps is as a source for permanent employees. Businesses will often hire temps to fill a new opening in the company. If the person is good at the job, the company arranges with the temp service to hire the person on a permanent basis.

Types of positions
Temporary work has broadened since its inception to include a wide range of fields and industries. Clerical and office positions continue to be the largest segment of all temp jobs, comprising almost 40% of all temporary positions. These positions commonly include secretaries, general office clerks, filing clerks, receptionists, typists, word processing operators, data entry clerks, and cashiers.

The second largest category, with one-third of all placements, are those involving industrial work, such as shipping/receiving and assembly line work.

A third category, with just over 15% of all placements, consists of technical workers such as computer programmers, analysts, or engineers, and professional workers in the accounting, legal, sales and marketing, and management areas. This ranks among the fastest growing categories, with specially trained temps becoming an important resource for many firms.

Differences between agencies
Most temporary help companies use newspaper advertisements, job fairs, and word of mouth to recruit candidates. National firms may attract greater numbers of candidates due to the brand name, but large, local firms are often equally well known within their region.

There are much greater differences, however, in how firms screen candidates before hiring. Some firms use computer testing to evaluate candidates, while others supplement this with psychological evaluations or personal interviews to select temps for the right jobs. If you need a temp who possesses specific skills, computer matches are usually adequate, but personal interviews can help ensure that workers are better suited for your needs.

Pricing
Temporary help firms generally charge a fixed percentage of the hourly cost of a worker. For basic jobs, this can translate to total

charges of $9 to $18 per hour. Skilled temps tend to be much more expensive. Technical or professional temps may cost up to $30 per hour.

Most firms offer discounts off their published rates. Even if you plan to use temporary services infrequently, it is usually worth negotiating rates upfront to reduce the overall cost.

Special tips

Even if the temporary help firm will not give you an across-the-board discount for temporary help, you should negotiate rates for specific types of workers and jobs, such as those that require little skill.

If temporary workers will be hired for a specific long-term project, see if you can provide training without being charged for this time.

Ask about guarantees from services for the workers they place. Reputable services generally guarantee satisfaction, waiving fees for workers who do not work out.

If security is of concern, see that the service is bonded to cover the theft or destruction of property by temporary workers.

Make sure to inquire about the cost of hiring a temporary for a permanent position before working with a service. Doing this ahead of time can put you in a much stronger position if you subsequently decide to permanently hire a temporary employee.

If you are looking for a temporary help companies in your area, you can contact the National Association of Temporary and Staffing Services (703/549-6287) for a listing of members in your area.

See also
Executive Recruitment Agencies

Time Clocks

*A*lmost any business with hourly workers uses time clocks. These clocks provide a simple yet reliable way to record how long each person works during the week. Newer models not only ensure accurate recording of work hours, but also can be tied to accounting systems for easier payroll processing.

VENDORS		
Company	Headquarters	Phone number
Acroprint Time Recorder	Raleigh, NC	800/334-7190
Amano Cincinnati	Roseland, NJ	800/842-6266
Kronos	Waltham, MA	617/890-3232
Lathem	Atlanta, GA	800/224-1881
OTR	Portland, OR	800/322-0674
Simplex	Gardner, MA	508/632-2500
Stromberg	New Haven, CT	203/387-2572
Time America	Phoenix, AZ	800/227-9766

Buying points

Types of time clocks

There are currently two main types of time clocks. Most of us are familiar with the older electromechanical clocks. These consist of an internal clock, a stamping device, and a slot into which time cards can be inserted to be stamped with the time. The electromechanical time clock does not actually record time worked, but does create an accurate system of measuring work hours from the stamped cards.

More sophisticated automated time and attendance (ATA) systems first emerged in the 1980s. These systems are electronic, computer-based time keeping systems. Unlike electromechanical systems, ATA systems can often perform more complex recording functions, such as keeping track of each employee over the week. To operate their many functions, ATA systems are often designed to work in concert with computer software packages.

How an ATA system works

ATA systems gather information by reading either time cards or identification cards carried by each employee. Workers simply insert a time card into the designated reading slot or swipe an electronically-coded plastic card through the ATA reader. A few systems provide a keypad for employees to input their identification numbers as they enter or exit the building.

Most ATA systems are designed to interface directly with a PC. The ATA system will generally be equipped with DOS- or Windows-based software programs for examining time data and creating management reports. These systems usually allow data to be exported to other formats or applications. There are also a few ATA systems that use standalone microprocessors, but these have become less common with the rise of PCs.

Advantages of ATA systems

The biggest drawback of electromechanical systems is that each time card must be manually tallied to calculate the hours worked. ATA systems automate this process, tallying the number of hours an employee works and adjusting payment for overtime or other special circumstances. These systems can reduce or eliminate the need for staff to spend time tracking hours and calculating payroll.

A second benefit of ATA systems is that a great deal more data can be recorded than is practical by hand. For example, many firms use ATA systems for job costing, which means recording the time it takes a person to complete a specific task. By analyzing job costing across employees, a firm can identify efficiency problems with individuals or specific departments.

ATA systems also have some side benefits. First, ATA systems will generally eliminate clerical errors in calculating paychecks. They also store work hours within the system, keeping records private.

Purchasing considerations
Before purchasing an ATA, you should carefully analyze how your current time clock is used and how this information is used. This can help determine the most effective type of time entry system and the type of PC interface required.

Most businesses will probably want a system that can interface with their existing payroll system. Make sure you can export data directly into a payroll program, or print reports that can be faxed to a payroll service. You may also want to ask a payroll service if there are specific ATA systems they recommend or prefer using.

Pricing
A conventional electromechanical time recorder will cost between $400 and $600. PC-based time clocks typically cost from $800 to $2,500.

According to industry estimates, a company with up to 500 employees can spend as little as $1,000 or as much as $10,000 on a PC-based ATA system, depending on the type and number of data-collection units, software packages, and reporting options.

Special tips

Avoid time and attendance systems that use proprietary databases. Look for systems that adhere to ODBC standards. This will allow you to use the data in other ODBC-compliant programs.

Look for a company that is experienced and financially stable so you will be able to get upgrades and support over the years.

Password protection is necessary to prevent unauthorized individuals from accessing private information in your ATA system.

Most software systems allow you to customize various parameters to best suit your company's specific needs. Most ATA systems at the lower price range allow only limited customization.

See also
Desktop Computers, Payroll Services

Toll Fraud Prevention

*T*oll fraud occurs when hackers break into a phone system and then use the equipment to place unauthorized calls. While toll fraud is illegal, current laws make your business responsible for paying all calling charges incurred by the hackers. In many cases, this can total hundreds of thousands of dollars in just a few weeks.

Toll fraud equipment is designed to monitor business phone systems to protect against toll fraud. These systems use a combination of passwords and traffic monitoring devices to prevent or minimize the damage caused by hackers.

\multicolumn{6}{c}{**VENDORS**}					
Company	Headquarters	Phone number	Equipment	Service	Software
Mer	New York, NY	800/933-TABS	●		●
Telco Research	Nashville, TN	800/48-TELCO	●	●	●
Teltone	Bothell, WA	800/426-3926	●		
TSL	New York, NY	212/248-2000		●	
Western Telematic	Irvine, CA	800/854-7226	●		
Xiox	Burlingame, CA	415/375-8188	●	●	●
Xtend	New York, NY	800/231-2556	●		●

Buying points

Vulnerable phone systems
Any company with a phone system that can be accessed from outside the office is vulnerable to toll fraud. Hackers can access phone systems through features such as voice mail, DISA, and remote maintenance ports, even when they are not activated.

Toll fraud can also refer to unauthorized usage of a phone system. Hackers often take over unused voice mail boxes for their own purposes. This can tie up your system and result in high charges if the voice mail system can be accessed with a toll free number.

Although toll fraud seems like an unlikely threat, the cost of toll fraud is enormous. Experts estimate that toll fraud costs U.S. businesses several billion dollars each year. Many businesses, including small businesses, have found themselves hit with thousands of dollars in fraudulent charges in just a few days.

How they work
Toll fraud equipment consists of software and hardware that is networked to your phone system via computer.

During installation, the phone system administrator indicates what types of calls are acceptable and unacceptable. Normal calling parameters can be defined according to the areas called, the time of day calls are placed, and the types of remote calling that are acceptable. Unacceptable calls may include 900 calls, calls to certain countries, or multiple calls made from a remote location.

The equipment then monitors all calls to detect fraudulent usage. Calls are analyzed on an ongoing basis to detect suspicious calling patterns. In addition, the system will note when callers attempt to access restricted calling areas.

Once the system detects possible fraudulent usage, it notifies the phone system administrator, who can then decide what action to take. This notification can occur via beeper, fax or computer. For the more vigilant, the toll fraud system can even be designed to shut down the phone system to prevent further misuse.

Buying a toll fraud system
When purchasing a toll fraud system, make sure you know all the details about your current phone system, including the model type as well as the software version. In some cases, a toll fraud system may be compatible with a phone system but will require a certain software version in order to work. For the most part, however, toll fraud systems should work with most phone systems.

One important aspect to consider when evaluating systems is the type of monitoring and protection the system provides. Some simply alert administrators of unusual calling patterns. Others can take a more active role by actively reassigning passwords, preventing access to other areas of a phone system, or even shutting down a system. Since increasing functionality usually results in higher prices, you will need to decide how much security is enough.

Another aspect to examine concerns how easy the system is to use. Even if someone else installs the system, the phone system administrator should be the one responsible for maintaining the system on an ongoing basis. Review the software and instruction manuals ahead of time to ensure the program can be easily modified by the administrator.

Also consider what accessories may be required with the purchase. Many toll fraud systems can be purchased on a standalone basis. However, some vendors require a call accounting system to be purchased at the same time, or recommend this product for better reporting. Call accounting systems provide detailed information about each call that is placed, with data that can pinpoint which extension was used to place a call. Even if you do not purchase a call accounting system at this point, make sure that you can still install your choice of systems if you decide to purchase one later.

Monitoring services

Toll fraud monitoring services offer the same type of oversight you would normally find with toll fraud equipment. The primary difference is that the service is responsible for reviewing calling reports and entering modifications to calling parameters.

Keep in mind that the cost for these services can be much greater than the equipment over time. However, they are a reasonable alternative for offices where there is no person available to review the calling information.

Preventing toll fraud

Companies can take several simple steps to minimize the likelihood of toll fraud. First, check into any remote maintenance port activity. These ports are used by dealers or manufacturers to program or diagnose your communication system without actually coming on-site. Unfortunately, these ports also allow hackers to alter the basic configuration of your system. Ideally, you should disable these ports altogether. Alternatively, you may want to ask the dealer to use a secure password system to access the port.

Companies that allow traveling employees to dial into the phone system and make long distance calls should be diligent about regularly updating passwords. You may even want to purchase a program that requires complex and frequently changing passwords. Also think about restricting access to this feature after hours or during holidays.

Block calls to all area codes and countries that are not called by your business to decrease the likelihood of large losses. 900 numbers, 976 numbers, overseas calls, and calls to the 809 (Caribbean) area code are most likely to be abused.

Pricing

The cost of a toll fraud system varies tremendously, from $500 on the very low end, to as much as hundreds of thousands of dollars for the most sophisticated equipment. Expect to pay between $1,000 and $3,000 for a basic system that includes call accounting.

Terms

Call detail recording (CDR) This feature allows a phone system to collect relevant data on both incoming and outgoing calls. It is used with both call accounting and toll fraud detection systems.

Direct Inward System Access (DISA) This feature allows callers to dial in and use a company's phone system from a remote location. DISA makes a phone system very vulnerable to toll fraud, since outbound calling capabilities are just a password away.

Station Message Detail Reporting (SMDR) Found on many phone systems, this type of CDR electronically records the length and location of every incoming and outgoing call.

Special tips

Activate system software that will disconnect callers after three failed attempts to access the system. This will make it much more difficult for hackers to break passwords by trying thousands of combinations.

Shred all call accounting reports before throwing them out so that a hacker cannot easily obtain this valuable information from the garbage.

Verify that remote maintenance ports are disconnected after service technicians work on your system.

For the cautious, there is insurance available that will indemnify your business in case of a phone system break-in.

While SMDR can alert the company of toll fraud, some hackers can even shut SMDR off so that no suspicious call accounting reports are produced. To prevent such a break-in, consider a system that notifies the administrator if no call records are received for 15 minutes.

See also
Paper Shredders, Telephone Systems, Voice Mail Systems

Toll Free Service

A toll free number gives callers a way to contact your firm without having to pay for the call themselves.

In the past, toll free numbers were primarily used by large firms, or those doing extensive business in catalog sales. The high startup costs of installing a toll free line placed the service out of reach for all but the highest volume users.

Today, toll free, or "inbound," service is available to businesses of all sizes. New programs with low monthly fees have made the service cost-effective for even the smallest businesses.

Company	Headquarters	Phone number
AT&T	Basking Ridge, NJ	800/222-0400
Cable & Wireless	Sterling, VA	800/486-8686
Frontier	Rochester, NY	800/836-7000
LCI	McLean, VA	800/860-1020
LDDS WorldCom	Jackson, MS	800/737-8423
MCI	Washington, DC	800/950-5555
Sprint	Overland Park, KS	800/877-7253

Buying points

Uses for a toll free number

Toll free numbers are most often used in connection with sales and marketing efforts. They are commonly used for taking orders and fielding customer inquiries.

Toll free numbers can also be used for support functions, such as technical help or assistance lines. Customers appreciate a toll free number, particularly during busy times when they are placed on hold.

Toll free numbers can also be used internally. A toll free number gives traveling employees an easy and inexpensive way to call back to the office from any phone. In many cases, inbound calling is less expensive for the company than paying for a calling card call.

Toll free service vendors

Long distance companies and resellers are the largest providers of inbound calling services. You can generally obtain inbound service from any firm that offers long distance service in your area.

Local telephone companies also offer inbound service for calls that originate from within their calling area. This can be combined with service from a long distance carrier to handle all types of calls.

Required equipment

Unless you expect a very high volume of calls, toll free service typically utilizes your existing phone lines. This means no new equipment is necessary, since the toll free call will ring into the office phone system just like any normal call.

Higher volume users often prefer to purchase a dedicated line that will only carry inbound calls. Dedicated lines require custom installation; however, these charges are usually offset by lower per-minute charges.

Comparing programs

The two main considerations when choosing a toll free calling program are the rates you will pay and the features you require.

Rates range from nearly 30¢ per minute on some plans, to less than 10¢ per minute with some high-volume programs. As a result, the plan you choose can have a tremendous effect on how much you end up paying for the service.

Most plans offer a similar set of basic calling features, although monthly charges and set-up charges may differ. You may want to look for options such as call blocking, which ensures that you do not get (and pay for) calls from areas you do not serve, or account codes, which restrict inbound access to employees or customers who know the correct code.

Larger businesses with dedicated inbound service can also consider more sophisticated features. If a business has more than one toll free number, Dialed Number Identification Service (DNIS) identifies the particular toll free number that was dialed. This can be used to distinguish between different marketing campaigns that all ring at a central location.

Another identification feature, called ANI, is similar to caller ID service for the home. ANI allows a business to see the caller's number as the call is received. Some businesses use this information to bring up the matching customer record on a computer as the call comes through.

Switching carriers
Portability, a program instituted by the FCC in May 1993, gives ownership of a particular toll free number to the company using it, not the carrier. As a result, any company can switch carriers without losing the marketing equity invested in a particular number. Switching carriers is as simple as calling a new carrier and signing up for service.

Portability also allows businesses to split toll free traffic on a given number across multiple carriers. For example, all in-state calls could be handled by the local telephone company while out-of-state calls could be handled by a national carrier.

888 numbers
In March 1996, the FCC released the 888 area code to supplement the diminishing supply of 800 numbers. 888 numbers function in exactly the same way as 800 numbers, billing the recipient rather than the caller. Billing programs are also exactly the same.

However, there is still a lack of public understanding about 888 numbers, which means that 888 numbers will not be particularly well suited for marketing campaigns in the immediate future. Expect 888 numbers to become more commonplace and better understood by the public in the coming years.

Pricing
The cost of toll free service includes a monthly fee and a per-minute charge. Monthly fees typically do not exceed $20 per month, although special features may add slightly to this figure.

The per-minute charge can be a flat rate, or it can be banded, which means it varies according to the distance a particular call travels. In either case, a calling plan's per minute charges often decreases for firms with higher calling volumes. Businesses receiving just a few calls a day can expect to pay about 20¢ per minute. Firms receiving thousands of minutes of calls per month should expect to pay 14¢ per minute or less.

Companies receiving more than 20,000 minutes per month on their toll free line may find a dedicated line to be more cost-effective. Although installation fees can be high, per minute rates are much lower.

Terms

Call rounding Indicates how the length of a call is determined for billing purposes. This is usually expressed in terms of the minimum billing period and the billing increment. For example, 30/6 means that all calls will be billed for a minimum of 30 seconds, with calls that are longer than 30 seconds billed in 6 second increments.

Dedicated service A type of service that requires a direct connection between your phone system and a long distance carrier. It is designed for high-volume users.

Inbound service Another term for toll free service. Most carriers use the term "inbound" to indicate that the recipient actually pays for "toll free" calls.

Switched service A type of service that routes toll free numbers into your phone system through regular phone lines.

Term agreement An agreement that locks clients into a fixed contract for the length of a term. Most term agreements guarantee a fixed percentage discount, but not specific rates.

Special tips

When choosing an inbound service provider, do not assume that well-known companies are necessarily the best choice. In fact, well-known providers are often considerably more expensive than smaller national and regional companies.

Watch out for term agreements. These programs lock you into a fixed rate for one to three years. With increased competition putting downward pressure on rates, now is not the time to lock yourself into a commitment of more than one year.

Be careful about agreeing to minimum monthly volume requirements. In many cases, your firm will be penalized if you fall below the minimum volume. In most cases, you can be penalized for any month that falls below the minimum, even if your monthly volume averages more than the minimum requirement.

Look for programs that bill calls in the smallest possible increments. Programs using 6 or 1 second rounding will end up being 10% to 20% less expensive than those using full-minute call rounding.

See also
900 Service, Calling Cards, Cellular Service, International Calling, Long Distance Service, Prepaid Phone Cards, Telemarketing Services, Telephone Systems

---

For more information, visit
BuyersZone
http://www.buyerszone.com/

Did you know?

Some $135 billion in goods and services were traded on toll free lines last year, according to National Telemarketing, Inc.

Toner Supplies

*T*oner is a dry, powder-like substance that acts as the "ink" for a wide range of office equipment, including copiers, laser printers, and many fax machines.

While most businesses spend a great deal of time deciding how much to pay for office equipment, they pay much less attention to the toner used in the machine. However, over the life of the equipment, the cost of toner needed to operate a copier, laser printer, or fax can be many times the cost of the equipment itself.

VENDORS

Company	Headquarters	Phone number	OEM	Generic
American Ribbon & Toner	Fort Lauderdale, FL	800/327-1013	●	●
Databyte Office City	Morpark, CA	800/992-2679	●	
Diskette Connection	Oklahoma City, OK	800/654-4058	●	●
Laser Gold	Federal Way, WA	800/626-2060		●
Nashua	Nashua, NH	800/258-1370		●
Nu Kote International	Dallas, TX	800/448-1422		●
Office America	Miami, FL	305/625-9035	●	●
PM Company	Cincinnati, OH	800/554-8053		●
Supply Depot	Providence, RI	800/331-3810	●	●
Toner Cartridge Services	Dallas, TX	800/633-4935	●	●

Buying points

Types of toner
There are two major types of toner on the market: bottled toner and toner cartridges. Bottled toner is plain toner in a plastic bottle. It is typically used with photocopiers and is simply poured into a toner container within the machine.

Toner cartridges are more complex units, consisting of toner plus an imaging drum, all packaged in a plastic case. Laser printers and fax machines most often use toner cartridges, although many low-end copiers do as well. Toner cartridges cost more than bottle toner, but are also usually easier to find.

Matching toner and equipment
Although toner can look quite similar to the bare eye, toners can differ greatly in terms of their properties and actual makeup. As a result, toner that works in one machine may not necessarily work in a different machine.

However, this does not mean that you are limited to the specific type of toner specified by the manufacturer. Many models, particularly laser printers, often use the same toner. In addition, there are vendors that produce generic versions of popular types of toner.

Toner vendors
Toner is sold through many different sources, including office equipment dealers, office supply stores, computer stores, and toner dealers.

Office equipment dealers are typically expensive sources for toner. Dealers usually derive a good percentage of their profits from supplies such as toner and parts, and are not very willing to cut margins. Instead, dealers often focus on scare tactics, describing all other toner as being unsuitable for the machines.

Office supply stores and computer stores usually sell only toner cartridges. This is because there are comparatively fewer varieties of toner cartridges than bottled toner, which allows these stores to stock fewer items. Pricing from these outlets can be quite good, particularly for popular brands.

Toner dealers are businesses that specialize in selling toner and other office equipment supplies. These stores typically sell both bottle toner and toner cartridges, often at prices that are significantly below those of an office equipment dealer.

Risking damage to office equipment
Using toner from alternate sources is unlikely to cause damage to office equipment, despite what many dealers claim. Generally, the worst that can happen is that the toner can contaminate the reservoir, requiring a professional cleaning. Usually the only problem is inferior image quality, a problem that can easily be solved by switching to a better toner.

Checking the quality of toner
Before you buy toner, document the quality and cost effectiveness of your current brand, noting how long a cartridge or bottle lasts and the quality of printing.

When you buy new toner, make sure it properly fits into your machine, and then test some pages. Compare the output with pages from the old batch, watching for streaking or gray areas.

As you use the toner, note how many pages it produces. If it does not last as long as previous supplies, make sure the price is low enough to make up for the shortage.

Pricing

Depending on the model, toner can range in cost from $30 to more than $100 per bottle or cartridge. Shopping around, buyers can look for 10% to 20% in savings.

Terms

Bundling The practice of combining products and services/supplies into a single package deal.

OEM (original equipment manufacturer) toner The type of toner that is manufactured by or for a specific equipment manufacturer.

Counterfeit toner A low-grade toner falsely labeled as being made by the original equipment manufacturer. Some dealers and stores try to sell counterfeit toner at OEM prices.

Compatible or generic toner A type of toner that is made for a specific model but is not manufactured by the original equipment manufacturer.

Special tips

Watch out for mail order equipment dealers that offer great deals on toner. Some may be scams that try to sell large volumes of counterfeit or poorly-made toner at greatly discounted prices.

It can be smart to check references and ask for guarantees when buying toner from a new supplier.

If you find a compatible brand that sells good toner for one piece of equipment, do not assume that their toner is good for all your machines. Many firms re-brand toner from other manufacturers, making it necessary to evaluate toner on a model by model basis.

Compatible brands should have a money-back guarantee in case the toner is of poor quality. Also look for a guarantee to cover damage caused by the toner.

Recycled toner cartridges can save you as much as $30 per cartridge. Recycled means that the cartridge case and some of the internal parts come from used OEM cartridges. This is a relatively easy business to enter, so watch for bad deals and poor quality cartridges.

Two ways to avoid toner phone scams are to never give someone your machine's model number and never make a purchase from an incoming caller.

See also
Color Printers, Copy Paper, Fax Machines, Ink-jet Printers, Laser Printers, Multifunctional Devices, Office Supplies, Photocopiers, Recycling

---

For more information, visit
BuyersZone
http://www.buyerszone.com/

Trade Show Displays

For many businesses, trade shows offer a simple and convenient way to directly target relevant buyers in the industry. Probably the greatest challenge in putting on a trade show display is making a statement that rises above the visual roar of neighboring booths. You need to convey your message forcefully and effectively in just the few seconds that someone spends walking by your booth.

VENDORS

Company	Headquarters	Phone number	Pop-up	Panel	Modular
Abex Display Systems	North Hollywood, CA	800/537-0231	●	●	●
Downing Displays	Milford, OH	800/883-1800	●		
Expo Systems	Tampa, FL	800/367-3976	●	●	●
Featherlite Exhibits	Minneapolis, MN	800/229-5533	●	●	●
Foga Systems	Oxnard, CA	800/488-3642		●	
The Godfrey Group	Raleigh, NC	919/544-6504	●		●
Hanna Design Group	Don Mills, Ontario	716/247-6240	●	●	●
Heritage Display Group	St. Paul, MN	612/646-7865			●
Laarhoven	Norcross, GA	800/825-2223	●	●	●
Nimlok	Niles, IL	800/233-8870	●	●	●
Nomadic Display	Springfield, VA	800/336-5019	●	●	
Professional Displays	Ontario, CA	800/222-6838	●	●	●
Skyline	Burnsville, MN	800/328-2725	●	●	●
Tiger Mark	Framingham, MA	800/338-8465		●	

Portable trade show displays offer a cost-effective way to make such a statement. Portable exhibits get their name because they can be packed into cases that can be checked onto airlines or sent via standard ground shipping services. This portability allows exhibitors to bring in and set up the displays themselves, avoiding the added complexity and expense of professional movers and builders. Portable displays usually require no tools for assembly, and can be set up by just one or two people.

Buying points

Types of portable trade show displays

There are two basic types of portable exhibits: pop-up exhibits and panel displays. Pop-up exhibits use an accordion-style folding frame, which is then covered with magnetic-backed fabrics or plastic panels. Panel displays typically consist of fabric-covered solid segments that are connected together to make a wall.

A variety of materials can be used for the display panels, including plastic and fabric. Heavier carpet-like fabric tends to withstand wear much better than smooth fabrics.

Advantages and disadvantages of pop-up displays

Pop-up displays are fairly lightweight and compact. A 10-foot display can fold into one or two cases, each about the size of a large golf bag, and weighs under 70 pounds. These displays are also fairly easy to set up.

The primary downside of these displays is that they offer little in the way of size flexibility. Since the frame must be fully opened to be stable, users cannot adjust the frame to fit smaller or larger spaces.

Advantages and disadvantages of panel displays

A panel display is composed of many separate folding panels that can be arranged in different configurations. As a result, companies can use the same display for different exhibition spaces. A tabletop display can be created by using only part of the display, or panels can be folded in and out to fit smaller or larger spaces.

Although it offers more setup flexibility, panel displays can be a bit unwieldy, and often require more than one person to assemble.

What can be displayed

Both text and images can be shown on a display. The most flexible way of doing so is to produce mounted graphics and back them with Velcro. These can then be attached to fabric-covered displays.

While panel displays can support large, flat images, pop-up displays will either require graphics that are small in size or that can be applied to a flexible curved surface.

Displays can also incorporate text and images as the surface of the display. This is typically done by creating a large photomural that is then applied to the display.

Most systems can also be equipped with shelving to display products.

Warranties

Displays receive a lot of rough treatment from shippers, customers, and those setting them up. You should expect a lifetime warranty on pop-up frames. Warranties on panel displays vary a bit more, lasting anywhere from two to five years.

Display vendors

Trade show displays are sold by dealers and direct from the manufacturer. The advantage of working with dealers is that they will typically carry models from multiple manufacturers, allowing you to make direct comparisons.

Graphics for the display can usually be purchased from the vendor selling the display. Firms can also turn to designers who specialize in producing artwork for trade show displays.

Pricing

A basic 10-foot, fabric-covered display will run about $3,500, while high end displays can easily cost $7,000. There is usually not a large price difference between similarly configured pop-up and panel systems.

On top of the basic display cost, you should expect to pay an additional 40% to 80% for graphics and accessories. Individual graphics that are attached via Velcro can cost $5 to $300 depending on the size. A full photomural that attaches directly to a display can cost about $1,200.

Terms

Backlighting Lights inside the display that shine through your graphics. Backlit displays can often create a high-impact visual image.

External frames These panel systems encase the fabric of the display in metal or plastic. These systems emphasize the individuality of each panel, and are useful for displaying multiple pictures or segmenting your product offerings.

Header A banner that is placed above the display that announces your message or company name.

Internal frames Hidden beneath the fabric, this type of frame allow panel systems to join closely together, providing a single consistent surface.

Special tips

Before you buy a display unit, you should consider renting one. An estimated 40% of first-time exhibitors never return to another show. Keep in mind that some dealers will allow you to apply 50% to 100% of the approximately $500 rental cost towards a purchase.

If you like the look, but not the cost, of a photomural, consider having one that only covers part of the frame. The remainder of the display can be backed by the regular fabric covering.

Buying a refurbished display can be a less expensive alternative to buying a new one.

One inexpensive, lightweight alternative for trade show displays is an exhibit made entirely of fabric, which clips directly to the pipes used at most trade shows. One of the larger vendors of fabric displays is Snap-Drape (800/358-9215).

If you would like to exhibit your company's products on the display, make sure to try before you buy. Not all systems can bear weight equally well.

Begin the shopping process about two months before the show to allow time to create the proper artwork.

Keep all your shipping options in mind when buying a display. Think about airplane, ground shipping, and personal car requirements when determining the overall cost of a particular system.

To ensure longer life for a display, make sure it can be securely packed. Look for a display with a case that has separate space for each display component. Avoid tucking non-display components in the case.

The best way to test a system is to try and set it up yourself. Start from the beginning and set it up with the extra components you may want.

See also
Advertising Agencies, Graphic Designers, Public Relations Firms, Signs

For more information, visit
BuyersZone
http://www.buyerszone.com/

Did you know?
The average trade show visitor spends only three seconds viewing your booth at a trade show.

Travel Agencies

*T*ravel agencies help businesses book travel reservations, obtain airline tickets, and plan trips. These firms have access to computer reservation systems that allow them to instantly compare rates and make reservations. In addition, many travel agencies obtain discounts from major travel providers, allowing you to reduce travel costs.

VENDORS

Company	Headquarters	Phone number	Air travel sales (1995)
American Express	New York, NY	800/AXP-TRIP	$7,300,000
BTI Americas	Northbrook, IL	800/888-8225	$1,634,933
Carlson Wagonlit Travel	Minneapolis, MN	800/227-5766	$2,426,947
Maritz Travel	Fenton, MO	800/325-4098	$1,001,000
Omega World Travel	Fairfax, VA	800/75-OMEGA	$413,000
Rosenbluth International	Philadelphia, PA	800/553-4893	$1,800,000
Sato Travel	Arlington, VA	800/SATO-911	$1,107,141
Travel and Transport	Omaha, NE	800/228-2545	$381,000
Travel One	Mt. Laurel, NJ	800/243-1600	$355,000
WorldTravel Partners	Atlanta, GA	404/814-2990	$505,000

Source: *Business Travel News*, "1996 Business Travel Survey" (May 27, 1996)

Buying points

Available services
Travel agencies help businesses and individuals prepare for travel, issuing airline tickets, making hotel reservations, and reserving rental cars or other types of transportation.

In addition to offering these basic functions, travel agents can offer a range of services such as ticket delivery, detailed travel expense reports, and 24 hour emergency service to handle problems. For larger accounts, travel agencies can also help negotiate custom discounts with travel vendors. Some agencies even provide complimentary copies of air flight guides and detailed information about destinations to help businesses plan their travels.

Agency size
One of the factors to consider when choosing a firm to work with is the size of the agency.

Small, independent travel agencies are best equipped to provide personalized attention. Their small size often allow the firms to accommodate unusual traveler needs and preferences. These firms are typically positioned to best serve firms that spend up to $100,000 in yearly travel bookings.

A medium-sized agency, usually a larger local agency, handles enough business travel to obtain significant discounts from hotels and a sizable number of free perks from airlines that can be shared with clients. Medium-sized agencies can also provide added travel conveniences, such as an airline ticket printer in your office. Firms with billings between $100,000 and $1 million should find such an agency to offer the appropriate level of support.

A large agency, usually a regional or national firm, is able to negotiate the largest discounts with suppliers, and will also be very familiar with rebating arrangements. Companies with multiple offices may especially want to consolidate their account with a national agency for increased bargaining power and ease in travel arrangements and reporting. Corporations with more than $1 million in yearly bookings should consider using a regional or national travel agency.

The bidding process
If your firm has travel bookings of a few hundred thousand dollars a year, it is generally worth the effort to ask travel agencies to bid for your business.

Begin the process by screening travel agencies in your area. You should initially ask whether the travel agency can offer the services you require and whether the agency's client base matches your demands and travel volume.

Once you have narrowed your choices to two or three agencies, you can request that they provide you with written proposals. You will need to give the agency a complete breakdown of your travel expenses, including information on how your firm currently makes its travel arrangements. In return, the agency should provide a proposal that details how they can save money and simplify your current travel booking process. This may include giving you access to special discounts that the agency has negotiated, or providing features such as an on-site ticket printer.

Online reservation services

In the past few years, online and World Wide Web-based reservation systems have emerged as an alternative to travel agents. Essentially, they offer travelers the opportunity to compare travel options and directly reserve tickets.

Since most small businesses do not pay travel agencies for their services, online reservations do not offer any real price savings. They are best suited for those who feel it is easier to compare travel options on their own or prefer the ability to check fares at any time.

Pricing

Travel agencies have traditionally worked on commission, earning 5% to 15% of charges paid by travelers. However, recently imposed caps on commissions have forced some agencies to reconsider this revenue model.

Alternative revenue structures include a flat fee for all services, a transaction fee for each service rendered, or a combination of the two.

Terms

Commission model A revenue model which gives agencies a certain percentage of the ticket's value. The commission model makes travel agencies "free" for travelers, but can decrease the agency's incentive to find the lowest fare.

Override An incentive program used by a travel vendor to encourage the use of its offering over other vendors. These incentives usually take the form of additional commissions that are paid as an agency achieves greater volumes of business with the vendor.

Rebating A process by which travel agencies share a percentage of their commission with their largest clients. Rebates generally range from 1% to 3% of the ticket price, and are typically supplemented by a flat fee for services.

Special tips

Look for an agency that earns at least half of its revenue from business travelers. Vacation-oriented travel agencies may not be as well equipped to dealing with the more urgent demands of corporate travelers.

Travel auditors can be hired to check how effective a travel agent is at finding the lowest available fares.

Ask if there are particular airlines or other vendors that the travel agency primarily represents. Agencies often want to book travel with their primary vendors to earn incentive rewards. In some cases, you will be able to share in these benefits by agreeing to use the same providers.

Although all travel agents have access to the same few computer reservation systems, not every travel agent will find the same fares. The skill of the agent, the time invested in the search, and the availability of low fare finders can all affect the rate they obtain.

See also
Car Rental Agencies, Corporate Cards, Frequent Flyer Programs, Hotels

Typewriters

Since the introduction of the personal computer, the typewriter has increasingly been relegated to the back corner of the office. Yet typewriters are still the most efficient tool for many tasks, particularly when using odd-sized pages or preprinted forms. As a result, businesses usually find they need to keep at least one good typewriter on hand for the occasional form or label.

VENDORS		
Company	Headquarters	Phone number
Brother	Somerset, NJ	901/373-6256
Canon	Lake Success, NY	516/488-6700
Lexmark	Lexington, KY	800/358-5835
Olivetti	Bridgewater, NJ	800/243-3185
Olympia	Dallas, TX	800/832-4727
Panasonic	Secaucus, NJ	201/392-4581
Sharp	Mahwah, NJ	800/237-4277
Smith Corona	New Canaan, CT	800/448-1018
Swintec	Moonachie, NJ	800/225-0867

Buying points

Why buy a typewriter
Typewriters have three main advantages over the laser printers most often used in the office. First, typewriters print by impact, allowing multi-part forms to be completed without separately printing each sheet.

A second advantage is that words can easily be lined up with blanks on a page. This makes a typewriter better equipped to handle preprinted forms or other documents where type placement is very important.

A third advantage of typewriters is its ability to handle unusually shaped sheets. The rollers in a typewriter generally can handle these pages much better than a standard printer.

Types of typewriters
Typewriters are generally available in basic and display versions. Basic versions type directly on the page, while display versions have built-in displays for making corrections before words are typed. Some display models are quite sophisticated, with full sized screens and advanced word processing features. However, at a certain point, users may just be better off using a full-fledged computer with a word processing program.

Choosing a typewriter
One of the most important features to examine when choosing a typewriter is the unit's erasing capabilities. Most modern typewriters store a few hundred characters in memory after typing, allowing letters or even whole lines of text to be erased at the touch of a button. Typewriters should also be equipped with a manual erase key, so the typist can correct mistakes no longer in memory.

A second concern is what size paper the typewriter will hold. Most typewriters hold paper that is up to 14 inches wide. However, there are some models that have much narrower maximum capacity. Other extra-wide models can accept sheets as large as 21 inches wide.

Also check whether very thick sheets will feed through the typewriter. Labels and file cards are sometimes too thick for some typewriters, particularly those designed for home use. Others can feed thick sheets, but are not able to hold a sheet when you get near the bottom of the page.

Finally, if you commonly print on multi-part forms, make sure the typewriter can print hard enough to transfer an image through four- or five-part forms. Some models are equipped with an impression control setting, that allows you to increase pressure for multi-part forms.

About memory features
If you use the typewriter for complex forms or long documents, it can be important to have a display typewriter with some basic memory capabilities.

One of the most useful memory features is one that handles forms. This records where each field in a form appears on a page. The next time you complete the same form, the typewriter will automatically advance to the appropriate section.

A text memory feature allows specific information such as a name or address to be saved in memory, and typed on demand. This feature can be useful for creating labels for commonly used addresses.

Other memory features are designed for longer documents. Options such as cut and paste, global search and replace, and right justifying text are reasonable features, but are usually more useful as part of a full word processing package.

Maintaining a typewriter
Office typewriters usually last 10 to 15 years if properly maintained. Proper maintenance consists of covering the typewriter when not in use and cleaning it about once a year. Users should also be careful not to use correction fluid in such a way that it gets inside the machine.

Cleaning is offered by many typewriter repair shops, and costs about $50 to $100.

Purchasing supplies
Typewriter supplies tend to be fairly inexpensive, particularly given the light use most typewriters receive. Instead, a greater concern is finding a steady source of supplies. Most stores do not stock ribbons or wheels for less popular brands, requiring you to turn to the dealer or the manufacturer for each round of supplies. Supplies for more popular brands such as IBM/Lexmark and Olivetti are widely available from office supply stores.

Pricing
Typewriters range in price from $100 to $1,500. Units costing less than $250 are generally designed for light home use, while heavy-duty office units typically cost $400 to $600.

There are also refurbished models available for sale. In particular, the long discontinued IBM Selectric typewriter can be found for a few hundred dollars.

Terms

Automatic paper insertion A feature that automatically scrolls a sheet of paper into place by pressing just one button.

Characters per second (cps) A measurement of the printing speed of the typewriter. This figure is only relevant when measuring how fast the model can print from memory, since human typists cannot attain such speeds.

Correction memory A memory buffer that allows recently typed characters to be corrected with the touch of a button. The size of the memory and the speed at which corrections are made can vary considerably from one typewriter to the next.

Pitch A term that refers to the number of characters that appear in a horizontal inch of text. Most typewriters feature a 10-point, 12-point, and 15-point options. This means 10, 12, and 15 characters, respectively, typically appear in an inch of text.

See also
Business Forms, Copy Paper, Desktop Computers, Dot Matrix Printers, Laser Printers, Notebook Computers

---

Did you know?

The last manual typewriter was made in 1983 by Smith Corona.

Uniforms

*M*ore than 32 million U.S. workers go to work each day wearing uniforms. Uniforms can project a consistent and unified image for companies that regularly interact with the public.

VENDORS

Company	Headquarters	Phone number	States served	Number of offices
American Industrial Service	Salt Lake City, UT	801/328-8831	7	8
Amertex Service Group	Farmington Hills, MI	810/539-9300	2	9
Apparelmaster USA	West Chester, OH	513/772-7721	5	8
Aramark Uniform Service	Burbank, CA	818/973-3700	33	157
Arrow Uniform	Detroit, MI	313/365-1100	5	15
Coyne Textile Services	Syracuse, NY	315/475-1626	16	33
G & K Service	Minnetonka, MN	612/912-5500	20	53
Morgan Services	Chicago, IL	312/346-3181	8	19
National Linen Service	Atlanta, GA	404/853-6000	22	79
Prudential Overall Supply	Santa Ana, CA	714/250-4855	3	21
Todd Uniform	St. Louis, MO	314/984-5606	22	36
Van Dyne-Crotty	Dayton, OH	513/236-1500	6	12

Source: Uniform Textile & Service Association, *1995-96 Guide to UTSA*

Buying points

Benefits of uniforms
Uniforms allow customers to quickly identify employees for assistance. Additionally, uniforms allow employers to control the appropriateness and condition of the clothes worn by employees. For employees, uniform programs help them avoid having to buy, clean and repair their work clothes.

Types of uniforms
Most uniforms are made from a blend of polyester and cotton fabrics. While uniforms have traditionally been associated with plain, matching, single-color shirts and pants, you can generally get whatever you want. In recent years, more firms are opting for coordinating shirts and pants that match but are of different colors. "Executive wear," such as Oxford-type shirts and dress pants, are also gaining in popularity.

Uniforms can also be worn over regular street clothes. Garments such as lab coats, smocks, aprons, or vests promote a more consistent image without requiring each person to be outfitted in the same clothes.

Most uniforms require regular washing and do not require ironing. The life expectancy of these garments is three to five years with regular wear.

Buying vs. renting
Firms can choose either to buy or rent uniforms.

Buying is generally the less expensive option. Not surprisingly, about 80% of uniforms are bought rather than rented.

However, buying uniforms means that you will need to manage cleaning and maintenance. You will either have to trust your workers to keep up their uniforms or hire an industrial launderer to deal with the garments.

A uniform rental firm supplies and cleans uniforms. Working with a service may be preferred in situations where employees may not wash their uniforms on a regular basis. In addition, renting can be a better option for companies that have a high turnover rate. That way, the firm will not have to pay for uniforms that are no longer needed.

About uniform vendors
Uniforms are sold through retail outlets, direct sales, and mail order catalogs.

Generally, the offerings do not vary very much among vendors. However, some vendors specialize in a particular type of uniform, such as lab coats, which can mean better prices for the buyer.

Vendors can also differ in terms of their service levels. For example, firms can vary in terms of their turnaround time for delivery, availability of custom embroidering of logos and/or names, and handling of emergency requests for uniforms.

Choosing a uniform rental firm
Each week, uniform rental companies provide employees with up to five changes of work clothes and pick up a set of uniforms from the previous week for cleaning.

These services generally require a minimum order of garments to be delivered each week. Services also typically require a minimum two-year commitment, with three- and four-year terms becoming quite common.

Generally, it will be cheaper for a uniform rental firm to handle your account if you are located nearby or along a route already being served. In addition, it can be more cost effective to work with a firm that already supplies the same garments to other firms. That way, the rental service can better manage their inventory and can obtain better pricing from uniform manufacturers.

Pricing

Purchasing five or six sets of uniforms, which should each last 3 to 5 years, will cost approximately $150 to $250. Note, however, that this figure does not incorporate the cost of cleaning or repairs.

Most uniform rental services bill a flat rate based on a negotiated contract. Generally, rates are based on the number of garment changes provided for each worker; this usually ranges from $1 to $1.50 per day's worth of clothing. This rate remains the same regardless of whether garments are returned for cleaning, with an additional per-piece rate typically charged when uniform delivery goes above a contracted maximum. Altogether, uniform rental will cost between $200 to $300 per employee per year.

Terms

Add man Term used when an employee is added to your uniform service contract.

Bulk items (flat goods) Products that are not customized, such as aprons, smocks, towels, and lab coats.

Industrial launderer The traditional name for a uniform rental service. The bulk of the business for these companies consists of renting customized garments and entrance mats.

Quit man Term used when an employee is removed from the contract.

Tunnel finishing The process most commonly used by industrial launderers to remove wrinkles from garments. After being washed and spun, the garments are placed on hangers and conveyed through a steam chamber for wrinkle-free drying.

Special tips

When choosing garments from a rental firm, it is more economical to choose those that can also be used by other businesses. That way, when you have turnover or need additional garments, replacement uniforms can come from the rental service's used garment inventory.

A recent technology allows small patches to be heat-sealed onto clothing. Logos printed on these patches can be removed with little problem, so clothing can be easily reused.

See also
Temporary Help Services

Uninterruptible Power Supplies

*U*ninterruptible power supplies (UPS) are designed to protect electronic equipment against problems stemming from a temporary failure in the power supply. By providing a constant source of electricity, UPS can help prevent damage to computers, phone systems, and other sensitive electronic equipment.

VENDORS		
Company	Headquarters	Phone number
Acme Electric	Cuba, NY	716/968-2400
American Power Conversion (APC)	W. Kingston, RI	800/800-4APC
Best Power	Necedah, WI	800/356-5794
Deltec	San Diego, CA	619/291-4211
Exide Electronics	Raleigh, NC	919/872-3020
Liebert	Columbus, OH	614/888-0246
Merlin Grein	Costa Mesa, CA	714/557-1636
Toshiba	Houston, TX	713/466-0277
Tripp Lite	Chicago, IL	312/755-8741

Buying points

How UPS systems work

UPS systems work by detecting decreases in the amount of electricity coming from the wall circuit, and boosting power to maintain a constant flow of electricity to connected equipment. This power boost is provided either by a transformer which enhances a weak electrical flow, or from an internal battery which substitutes for the normal power source in the event of failure. The battery is then recharged when the power flow returns to normal.

Most UPS units also contain surge protectors which help prevent equipment damage whenever there are power surges or sudden increases in the flow of voltage.

Types of UPS

There are three basic types of UPS available.

Standby, or off-line, units switch from the regular power source to an internal battery when they sense a power disturbance. There is a brief lag time before the internal battery comes on-line. This downtime should be brief enough, however, to avoid causing a computer to shut down.

Line-interactive UPS systems add a transformer to minimize the need to use an internal battery with every power fluctuation. These units monitor the line voltage at all times, activating the power transformer when the voltage falls below manufacturer-specified parameters. The battery is activated when even lower voltages are recorded.

On-line UPS units constantly supply power to connected equipment from an internal battery, with battery recharging occurring on an ongoing basis. There is no lag time when power failures occur since these units serve as the primary source of power to equipment. In the case of a blackout, the UPS will continue to generate power until the battery runs out.

Choosing the right UPS

When deciding what type of UPS to purchase, you have to determine how much an unexpected power failure would impact your business.

On-line units offer the most protection, since they run constantly. The additional cost of these systems is often deemed worthwhile for key equipment where a shutdown is unacceptable. They are usually recommended for mission critical applications such as a phone system or a computer server.

Standby and line-interactive UPS are more appropriate when an unexpected power outage, and the resulting loss of data or other information, would be more of an inconvenience than a major problem. These systems should be able to keep equipment going during most power fluctuations, but there may be the occasional situation where they do not quite work as expected. They can be a more cost-effective solution for equipment such as standalone computers or a fax machine.

Line-interactive UPS are best suited for situations where power fluctuations are common occurrences. Power fluctuations occur when "power-hungry" equipment such as an air conditioner is frequently turned on and off, causing temporary voltage drains and surges. With line-interactive UPS, these fluctuations can be handled by the transformer instead of the internal battery.

Calculating UPS needs

The power requirements of your equipment will determine the amount of backup power you will need. It is generally recommended that a UPS have a capacity that is at least 25% greater than the total power capacity requirements of the connected equipment.

Firms will also need to decide whether they want to centralize or distribute their UPS. Offices that have multiple computers housed in one room will generally find that connecting all the equipment to a central UPS will be more cost effective than purchasing individual UPS units. However, this may not be a reasonable option when the equipment is spread over multiple rooms.

How long backup power lasts

Most UPS units are designed to provide about ten minutes of backup power. This should be enough time to appropriately shut down the connected equipment and avoid data loss. Since blackouts typically last no more than two minutes, this should also be enough time to work right through most power failures.

Manufacturers report how long a battery will last under full-load or half-load conditions. Running under full load signifies that a UPS is working at its maximum capacity. A typical UPS should report a full-load time duration of about ten minutes. Under half-load conditions, when the UPS only provides half the power it is capable of generating, the time duration is often more than three times as long.

If ten minutes is not enough security for your company's needs, there are also units that can last as long as a day on backup power. This is ideal if you need a system to operate overnight. While this amount of backup may seem much more desirable, however it can cost significantly more.

Another option is to purchase extra battery attachments. Expect these extra batteries to cost about one-fourth to one-half the price of the UPS itself.

Pricing

Individual UPS units cost between $100 and $500. If you plan on using the UPS for multiple computers, expect to pay between $600 and $1,500.

Terms

Blackouts Periods of time where there is a complete loss of power.

Brownouts (or sags) Periods of time where there are decreases in the amount of voltage coming through a power line.

Double conversion A term which means that an AC current is transformed to a DC current and then back to AC for connected equipment. On-line UPS units typically use double conversion.

Spike A very strong surge of power, often caused by lightning strikes.

Surge A brief increase in voltage coming through a power line.

Volt Ampere (VA) Volt Ampere, or Watt, is the unit used to quantify power.

Special tips

If computers run unattended, you may want to look into software that will automatically shut down the computer if the UPS begins to reach the end of its battery power.

Batteries cannot be recharged forever. You should plan to replace the battery in the UPS every three to five years. Check ahead of time to find where you can purchase additional batteries.

Look for features that communicate the status of the UPS. At minimum, there should be a visual signal indicating when the unit is drawing upon its internal battery for power. Audible signals are preferred when the battery power is almost depleted. It is also a good idea to look for a battery run-time display.

Surge suppressors are an inexpensive way to protect against surges and spikes that can destroy equipment. Surge suppressors are very inexpensive, starting at less than $10. Two leading vendors include Atlanta Scientific (800/544-4737) and Panamax (800/472-5555).

See also
Computer Backup Systems, Desktop Computers, Telephone Systems

Video Conferencing Services

Video conferencing technology is designed to provide the immediacy of a face-to-face meeting without the expense and hassle of long distance travel. These systems use video cameras and monitors to provide an experience that can be eerily realistic.

Unfortunately, video conferencing equipment remains quite expensive, particularly for firms that rarely use the technology. Service bureaus allow any firm to take advantage of video conferencing without requiring a large investment in the technology.

SERVICE CENTERS			
Company	Headquarters	Phone number	Number of total locations
Affinity VideoNet	Essex, MA	800/370-7150	143
Connexus	Dallas, TX	800/938-8888	77
Kinko's	Ventura, CA	800/669-1235	145
MRI	Cleveland, OH	800/875-4000	630

Buying points

How video conferencing works
Video conferencing involves the real-time transmission of audio and video signals to a distant location. Systems use video cameras and microphones to capture the necessary information, while monitors and speakers relay the information to participants on the other end.

Video conferencing typically requires ISDN or other high-speed digital lines in order to transmit the required amount of data. However, it is also possible to use satellite technology or regular telephone lines.

Working with a service bureau
Service bureaus rent video conferencing services to companies. This can be a cost-effective option for firms that do not hold video conferences on a regular basis.

One of the greatest advantages of working with bureaus is their expertise. Since these providers generally have more experience linking locations, they are often better suited to troubleshoot problems. They also have backup equipment they can turn to in case of trouble.

In addition, set up requirements are fairly minimal. These services often have meeting rooms already prepared to go. In contrast, in-house setups usually require people to prepare a specific room for a conference.

Bandwidth
Most video conferences are conveyed using digital phone lines. These lines come in varying sizes, with larger sizes capable of transmitting more information at a time.

Conferences that involve movement or multiple cameras will require larger digital lines to handle the higher amounts of data. This is needed so the information can be relayed at a fast enough speed to ensure a natural-looking broadcast. With too small a data pipe, you risk a choppy-looking and -sounding conference. A service bureau should be able to help estimate your particular data traffic needs.

Keep in mind that greater bandwidth does come at an additional cost. Bandwidth that is three times greater than normal will generally be about three times more expensive.

Choosing a service bureau
In addition to bandwidth considerations, identifying the appropriate provider depends on what services you require to make your video conference a success.

Firms should first look for a service bureau that has offices in the locations you need to connect. This can reduce the cost of holding the video conference, since most service bureaus charge extra for conferences that connect to non-company locations. Also look into the hours of operation, as additional charges may be assessed for after-hours conferences.

Next, check that conference rooms are large enough to comfortably seat everyone in view of the camera and monitor. If you have a particularly large group, you may want to ask about the availability of multiple monitors and cameras.

You may also want to check if the service can provide a separate camera to focus on any items being presented. This allows documents, still photos and overhead presentations to be shown more clearly without requiring readjustment of a single camera. If you want to use equipment such as whiteboards or presentation screens, make sure they are available for use and can be seen on screen. Some centers also have the ability to directly broadcast a videotape or images from a computer screen.

If you want to distribute materials at the start of a meeting, check whether the bureau offers fax broadcasting capabilities. This will allow you to quickly distribute materials before the meeting.

Pricing

Pricing is normally charged on a per-minute, per fifteen minutes, or per half-hour rate. Some vendors may have no minimum usage requirements, while others set a half hour minimum.

A basic one hour, two-site video conference will cost between $200 and $500. A video conference involving multiple locations and multiple vendors can easily cost more than $1,000 per hour.

Market terms

Bandwidth   Refers to the amount of digital data that can be transmitted during a connection. Wider bandwidths are preferable to narrow bandwidths because they allow for more information to be transferred at greater speeds.

Bridging   The ability to connect more than two sites together.

Roll-about   A complete set of video conference equipment placed on a cart, which allows the equipment to be "rolled-about" from room to room.

Special tips

Schedule conferences that involve multiple locations and multiple vendors well in advance so the video conferencing centers can work out any compatibility issues.

People who often wave their hands around when speaking will require greater bandwidth to handle the data traffic. Participants may want to make a conscious effort not to use their hands to lessen bandwidth requirements.

One way to save money on a video conference is to offer a phone hookup. With this setup, participants speak over regular phone lines instead of having the conversation relayed over the digital lines. This can help reduce the bandwidth requirements for a conference.

When dressing for a video conference, it is generally better to wear solid color clothing. White and red, however, do not work so well. Avoid wearing plaids or other complex prints.

Avoid coughing into microphones, shuffling papers, and carrying on

Video Conferencing Services

side conversations when video conferencing. Such sounds are often very noticeable.

Buying and maintaining your own equipment in-house is probably a better option for firms that video conference regularly to a limited set of locations. This may be the only option for firms that do not have a service located within close driving distance.

See also
Conference Calling Services, Conferencing Equipment, ISDN

> **Did you know?**
>
> Video conferencing was first introduced by AT&T at the 1964 World's Fair.

Voice Mail Systems

*A*lmost everyone has faced the frustration of playing telephone tag with another person. Just trying to communicate a simple message can entail a long series of phone calls back and forth. The result is wasted time and lost productivity.

Voice mail is designed to address this very problem. A voice mail system acts as a corporate answering machine, recording messages from people both inside and outside the company.

VENDORS

Company	Headquarters	Phone number	Proprietary hardware	Standard PC with voice card
Active Voice	Seattle, WA	206/441-4700		●
Applied Voice Technology	Kirkland, WA	206/820-6000		●
Centigram	San Jose, CA	408/944-0250		●
Lucent Technologies	Basking Ridge, NJ	800/247-7000	●	●
Nortel	Richardson, TX	800/4-NORTEL	●	●
Octel	Milipitas, CA	800/284-4869	●	●
Siemens Rolm	Santa Clara, CA	800/ROLM-123	●	
Voysys	Fremont, CA	800/7-VOYSYS	●	

Buying points

How voice mail systems work

Voice mail systems use centralized recording equipment to record, store, and play back messages for each person in a company. Each person has access to an individual mailbox, which allows messages to be kept private.

These systems are sized according to the number of ports, or connections, that are established between the phone system and the voice mail system. Having more ports on a voice mail system means more people can simultaneously leave or pick up messages.

Advantages of a voice mail system

Compared to written notes, voice recording allows longer and more complex messages to be accurately relayed. The ability to leave detailed, private messages frequently means that callers can relay information without the need for a return call. This is especially useful when you consider that half of all calls are for one-way transfers of information.

Voice mail systems also guarantee a common messaging platform within a company. Features such as broadcasting allow employees to send messages to multiple people at once, allowing a voice mail system to serve as a central messaging center for a workgroup or the entire company.

Types of systems

Voice mail systems come in two basic designs. Most newer systems are PC-based, meaning they use a standard desktop PC as the core of the system. Manufacturers then add voice boards to peripheral slots in the back of the computer, and write software that can run on OS/2, Windows NT, or other high-end desktop operating systems. These systems are then integrated to work with phone systems.

The greatest advantage of PC-based systems is their low cost. Because these systems use widely available PC components, they benefit from the lower prices associated with mass-produced parts.

Most older systems are based on proprietary hardware. These systems are designed from scratch to store voice messages, and typically use operating systems developed specifically for messaging. Today, proprietary systems are strongest at the high-end of the market, where concerns of stability and size outweigh the lower cost of PC hardware. There are also a few proprietary systems designed for the low end of the market. These are usually non-expandable systems designed for very small businesses.

Choosing a system

Voice mail systems are designed to work with a phone system. The term "integration" is used to refer to a high level of phone system and voice mail system interactivity.

In most cases, integration comes down to three features. First, a light on the phone indicates when messages are waiting in the mailbox. This notifies users when to check the system.

A second integration feature is the ability to automatically forward calls to the correct mailbox when a call is not answered. This alleviates the need for the caller to remember the correct mailbox number to leave a message.

A third integration feature is known as return to operator. This allows a caller to exit the voice mail system and reach a live attendant at any time.

Not all voice mail and phone system combinations can attain this level of integration. Before buying, you need to check that the particular combination you are considering will at least handle these three tasks.

About system vendors

Many phone systems can be equipped with a voice mail system manufactured or relabeled by the phone system vendor. In most cases, this means you must choose between this same-brand system and one of the many available systems from third-party manufacturers.

Same-brand systems are generally easy to install, since the systems do not have to be compatible with a wide range of phone systems. Debates about which part of the system is at fault when breakdowns occur are also less of a concern, since both components come from the same manufacturer.

On the other hand, third-party systems tend to be more competitively priced and do not lock firms into the same brand phone system in the future. For some applications, third-party systems may offer more capabilities than a same-brand system can provide.

Finding the right dealer

The key to choosing a dealer is finding one who has previously installed the voice mail system you are considering with the same type of phone system you currently use. Nothing eases the installation and integration process as much as past experience in performing the same job.

In addition, firms should judge the dealer's responsiveness to service calls and the firm's general expertise in the voice mail arena. This can be done by inquiring about the dealer's history, asking about the staff, and visiting their office. You can also check a dealer's references, making sure to talk to companies that are similar in size to yours.

Pricing

In general, you will find PC-based systems to be less expensive than expandable standalone models. You can expect to pay $5,000 to $6500 for a basic four-port voice mail system with an automated attendant. Each additional port (and accompanying storage hours) will add about $1,000 to $2,000 to the price tag. Expect to bargain 10% to 20% off the asking price for most systems.

For companies of less than five people, buying a full-fledged voice mail system is often prohibitively expensive. However, it is possible to purchase a no-frills system that will offer individual mailboxes for under $1,000.

Terms

Automated attendants A phone system accessory that answers the phone automatically, allowing callers to route themselves to the appropriate department or extension. Automated attendant capabilities are built into most modern voice mail systems.

Blocking levels A statistical term which refers to the percentage of calls that will be blocked from accessing the voice mail system during peak usage. Most companies consider a blocking level of 2% to be acceptable, but organizations such as hospitals or security firms may require blocking levels as low as 1% or 0.1%.

Port A connection between the phone system and the voice mail system. The number of ports needed depends on how many people will simultaneously use the system.

Unified messaging system A type of storage system that combines incoming e-mail, fax, and voice mail messages for one user into a common mailbox. This mailbox, commonly displayed on a computer screen, allows users to access all messages at once.

Special tips

Make sure that callers in the voice mail system can reach a human at any time. In general, it is a good idea to assign the zero key for access to a live operator.

One alternative to buying a voice mail system is to rent mailboxes from a service bureau. This can be particularly helpful for companies that do not have phone systems designed to work with voice mail. Service bureaus typically charge each subscriber on a monthly basis, with some adding charges for connection time, saved messages, or the number of messages you receive.

A voice mail system will require occasional reprogramming, as well as (hopefully infrequent) emergency repairs. Your maintenance costs should typically not exceed 5% to 10% of the purchase price per year.

See also
Answering Machines, Centrex Service, Fax on Demand, KSU-less Phone Systems, Music on Hold Systems, Telephone Systems

For more information, visit
BuyersZone
http://www.buyerszone.com/

Workers Compensation Insurance

*E*very state has workers compensation laws that require payment to employees that suffer work-related injuries. To ensure adequate compensation, states typically require that firms purchase liability insurance for workers compensation claims. This insurance is generally sold and classified separately from other forms of liability.

WORKERS COMPENSATION INJURIES

Type of injury	% of claims
Amputation	1.1
Burn	2
Carpal tunnel	1.7
Contusion/concussion	9.7
Fracture/dislocation	10.3
Infection/inflammation	2
Laceration	8.9
Occupational disease/cumulative injuries	2.7
Other traumatic injuries	8.8
Strain/sprain	52.8

Source: NCCI *Call for Detailed Claim Information (DCI)*

Workers Compensation Insurance

Buying points

Insurance requirements
Virtually every business is required to purchase workers compensation insurance. Larger companies may be able to exempt themselves from purchasing insurance if they provide adequately funded self-insurance program.

Types of coverage
Workers compensation policies typically provide two types of coverage. The first type provides the basic level of workers compensation coverage mandated by the state. A second type of coverage, known as employer's liability insurance, covers the costs associated with the defense of lawsuits brought by employees for work-related injuries. In general, workers who receive compensation benefits are required to forfeit their rights to solicit litigation against their employers.

Calculating premiums
Workers compensation premiums are calculated by taking your business classification, the size of the firm, and your past claims history. This rate is usually fixed and is not negotiable on a case-by-case basis.

Insurers first place your company into a specific business classification. This classification results in a different charge based on the type of work you perform. For example, firms that regularly expose their employees to physical hazards, such as those common in the construction and trucking industries, have substantially higher insurance premiums than businesses with large numbers of clerical workers.

The second consideration is the size of your firm, which is called your exposure base. Depending on how your business is classified, the exposure base may be measured in terms of payroll, gross sales or square footage.

The final factor is your claims history. Companies with a large exposure base are subject to an experience rating, which compares the firm's claims history against the average in the industry. Based on the comparison, the premium may be adjusted accordingly. Companies with a limited exposure base are subjected to the merit rating system, where the total number of claims made by similar companies is used as to adjust premiums.

For the most part, basic rates are calculated by a rating bureau called the National Council on Compensation Insurance (NCCI). A number of states also have their own rating bureaus that calculate the appropriate rates for all business classifications.

Coverage levels
There are conflicting views on the optimal level of coverage a company should purchase. While some brokers recommend that your coverage match the largest awarded settlement for a case relevant to your business, others base their recommendations on company assets.

Sources for coverage
Depending on the state, workers compensation coverage can be

obtained from either a state fund or a private carrier. A small number of states may require your firm to subscribe to state workers compensation funds.

Your choice of insurance agencies may be considerably limited if your company is small or if you have a poor claims history. For those companies that are left in this "residual market," there are a number of states that offer special assistance programs. For example, the Quality Loss Management Program (QLMP) in Massachusetts matches companies with insurers who provide coverage. Small companies who find themselves scrambling for underwriters should get in touch with their state insurance department to learn about their options.

Pricing

It is difficult to estimate the costs of workers compensation insurance, since premiums can vary in so many ways. However, no matter what your business, there are a number of strategies you can use to lower your insurance costs.

First, some private insurers offer rates that are lower than the standard market rates. Unless your state heavily regulates workers compensation policies, it usually pays to shop around.

Additionally, premiums can often be reduced by checking and clarifying mistakes in your company profile. Some businesses can be classified under one of many different business listings. In some cases, your insurance premiums may be based on a classification that is relevant for only a small portion of your operations. By making sure the classification assigned to your business accurately reflects your operations, premiums can potentially be significantly lowered.

A third area to investigate is whether your exposure base is calculated correctly, with all appropriate exemptions taken into account. For example, if payroll is used to calculate the exposure base, you may want to find out if you can exclude employees whose positions are unrelated to the coverage type. If the exposure base is sales, you may want to exclude amounts that do not appropriately reflect your exposure to claims.

Finally, while your business classification and exposure base are fixed, your experience rating need not be static. Needless to say, a safe record always lowers insurance premiums. A good claims history can be accomplished by instituting measures to promote a safe working environment.

Terms

Business classification A classification used to calculate premiums that categorizes businesses according to their industry. Businesses that do not clearly fit in one category may be able to lower premiums by switching their classification to a less costly category.

Claims-based insurance Insurance policies that pay claims based on the policy in force when a claim is filed and reported. This method minimizes the tracking and claim inflation problems that can arise with occurrence policies.

Exposure base A measurement of the size of your firm used to calculate workers compensation premiums. This can be measured in terms of employees, payroll, square footage or other relevant figures.

Occurrence-based insurance Insurance policies where claims are paid by the policy in place at the time of the incident. Coverage is provided even if you are no longer with the insurance firm that originally provided coverage. Keeping track of your policies with this type of coverage is extremely important.

Special tips

The U.S. Chamber of Commerce (800/638-6582) offers the *Analysis of Workers Compensation Laws* for $25.

The National Council on Compensation Insurance (800/NCCI-123) offers additional information about workers compensation. The Occupational Safety & Health Administration (202/606-5100) offers information on implementing safe workplace programs.

See also
Business Insurance, Employee Drug Testing, Health Insurance

World Wide Web Site Setup

*O*nly five years after its conception, the World Wide Web has emerged as the hottest new area for business development and growth. For businesses that establish a site, the Web can be a successful medium for distributing product information, attracting new prospects, or supporting existing customers.

Buying points

Untangling the World Wide Web
The World Wide Web (hereafter referred to as the "Web") is nothing more than a set of protocols for accessing information over the computers that make up the Internet.

The essence of the Web is the notion of hypertext links. This means that any bit of information on the Web can be linked to any other bit of information. For example, a page (really just a computer file) on the Web that discusses sailing could offer links to other pages related to sailing, no matter where in the world they might be located. Each of these sites, in turn, could provide links to other related sites.

Another key feature of the Web is that information can be accessed via a graphical interface. This means that users can point and click their way through the Internet, rather than having to type the text commands required by most Internet applications.

Explaining a Web site
A Web site is simply a collection of computer files stored on a computer that is connected to the Internet. Sites can be as basic as a single text file or as elaborate as a group of several thousand files incorporating video and audio.

The computer that stores the files is called an Internet, or Web, server. These computers generally run UNIX as the operating system, although there is an increasing numbers of servers using the Macintosh or Microsoft Windows NT operating systems.

Setting up a Web site
There are many positive aspects of setting up a Web site. Probably the

main advantage of a Web site is that it offers a very easy, inexpensive way for anyone to get information about your company 24 hours a day. With relatively little effort, Web sites can offer small companies a "big company" feel. Even if you conduct no promotion, you can expect some new prospects to visit your site each month. Finally, having a Web site carries some prestige, indicating that your firm is a technologically savvy player.

On the downside, having a Web site can never serve as an easy substitute for marketing, since the vast majority of Internet users will never visit your site. In addition, with plenty of students, retirees, and foreigners browsing the Web, you may not attract the right kind of visitors. Finally, Web sites are not only costly to develop, but must be changed and updated on a frequent basis to keep users coming back to the site.

Web site strategies

The most complex way to establish a Web site is to set it up yourself. To do so, you will need a Web server, which is basically a high-end computer equipped with Web server software. You will also need to purchase a dedicated link to an Internet service provider (ISP) in your area. Regular dial-up modem connections are not acceptable, since you will want to provide 24-hour access for visitors.

You can also set up a Web site by renting server space from an ISP. These firms are already connected to the Internet, and have Web servers up and running. Renting gives you the additional advantage of having technical problems handled by the ISP.

Businesses looking for a more complex Web site often hire outside developers to create a site that will do whatever the business requires. This tends to be much more expensive than setting up a site yourself. Fees range from a few hundred dollars for a few pages, to tens or hundreds of thousands of dollars for a large, innovative site.

Advertising your Web site's existence

Once your site is up and running, make sure to register it with search engines that can point our your site to interested users. One way to register is to use a meta-registry, such as Submit It! (http://www.submit-it.com), SubmitAll (http://www.home.team.com/addurl) or wURLd Presence: One-stop Registration (http://www.ogi.com/wurld). These ask you for specific information about your site, and then automatically submit it to several dozen locations.

To attract more targeted users, you may want to consider buying advertising from relevant sites or promoting your site via direct mail efforts.

Pricing

Virtually all providers charge a set monthly fee for operating your Web server. This fee can be as little as $20 per month for a small site on a local provider, but is more often $50 to $100 per month. Larger providers offering a greater set of features and a more robust network typically charge several times as much as smaller services.

Setting up a Web server in your office requires an investment of at least a few thousand dollars for the appropriate hardware and software. In addition, dedicated line charges start at a few hundred dollars per month.

Terms

Domain name This is the address browsers will use to access your site. This name, which you have probably seen in advertisements, is usually written as something like http://www.buyerszone.com/

Firewall A software product designed to prevent data stored on a Web server or connected computer from being accessed by unauthorized users on the Internet. Firewalls block outsiders from downloading private information or altering your Web site.

HTML The programming code used to create a Web page. HTML can be written on a regular word processor or with special HTML programs.

Internet A worldwide network of interconnected computers. The Internet is not monitored or administered by one company, although groups do meet to set technical standards for accurate and timely communication.

Internet service provider (ISP) A business that provides Internet access to users. Many ISPs also host Web sites for companies.

Search engines These are sites designed to help people find Web sites of interest. They use key word searches or full text searches to match requests with relevant sites.

Special tips

Make sure to answer the question "Why do I need a Web site" before plunging in and setting one up. "Why not?" is a response that can result in thousands of dollars being needlessly wasted.

Most advanced sites incorporate features that use CGI (Common Gateway Interface) scripts. Some of the most popular scripts include counters that can track the number of visitors to a certain page; imagemaps, which enable users to link to various pages by clicking on different parts of an image; and e-mail forwarding, which automatically sends messages to a company's e-mail account.

If you are considering setting up a Web site with an ISP, make sure to learn about all charges. Beyond a monthly fee, providers may assess fees for handling more than a set number of visitors or for implementing advanced features.

Be careful when transmitting or receiving sensitive information such as a credit card number through your site. Because data on the internet passes through many computers on its journey, there are ample opportunities for information to be stolen or copied. Look for a secure server to lessen the risk of fraud

The Internet craze has spawned a cottage industry of providers and consultants. Make sure to check a company's references thoroughly before signing up with any service.

See also
Advertising Agencies, Desktop Computers, E-mail Services, Graphic Designers, Internet Service Providers, ISDN, Modems, Notebook Computers

For more information, visit
BuyersZone
http://www.buyerszone.com/

Did you know?

In 1990, a physicist at CERN in Switzerland devised the standards for what would become the World Wide Web. The first Web sites were developed in 1991, and the first graphical interface for it was developed in 1993.

Topic Listing By Category

Benefits

401(k) Plans 1
Health Insurance 161
HMOs 165
Pension Plans 276
PPOs 304
Workers Compensation Insurance 404

Computer Equipment

CD-ROM Drives 43
Color Printers 76
Computer Backup Systems 85
Desktop Computers 108
Dot Matrix Printers 118
Fax Servers 144
Ink-jet Printers 174
Keyboards 196
Laser Printers 209
LCD Systems 213
Modems 230
Monitors 234
Notebook Computers 244
PDAs 272
Pointing Devices 289
Portable Printers 292
Recordable CD Drives 314
Scanners 329
Uninterruptible Power Supplies 392

Computer Services

E-mail Services	122
Internet Service Providers	188
ISDN	192
Telephone Directory Software	351
World Wide Web Site Setup	408

Financial/Back Office

Accountants	9
Business Forms	29
Checks	63
Collection Agencies	72
Corporate Cards	102
Fax Broadcasting Services	133
Paper Shredders	265
Payroll Services	268
Photocopier Controls	280
Safes	323
Time Clocks	364

Furnishings

Chairs	59
Desks	105
File Cabinets	148
Systems Furniture	343

Human Resources

Employee Drug Testing	126
Executive Recruitment Agencies	129
Temporary Help Services	361
Workers Compensation Insurance	404

Mailing/Shipping

Ground Shipping	157

Topic Listing By Category 415

International Expedited Delivery 184
Letter Folding Equipment 217
Letter Opening Equipment 220
LTL Shipping 226
Overnight Delivery Services 259
Postal Scales 301
Postage Meters 296
Same Day Delivery Services 326
Telephone Directory Software 351

Marketing

Advertising Agencies 12
Clipping Services 69
Fax on Demand 140
Graphic Designers 154
Public Relations Firms 311
Stock Photography 340
Telemarketing Services 347
World Wide Web Site Setup 408

Office Equipment

Answering Machines 15
Automatic Staplers 19
Dictation Equipment 114
Fax Machines 136
Lamination Equipment 203
Multifunctional Devices 238
Paper Shredders 265
Postage Meters 296
Photocopier Controls 280
Photocopiers 284
Typewriters 386
Uninterruptible Power Supplies 392

Office Operations

Beverage Services 22
Business Insurance 32
Cleaning Services 66
Computer Backup Systems 85
Fax Broadcasting Services 133
Off-site Storage 248
Recycling 319
Time Clocks 364
Uniforms 389

Office Supplies

Business Cards 25
Business Forms 29
Checks 63
Commercial Printing 81
Copy Paper 95
Office Supplies 251
Signs 333
Toner Supplies 375

Presentation

Conference Calling Services 89
Conferencing Equipment 92
Graphic Designers 154
Laser Pointers 206
LCD Systems 213
Overhead Projectors 255
Slide Projectors 337
Stock Photography 340
Trade Show Displays 378
Video Conferencing Services 396

Topic Listing By Category

TELECOMMUNICATION EQUIPMENT

Answering Machines 15
Cellular Telephones 51
Conferencing Equipment. 92
Cordless Telephones. 99
Fax Machines 136
Fax on Demand 140
Fax Servers 144
KSU-less Phone Systems 200
Modems. 230
Multifunctional Devices. 238
Music on Hold Systems 241
Pagers 262
Telephone Headsets 353
Telephone Systems. 356
Toll Fraud Prevention 367
Voice Mail Systems. 400

TELECOMMUNICATION SERVICES

900 Service 5
Calling Cards 36
Cellular Service. 47
Centrex Service. 55
Conference Calling Services 89
E-mail Services 122
Fax Broadcasting Service. 133
International Callback 177
International Calling 180
Internet Service Providers 188
ISDN 192
Long Distance Services 222
Pagers 262
Prepaid Phone Cards 308

Telemarketing Services 347
Toll Fraud Prevention 367
Toll Free Service 371
Video Conferencing Services. 396

TRAVEL
Calling Cards 36
Car Rental Agencies. 39
Cellular Service. 47
Cellular Telephones 51
Corporate Cards 102
Frequent Flyer Programs. 151
Hotels 169
Pagers 262
Prepaid Phone Cards 308
Travel Agencies. 382

INDEX

!nfaxamation, 140
128,000 bits per second, 189, 193, 195
14,400 bits per second, 137, 139, 142, 146, 147, 232, 233
1964 World's Fair, 399
1994 National Survey of Employer-Sponsored Health Plans, 163, 167, 306
1995-96 Guide to UTSA, 389
1996 Business Travel Survey, 382
24-pin printer, 119
28,800 bits per second, 189, 193, 232, 233
3Com, 192
3M, 76, 255
4 mm cartridge, 87

401(K) PLANS, 1-4, 269, 278
  see also
    accountants, 9-11
    payroll services, 268-271
    pension plans, 276-279

401(k) Association, The, 1
401(k) Provider Directory: A Small Plan Guide, 4
403(b) plans, 4, 279
4,800 bits per second, 146
8 mm videotapes, 85, 87
800 number, *see* toll free service
888 number, *see* toll free service
9-pin printer, 119
9,600 bits per second, 137, 146, 232, 274

900 SERVICE, 5-8, 369
  service bureaus, 7, 8
  see also
    calling cards, 36-38
    cellular service, 47-50
    conference calling services, 89-91
    fax on demand, 140-143
    international callback, 177-179
    international calling, 180-183
    long distance service, 222-225
    prepaid phone cards, 308-310
    telemarketing services, 347-350
    telephone directory software, 351-352
    toll free service, 371-374

A

A.M. Best Company, 32, 34, 162, 168

A Better Conference, 89
AAA, *see* American Automobile Association
Abaddon, 280
Abex Display Systems, 378
ABF, 226
Accent, 72
access controls, 282
access number, 309-310
accessorial charges, 228
Acco USA, 19, 265

ACCOUNTANTS, 9-11, 64, 280, 362
  records retention, 11
  see also
    401(k) plans, 1-4
    corporate cards, 102-104
    payroll services, 268-271
    pension plans, 276-279

Accountemps, 361
accounting codes, 299,
  see also billing codes
accounting software, 64-65, 365
Accountor Systems, 280
Accu-Weather, 140
Acer, 108
acetates, 287, 292
acid-free sheets, 97
Acme Electric, 392
acoustic modems, 231
Acroprint Time Recorder, 364
ACS, 353
ACT, 89
active matrix, 245, 247
Active Voice, 140, 400
ADA, *see* Americans with Disabilities Act
ADB, 197
Adesso, 196
ADF, 285
ADI, 234
Adia, 361
ADP, 1, 268
ADSL, 194
Advanced Telecom Services, 5
Advantage, 268

ADVERTISING AGENCIES, 12-14, 77, 410
  see also
    clipping services, 69-71
    digital stock photography, 340-342
    graphic designers, 154-156
    public relations firms, 311-314
    signs, 333-336
    trade show displays, 378-381

World Wide Web site setup, 408-411

Advertising Agency Register (New York, NY), 14
Advertising Red Books, 13
Adweek Directories (Lakewood, NJ), 13
Affinity VideoNet, 396
Africa, 181, 185
Agfa, 329
aggregators, 181
air couriers,
  see same delivery services
air freight forwarders, 186, 228
Air Travel Card, 102, 103
Airborne, 185, 259, 261, 326
Airborne International Express, 184
Airborne Sky Courier, 326
airlines, 327, 381, 383,
  see frequent flyer programs
AirTouch, 262
Alabama, 165
Alamo, 39, 40, 41
Alaska, 160, 165
Alaska Airlines, 151
Alaska Mileage Plan, 151
alcohol testing, 126
Alcom, 144
Allegheny, 265
Allen's Press Clipping Bureau, 69
Allerton Heneghan & O'Neill, 129
Alliance Capital, 1
Allied Payroll Service, 268
Allsteel, 105, 343
AlphaGraphics, 81, 82
alphanumeric pagers, 263
Alps, 289
Amano Cincinnati, 364
ambient lighting, 339
ambulance service, 166
AMD, 110
Ameri-shred, 265
America Online, 122, 123
America Telefone, 177
America West, 151, 152, 153
America West FlightFund, 151
American AAdvantage, 151
American Airlines, 151
American Association of Advertising Agencies (New York, NY), 14
American Automobile Association (AAA), 171
American Board of Medical Specialties, 166, 305
American Business Information (ABI), 351

American Collectors Association
  (Minneapolis, MN), 74
American Express,
  102, 104, 153, 382
American Funds, 1
American Industrial Service, 389
American Institute of Certified
  Public Accountants (AICPA)
  (New York, NY), 10
American Institute of Graphic
  Arts (New York, NY), 155
American Motor Carrier
  Directory, 228
American Paging, 262
American Payroll Association
  (APA) (New York, NY), 270
American Plastics Council
  (Washington, DC), 322
American Power Conversion,
  see APC
American Ribbon & Toner, 375
American Speedy, 81
American Telnet, 5
American Trucking Association
  (Alexandria, VA), 228
American United Life, 1
Americans with Disabilities Act
  (ADA), 333, 335
Ameritech, 192, 262
Amertex Service Group, 389
Amex, see American Express
amplifier, 355
amputation, 404
Amsec, 323
AMT, 118
Anaheim, 169
Analysis of Workers
  Compensation Laws, 407
ANI, see automatic number
  identification
ANS, 188
Ansaphone, 133
ANSI lumens 62, 214, 215

ANSWERING MACHINES,
  15-18, 202, 400
  see also
    voice mail systems, 400-403

AOC, 234
AOL, see America Online
APC, 392
aperture grill, 237
Apollo, 203, 206, 255
Apparelmaster USA, 389
Apple, 43, 76, 108, 118, 174, 196,
  209, 244, 245, 272, 273, 289, 292
Apple Newton, 273
Apple PowerBook, 245, 293
Applied Voice Technology, 400
Aramark Uniform Service, 389
Arch, 262
Archive Photos, 340
Arcus, 248
Arizona, 165
Arkansas, 165
Arrow, 389
Arrowhead, 22

Artisoft LANtastic, 145
ASCAP (New York, NY), 243
Ascend, 192
Ascom Hasler, 217, 220, 296, 301
Asia, 181, 184, 185
ASK LCD, 213
Association of Commercial
  Records Centers (Raleigh,
  NC), 250
Association of Executive Search
  Consultants (New York, NY),
  130
AST, 108, 244
Astarte, 316
Astarte Toast, 316
Asymmetric Digital Subscriber
  Line, see ADSL
AT Products, 92
AT&T, 5, 36, 48, 89, 308, 122, 123,
  133, 180, 181, 183 188, 222, 223,
  230, 262, 371, 399,
  see Lucent Technologies
AT&T WorldNet, 122, 123
ATC, 200
Atlanta, 169, 185
Atlanta Scientific (West
  Melbourne, FL), 395
Atrix, 280
ATS, 89
auctions, 150
audio/visual equipment, 324,
  325, 338
Audiomax, 241
Audiotex News, 8
Audiovox, 51
Austin (IPC), 108
auto postage reset, 299
auto rental, see car rental agencies
automated attendant,
  201, 359, 403
automated time and attendance
  (ATA) systems, 365, 366
automatic access-protection
  code, 101
automatic check signatures, 269
automatic call distributor
  (ACD), 349, 359
Automatic Data Processing,
  see ADP
automatic document feeder,
  see ADF
automatic lock, 303
automatic mail openers,
  see letter opening equipment
Automatic Number
  Identification (ANI), 8, 373
automatic paper insertion, 388
automatic tape dispenser, 298

AUTOMATIC STAPLERS, 19-21
  cordless, 19
  saddle stapler, 19, 21
  type of paper, 20
  see also
    copy paper, 95-98
    letter folding equipment,
      217-219
    photocopiers, 284-291

Avis, 39, 40, 41
Avoiding Legal Liability: The 25
  Most Common Employer
  Mistakes in Addressing Drug
  Abuse, 128

B

B channels, 195
backlighting, 335, 379
backup power, 394
backup systems,
  see computer backup systems
Bacon's Clipping Bureau, 69, 70
Badger Paper Mills Co., 319
Bain, Alexander, 139
banded rate programs, 224, 373
bandwidth, 397, 398
bankruptcy, 277
banks, 1-4, 63-64
banners, 334, 380
Banyan Vines, 145
base, see postage meters
basic rate interface, see BRI
basis weight, 97
batch counter, 218
batteries, 52, 100, 202, 207, 220,
  246, 264, 274, 294, 355, 393-395
BBN Planet, 188
bearer channels, see B channels
Bell & Howell, 329
Bell Atlantic, 192
Bell South, 48, 192
benefits, 9, 161, 304
Best Power, 392
Best Western, 170
Beta Electronics, 206

BEVERAGE SERVICES, 22-24
  see also
    cleaning services, 66-68

Bevis (Hunt Mfg.), 105
BFD Productions, 5
BIFMA, 62
billing codes, 280, 373,
  see accounting codes
billing reports, 182
Binaural design, 355
Biscom, 144
Bishop Partners, 129
bit depth, 329, 331
bits per second (bps), 137, 139,
  193, 232
blackout, 393, 394
blocking levels, 403
Blue Cross/Blue Shield, 163
BMI (East Nashville, TN), 242-243
Boca Research, 192, 230
Bodybilt, 59
Bogen, 15, 140
Boise Cascade, 251, 319
bond paper, 97
bonding, 195
book platen, 240
boom, 355
BOP, see businessowners policy

Index

Bostitch, *see* Stanley Bostitch
Boston, 185
Boston/Eberhard Faber (Hunt Mfg.), 19, 203, 220
bottled water,
  see beverage services
boutique firms, 131, 132
bps, *see* bits per second
braille, 333
Brambles, 248
Brazil, 180
BRI, 194
bridging, 398
brightness, 96
Britain, *see* England
brochures, 143, 154, 219, 330, 341
brokers, 33, 161, 162, 163, 164, 186
Brooktrout, 140, 144
Brother, 118, 136, 209, 238, 329, 386
brownouts, 394
browsers, 190, 409
BT Office Products Int'l., 251
BTI Americas, 382
Bubblejet, 175, 176, 294,
  see ink-jet printers
Buckstaff Co., The, 105
Budget, 39, 40
Budgetel, 170
Buhl, 213, 255
Building Owners and Managers Association (BOMA) International (Washington, DC), 68
bulbs, 338, 339
bulk items, 391
bundling, 377
burglar alarms, 35
burglaries, 86, 324, 325
Burlington Air Express, 184, 185, 259, 261
Burlington International Express, 184
Burlington Time Definite Premier, 184
burn, 404
Burrelle's Press Clipping Service, 69, 70
business card, *see* corporate cards

BUSINESS CARDS, 25-28, 203
see also
  business forms, 29-31
  commercial printing, 81-84

business classification, 405-407

BUSINESS FORMS, 29-31, 119-121, 387, 388
  electronic invoicing, 30
  preprinted forms, 30
  see also
    business cards, 25-28
    checks, 63-65
    commercial printing, 81-84
    dot matrix printers, 118-121

Business Forms Management Association (Portland, OR), 31

BUSINESS INSURANCE, 1-4, 32-35
  see also
    employee drug testing, 126-128
    health insurance, 161-164
    workers compensation insurance, 404-407

Business Products Industry Association (BPIA) (Alexandria, VA), 322
Business Travel News, 382
businessowners policy (BOP), 33, 35
button lock, 291
buyers protection insurance, 104
bypass tray, 287
BZ/Rights & Permissions (New York, NY), 332

C

C. Itoh, 118
cabinets, *see* file cabinets
Cable & Wireless, 36, 133, 180, 181, 222, 371
cable modems, 194, 231
Caere OmniPage, 240, 332
California, 53, 165
caliper, 97
Calistoga, 22
call accounting, 369, 370
call centers, 242, 348
call detail recording (CDR), 349, 370
Call for Detailed Claim Information (DCI), 404
call forcing, 349
call forwarding, 49
call rounding, 310, 373
call sequencer, 349
callback,
  see international callback
caller ID, 57, 101, 143, 357, 359, 373

CALLING CARDS, 36-38, 173, 309
  fraud, 37
  see also
    900 service, 5-8
    cellular service, 47-50
    conference calling services, 89-91
    international callback, 177-179
    international calling, 180-183
    long distance service, 222-225
    prepaid phone cards, 308-310
    telephone directory software, 351-352
    toll free service, 371-374

camcorders, 214
Canada, 183, 184
Canon, 76, 136, 174-176, 209, 238, 244, 284, 292, 294, 329, 386

capitation, 167

CAR RENTAL AGENCIES, 39-42, 152, 383
  on-airport, 40
  see also
    corporate cards, 102-104
    frequent flyer programs, 151-153
    hotels, 169-173
    travel agencies, 382-385

carbonless paper, 31
card stock, 287
cards, *see* business cards
Career Horizons, 361
Caribbean, 183
Carlson Wagonlit, 382
Carmel Connection, 140
Carolina Clipping Service, 69
Carpal tunnel syndrome (CTS),
  see repetitive stress injuries
cartridge drives,
  see removable storage
cash balance plans, 279
Casio, 15, 99
Castelle, 144
catastrophes, 56, 86
cathode ray tube (CRT), 237
CCS, 72
CD jukeboxes, 46
CD-Interactive (CD-I), 316
CD-R, *see* recordable CD drives

CD-ROM DRIVES, 43-46, 87, 246, 314, 315, 330, 341, 342, 352
  see also
    computer backup systems, 85-88
    desktop computers, 108-113
    digital stock photography, 340-342
    notebook computers, 244-247
    recordable CD drives, 314-318

CD-ROM XA format, 316, 317
CDW, *see* collision damage waiver
ceiling materials, 344
Cejka & Company, 129
Cellular One, 48

CELLULAR SERVICE, 47-50, 53, 54, 101, 232, 263, 264, 274
  see also
    900 service, 5-8
    calling cards, 36-38
    cellular telephones, 51-54
    conference calling services, 89-91
    international callback, 177-179
    international calling, 180-183
    long distance service, 222-225
    pagers, 262-264
    prepaid phone cards, 308-310
    telephone directory, software, 351-352
    toll free service, 371-374

CELLULAR TELEPHONES,
  36, 47-49, 51-54, 101, 231, 232,
  264, 355
  car adapter, 54
  see also
    cellular service, 47-50
    cordless telephones, 99-101
    pagers, 262-264
    telephone systems, 356-360
Center for Substance Abuse
  Prevention (Rockville, MD), 127
Centigram, 400
Centrex-compatible telephones, 57
CENTREX SERVICE, 55-58
  see also
    KSU-less phone systems,
      200-202
    telephone systems, 356-360
    voice mail systems 400-403
Ceridian, 268
CERN, 411
certified mail, 302
Certified Payroll Professional
  (CPP), 270
Certified Public Accountants
  (CPA), 9-11
  see accountants
CGI, 410
CGL form, see commercial
  general liability form
chadders, 221

CHAIRS, 59-62
  see also
    desks, 105-107
    file cabinets, 148-150
    systems furniture, 343-346
Chambers of Commerce, 173, 407
characters per inch (cpi), 120
characters per second (cps),
  120, 388
chat rooms, 123
Check Store, The, 63
Checkrite, 72

CHECKS, 63-65, 365
  fraud, 64
  direct sales, 65
  see also
    business forms, 29-31
    laser printers, 209-212
    payroll services, 268-271

Checks in the Mail, 63
Cheyenne, 144
Chicago, 41, 169, 187, 262
China, 180
Chinon, 43
chording, 198
Cincinnati Bell, 192
Cirque, 289
CIS (Syracuse, NY), 360
Citizen, 292
city code, 181

Civil War, 342
claims based insurance, 407
claims history, 405, 407
claims/damage ratio, 227
Clarion, 170
Class 1.0, 147
Class 2.0, 147

CLEANING SERVICES, 66-68
  supplies, 67, 68
  see also
    office supplies, 251-254
    recycling, 319-322

CleanNet USA, 66
climate control, 249
Clipping Bureau of Florida, 69

CLIPPING SERVICES, 69-71, 312
  see also
    advertising agencies, 12-14
    public relations firms, 311-313

clock speed, 112, 245, 247
clocks, see time clocks
clothing, see uniforms
co-insurance, 162, 163, 305, 306
co-polymer film, 205
Cobra, 15, 99
coffee service,
  see beverage services
Coherent, 92
Coleman Lew & Associates, 129
collect calling, 223

COLLECTION AGENCIES,
  7, 72-75
  see also
    accountants, 9-11
collision damage waiver (CDW),
  41

COLOR PRINTERS, 76-80, 175,
  240, 293
  continuous tone printing, 78
  see also
    desktop computers, 108-113
    dot matrix printers, 118-121
    ink-jet printers, 174-176
    laser printers, 209-212
    notebook computers, 244-247
    stock photography, 340-342

color ribbons, 121
Colorado, 165
Colorado Press Clipping
  Service, 69
Comdial, 55, 356
commercial general liability
  (CGL) form, 34
commercial online services,
  see online services

COMMERCIAL PRINTING,
  77, 81-84, 155
  see also
    business cards, 25-28

business forms, 29-31
lamination equipment,
  203-205

commission, 349, 350, 384
Common Gateway Interface,
  see CGI
compact disc players, 315
Compaq, 108, 236, 244
"comparison shopping" option,
  302
completion rate, 131
composite safe, 325
Comprehensive, 268
compression,
  see data compression
compression protocols, 137
Compupay, 268
CompuServe, 122, 123

COMPUTER BACKUP
  SYSTEMS, 85-88
  see also
    CD-ROM drives, 43-46
    desktop computers, 108-113
    notebook computers, 244-247
    recordable CD drives, 314-318

computer printout (cpo),
  see continuous paper
computer programmers, 362
computer viruses, 86
computer-telephone integration
  (CTI), 359, 360
computers,
  see desktop computers
Computing Resources, Inc.
  (CRI), 268
Comstock, 340
Conair, 15, 99

CONFERENCE CALLING
  SERVICES, 89-91, 93, 94, 201
  see also
    900 service, 5-8
    calling cards, 36-38
    cellular service, 47-50
    conferencing equipment,
      92-94
    international callback, 177-179
    international calling, 180-183
    long distance service, 222-225
    prepaid phone cards, 308-310
    telephone systems, 356-360
    toll free service, 371-374
    video conferencing services,
      396-399

Conference Center, The, 89
Conference Pros, 89
conferencing bridge, 91

CONFERENCING EQUIPMENT,
  92-94
  see also
    conference calling services,
      89-91
    desktop computers, 108-113

Index

ISDN, 192-195
 modems, 230-233
 telephone systems, 356-360
 video conferencing services, 396-399

Confertech, 89
Connecticut, 165
connectivity, 275
construction industry, 405
Connex International, 89
Connexus, 396
consignee, 228
Consolidated Delivery & Logistics, 326
Consolidated Freightways, 226
consolidator, 260
consumables, 79, 120, 211, 239, 286, *see* toner supplies
Continental Airlines, 151
Continental OnePass, 151
contingency firms, 130, 131
continuous paper, 120
continuous tone, 79
contract stationers, 248-250
convention and visitor bureaus (CVBs), 173
Conway Transportation Systems, 226
Copia International, 140
copier controls,
 see photocopier controls
copies per minute, 287
Copy Guard, 280

COPY PAPER, 95-98, 266, 287
 see also
  color printers, 76-80
  ink-jet printers, 174-176
  laser printers, 209-212
  paper shredders, 265-267
  photocopiers, 284-288
  portable printers, 292-295
  recycling, 319-322

copy writers, 155
copyright, 155, 242, 332

CORDLESS TELEPHONES, 99-101
 call interference, 100
 see also
  cellular telephones, 51-54
  KSU-less phone systems, 200-202
  telephone systems, 356-360

Corel, 316, 340
Corel CD Creator, 316
corona wires, 211

CORPORATE CARDS, 102-104
 see also
  accountants, 9-11
  car rental agencies, 39-42
  frequent flyer programs, 151-153
  hotels, 169-173
Corporate Express, 251

corporate rate, 172, 384
correction fluid, 388
correction memory, 388
Cortelco, 55
counseling, 127, 128
counterfeit toner, 377
country code, 181
couriers,
 see same delivery services
Courtyard, 170
Coverall, 66
Coyne Textile Services, 389
CPA, *see* accountants
CPE, 58
cpi, *see* characters per inch
cpm, *see* copies per minute
cps, *see* characters per second
CPU, *see* processor chip
Crash printing, 31
Creative Audio Network, 241
Creative Office Seating, 59
credenzas, 149
credit, 73
credit cards, 8, 152, 153
crime, 336
crisis, 311
cross-cut shredders, 265-267
CRW, 72
CTI, *see* computer-telephone integration
CTX, 234, 236
Cummins-Allison, 265
Current, 63
Custom Direct, 63
Custom On-Hold Services, 241
customer premise equipment (CPE), *see* CPE
customs, 185, 186
cut-sheet feeders, 120
Cyrix, 110

D

D&S (Elgin, IL), 360
D channels, 195
Dahle, 265
daisy wheel printer, 119
Danyl, 280
DAT drives, *see* digital audio tape drives
data channel, *see* D channels
data compression, 87
Data Documents (Omaha, NE), 65
Database, 248
databases, 86, 275, 282, 315, 342, 348, 352, 359, 366
Databyte Office City, 375
Datadesk, 196
Dataproducts, 118
Datarite Payroll Service, 268
Datatech, 265
Days Inn, 170
DBA Telecom, 55, 200
debt collection, 73, 74
DEC, *see* Digital
deductibles, 34, 35, 161, 163, 167, 306

dedicated lines, 189, 190, 194, 224, 372, 374
Deer Park, 22
defined benefit plans, 277, 278
defined contribution plans, 277, 278
Deka, 55
Delaware, 165
delinquent accounts,
 see collection agencies
Dell, 108, 111, 236, 244
Delta Airlines, 151, 152
Delta Platinum Medallion, 152
Delta SkyMiles, 151
Deltec, 392
Deluxe, 29, 63
Department of Defense, 191
Department of Health and Human Services, 127
Department of Transportation, 126, 128
depository safe, 325
designers, *see* graphic designers

DESKS, 105-107, 344, 346
 remanufactured, 107
 see also
  chairs, 59-62
  file cabinets, 148-150
  systems furniture, 343-350

DESKTOP COMPUTERS,
 85-88, 106-107, 108-113, 115, 117, 139, 141, 170, 176, 197, 208, 210, 214, 231-233, 234-237, 238-240, 244-247, 256, 260, 270, 273-275, 281, 282, 289-291, 295, 314-318, 329-332, 339, 342, 346, 348, 351, 352, 360, 363, 365, 368, 387, 393, 394, 398, 400-403, 408-411
 storage, 110
 see also
  CD-ROM drives, 43-46
  color printers, 76-80
  computer backup systems, 85-88
  dot matrix printers, 118-121
  fax servers, 144-147
  ink-jet printers, 174-176
  keyboards, 196-199
  laser printers, 209-212
  LCD systems, 213-216
  modems, 230-233
  monitors, 234-237
  multifunctional devices, 238-240
  notebook computers, 244-247
  PDAs, 272-275
  pointing devices, 289-291
  recordable CD drives, 314-318
  scanners, 329-332
  stock photography, 340-342
  telephone directory software, 351-352
  typewriters, 386-388
  World Wide Web site setup, 408-411

Destroyit, 265
Detecto, 301
developer, 256, 286, 376,
 see toner supplies
DHL, 184-187, 259, 302, 326
DHL Same Day, 326
DHL Worldwide Priority
 Express, 184
Dial A Check, 268
Dialed Number Identification
 Service (DNIS), 8, 372
Diamondtron, 236
Dictaphone, 114, 117

DICTATION EQUIPMENT,
 114-117, 355
 indexing, 115
 see also
  desktop computers, 108-113
  telephone headsets, 353-355

DID, see direct inward dialing
Digital (DEC),
 76, 108, 118, 209, 244, 292
digital audio tape (DAT) drives,
 85, 87
Digital Directory Assistance
 (DDA), 351
digital linear tape (DLT) drives,
 85, 87
digital phones, 54, 357
digital service,
 50, 54, 139, 193, 357, 397
Digital Stock, 340
digital stock photography,
 see stock photography
digital video disc, see DVD
Diners Club, 102, 151
Direct, 350
direct deposit, 269
direct inward dialing, 58, 146
Direct Inward System Access,
 see DISA
direct mail, 409
directory assistance services, 351
Directory of 900 Service
 Bureaus: How to Select One, 8
Directory of Executive
 Recruiters, 130
Directory of Personnel Consultants by Specialization, 130
DISA, 368, 370
disk drives, 86, 109
Diskette Connection, 375
dissolve rates, 339
dithering printers, 78
Diversified Search, 129
DLT drives, see digital linear
 tape drives
DNIS, see dialed number
 identification service
Document Management
 Industries Association
 (Alexandria, VA), 31
Dollar, 39-41
domain name, 124, 410
DOS, 110, 145, 293, 365, 401

DOT, see Department of
 Transportation

DOT MATRIX PRINTERS,
 64, 65, 118-121
 acoustical cover, 121
 wide format, 121
 see also
  business forms, 29-31
  color printers, 76-80
  desktop computers, 108-113
  ink-jet printers, 174-176
  laser printers, 209-212
  notebook computers, 244-247
  typewriters, 386-388

dot pitch, 237
Doubletree, 170
Downing Displays, 378
draft mode, 119, 120
Dragon Systems (Newton, MA),
 117
dread disease policies, 164
Dreyfus Retirement Services, 1
drug testing programs,
 see employee drug testing
drugs,
 see employee drug testing
drum, see photoconductor
DTP Direct (Edina, MN), 331
dual scan, 138, 245, 247
"dual standard" modems, 233
Duff & Phelps, 32, 162
Dukane, 213, 255
Dun & Bradstreet, 72
dunning, 74
Duplex (Sycamore, IL), 65
duplexing, 93, 287, 288
Duplo, 217
dutiable shipments, 186
DVD, 45, 317
DVD-ROM drive, 317
Dvorak, 198
dye sublimation printers,
 76, 77-80
Dynamex, 326
Dynatek, 314

E

E-MAIL SERVICES,
 31, 108-113, 122-125, 189-191,
 231, 273, 403, 410
 see also
  Internet service providers,
   188-191
  modems, 230-233
  same day delivery services,
   326-328
  World Wide Web site setup,
   408-411

Earth Day, 321
EBA, 265
Eberhard Faber/Boston (Hunt
 Mfg.), 19
echo canceller, 93

Eck Adams, 59
ECM, 142
EDI, 31, 253
Edward Blank Associates, 347
Eiki, 213, 255
electricity, see uninterruptible
 power supplies
electromechanical clocks, 365
electronic invoicing, 30, 31
electronic mail, see e-mail services
electronic organizers, see PDAs
electronic scales, see postal scales
electrostatic printing, 83
Elmo, 255, 337
embossed mount, 339
Emerging Technology, 206
Emery, 184, 185, 259, 261
Emery Time Definite Express, 184
Employee Benefit Research
 Institute (Washington, DC),
 279

EMPLOYEE DRUG TESTING
 126-128
 occupational health clinics, 127
 see also
  business insurance, 32-35
  health insurance, 161-164
  workers compensation
   insurance, 404-407

employer matching contribution,
 4
employers liability insurance, 405
emulation, 211
encapsulation, 205
end-of-tape alert, 116
Energy Star, 212
England, 178, 180
Enhanced CD format, 316
Ennis Forms (Ennis, TX), 65
Enterprise, 39, 40
envelopes, 120, 211, 220, 221,
 239, 269, 294, 297, 299, 302
Epson, 76, 118, 174, 209, 213, 329
Equitrac, 280
erasures, 86
Ergonomixx, 196
Ericsson, 51
ethernet, 176
Europe, 308, 184, 185
Evcor (Aurora, IL), 300
Evian, 22
Exabyte, 85
exclusive provider organizations
 (EPO), 167
Executive Recruiter News, 129

EXECUTIVE RECRUITMENT
 AGENCIES, 129-132
 see also
  temporary help services,
   361-363

Executone, 356
Exide Electronics, 392
expedited delivery, 227
experience rating, 34, 405, 406

Index

Expert Systems, 140
Expo Systems, 378
exposure base, 34-35, 405-407
Express, 361
Express Direct (Chicago, IL), 331
Express Mail, 261,
  see United States Postal Service
external frames, 380

F

Fair Debt Collection Practices Act (FDCPA), 73-75
Fairfield Inns, 170
fallout, 131
fanfold paper,
  see continuous paper
Fargo, 76
fax boards, 146, 147, 232

FAX BROADCASTING SERVICES, 133-135, 398
  see also
    fax machines, 136-139
    fax on demand, 140-143
    fax servers, 144-147
    international calling, 180-183
    long distance service, 222-225

FAX MACHINES, 15, 123, 133-135, 136-139, 140-143, 171, 181, 232, 233, 238-240, 270, 273, 282, 293, 295, 330, 354, 376, 393, 403
  see also
    fax broadcasting services, 133-135
    fax on demand, 140-143
    fax servers, 144-147
    ink-jet printers, 174-176
    laser printers, 209-212
    modems, 230-233
    multifunctional devices, 238-240

FAX ON DEMAND, 140-143, 309
  service bureau, 140, 142
  see also
    fax broadcasting services, 133-135
    fax machines, 136-139
    fax servers, 144-147
    long distance service, 222-225
    toll free service, 371-374

FAX SERVERS, 105-107, 136-139, 144-147
  see also
    desktop computers, 108-113
    fax broadcasting services, 133-135
    fax machines, 136-139
    fax on demand, 140-143

faxmodems, 15, 147, 232, 295
FCC, *see* Federal Communications Commission

Featherlite Exhibits, 378
"feathering", 221
featherweight copier, 284
Federal Communications Commission, 222, 263, 373
Federal Express, 184, 185, 187, 259-261, 302, 326
Federal Express International Priority, 184
Federal Trade Commission (FTC), 7
Federated Investors, 1
FedEx, *see* Federal Express
feeders, 285-288, 294, 295, 296, 297, 299, 332
Fellowes, 265
fiber optics, 181
FICA/FUTA, 270
Fidelity Investments, 1
file attachment, 123-124

FILE CABINETS, 148-150, 324
  locks, 149
  see also
    chairs, 59-62
    desks, 105-107
    systems furniture, 343-346

filing, *see* off-site storage
film footage, 342
finishing features, 239
fire extinguishers, 35
Fireking, 148
fires, 86, 150, 324, 325
firewall, 410
First Bank, 102
First Class Mail, 157-160, 302
flat fee, 384
flat rate programs, 224
flatbed scanners, 330-332
flexographic presses, 83
float, 270
floppy discs, 44, 86
Florida, 41, 165
focal length, 256, 257
Foga Systems, 378
fonts, 210, 239, 331
Form and Function, 340
Fort Knox, 323
Fortune 500, 125
forwarding, 74
Foster Higgins (New York, NY), 163, 167, 306
FPG International, 340
France, 180
franchise, 68
Francotyp-Postalia, 217, 220, 296, 301
FreeMark (Cambridge, MA), 125
Freightways, 226
Frequent Flyer, 152-153

FREQUENT FLYER PROGRAMS, 104, 151-153, 171, 173
  upgrades, 152
  prestige programs, 152
  see also
    car rental agencies, 39-42

corporate cards, 102-104
hotels, 169-173
travel agencies, 382-385

friction feeders, 120, 218, 219
Frontier, 36, 308, 180, 181, 222, 371
Frost-Arnett, 72
Fujitsu, 85, 329, 356
full bleed, 79
furniture, *see* office furniture
FutureCall Telemarketing West, 347

G

G & K Service, 389
Gabelli Funds, 1
GammaLink (Dialogic), 144
Gandalf, 192
Ganging, 83
Gardall, 323
Garden State Press Clipping Bureau, 69
garment rental, *see* uniforms
Gateway 2000, 108, 111, 236, 244
GBC Bates, 19, 203, 265
GC, 72
GE, *see* General Electric
GE Capital, 102
Geiger Brickel, 343
General Business Forms (Skokie, IL), 65
General Electric, 15, 99
General Metalcraft, 148
Genicom, 118, 209
Genovation, 196
Gentner, 92
Georgia, 165
Germany, 180
Gestetner, 284
GF Office, 105, 343
gigabyte (GB), 112
Girsberger, 59
glass, 320
Global, 59, 61, 203, 251
Global Priority Mail, 184
Global Village, 144, 230
Globaltel, 177
glues, 320
GM Productions, 241
GN Netcom, 353
GNN, 188
Godfrey Group, The, 378
Goldstar, 234
Government Executive, 283
Grahl, 59
grain, wood, 97

GRAPHIC DESIGNERS, 77, 154-156, 332, 342, 380
  see also
    advertising agencies, 12-14
    public relations firms, 311-313
    stock photography, 340
    trade show displays, 378-381
    World Wide Web site setup, 408-411

The Essential Business Buyer's Guide

graphics, 154, 210, 293, 294, 315, 330, 332, 379, 380
gravure printing, 26, 83
Green Book Format, 316
grievance board, 167, 305

GROUND SHIPPING, 157-160, 381
  negotiating rates, 158
  zones, 159
  see also
    international expedited delivery, 184-187
    LTL shipping, 226-229
    overnight delivery services 259-261
    postage meters, 296-300
    postal scales, 301-303
    same day delivery services, 326-328

Group 3, 139
Group 4, 139
GTE, 48, 192
Guide to State Drug Testing Law, 128
Guide to Recycled Office and Business Paper Containing 20% Post Consumer Fiber, 319
Gyration, 289

H

HAG, 59
halogen lamps, 215, 257
Hammermill Papers, 319
Hampton Inns, 170
handheld phones, 52, 54
handheld scanners, 329-331
handwriting recognition, 273
Hanna Design Group, 378
hard drives, 86, 109, 110, 115, 142, 245, 247, 275, 315, 330, 346
hardware, 109, 144, 146, 368, 400, 401
Hardware Xenon, 337
Hawaii, 160, 165
Haworth 59, 105, 343
Hayden Group, 129
Hayes, 230
header, see banners
headsets, see telephone headsets
Health Care Keyboard, 196

HEALTH INSURANCE, 161-164, 165-168, 276, 305
  computer searches, 162
  see also
    business insurance, 32-35
    employee drug testing, 126-128
    HMOs, 165-168
    PPOs, 304-307
    workers compensation insurance, 404-407

Hecon, 280

helical recording, 88
helical scan drive, 88
Hello Direct, 353
Heritage Display Group, 378
Herman Miller 59, 105, 343
Hertz, 39-41
Hewlett-Packard, 76, 78, 85, 108, 136, 174, 176, 209, 210, 238, 244, 272, 292, 314, 329
Hilton, 170
hiring,
  see temporary help services
Hitachi, 43, 356
HMOs, 161, 163, 165-168, 304, 306
  purchasing coalitions, 168
  see also
    business insurance, 32-35
    employee drug testing, 126-128
    health insurance, 161-164
    PPOs, 304-307
    workers compensation insurance, 404-407

Hockett Associates, 129
Holiday Inn, 170
home page, 123
HON, 105, 148, 343
hospital indemnity policies, 164
hotel calling, 36
HOTELS, 152, 169-173, 295, 383
  extended-stay, 169, 171
  limited service, 169, 170
  luxury, 170
  suite, 169, 171
  see also
    beverage services, 22-24
    car rental agencies, 39-42
    corporate cards, 102-104
    frequent flyer programs, 151-153
    travel agencies, 382-385

Howard Johnson, 170
HP, see Hewlett-Packard
HR Investment Consultants (Baltimore, MD), 4
HTML, 410
Hunt Mfg., 19, 105, 203, 220
Hyatt, 173, 170
hybrid phone systems, 357
hypertext links, 408

I

Ibex Systems, 140
IBICO Binding, 203
IBM, 76, 108, 109, 145, 192, 234, 236, 244, 388
IBM Selectric, 388
IBM OS/2 Warp Server, 145
ICT Group, 347
Idaho, 165
IDE, 88

IDT, 188
Illinois, 165
illness, 162, 164
illustrations, 342
Image Bank, 340
Image Checks, 63
impact printing, 29, 65
In Focus, 213
inbound service,
  see toll free service
Incentive, 258
incentives, 385
incremental backup, 88
Indiana, 165, 262
Indicia, 299
individual retirement accounts,
  see IRAs
industrial launderer, see uniforms
Info Systems, 140
Infogrip, 196
infrared, 208, 274, 291
injuries, see workers compensation insurance

INK-JET PRINTERS, 76-80, 97, 136, 138, 174-176, 238, 240, 292-294
  cartridges, 174-176
  see also
    color printers, 76-80
    copy paper, 95-98
    desktop computers, 108-113
    fax machines, 136-139
    multifunctional devices, 238-240
    notebook computers, 244-247
    portable printers, 292-295
    toner supplies, 375-377

Innerface Architectural Signage (Lilburn, GA), 333
inserters, 218
InsideFlyer, 153
INTERIM, 361
internal frames, 380
International Papers, 319
Interpay, 268
Intimus, 265
Institute for a Drug-free Workplace (Washington, DC), 128
insurance, see business insurance, see health insurance
Insurance Information Institute (New York, NY), 35
insurance premiums, 33, 34
Integrated Services Digital Network, see ISDN
Intel, 109-110, 144, 195, 245
Intelemedia, 140
"intelligent" cards, 281, 282
IntelliSell, 347
Inter-Tel, 356
Interactive Strategies, 5
interlining, 227
Interlink, 289
Internal Revenue Service (IRS) 3, 4, 11, 271, 277, 279
international access code, 181, 183

Index

427

International Association of Corporate and Professional Recruiters (Louisville, KY), 130
International Bottled Water Association (Alexandria, VA), 23

INTERNATIONAL CALLBACK, 177-179
see also
   900 service, 5-8
   calling cards, 36-38
   conference calling services, 89-91
   international calling, 180-183
   long distance service, 222-225
   prepaid phone cards, 308-310
   toll free service, 371-374

INTERNATIONAL CALLING, 135, 180-183, 223, 352
   compression, 181
see also
   900 service, 5-8
   calling cards, 36-38
   international callback, 177-179
   long distance service, 222-225
   prepaid phone cards, 308-310
   toll free service, 371-374

INTERNATIONAL EXPEDITED DELIVERY, 184-187
see also
   ground shipping, 157-160
   LTL shipping, 226-229
   overnight delivery services, 259-261
   postage meters, 296-300
   postal scales, 301-303
   same day delivery services, 326-328

International Express Mail, 184
International Telecommunication Union (ITU), 232, 233
Internet, 86, 124, 188-191, 193, 260, 408-410
Internet server, *see* Web server

INTERNET SERVICE PROVIDERS, 122-124, 188-191, 409, 410
   shell accounts, 190
see also
   E-mail services, 122-125
   ISDN, 192-195
   modems, 230-233
   World Wide Web site setup, 408-411

Interpay, 268
interpreters, 90, 183
Invar shadow mask, 237
Invesco Retirement Plan Services, 1
investments, 2, 3
Invincible, 105
invoices, 119, 218, 315

Iomega, 85, 86
Iowa, 165
Iron Mountain, 248
IRAs, 278
IRS, *see* Internal Revenue Service
ISDN, 57, 189, 192-195, 231, 397
see also
   conference calling services, 89-91
   conferencing equipment, 92-94
   desktop computers, 108-113
   E-mail services, 122-125
   international calling, 180-183
   Internet Service Providers, 188-191
   long distance service, 222-225
   modems, 230-233
   notebook computers, 244-247
   telephone systems, 356-360
   video conferencing services, 396-399
   World Wide Web site setup, 408-411

ISO 9660, 317
ISP, *see* Internet service providers
Itac Systems, 289
ITC, 133, 177
ITI Marketing Services, 347
Iwatsu, 356

J

J. R. O'Dwyer Company (New York, NY), 313
JABRA, 353
James River Corp., 319
JaniKing, 66, 68
Japan, 180
Jaz drives, 86
JetFax, 238
joggers, 219, 221
John Harland, 29, 63
Juno (New York, NY), 125
JVC, 314, 316
JVC Personal RomMaker, 316

K

K.I., 343
Kallback, 177, 178
Kansas, 165
Kbps, *see* kilobits per second
Kelly, 361
Kennedy Publications (Fitzwilliam, NH), 129, 130
Kensington, 289
Kentucky, 165
key system unit (KSU), 201, 202
key phone systems, 201, 242, 356, 357
Key Tronic, 196

KEYBOARDS, 60, 106, 196-199, 245, 246, 274, 282, 290, 291, 345
see also
   desktop computers, 108-113
   notebook computers, 244-247
   pointing devices, 289-291

keystoning, 257
Kilobits per second (Kbps), 195
Kimball Int'l., 343
Kinko's, 81, 396
Knoll Group, 343
Kodak, 76, 238, 284, 337, 342
Kodak Picture Exchange (KPX), 342
Konica, 238, 284
Kronos, 364
Krueger Int'l., 105
KSU, *see* key system unit

KSU-LESS PHONE SYSTEMS, 200-202
see also
   cellular telephones, 51-54
   cordless telephones, 99-101
   telephone systems, 356-360

Kwik Copy, 81, 82
Kyocera, 209

L

La-Z-Boy, 105
Laarhoven, 378
Labor World, 361
LaCie, 329
laminate, 105, 106, 344

LAMINATION EQUIPMENT, 203-205
see also
   business cards, 25-28
   business forms, 29-31
   commercial printing, 81-84

lamps, *see* bulbs
LAN, 281, 282
Lanier, 114, 238, 284
Las Vegas, 169
laser beam, *see* laser pointers
Laser Gold, 375

LASER POINTERS, 206-208
see also
   LCD systems, 213-216
   overhead projectors, 255-258
   slide projectors, 337-339

LASER PRINTERS, 76-80, 118, 119, 136, 138, 139, 175, 209-212, 238, 256, 282, 293, 319, 376, 387
see also
   color printers, 76-80
   desktop computers, 108-113
   dot matrix printers, 118-121
   fax machines, 136-139
   ink-jet printers, 174-176

The Essential Business Buyer's Guide

multifunctional devices, 238-240
notebook computers, 244-247
portable printers, 292-295
toner supplies, 375-377
typewriters, 386-388

laserdisc, 214
Laserex, 206
LaserMaster, 76, 209
lateral filing cabinets, *see* filing cabinets
Lathem, 364
lawsuits, 405
law firms, 280
LCD panels *see* LCD systems
LCD projectors, *see* LCD systems

LCD SYSTEMS, 207, 213-216, 255-258, 338
 remote controls, 215
 see also
  laser pointers, 206-208
  notebook computers, 244-247
  overhead projectors, 255-258
  slide projectors, 337-339

LCI, 36, 180, 181, 222, 308, 371
LDDS WorldCom, 36, 133, 180, 181, 222, 371
Leader/General Metalcraft, 148
LED, 136, 138, 211, 238
less than truckload shipping *see* LTL shipping

LETTER FOLDING EQUIPMENT, 217-219
 see also
  automatic staplers, 19-21
  letter opening equipment, 220-221
  photocopiers, 284-288

LETTER OPENING EQUIPMENT, 220-221
 see also
  postage meters, 296-300
  postal scales, 301-303

letterhead, 120
lettering, 335
Lexmark, 76, 118, 174, 209, 386, 388
liability insurance, 33
library, 283, 313
Liebert, 392
lighting, 336, 339
Lincoln National Life, 1
line-interactive UPS, 393, 394
lines per minute (lpm), 120
"links", *see* hypertext links
lithium ion (Li), 246
Lithographic printing, 31
local area network, *see* LAN
locks, 325
logistics management company, 228
Logitech, 289

logos, 154, 390, 391

LONG DISTANCE SERVICE, 37, 49, 135, 152, 181, 195, 222-225, 369, 372
 see also
  900 service, 5-8
  calling cards, 36-38
  cellular service, 47-50
  conference calling services, 89-91
  fax on demand, 140-143
  international callback, 177-179
  international calling, 180-183
  prepaid phone cards, 308-310
  telemarketing services, 347-350
  telephone directory software, 351-352
  toll free service, 371-374

Los Angeles, 169, 185, 187
lost baggage insurance, 104
Louisiana, 165
lpm, *see* lines per minute

LTL SHIPPING, 226-229
 see also
  ground shipping, 157-160
  overnight delivery services, 259-261
  postal scales, 301-303
  same day delivery services, 326-328

Luce's Press Clipping, 69
Lucent Technologies, 15, 51, 99, 101, 356, 400, *see* AT&T
lumbar support, 60
lumens, 214, 215, 257, *see* ANSI lumens
Lyte Optronics, 206

M

Mac, *see* Macintosh
Macintosh, 78, 109, 110, 141, 145, 210, 234, 238, 289, 292, 293, 329, 351, 408
 see Apple
MacOS, 112
MacroTel, 200
MacroVoice, 140
MAG Innovision, 234, 236
magazines, 312, 332
Magnavox, 234
magnetic cards, 281
magneto-optical (MO) drives, 87
magnets, 346
Maid Brigade, 66
Maid to Perfection, 66
mailing equipment, *see* postage meters
mailing house, 300
Maine, 165
Malibu, 140
managed care, 163, 165, 306

Mannesman Tally, 118, 174, 292
Manpower, 361
Maritz Travel, 382
Market USA, 347
marketing, *see* public relations
Marketing Messages, 241
Marriott, 170
Martin, 148
Martin Yale, 217, 220
Maryland, 165
Massachusetts, 165, 406
MasterCard, 102, 103, 151
maternity care, 166
Max USA, 19
MBM, 217
MC, *see* MasterCard
McBee, 29, 63
MCI, 36, 89, 122, 123, 133, 180, 181, 188, 222, 262, 308, 371
MDI, *see* Micro Design Int'l.
media, *see* public relations
media safes, 324, 325
Mediatel, 133
Medicare, 270
megabyte, 110, 112, 245, 318
megahertz, 112, 247
Megahertz, 230
Meilink, 148, 323
memory, 109, 110, 176, 219, 240, 242, 245, 264, 274, 387, 388
mental health, 166
Mer, 367
Merchant Shippers Cooperative Association (Concord, NH), 228
Merlin Grein, 392
message on hold, *see* music on hold (MOH) systems
messenger couriers, *see* same day delivery services
metal, 320
metal halide lamps, 215, 257
Metrocall, 262
MEWA, 307
Mexico, 180, 184
MH, *see* Modified Huffman
MHz, *see* megahertz
Miami, 185, 187
Michigan, 165
Micro Design Int'l., 85
Micro General, 301
microcassettes, 115, 116
Microcom, 230
microfiche, 249
microfilm, 249
Micron, 108
microphone, 93, 115, 116, 355, 397
Microsoft, 145, 190, 196, 214, 289, 408
Microsoft Internet Explorer, 190
Microsoft Network (MSN), 122, 123
Microsoft PowerPoint, 214
Microsoft Server NT Advanced Server, 145
MicroSpeed, 196, 289
Microtek, 329
Midnite Express, 326
Midwest Express Airlines, 151

Index

Midwest Express Frequent Flyer, 151
MidWest Micro, 108
military addresses, 158
Miller Desk, 105
milliwatts (mW), 207
Mindpath, 289
Minidata, 268
Minnesota, 165
Minolta, 238, 284
Minuteman, 81
Mississippi, 165
Missouri, 165
Mita, 238, 284
Mitel, 356
Mitsubishi, 51, 76, 234, 236
Mitsumi, 43
MMR,
 see Modified Modified Read
MO drives,
 see magneto-optical drives
Mobil, 171
mobile phones, 52
Mobilecom, 262

MODEMS, 15, 134, 189, 193, 194, 202, 230-233, 246, 247, 263, 270, 273, 274, 354
 proprietary protocols, 233
 see also
  desktop computers, 108-113
  E-mail services, 122-125
  Fax machines, 136-139
  Internet service providers, 188-191
  ISDN, 192-195
  notebook computers, 244-247
  video conferencing services, 396-399
  World Wide Web site setup, 408-411

Modified Huffman (MH), 137, 147
Modified Modified Read (MMR), 137, 139, 142, 146, 147
Modified Read (MR), 137, 147
modular, 344, 345, 378
modulation, 232
monaural design, 355

MONITORS, 111, 234-237, 245, 247, 282, 397
 see also
  desktop computers, 108-113
  notebook computers, 244-247

Monroe, 284
Montana, 165
Moody's, 32, 162
Moore, 29, 63
Morgan Services, 389
Motorola, 51, 110, 192, 230, 262, 272
Mountain Valley, 22
mouse, see pointing devices
MR, see Modified Read

MRI, 396
MSN, see Microsoft Network
MTA-EMCI (Washington, DC), 262
multi-part checks, 64
multi-part forms, 30, 119, 387
Multi-tech, 230
multichannel operation, 100

MULTIFUNCTIONAL DEVICES, 139, 238-240
 see also
  answering machines, 15-18
  color printers, 76-80
  desktop computers, 108-113
  fax machines, 136-139
  ink-jet printers, 174-176
  laser printers, 209-212
  modems, 230-233
  notebook computers, 244-247
  scanners, 329-332

multimedia, 316
multisession recording, 317
multiple employer welfare association, see MEWA
Muratec, 136
muscle strain, 196

MUSIC ON HOLD SYSTEMS, 241-243
 licenses, 242, 243
 see also
  telephone systems, 356-360
  voice mail systems 400-403

Mustek, 329
mute, 355
mutual funds, 269, 278
Mutual Press Clipping Service, 69
Muzak, 241
mW, see milliwatts

N

Nady, 353
NAM, 53
Nanao (Eizo), 234
nanometer (nm), 207
Nashua, 375
Nashuatec, 284
NASSTRAC (Washington, DC), 228
National, 39, 40
National Association of Health Underwriters (Washington, DC), 164
National Association of Personnel Services (Alexandria, VA), 130
National Association of Temporary and Staffing Services (Alexandria, VA), 363
National Business Coalition on Health (Washington, DC), 168
National Business Furniture, 61
National Coffee Service Association (Fairfax, VA), 23

National Committee on Quality Assurance (NCQA) (Washington, DC), 168
National Council on Compensation Insurance (NCCI) (Boca Raton, FL), 404, 405, 407
National Highway Carriers Directory, 228
National Linen Service, 389
National Motor Freight Classification, 228
National Office Paper Recycling Project (Washington, DC), 319, 321
National Register Publishing (New Providence, NJ) 13
National Telemarketing, Inc. (New Orleans, LA), 374
National Underwriter Co. (Cincinnati, OH), 279
Nationsway, 226
Nationwide, 72
Nationwide Life Insurance Co. 1
Nationwide Papers, 95, 319
native capacity, 88
Navitar, 337
NCQA, see National Committee on Quality Assurance
Nebraska, 165
NEBS, 29, 63
NEC, 43, 51, 92, 209, 213, 234, 236, 244, 262, 356
Neopost, 217, 220, 296, 301
Netcom, 188
Netscape Navigator, 190
networks, 86, 87, 56, 145, 146, 176, 189-191, 209-211, 247, 281, 282
Network Courier, 326
network laser printers, 209
Network Telephone Services, 5
Nevada, 165
Nevada Bell, 192
New England Newsclip Agency, 69
New England Retirement Services, 1
New Hampshire, 165
New Jersey, 165
New Mexico, 165
New York, 41, 165, 185, 187
New York City, 169
news wire services, 70
newsletters, 70, 313
Newspaper Association of America (Kearneysville, WV), 14
newspapers, 70, 321, 320, 321
Newtronix, 55
nickel cadmium (NiCad), 246, 274, 294
nickel metal hydride (NiMH), 246, 274, 294
Nightrider, 81
Nikon, 329
Nimlok, 378
Nitsuko, 356

noise canceling, 354
Noise Reduction Coefficient (NRC), 346
Nokia, 51
Nomadic Display, 378
non-profit organizations, 4, 279
Norcom (Norwalk, CT), 117
Norelco, 114
Norman Roberts & Associates, 129
Norrell, 361
Nortel, see Northern Telecom
Northern Telecom, 99, 101, 356, 400
North Carolina, 165
North Dakota, 165
Northwest Airlines, 151, 152, 326
Northwest VIP Same Day, 326
Northwest WorldPerks, 151

NOTEBOOK COMPUTERS, 216, 231, 244-247, 263, 273, 274, 281, 291, 292, 293, 295
see also
   CD-ROM drives, 43-46
   color printers, 76-80
   computer backup systems, 85-88
   desktop computers, 108-113
   dot matrix printers, 118-121
   ink-jet printers, 174-176
   keyboards, 196-199
   laser printers, 209-212
   LCD systems, 213-216
   modems, 230-233
   monitors, 234-237
   multifunctional devices, 238-240
   PDAs, 272-276
   pointing devices, 289-291
   portable printers, 292-295
   recordable CD drives, 314-318
   scanners, 329-332
   typewriters, 386-388
   World Wide Web setup, 408-411

Novell, 145
Novell Netware, 145
NTC, 308
Nu Kote International, 375
numeric assignment module see NAM
numeric keypad, 197
numeric pagers, 263
nView, 213
Nynex, 192

O

O'Sullivan, 148
OAZ, 144
Oce, 284
OCR, 147, 240, 330, 331
Octel, 400
OEM toner, 375, 377
off-limits policy, 131

off-line UPS, 393
off-line composing, 124

OFF-SITE STORAGE, 35, 86, 248-250
see also
   accountants, 9-11
   computer backup systems, 85-88
   file cabinets, 148-150

off-peak rates, 91, 224
Office America, 375
Office Depot, 251
office furniture, see desks
   see office chairs
   see systems furniture
Office Paper Recycling Guide, 321
office superstores, 61, 150, 204, 219, 240, 251-253, 267, 376

OFFICE SUPPLIES, 251-254
see also
   beverage services, 22-24
   copy paper, 95-98
   recycling, 319-322
   toner supplies, 375-377

OfficeMax, 251
Official Motor Freight Guide, 228
offset printing, 83, 84
Ohio, 165
Oki telecom, 51
Okidata, 76, 118, 174, 209
Oklahoma, 165
Olivetti, 174, 203, 292, 386, 388
Olsten, 361
Olympia, 265, 386
Olympus, 85, 114, 314
Omation, 220
Omega World Travel, 382
On Paper (Malvern, PA), 98
On-Hold America, 241
on-line UPS, 393
on-time delivery, 227
Oneil Product Development (Irvine, CA), 248
online services, 122-124, 193, 233, 273, 384
opacity, 96
OPEN Cleaning Systems, 66
Open Database Compliance (ODBC), 366
optical character recognition, see OCR
optical drives, 87
optical mark recognition (OMR), 218
Optus, 144
Oregon, 165
Orlando, 169
OS/2, 401
OTR, 364
out-of-paper reception, 138
Output Technology, 118
overdue accounts, see collection agencies

OVERHEAD PROJECTORS, 171, 207, 214, 215, 255-258, 338, 398
see also
   color printers, 76-80
   laser pointers, 206-208
   LCD systems, 213-216
   slide projectors, 337-339

OVERNIGHT DELIVERY SERVICES, 137, 158, 184, 185, 226, 259-261, 327, 328
see also
   ground shipping, 157-160
   international expedited delivery, 184-187
   LTL shipping, 226-229
   postage meters, 296-300
   postal scales, 301-303
   same day delivery services, 326-328

Overnite, 226
overrides, 384
Ozarka, 22
ozone filters, 211
Oztec, 265

P

P.F.E., Int'l., 217
P.O. box, see Post Office box
Pacific Bell (San Francisco, CA), 192
Packard Bell, 108
PageMart, 262
PageNet, 262

PAGERS, 262-264
see also
   cellular service, 47-50
   cellular telephones, 51-54
   PDAs, 272--275
   telephone systems, 356-360

paging systems, 57, 201
Panamax (San Rafael, CA), 395
Panasonic, 15, 19, 43, 51, 99, 114, 136, 200, 209, 220, 234, 238, 262, 284, 329, 356, 386
panel, 344, 346
panel displays, see trade show displays
Pantographs, 64
paper, 79, 84, 95-98, 137-139, 175, 218, 319, 320, 322, 325, 377, 387, see copy paper
paper clips, 251, 320
Paper Direct (Secaucus, NJ), 98
Paper Mart, The, 95
Paper Showcase (Mankato, MN), 98

PAPER SHREDDERS, 265-267
see also
   business forms, 29-31
   checks, 63-65
   copy paper, 95-98

Index

photocopiers, 284-288
safes, 323-325

paper trays, 176, 239, 3301
parallel port, 88, 176, 293
Parcel Post, 158
passwords, 303, 366, 368-370
Paychex, 268
Payco, 72
Payless, 39, 40
Payroll 1, 268

PAYROLL SERVICES,
268-271, 349, 365, 366, 405-407
see also
401(k) plans, 1-4
accountants, 9-11
health insurance, 161-164
pension plans, 276-279

PBX phone systems,
6, 100, 56-58, 242, 357, 360
PC Card, see PCMCIA
PCL, 78, 176, 210, 211
PCMCIA, 216, 231, 247, 275
PCs, see desktop computers
PCS, 50, 53, 100, 231, 263

PDAs, 272-275
see also
desktop computers, 108-113
modems, 230-233
notebook computers, 244-247
portable printers, 292-295

peak rates, 183, 224, 225
Pelouze, 301
Pendleton James & Associates, 129
Pennsylvania, 165
Penny Wise, 251
pens, see office supplies
Pension Benefit Guarantee
  Corporation (PBGC), 279

PENSION PLANS, 2, 276-279
administrators, 278
see also
401(k) plans, 1-4
accountants, 9-11
health insurance, 161-164
payroll services, 268-271

pen-style, 206
Pentax, 292
Pentium, 109, 110, 245
Pentium Pro, 110
perfect binding, 84
Personal communications system,
  see PCS
personal computers,
  see desktop computers
personal digital assistants,
  see PDAs
personal identification number,
  309, 281, 282
Philadelphia, 185
Philips, 114, 117, 234, 314

Phoenix Funds, 1
phone books, 352
phone systems,
  see telephone systems
PhoneMate (Casio), 15, 99
photoconductor, 286

PHOTOCOPIER CONTROLS,
280-283
see also
  copy paper, 95-98
  paper shredders, 265-267
  photocopiers, 284-288
  recycling, 319-322

PHOTOCOPIERS,
136, 171, 210, 239, 240, 256,
280-288, 319, 330, 376
leasing, 287
repairs/service, 286-288
see also
  copy paper, 95-98
  multifunctional devices,
    238-240
  paper shredders, 265-267
  photocopier controls,
    280-283
  recycling, 319-322
  toner supplies, 375-377

PhotoDisc, 340
photographer, 341, 342
photographs, 330, 331, 341, 342,
  398, see stock photography
physician turnover rate, 167
physicians,
  see primary care physicians
Picture Agency Council of
  America (Northfield, MN), 342
Pierce Leahy, 248
PIN, see personal identification
  number
pins, 119
Pinnacle Micro, 85, 314
Pioneer, 314
PIP Printing, 81, 82
pitch, 388
Pitney Bowes, 136, 217, 220, 221,
  280, 284, 296, 301
Pittsburgh, 157
pixels per inch (ppi), 331
Plantronics, 353
plastic, 320, 322
platen, see book platen
Plextor, 43
PM Company, 375
pocket recorders, 115

POINTING DEVICES,
197, 245, 246, 289-291
see also
  desktop computers, 108-113
  keyboards, 196-199
  notebook computers, 244-247

points of presence, 124, 190, 409
point of service plans,
  167, 167, 306

Poland Springs, 22
Polaroid, 329
Polycom, 92
pop-up exhibits,
  see trade show displays
POPs, see points of presence
portability, 373
portable phones,
  see cellular telephones

PORTABLE PRINTERS, 292-295
see also
  color printers, 76-80
  copy paper, 95-98
  desktop computers, 108-113
  dot matrix printers, 118-121
  ink-jet printers, 174-176
  laser printers, 209-212
  notebook computers, 244-247
  PDAs, 272-275
  recycling, 319-322
  scanners, 329-332

ports,
  116, 231, 242, 357, 369, 401, 403
Post Office Box, 158
postage, 298, 299, 302, 303

POSTAGE METERS, 282, 296-300,
302, 303
see also
  ground shipping, 157-161
  international expedited
    delivery, 184-187
  letter opening equipment,
    220-221
  LTL shipping, 226-229
  overnight delivery services,
    259-261
  postal scales, 301-303
  same day delivery services,
    326-328

POSTAL SCALES, 299, 301-303
see also
  ground shipping, 157-160
  international expedited
    delivery, 184-187
  letter opening equipment,
    220-221
  LTL shipping, 226-229
  overnight delivery services,
    259-261
  postage meters, 296-300
  same day delivery services,
    326-328

Postal Service,
  see United States Postal Service
postmarks, see postage meters
PostScript, 78, 210, 212
pouches, 205
power failure, 393
PowerPC chip, 110, 245

PPOs, 161, 163, 168, 304-307
see also
  business insurance, 32-35

employee drug testing,
    126-128
health insurance, 161-164
HMOs, 165-168
workers compensation
    insurance, 404-407

PPP, 190
PR, *see* public relations
Practical Peripherals, 230
Prairie Systems, 140
pre-existing conditions, 162
preferred provider organization,
    see PPO
preferred rates, 172, 384-385
premastering software, 316
premium, 33-35, 304, 405-407
Preng & Associates, 129

PREPAID PHONE CARDS,
    308-310
see also
    calling cards, 36-38
    cellular service, 47-50
    international callback, 177-179
    international calling, 180-183
    long distance service, 222-225
    toll free service, 371-374

PrePRESS Direct (East Hanover,
    NJ), 331
prescription drugs, 166
press clippings, 312
press releases, 155, 312
primary care physicians,
    161-164, 165-168, 304-307
PrimeCall, 177
print resolution, *see* resolution
Printer Control Language,
    see PCL
Printer Systems Int'l., 118
printhead, 119, 175, 176
Priority Mail, 158
private branch exchanges,
    see PBX phone systems
Pro CD, 351
Pro Staff, 361
processors, 109-112, 210, 245-247
Prodigy, 122, 123
Professional Displays, 378
Profold, 217
projectors, *see* LCD systems,
    see overhead projectors ,
    see slide projectors
Promoting Your 900 Number, 8
property insurance, 33, 35
"prototype" plans, 279
Proxima, 213
Prudential Overall Supply, 389
PS/2, *see* serial port
PSINet, 122, 188
Psion, 272, 273
Psion Series 3a, 273

PUBLIC RELATIONS FIRMS,
    71, 311-313
see also
    advertising agencies, 12-14

clipping services, 69-71
graphic designers, 154-156
stock photography, 340-342
trade show displays, 378-381

Public Relations Society of
    America (PRSA) (New York,
    NY), 312, 313
purchase orders, 119
Purchasing Recycled Plastic
    Products, 322
purity, 320

Q

QIC, *see* quarter inch cartridges
QMS, 76, 209
Quality, 170
Quality Loss Management
    Program (QLMP), 406
Quantex, 108
Quantum, 85
quarter inch cartridges, 87
quick disconnect, 354
Quick Print, 81
quick printers, 82
quick scan, 138
Quill, 61, 251
QWERTY, 198, 199

R

Rack rates, 172, 385
RADF, 286
radio, 70, 243
Radio Shack (Tandy), 15, 99, 310
Radisson, 170
Radius, 234, 236
RAM, 110, 111, 212, 245
Ramada, 170
random access, 339
Random Access Memory,
    see RAM
Rapidforms, 29, 63
rating services, 162
RDH, 286
ream, 97
rebates, 384
"recirculating" document
    handler, *see* RDH
"recirculating" feeder, *see* RADF
record safes, 324

RECORDABLE CD DRIVES,
    85, 314-318
CD formats, 316
see also
    CD-ROM drives, 43-46
    computer backup systems,
        85-88
    desktop computers, 108-113
    notebook computers, 244-247

recording software,
    see premastering software
records center, *see* off-site storage

records storage,
    see off-site storage
recruitment, *see* executive
    recruitment agencies
    see temporary help services
Recycled Plastic Products
    Source Book, 322

RECYCLING,
    98, 176, 319-322, 377
see also
    cleaning service, 66-68
    copy paper, 95-98
    off-site storage, 248-250
    office supplies, 251-254
    paper shredders, 265-267
    photocopiers, 284-288
    toner supplies, 375-377

Recycling at Work: Guide for
    Building Managers, 321
reflective projectors, 256, 257
Registered Health Underwriters
    (RHU), 164
registered mail, 302
reimbursement levels, 162
Reliable, 61, 251
Remedy, 361
remote diagnostics, 287, 368-370
removable storage, 85, 86
rental insurance, 41, 104
repetitive stress injuries (RSI),
    197, 198, 291
reproduction rights, 342
request for proposal, *see* RFP
resellers, 181
Residence Inn, 170
residential directories, 351
resolution, 78, 79, 112, 175, 176,
    211, 212, 216, 235, 240, 247,
    293, 294, 331, 332
Resource Guide to Business
    Products Manufacturers'
    Recycling Products, 322
ResourceNet Int'l., 95
restaurants, 170
retainer, 130-132
retirement savings, 276
"reversing" feeder, *see* RADF
RFP, 358
Rhode Island, 165
RHU, *see* Registered Health
    Underwriters
ribbons,
    120, 121, 293, 294, 320, 388
Ricoh, 136, 238, 284, 314, 329
RightFAX, 144
RIS Paper, 95
RISC, 212
RMH Teleservices, 347
RMS, 248
Roadway Express 226
Roadway Package Service (RPS),
    157-160, 184, 228, 259, 302
Rochester Telephone, 192
roll-about, 398
rolling cabinets, 149
Rosenbluth International, 382

Index

Royal/Olivetti, 203
Royal Copystar, 284
RPS, *see* Roadway Package Service
RPS Multiweight, 228
RPSAir, 184
RSIs, *see* repetitive stress injuries

S

SAFES, 150, 323-325
  see also
    file cabinets, 148-150
    off-site storage, 248-250
    paper shredders, 265-267

Safesite, 248
sags, *see* brownouts
salary-reduction simplified employee pension, *see* SAR-SEP
sales, *see* telemarketing services

SAME DAY DELIVERY SERVICES, 326-328
  see also
    e-mail services, 122-125
    ground shipping, 157-160
    international expedited delivery, 184-187
    LTL shipping, 226-229
    overnight delivery services, 259-261
    postage meters, 296-300
    postal scales, 301-303

sampling rate, 242
Samsung, 234, 262
Samtron, 234
San Diego, 169
San Francisco, 169, 185, 187
Sanyo, 114
SAR-SEP, 277, 278
satellite transmission, 231, 397
Sato Travel, 382
Sauder, 148
Savin, 238, 284
SBC, 200
scales, *see* postal scales

SCANNERS, 137, 138, 238, 239, 329-332
  see also
    computer backup systems, 85-88
    desktop computers, 108-113
    fax machines, 136-139
    multifunctional devices, 238-240
    notebook computers, 244-247

school, 283
Schwab, 323
screens, *see* monitors
screen markup, 216
screen printing, 84
SCSI, 45, 88
Seagate Technology, 85

Seal Products, 203
sealers, 298
search engines, 410
secretaries, 344, 362
Section 125 mutual fund plans, 269
Seiko, 76
SEM, 265
Sentry, 148, 323
SEP, 277, 278
serial port, 176, 197, 231, 274, 293
server software, 145
service contracts, 139
ServiceMaster, 66, 68
settlement, 405
Sharp, 15, 99, 136, 213, 238, 244, 272, 274, 284, 386
sheet-fed scanners, 329-331
sheets per pass, 267
Sheraton, 170
shredders, *see* paper shredders
Shredex, 265
Shure, 92
Siemens Rolm, 356, 400
Signature, 84

SIGNS, 333-336
  see also
    advertising agencies, 12-14
    color printers, 76-80
    graphic designers, 154-156
    public relations firms, 311-313
    stock photography, 340-342
    trade show displays, 378-381

SIIG, 196
Silicon Valley Bus Company (San Juan Bautista, CA), 291
Simplex, 364
simplified employee pension, *see* SEP
Sir Speedy, 81
Sisco, 323
SITEL Corporation, 347
skiptracing, 73
Skyline, 378
SkyTel, 262

SLIDE PROJECTORS, 207, 256, 337-339
  auto focus, 338, 339
  built-in screen, 339
  lenses, 338
  see also
    commercial printing, 81-84
    LCD systems, 213-216
    overhead projectors, 255-258

slide scanners 329, 331
SLIP, 190
slitters, 220, 221
Smart & Friendly, 314
Smed, 343
SMG Marketing Group (Chicago, IL), 165
Smith Corona, 203, 386, 388
Smith Travel Research (Hendersonville, TN), 169

smoothing, 212
smoothness, 96, 97
Snap-Drape (Carrollton, TX), 381
snap-set forms, 31
Snelling & Snelling, 361
SNET, 192
Social Security, 270
Society for Human Resources Management (Alexandria, VA), 125
solid ink printers, 76, 77, 79, 80
Sony, 15, 43, 99, 114, 234, 236, 272, 273, 314
Sony MagicLink, 273
sorting, 239, 285
sound, 110
Sound Control, 92
Sound Transmission Class (STC), 346
South America, 178, 184, 185
South Carolina, 165
South Dakota, 165
Southwest Airlines, 151, 152, 326
Southwest Airlines Cargo, 326
Southwest Rapid Rewards, 151
Southwestern Bell, 15, 48, 99
Soviet Union, 181
Sparkletts, 22
Speak-EZ Productions, 241
speakerphone, 93
speakers, 93, 215
specialty paper, 98
SpectraFax, 140
SpectraLink, 99, 101
spike, 395
Sprint, 36, 89, 122, 123, 133, 180, 181, 222, 308, 371
sprinkler systems, 35
stackers, 218, 297
staff model, 167
stamps, 296, 297, 299
standby UPS, 393
Standard & Poor's, 32, 34, 162, 168
Standard Register (Dayton, OH), 65
Stanley Bostitch, 19
staplers, *see* automatic staplers
Staples, 251
Staplex Co., The, 19
Star Micronics, 118
Starkey, 353
Station Message Detail Recording (SMDR), 370
Steelcase, 59, 343
Steelworks, 148
stock forms, 31

STOCK PHOTOGRAPHY, 340-342
  see also
    advertising agencies, 12-14
    CD-ROM drives, 43-46
    color printers, 76-80
    computer backup systems, 85-88
    desktop computers, 108-113
    graphic designers, 154-156

The Essential Business Buyer's Guide

ink-jet printers, 174-176
notebook computers, 244-247
public relations firms, 311-313
signs, 333-336
trade show displays, 378-381

STN, *see* dual scan
storage areas, 344
strip-cut shredders, 265-267
Stromberg, 364
subscription, 352
substance abuse, 126, 166
substrates, 334, 335
Submit It!, 409
SubmitAll, 409
"Super A" pages, 79
"Super B" pages, 79
super-VGA, 235
superstores, *see* office superstores
Supply Depot, 375
Supra, 230
Supreme Court, 267
surge, 395
surge suppressor, 107, 395
surveillance systems, 249
switched service,
  see long distance service
Swingline (Acco USA), 19
Swintec, 386
switches, 56-58, 183
Switzerland, 411
SyQuest, 85, 86
system crashes, 86

SYSTEMS FURNITURE, 150,
  343-346
  see also
    chairs, 59-62
    desks, 105-107
    file cabinets, 148-150

T

T.30, 147
T1, 6, 189, 190, 225
T3, 189, 190
T&E expenses
  see corporate cards
Tadiran, 356
tailored call coverage, 8
Talent Tree, 361
Tamarack, 329
Tandy, *see* Radio Shack
tape drives, 85-88, 315
tape recorders, 115, 242
target benefit plans, 277
tax records, 86, 269, 270, 276, 315
Teac, 43
Tektronix, 76
Telco Research, 367
Telebit, 230
telecommuting, 193
Telecorp Systems, 241
TeleDebit, 308
telegraph, 139
Telegroup, 177, 178
Telekol, 140

TeleMark, 347
Telemarketing & Call Center
  Solutions, 347, 350

TELEMARKETING SERVICES,
  347-350
  see also
    900 service, 5-8
    fax on demand, 140-143
    international calling, 180-183
    long distance service, 222-225
    telephone directory software,
      351-352
    telephone headsets, 353-355
    telephone systems, 356-360
    toll free service, 371-374
    voice mail systems, 400-403

Telematrix, 200

TELEPHONE DIRECTORY
  SOFTWARE, 351-352
  see also
    international calling, 180-183
    long distance service, 222-225
    telemarketing services,
      347-350
    toll free service, 371-374

Telephone Disclosure and
  Dispute Resolution Act
  (TDDRA), 7

TELEPHONE HEADSETS,
  353-355
  hygiene, 355
  wireless, 355
  see also
    dictation equipment, 114-117
    telemarketing services,
      347-350
    telephone systems, 356-360

telephone sales representatives
  (TSR), 348-350

TELEPHONE SYSTEMS,
  7, 8, 56, 57, 90, 93, 100, 101, 116,
  171, 182, 183, 201, 202, 242, 349,
  356-360, 368-370, 372, 374, 393,
  401-403
  see also
    answering machines, 15-18
    cellular telephones, 51-54
    centrex service, 55-58
    conference calling services,
      89-91
    conferencing equipment,
      92-94
    cordless telephones, 99-101
    desktop computers, 108-113
    fax on demand, 140-143
    ISDN, 192-195
    KSU-less phone systems,
      200-202
    modems, 230-233
    music on hold systems,
      241-243

Toll fraud prevention, 367-370
video conferencing services,
  396-399
voice mail systems, 400-403

Telephonetics, 241
Telepublishing, 5
television, 70
telex, 123
Telex, 337
Telrad, 356
Teltone, 367

TEMPORARY HELP SERVICES,
  361-363
  see also
    executive recruitment
      agencies, 129-132

temps,
  see temporary help services
Tennessee, 165
Texas, 165
Texas Instruments, 118, 209, 244
Texas Press Clipping Bureau, 69
text memory, 387-388
TFT, *see* active matrix
Thank You For Holding, 241
theft, 324, 363
thermal printing, 136-139, 292-294
thermal transfer,
  136, 138, 238, 292-294
thermal wax printers, 76-80
thermography, 25, 26, 28
Thomson & Thomson (North
  Quincy, MA), 332
Thrifty, 39-41
throat width, 267
throughput, 233
Tiger Mark, 378
Time America, 364

TIME CLOCKS, 364-366
  see also
    desktop computers, 108-113
    payroll services, 268-271

TNT, 184, 185, 187, 259, 326
Todays, 361
Todd Uniform, 389
token ring, 176

TOLL FRAUD PREVENTION,
  367-370
  service bureau, 367
  see also
    international callback, 177-179
    international calling, 180-183
    ISDN, 192-195
    KSU-less phone systems,
      200-202
    modems, 230-233
    telephone systems, 356-360
    voice mail systems, 400-403

TOLL FREE SERVICE, 38, 90,
  124, 143, 309, 352, 371-374

Index

see also
900 service, 5-8
calling cards, 36-38
cellular service, 47-50
conference calling, 89-91
fax on demand, 140-143
international callback, 177-179
international calling, 180-183
long distance service, 222-225
prepaid phone cards, 308-310
telemarketing services, 347-350
telephone directory software, 351-352
telephone systems, 356-360

Toner Cartridge Services, 375

TONER SUPPLIES, 79, 138, 210, 212, 286, 320, 375-377
see also
color printers, 76-80
copy paper, 95-98
fax machines, 136-139
ink-jet printers, 174-176
laser printers, 209-212
office supplies, 251-254
photocopiers, 284-288
recycling, 319-322

Tony Stone, 340
Toshiba, 43, 136, 238, 244, 284, 356, 392
touch tone, 310, 263
touchpads, *see* pointing devices
Tower Cleaning Systems, 66
trackballs, *see* pointing devices
tracking, 157, 159, 186, 227, 260
tractor feeds, 120

TRADE SHOW DISPLAYS, 334, 335, 378-381
see also
advertising agencies, 12-14
graphic designers, 154-156
public relations firms, 311-313
signs, 333-336

Traffic USA, 144
trailers, 116-117
transcription,
see dictation equipment
transfer rate, 45
transmissive projectors, 255-257
transparencies, 77, 79, 256-258, 294, 332
transparency adapters, 332
Transport Network, 326
transportable phones, 51, 52
Travan QIC format, 85, 87

TRAVEL AGENCIES, 172, 382-385
see also
car rental agencies, 39-42
corporate cards, 102-104
frequent flyer programs, 151-153

hotels, 169-173

Travel and Transport, 382
travel auditors, 384
Travel One, 382
Travelodge, 170
Trinitron, 236
Trio, 144
Tripp Lite, 392
truckload carriers, 228
TSI, 133
TSL, 367
TT Systems, 200
tunnel finishing, 391
TWA, 151, 152, 153
TWA Frequent Flyer Bonus, 151

TYPEWRITERS, 118-120, 199, 386-388
see also
business forms, 29-31
copy paper, 95-98
desktop computers, 108-113
dot matrix printers, 118-121
laser printers, 209-212
notebook computers, 244-247

Tyvek, 221

U

U.S.P.S.,
see United States Postal Service
U.S. Chamber of Commerce (Washington, DC), 407
U.S. Delivery Systems, 326
U.S. Office Products, 251
U.S. Robotics, 92, 144, 192, 230, 272, 273
U.S. Robotics Pilot, 273
U.S. West, 192
UARCO (Barrington, IL), 65
UL, *see* Underwriters Laboratory
UMAX, 329
umbrella insurance, 35
uncollectables, 8
underwriters, 406
Underwriters Laboratory (UL), 150, 324
UNEX, 353
Uniden, 99, 262
unidirectional printing, 120
unified messaging systems, 403
Uniform Textile & Service Association (UTSA) (Washington, DC), 389

UNIFORMS, 389-391
rental, 390
see also
temporary help services, 361-363

UNINTERRUPTIBLE POWER SUPPLIES, 392-395
see also
desktop computers, 108-113

modems, 230-233
telephone systems, 356-360

Union Camp Corp., 319
UniSource, 95
United 1K flyer, 152
United Airlines, 151, 152
United Mileage Plus, 151
United Parcel Service (UPS), 157-160, 184, 185, 187, 226, 228, 259-261, 302, 303, 326
United Parcel Service Hundredweight, 228
United Parcel Service SonicAir, 326
United Parcel Service Worldwide Expedited, 184
United Parcel Service Worldwide Express, 184
United States Postal Service, 157-160, 184, 259, 261, 297, 302, 326
United States Telecard Association (Washington, DC), 310
UNIX, 145, 408
UPS, *see* uninterruptible power supplies
UPS, *see* United Parcel Service
urinalysis, 127
upstream provider, 190-191
USA Global Link, 177, 178
USAir, 151, 152
USAir Frequent Traveler, 151
USI, 203
USPS,
see United States Postal Service
Utah, 165
utilization review, 163-164
UUNet, 122, 123, 188

V

V.17, 137, 147
V.34, 232, 233
vacuum feeders, 218
Value, 39, 42
value added resellers, 111
Van Dyne-Crotty, 389
Van Kampen American Capital, 1
variance, 335
Varifocal lenses, 257
VARs, *see* value added resellers
VCRs, 88, 214
VDI, 114
Velcro, 380
veneer, 106
Vermont, 165
vertical file cabinets,
see file cabinets
vertical refresh rate, 237
vesting, 4, 279
VGA, 216, 235
video, 109, 111, 207, 214, 215, 249, 266, 315, 317, 324, 397, 408
video cameras, 397
video cards, 111, 236

VIDEO CONFERENCING
  SERVICES, 193, 396-399
  see also
    conference calling services,
      89-91
    conferencing equipment,
      92-94
    desktop computers, 108-113
    international calling, 180-183
    ISDN, 192-195
    long distance service, 222-225
    modems, 230-233
    notebook computers, 244-247

video RAM, 111
videotapes, 87, 398
ViewSonic, 234, 236
Viking, 61, 251
Virginia, 165
viruses, see computer viruses
VISA, 102, 103, 151
Vodavi, 55
voice activation, 115
voice boards, 401

VOICE MAIL SYSTEMS,
  15, 48, 56-58, 171, 201, 264, 309,
  357, 359, 360, 368, 400-403
  service bureaus, 15
  see also
    answering machines, 15-18
    centrex service, 55-58
    fax on demand, 140-143
    KSU-less phone systems,
      200-202
    music on hold systems,
      241-243
    telephone systems, 356-360

voice recognition systems, 117
voice tubes, 355
Vogel Peterson, 105
Volt, 361
Volt Ampere (VA), 394, 395
voltage, 393, 394
Voysys, 400
VXI, 353

W

W-2 forms, 269
Wallace, 29, 61, 63
WAN, 281, 282
Ward Howell International, 129

warehouse clubs, 240, 253-254
Washington, 165
Washington, D.C., 169, 187
Wausau Paper Mills Co., 319
Web,
  see World Wide Web site setup
Web server, 408-410
Weiss Research (West Palm Beach,
  FL), 162
West Interactive, 5
West Virginia, 165
Western, 361
Western Telematic, 367
Western Union, 308
Westin, 170
Weyerhauser Corp., 319
"Who Writes What", 164
Wholesale Supply, 251
wide-area network, see WAN
Wildcard Technologies, 144
Wilson Jones (Acco), 265
Windows,
  141, 145, 236, 291, 293, 365, 401
Windows 95, 109, 112, 197, 291
Windows NT operating system,
  110, 408
wire services
  see news wire services
wireless phone systems,
  101, 93, 231, 262
wiring, 360
Wisconsin, 165
WiTec, 353
word processor, see typewriters
work clothes, see uniforms

WORKERS COMPENSATION
  INSURANCE, 33, 404-407
  see also
    business insurance, 32-35
    employee drug testing,
      126-128
    health insurance, 161-164

workstation, 345, 346
worksurface, 344-346
World Telecom, 308
World Travel Partners, 382
World War II, 132, 164
World Wide Web,
  123, 188, 190, 191, 232

WORLD WIDE WEB SITE SETUP,
  123, 154, 408-411

see also
  advertising agencies, 12-14
  desktop computers, 108-113
  e-mail services, 122-125
  graphic designers, 154-156
  Internet service providers,
    188-191
  ISDN, 192-195
  modems, 230-233
  notebook computers, 244-247

WorldCom
  see LDDS WorldCom
wrist pain, 198
write-off rate, 74
WWF Paper, 95
WWW, see World Wide Web
wURLd Presence: One-stop
  Registration, 409
Wyndham, 170
Wyoming, 165

X

Xerographic copier paper
  see copy paper
Xerox,
  76, 136, 238, 240, 284, 319, 332
Xerox TextBridge, 240, 332
Xiox, 367
Xircom, 230
Xpedite Systems, 133
Xtend, 367

Y

Yamaha, 314
Yellow Book Standard, 316
Yellow Freight, 226

Z

Zacson Corporation, 347
Zagat's, 171
Zellerbach, 95
Zephyrhills, 22
Zip drives, 86
Zip-to-zone conversion, 303
zoning regulations, 335
Zoom, 230

Visit BuyersZone

http://www.buyerszone.com/

for the best buying advice on the Internet

BuyersZone is a FREE site on the World Wide Web that contains all the information and advice you need to make well-informed purchases for your company. Whenever you are looking to buy for the office, BuyersZone gets you up to speed.

- Search product databases to find the models with the features you require

- Find out what others think about a product or service by posting your questions in the Buyers Forum

- Learn about the manufacturers and service providers serving the market

- Find the local dealers that offer the products and services you desire

- Electronically distribute requests for proposal

- Keep up with the latest deals and discounts, locate hard-to-find items, learn the industry lingo, and much, much more. . . at BuyersZone

Buy with confidence. Use BuyersZone.
From the authors of *The Essential Business Buyer's Guide*

**Visit BuyersZone at
http://www.buyerszone.com/**

For detailed, how-to buying advice Turn to the BUSINESS CONSUMER GUIDE!

America's leading reference for office buyers

Get your FREE sample issue

The Business Consumer Guide is a publication offering detailed buying advice on all types of office purchases, from phone systems and photocopiers to long distance service and overnight delivery.

- Insightful articles explain all you need to know about a particular product or service, updating you on the latest technologies and providing money-saving tips and advice.
- Vendor profiles give you a "who's who" rundown of the market, so you know who to call and who to avoid.
- Easy-to-read tables compare the critical buying features across dozens of options. No more wading through brochures to compare specifications.
- Decision trees highlight the best purchasing choices, with different recommendations to fit your particular needs.
- A toll-free buyer's hotline gives you direct access to our editorial staff for help with confusing purchasing questions.

Receive a FREE sample issue by returning the card on the next page

No cards left? Call (800) 938-0088 to receive your free sample issue.